This book belongs to Judy Couthern Wight

Mon.
12-6-2021   29.95

A History

OF

Tennessee and Tennesseans

The Leaders and Representative Men in Commerce,
Industry and Modern Activities

BY

WILL T. HALE

Author of "The Backward Trail: Stories of the Indians and Tennessee
Pioneers," "Great Southerners," "Marriage and Divorce, and
Land Laws of Tennessee," "True Stories of James-
town, Va.", "An Autumn Lane and Other
Poems" and "Folk-Tales of the
Southern Hill People,"

AND

DIXON L. MERRITT

VOLUME V

ILLUSTRATED

THE LEWIS PUBLISHING COMPANY
(Not Inc.)
CHICAGO AND NEW YORK
1913

pgs. 1207-1530.

Tennessee and Tennesseans

SAMUEL BENNETT WILSON. In the financial system which so facili-
tates the operations even of local trade, Cross Plains included among its
capable bank officials, the genial young cashier, Samuel B. Wilson. His
is a Tennessee family, identified with the interests of this state for several generations. Through his mother, Mr. Wilson is a descendant of
the Bennett line, of early Tennessee settlement, his grandfather, Bur-
rell Bennett, having been a prosperous farmer and slave-owner. His
daughter, Elizabeth (1849-1899), born in Sequatchie, Tennessee, was
united in marriage with William H. Wilson (1847-1897) and shared his
fortunes during their half-century of life together. William Wilson was
a school teacher and farmer. At one time he was was possessed of
abundant property and money, but his was the fate of the too kindly
man who signs security papers for the unreliable, for in that way he
sacrificed his means, very shortly before his death. He is remembered
as a man of particular intelligence and generous character. A Democrat
in politics, he took a lively interest in local affairs of a public nature.
He was active and honored in the organizations of the Ancient Free and
Accepted Masons, and was an esteemed member of the Cumberland Presbyterian church, as his wife was of the Baptist. William and Elizabeth
Wilson were the parents of five children, all of whom are yet living. Of
these the youngest was named Samuel B., and he it is whose life forms
the special subject of this sketch.

Born in Sequatchie county, Tennessee, on the important date of July
4, in 1880, Samuel B. Wilson followed the usual experiences of a well-
to-do farmer's son in the rural schools, with additional advantages from
the school systems of Knoxville and Chattanooga.

His education completed, as a young man Mr. Wilson first occupied
himself with farming occupations. Subsequently he accepted employment in a mercantile establishment. From that he passed to a position
as assistant cashier in the bank at Whitwell, Tennessee. There he remained for two and one-half years. In 1907 he came to Cross Plains,
Tennessee, where he assisted other public-spirited and enterprising citi-

zens in organizing a similar commercial institution. He was made first cashier of this bank at Cross Plains, which has a capital of $20,000, a surplus of $2,000 and an average deposit of $55,000. Mr. Wilson is a director and stockholder of the bank.

Other financial interests of Samuel B. Wilson include his farm of 300 acres, a part of the original homestead of his grandfather, Bennett, Besides a share with his brother-in-law, in a mercantile business near Chattanooga. Mr. Wilson is a wide-awake man about town and is honored in the fraternal circles of the Free and Accepted Masons, the Independent Order of Odd Fellows and the Modern Woodmen of America. He is a member of the Methodist Episcopal church, South.

LAWRENCE A. WARD. A well-to-do and leading business man of Obion, as a man who has in more than one line given worthy public service, and as a member of organizations that tend toward the betterment of humanity, L. A. Ward is one whose life is of interest to historian and reader. Of his forty odd years in the lumber industry more than a score have been spent in the city of Obion.

Greenwood, Indiana, was the place of L. A. Ward's birth and January 21, 1853, was his natal day. His parents were James and Martha Ward, the father a native of Xenia, Ohio, and the mother one of Indiana's daughters. They removed from the Hoosier state to Tennessee, where the boyhood of L. A. Ward was spent and where he has lived his subsequent life of usefulness. He early became interested in sawmills and lumber, entering this line of business when only sixteen years of age—in 1869.

The year 1887 was a doubly important one in the life of Mr. Ward, for it was marked both by his marriage and by his initial residence in Obion. On March 24, of the year mentioned, Miss Joe Thornton, of Weakley county, Tennessee, joined her life's fortunes with his. In the years that have followed, their home has been gladdened by the coming of three children. Cosler, the first born, and Miles Thornton the youngest, have passed from this life. Owen Stanley, the second son, was born February 21, 1893.

Mr. Ward and his family are connected with the Church of the Disciples, or Christian church, of which they are substantially helpful members. The fraternal society of Ancient Free and Accepted Masons is honored by his affiliation with the local lodge. His politics is that of almost every other son of "the solid south" and he has cheerfully and ably performed such public duties as have devolved upon him. For the past fifteen years he has served as an alderman of Obion and has also been an efficient member of the Obion school board.

The property of Mr. Ward includes about seven hundred acres of land, of which a tract of one hundred acres is devoted to the production of rice. His lumber business is of course the most significant feature of his property. His mill and yard cover a space of three acres in Obion. He employs ten men throughout the entire year and at busy times often has as large a force as thirty. In his plant the lumber manufactures include everything required for the building of a house, with the single exception of blinds. His business is of prime importance to Obion and the adjacent vicinity and he is personally a gentleman whose worth and influence are held in high esteem by his fellow-citizens of the community.

JAMES Q. SHIRES. One of the most attractive establishments in Obion is the jewelry establishment of J. Q. Shires. One of the finest stores in the city, it occupies three hundred and seventy-five feet of floor space and is filled with heavy and expansive glass cases containing every variety of jewelry. This stock is of the best and most modern workmanship and draws many customers. This business has been located in Obion since 1905.

Its proprietor, J. Q. Shires, is a native of Obion county, where his parents, Thomas and Lissie Shires, resided for many years. Thomas Shires was a mechanic, whose ability has been inherited by his son in a more highly developed form. The two children of the family were J. Q. Shires, the special subject of this review, and W. T. Shires, his younger brother. The date of birth of the former was the year 1885. J. Q. Shires grew to manhood in his parental home and in its vicinity received his opportunities for mental development. His mechanical genius was early evident and all his life's experiences have been turned to practical account. He had scarcely attained the years of his majority when he established his present business, which has been successful from the beginning.

After several years of prosperous business life Mr. Shires was united to his life's companion, who was well known in her girlhood days as Miss Maple Grissom. The Shires-Grissom nuptials were celebrated in 1912 and the young pair occupy an enviable place in their wide circle of friends. They are faithful and valued members of the Church of the Disciples of this place.

Mr. Shires is a man of intelligent interests in all lines. He is not, however, one who seeks conspicuous places in the limelight of life, preferring to devote his time and attention to his home, his church and his business. His large experience in his line, his natural gifts for grasping and executing the most intricate and complex pieces of workmanship—these are elements of his vocational life which guarantee his success in the work he has chosen.

VIRGIL J. JERNIGAN, M. D. The need of high regard is not the least of the world's tribute to that most helpful of all professions—that of the conscientious physician. And when, to his qualities as physician are added those of the practical Christian, such a man's usefulness is infinitely multiplied. One member of this profession, who has won both sincere appreciation and pecuniary success and who still continues to rise in the ranks of his fellows, is V. J. Jernigan, the well-known physician of Obion.

For five generations his family have resided in Tennessee. The doctor's paternal grandfather was Elisha Jernigan, who married Miss Stone. Robertson county, Tennessee, was the home of E. T. Jernigan and L. M. Jernigan, his wife. They were both natives of the state, E. T. Jernigan being a planter of considerable property. He was largely engaged in the production of tobacco and handled it also in a commercial way. He and his wife were the parents of six children, of whom the eldest was V. J. Jernigan, the subject of this biographical account. He was born in Robertson county in 1868.

V. J. Jernigan received his early training, both in books and in the practical things of life, in his native county. When he was fourteen years of age, Union City, in Obion county, became his home. Here his education was continued in the public schools of the place. When that period of his intellectual development was concluded, he entered Webb Brothers' Academy, at Bellbuckle, and later passed to the McTyre Institute at McKenzie.

Thus, well equipped with the general knowledge, which is ever valuable, the young man, V. J. Jernigan, entered temporarily the profession of teaching. In this useful occupation he continued for three years and at the end of that time made arrangements for beginning his preparation for the medical profession.

He matriculated at Vanderbilt University and entered upon the prescribed courses in the college of medicine in 1897, which is one of the strongest departments of that great institution. He was graduated in 1900, receiving his degree of doctor of medicine.

Doctor Jernigan chose the city of Obion as the field for his practice. Here he has built up a most desirable practice and has endeared himself in many ways to his numerous patrons. He is thoroughly interested in every branch of his science and is constantly increasing his breadth of knowledge. In 1906 he went to New York City, where he took a post-graduate course in the Polyclinic College of Physicians. In 1908 he returned to his alma mater, Vanderbilt University, for further post-graduate research. In the year 1912 he took yet more advanced and specialized work in the University of Chicago. The doctor fully realizes the almost infinite possibilities of present day medicine and it is not too much to say that truly great ones will be reached by him.

Doctor Jernigan is an important member of the county, state and tri-state medical associations. He is one of Obion's officers on the board of health and is medical examiner for several insurance companies. He finds time for fraternal and church associations. Of the former, he is a member of the orders of Knights of Pythias and Woodmen of the World. His religious affiliation is with the Methodist Episcopal church.

The doctor's attractive home is presided over by Mrs. Anna White Jernigan, his wife, to whom he was united in 1895, in Union City. Doctor and Mrs. Jernigan are the parents of two sons and one daughter. The family is one that ranks high in the social life of Obion and one whose friends are legion. Doctor Jernigan is, notwithstanding his busy life and his many interests, a very close student of both books and men and is intellectually broad as well as professionally conscientious and scientifically purposive.

JOHN W. BENNETT. Among the merchants of Obion county probably none is more widely or more favorably known than the subject of this review, who has been engaged in business in the city of Troy for a period of forty years. His parents, Wm. H. and Temperance (Jackson) Bennett, were both natives of North Carolina and were married after coming to Tennessee. In 1840 he came to Tennessee and settled in Decatur county, but after a residence of about twelve or thirteen years there they removed to Obion county in 1853, and here W. H. Bennett purchased a farm and was engaged in agricultural pursuits until his death, which occurred on May 22, 1896. He owned about five hundred acres at the time of his death. He and his wife were the parents of twelve children, ten sons and two daughters, ten of whom are now living, the sons being either farmers or merchants. The family is therefore well known throughout the county, where its members have wielded considerable influence upon the industries and political destinies of the county and state.

John W. Bennett was born April 1, 1851, in Decatur county, Tennessee, and came to Obion with parents when about three years old, where his entire life has been passed. He was educated in the local schools, and while still in his boyhood became interested in mercantile pursuits, with which he has ever since been associated. Beginning business for himself with a small stock of goods, he has gradually added to it until at the present time he has one of the best assortments and one of the best equipped mercantile establishments in the city of Troy. His store building is thirty by one hundred feet and two stories in height. It is considered one of the best brick buildings in Troy. Passing from the outside to the interior of the building the visitor is at once impressed with the well selected and carefully arranged stock of general merchandise, including a full line of general hardware and groceries. Here Mr. Bennett is "monarch of all he surveys." He has been in the business for so long a time that he knows just where everything is, so that his customers are sure of prompt attention and courteous treatment at all times. By assiduous attention to the needs of his trade and care in the selection of goods to meet the demand, he has built up a lucrative and permanent business. It is intended as no disparagement to the other retail dealers of Troy to say that he stands at the head, and it might be said that he is the Nestor of the mercantile business of the city.

Mr. Bennett, notwithstanding the demands of his personal affairs and his constantly growing trade, has found time to devote to the public welfare in an official capacity. He has served as a member of the town board, and is always a willing and intelligent helper of any and every movement for the improvement of Troy and the welfare of her people. His long residence there has rendered him familiar with conditions, and he is usually one of the first men to be consulted when any proposition for the advancement of Troy's material interests comes up for consideration, thus marking him as a man of public spirit and progressive ideas.

In 1874 Mr. Bennett married Miss Amanda Oliver, daughter of William Oliver, and to this union have been born two children—John O. and Clara. The son is now the manager of the Troy Flour Mills and is one of the promising young business men of the city. The daughter married G. R. McDade, of Troy.

CALVIN E. UPCHURCH, D. D. S. While medicine—and especially surgery—has made rapid strides in the ranks of science and has marked the successful physician as a most significant figure in modern civilization, no less remarkable achievements have been made in dental surgery. The restoration of health and the prolonging of life are often made possible through the preservation of teeth or the substitution of artificial ones.

The only dental surgeon of Obion is Dr. C. E. Upchurch, who has practiced here since 1904 and who enjoys a very wide patronage. Its extent and its constant growth are among the numerous evidences of the doctor's superior skill and wide knowledge of all phases of his science. By education and training he is well fitted to stand at the head of his profession.

Doctor Upchurch is of Alabama birth, that state being also the place of nativity of both his parents, Calvin and Sarah (Childers) Upchurch. Of the four children born in this home the fourth in order of birth was he whose name forms the caption of this sketch. He was born in 1877. In his native home he was reared and educated liberally.

After the preliminary years of general education he entered Vander-bilt University in Nashville, where in the college of dental surgery he pursued thorough courses and was graduated in 1904 with the degree of doctor of dental surgery. He then located in his present home and field of professional practice—the town of Obion.

In 1907 Doctor Upchurch was united in marriage to Miss Sadie Howell, of Obion, Tennessee. Mrs. Upchurch is a daughter of John W. Howell, who is a well-known citizen of this place. Doctor and Mrs. Upchurch are the parents of one child, a little daughter named Lulu Janette.

The church affiliation of Doctor Upchurch and his family is with the Baptist congregation of this place. For some years the doctor has served this church in the capacity of clerk, the duties of which office he ably performs. He is a man who has established wide friendly relations and is popular in various organizations, including the fraternal societies of Knights of Pythias and Ancient Free and Accepted Masons. The former body honors him with the status of past chancellor.

The business office and operating rooms of Doctor Upchurch are located at the corner of Broadway and Main street. They are finely finished rooms, elaborately furnished and thoroughly equipped with the best and most up-to-date apparatus for his work.

GORDON B. BAIRD. In the rapidly developing history of the modern era there is perhaps no one influence comparable to that of the press. Through this ubiquitous medium fleets each day's momentous news and the psychology of nations is carried round the world. The great metropolitan press, with its complex network of intellectual machinery, connecting myriad points on the globe, does its great work of disseminating universal information of importance to the world. No less valuable, in its less pretentious way, is the local press of county or town, which keeps in mental touch the citizens of county seat and remotest farm. A worthy exponent of our newspaper systems is Editor Gordon B. Baird, who conducts the *Obion County Enterprise*.

Mr. Baird is an energetic representative of the younger generation of the men who are doing things. He is a son of James M. and Rebecca (Smith) Baird, a former native of middle Tennessee and later of west Tennessee. They lived in Carroll county during their earlier married years and it was during their residence there that their third child, a son, whom they named Gordon, was born, on January 12, 1888.

Gordon Baird had excellent advantages from the first. His father was an attorney, who had acquired an enviable prestige for legal acumen in his native county. While Gordon Baird was yet a child the father died and his mother removed to Fulton, Kentucky, where the son's education was completed. In 1909 he returned to his native state, which has been the scene of Gordon Baird's vocational success. In 1909 he established himself in Obion, where he entered upon his present work as editor and publisher of the *Enterprise*. In 1910 he won as his life's closest companion Miss Anna Lee Pascall, well known in Fulton, Kentucky, as the daughter of T. T. Pascall. Mr. and Mrs. Baird have a small daughter, named Mary Gordon Baird.

Mr. Baird's most enthusiastic attention, as well as his choicest gifts, are devoted to his editorial work. *The Obion County Enterprise* is a six-column sheet, well constructed and finished, with editing of a particularly breezy and effective quality. Its circulation is one that will average well with that of any paper in the county. Mr. Baird also does the job printing for Obion and its vicinity, being in every way thoroughly well equipped for such responsible work. He is a Democrat in his political affiliation.

GEORGE A. DAVIDSON. Notwithstanding the fact that great fortunes are sometimes made in speculation and by manipulation of the markets, it is undeniable that there is no line of honest effort which offers greater or more certain returns than intelligent and, painstaking cultivation of the soil. In recent years, by scientific methods and careful management introduced among the best agriculturists of the country, it has been demonstrated that the fertility of the soil can be preserved and even increased, and that agriculture as an occupation can be made more profitable by what is known as intensive farming. By this method, the number of acres is not so much a factor as the amount produced upon a single acre. The man who cultivates eighty acres of wheat and harvests fifteen bushels to the acre does much more work and receives far less for his labor than the man who cultivates forty acres and harvests thirty bushels to the acre.

George A. Davidson is one of those progressive individuals who, profiting by experience, and past mistakes, are constantly endeavoring to increase the yield from their farms. He owns nine hundred and fifty acres in Obion county, Tennessee, and another farm of two hundred and twenty acres, on which he raises cotton, corn and wheat. Of his Obion county farm two hundred and fifty acres are under cultivation. Here he has been experimenting with rice culture, and on twenty-five acres he has raised one thousand bushels. This has convinced him that rice can be grown with profit in Tennessee, and he is preparing to increase the acreage devoted to rice culture to at least one hundred and twenty-five acres, the remainder of the land under cultivation to be devoted to the customary crops of this section of the state. He does not believe in "luck" as a factor in making farming a profitable occupation, but relies upon his industry and its thoughtful application.

Every plan on his farm is thoroughly worked out, and then, when it is matured, it is carefully executed. If it fails to accomplish what is expected of it, another plan is tried. He never makes the same mistake twice. By this course he has come to be known as one of the most progressive and successful farmers of west Tennessee.

Mr. Davidson was born in Obion county, January 7, 1861, and has lived there all his life so far. He was educated in the common schools and grew to manhood on his father's farm. He is the fourth of six children born to Josephus C. and Arabelle (Inman) Davidson, the former a native of Tennessee and the latter of Mississippi. His grandparents, George and Mary Davidson, were natives of North Carolina, but joined the tide of emigration from that state in early days and settled in Davidson county, Tennessee, not far from the city of Nashville.

On December 9, 1896, Mr. Davidson married Miss Anna E. Richardson, daughter of Dr. Elbridge G. and Josephine (Terrell) Richardson, and to this union have been born four children—Earl, Lena and Lara (twins), and Robert J. Mrs. Davidson's father was a native of Brewersville, Tennessee, and during the Civil war he served with distinction as captain in a Missouri artillery regiment. After the war he became a prominent physician of Obion, where he enjoyed a lucrative practice and had many friends. He married Josephine Terrell in 1860, and of the six children born to them Mrs. Davidson is the only one now living. Mr. Davidson is a Democrat, but never aspired to office. He is a member of the A. F. & A. M. of Glass, Obion county (Palestine Lodge, No. 296). He and his family are members of the Methodist Episcopal church, South.

BRICE P. MOFFATT. It seems to be a well-established fact, and one which has frequently been commented upon in the columns of the popular press, that during the last few years the young men of the country are annually coming to occupy positions of greater prominence and responsibility in the business world. As a rule these young men are both progressive and aggressive. Many of them have fitted themselves for their work by taking special courses in the leading educational institutions of the country, where they have become well grounded in the fundamental knowledge of the profession or occupation they have selected for their life's work. When they leave school and begin to apply the theories they have learned they are not slow to discard the obsolete methods of the past and conduct their business according to those of more modern times.

A fine example of this truth may be seen in Brice P. Moffatt. one of the best known druggists and rising young business men of Troy. Obion county, Tennessee, where he was born on April 23. 1891, and is a descendant of one of the oldest families of that section of the state. The first of the name to locate in Tennessee was John Moffatt, the great-grandfather of Brice. He was a native of South Carolina, where he married a Miss Strong, and in 1840 left Chester district and settled in Obion county, where he purchased four hundred acres of fertile land and became one of the leading agriculturists. His son James S., one of a family of twelve children, married Miss Martha Moffatt and engaged in farming, owning three hundred acres of land and a number of negro slaves. He was also one of the pioneer merchants of Troy, having established himself in business there as early as 1841. He was born in South Carolina in 1818, was a public-spirited man, a member of the Presbyterian church, and a liberal contributor to every worthy cause for the advancement of the community. The business he established passed to his sons, and from them to his grandsons, so that three generations of the family have been engaged in merchandising "at the old stand." James S. Moffatt died in 1890 and his wife died in 1859. Of their six children only one is now living. J. P. Moffatt, the grandfather of the subject of this sketch, was also born in South Carolina and succeeded to the business of his father upon the latter's retirement from active affairs. He served for more than three years in the Confederate army during the Civil war, was wounded at Rome, Georgia, in 1863, and rose to the rank of second lieutenant. His death occurred in 1873. He married Miss Mary Brice, a native of South Carolina, and to them were born six children, only two of whom are now living, James R. and Pressley W., who are now proprietors of the mercantile establishment founded by their grandfather in 1841. This business includes a complete line of dry goods, clothing, farming implements, etc., and is one of the leading mercantile houses of Troy, with a trade that extends over a large section of the adjacent territory.

James R. Moffatt was born in Troy, Tennessee, May 29, 1861. He was educated in the local schools and in 1878 succeeded to the business of his father. In 1889 he married Miss Lulu Marshall, daughter of R. H. Marshall, and of their five children two are now living, Brice P. and Maud. His brother and partner, Pressley W., was born in Troy on January 15, 1869. He married Miss Mary Maxey, and their four children are Maxey, Jennie, Pressley W., Jr., and Sarah.

Brice P. Moffatt, whose name introduces this review, acquired his elementary education in the public schools of his native city of Troy. He then entered the department of pharmacy in the Northwestern University, at Chicago, and there graduated as a member of the class of 1911. The same year he became a registered pharmacist and opened his drug store in Troy. His store, which is twenty-four by sixty feet in dimensions, is equipped with everything to be found in a model drug store of the present day. Besides the customary stock of drugs and medicines, he carries a complete line of paints, oils, perfumery, toilet articles, etc., and his close attention to business and the wants of his customers is bearing fruit in the way of a constantly increasing patronage. Mr. Moffatt is a member of the Masonic fraternity, Lodge No. 679, Benevolent and Protective Order of Elks, of Union City, Tennessee, and also of the Phi Delta Chi college fraternity. About the time he started in business for himself he was united in marriage with Miss Mary Whittaker, of Hopkinsville, Kentucky, and he and his wife are prominent in the social circles of Troy.

BENJAMIN H. SETTLE. Among the well-known and substantial business men of Troy, Obion county, Benjamin H. Settle occupies a prominent position as a dealer in dressed lumber and building materials of all kinds. He was born in North Carolina, August 11, 1849, and is a son of Benjamin and Sarah (Campbell) Settle, both natives of that state. The mother was of Scotch extraction and was a great-granddaughter of one of the dukes of Argyle. In 1855 Benjamin Settle removed with his family to Tennessee and settled in Fayette county, where he purchased eight hundred acres of land and engaged in agricultural pursuits upon a large scale for that period. He was also interested in real estate operations and in the slave trade, becoming in time one of the wealthiest men in the county. When the Civil war began he remained loyal to the government of the north, though he was opposed to the war. His attitude incurred the enmity of some of the southern sympathizers, and on January 20, 1864, he was killed by a party of Confederate guerrillas. He and his wife were the parents of seven children, five of whom are now living, Benjamin H. being the second child in the order of birth and the only son. Although not yet fifteen years of age at the time of his father's untimely death, he bravely took up the work of assisting his widowed mother in the support of her family. Under her direction and guidance he practically assumed the management of the estate, making ample provision for the family needs and selling considerable produce to the neighbors and in the adjacent towns. Thus his boyhood and youth were passed in Fayette county, where he managed to secure in the common schools a good practical education. In 1890 he became interested in the Ekdahl Furniture Company, for which he traveled over a broad territory. When the company failed, some time afterward, he took charge of the settlement of its affairs. While thus engaged he acquired a knowledge of the lumber business that led to his engaging in that line of activity in 1893. For several years he was both dealer in and inspector of lumber, and during this time he learned all the details pertaining to the manufacture and sale of building materials. In 1902 he located in Troy, where he opened his lumber yard two years later. His yards, including the space occupied by his dwelling, covers four acres of ground, upon which there are two small cottages that he rents. His past experience gave him an advantage in opening his new business in Troy, and his success was assured from the start. During the eight years that he has been thus engaged he has made money and gained a reputation as a square dealer in the materials he handles. He is public-spirited and takes a keen interest in everything that has a tendency to benefit the town.

Mr. Settle has been twice married. In 1873 he married Miss Mattie Pickens, and to this union were born five children, three of whom are still living. They are John C., a well-to-do business man of San Francisco, California; Thomas B. is traffic manager of E. Clemmons Horst Company of San Francisco, California; and Hugh L. of Memphis, Tennessee. All three of these sons are above the average type of business men in executive ability and resourcefulness. Mrs. Mattie Settle died in 1892, and subsequently Mr. Settle married Mrs. Sallie Weddington. No children have been born to this second marriage.

The Settle family is well connected and has furnished at least one man who has been recognized in political and legal circles. Thomas Settle, a second cousin of the subject of this review, was chairman of the Republican national convention that nominated General Ulysses S. Grant for the presidency. He was a prominent attorney of North Carolina and served for some time as United States minister to Peru. Upon his return to this country he was appointed federal judge for the district of Florida and took up his residence at Tallahassee, where he passed the closing years of his life. Benjamin H. Settle is a Democrat. Both his wives were Cumberland Presbyterians and he is a Methodist.

MRS. BONNIE S. MAXWELL. Among the old and honored pioneers who paved the way for the development of Obion county and the position that it occupies socially and financially at the present time, the name of Alexander W. Smith stands preeminent. He was a native of the Emerald Isle, but when a young man left Ireland with a brother to seek his fortune in the United States. They landed at New York in 1818 and the brother located in that state. Alexander, after some time in New York, made his way to South Carolina, locating in Chester district. Here he married Esther Graham, who was a relative of the celebrated Scottish chief, William Wallace. In 1840 he removed with his family to Tennessee and located in Tipton county, where he purchased two hundred acres of land and engaged in agricultural pursuits. He was a strict conformist and adhered to the dogma and teachings of that sect. He died in 1870, aged seventy-two years, after a long and useful life, during which he wielded great influence upon the destinies of his adopted county. Alexander and Esther (Graham) Smith were the parents of four children—three sons and one daughter.

One of his sons, James G. Smith, was the father of Mrs. Bonnie S. Maxwell. He was born in South Carolina, September 18, 1828, and became a resident of Obion county, Tennessee, in 1850. He was a well-educated gentleman and was a remarkable man in various respects. As a young man he taught school for several years, employing his spare hours in the study of law. Into this subject he went deeply, and soon after his admission to the bar he became recognized as one of the leading attorneys of west Tennessee. For fifty years he practiced his profession in Obion county, and at the time of his death on August 5, 1905, he was the oldest lawyer in the county. His funeral was a notable one in one particular. While many of his friends and acquaintances were in attendance, it was remarked that all the lawyers in the county had closed their offices on that occasion, in order to give them an opportunity to pay their respects to one whom they universally loved as a man and admired as an attorney. James G. Smith was everybody's friend. If he found a young man who desired to become a lawyer he was always ready to extend his aid, and a number of young attorneys owe him a debt of gratitude for his kindly words and advice, as well as more substantial assistance. Even the children on the street received his attention and he was universally popular. When the trouble between the north and south culminated in Civil war he espoused the cause of the Confederacy. On one occasion he was ordered to take the oath of allegiance to the federal government, but refused to do so. For his refusal he was treated as a prisoner of war and confined for some time in a military prison at St. Louis, Missouri.

On January 3, 1854. James S. Smith and Sarah E. Allen were united in marriage, and to this union were born six children. Wallace S., born October 3, 1854, became the wife of H. H. Crockett on March 16, 1871; Bonnie S., born June 2, 1856, was married to John B. Maxwell on March 24, 1875; Wm. A., born September 26, 1858, married Miss Sunie Pressley on April 17, 1889; Dora S. married Rev. Thos. P. Pressley and is now deceased; Lutheran A., born January 8, 1863, married Miss Annie Faulk on February 19, 1896; and Fitz James, born October 16, 1864, attorney in Union City, Tennessee.

John B. Maxwell was for many years a conspicuous figure in the affairs of Obion county. He was a native son of Tennessee, having been born on April 21, 1855. in Henry county, where his father was a well-known and influential citizen. After securing a good education he decided to enter the field of journalism, and for some time he was editor of the *Troy Times*. He was also deputy clerk of the county court and was a factor in politics. As an editor he always advocated measures for the advancement of the moral, material and social interests of Troy, and as a citizen he commanded the esteem and confidence of his fellow-townsmen in a marked degree. His death occurred on September 5, 1901, and was a distinct loss to the town where he had so long lived and labored. As stated above, he was married on March 24,'1875, to Miss Bonnie S. Smith, and to this union were born nine children, two of whom passed away in childhood. Those living, with the dates of birth, are as follows: Basil B., February 4, 1878; Luther M., July 17, 1882; Martha M., September 24, 1887; Fitz L., March 10, 1890; Dora W., December 7, 1892; Stonewall H., June 16, 1895, and John B., October 16, 1897.

In looking back over the lives of such men as Alexander W. Smith, James G. Smith and John B. Maxwell, the reader of the present generation may find a career worthy of emulation. They encountered many difficulties during the pioneer days, but with courage and fortitude overcame them and left to their posterity a better community and an untarnished name. A record of their deeds and achievement leads one to believe with Longfellow, that:

> "Lives of great men all remind us
> We can make our lives sublime;
> And, departing, leave behind us
> Footprints on the sands of Time."

MATTHEW McCLAIN, sheriff of Lewis county, Tennessee, and a resident of Hohenwald, is a native of that county, has been one of its representative agriculturists for a number of years and always has been worthily identified with its best citizenship. He first took up the duties of sheriff on October 3, 1910, in consequence of his election to that office by the county court and his services were of that efficient order that in August, 1912, he was returned to that official station by the vote of the citizens of Lewis county. The McClains were originally of Kentucky stock, and the grandfather and father of Matthew McClain were, respectively, soldiers in the War of 1812 and in the Civil war. the latter as a supporter of the southern cause. The former, John McClain, was the first of the family to locate in Tennessee. He was born in Kentucky April 4, 1777, and came to this state as a young man. He served throughout the second struggle for American independence and fought with Gen. Andrew Jackson at the battle of New Orleans in 1815. On coming to Tennessee he settled in Maury county, where he spent the remainder of his active years as a farmer. He lived to the remarkable age of one hundred and four years, passing away on April 4, 1881. In political adherency he was first a Whig and then later a Democrat. He wedded Elizabeth McMillian, also a Kentuckian by birth, who bore him seven sons and four daughters. Martin, the youngest of his sons and the father of Matthew, was born in Maury county, this state, March 2, 1833, and grew to manhood there, receiving such educational discipline as the public schools of the place and period afforded. When the Civil war broke out he espoused the cause of the southland and entered the Confederate service as a member of Captain Biffle's company, which was assigned to the Third Tennessee Regiment. At the battle of Fort Donelson he received a wound in his leg, from which he suffered severely and which caused him to return home. After the minnie ball causing the wound had been removed and he had recovered, which was some four months later, he returned to the service and remained with the army until its surrender. Returning to Maury county, he was married there in 1867 and shortly afterward removed to Lewis county, where he purchased a small farm and was engaged in agricultural pursuits until his retirement in 1890. He is yet living and is quite active for one of his years, though suffering from failing sight. He has always been a stalwart supporter of the Democratic party in political affairs. His wife was Miss Nancy J. Beckum prior to her marriage, a daughter of Alexander Beckum and a native of Maury county, where she was born April 20, 1848. She passed to rest on December 16, 1881, leaving a family of six children, all of whom are still living and are as follows: Felix, Matthew and Lavona, residents of Lewis county, Tennessee; Robert, whose home is in Maury county, this state; Knox, now located in New Mexico; and Martin, also a resident of Lewis county.

Matthew McClain, the second of this family, was born in the Fourth civil district of Lewis county, Tennessee, July 8, 1873. He received such educational advantages as the schools of Lewis county afforded at that time but which were very limited. He took up responsibilities at the early age of fourteen working a in a sawmill, first being employed in firing the engine and then later becoming a sawyer. At the age of twenty he bought a farm and took up agriculture, at the same time also running a sawmill. He carried on these industries jointly until October 3, 1910, when he became sheriff of Lewis county, which office he continues to fill with satisfaction to all concerned. Prior to becoming sheriff, however, he had served ten years as a magistrate of the Fourth district of Lewis county. He still retains his farming interests. Fraternally he is a member of Hohenwald Lodge, No. 293, Independent Order of Odd Fellows, and in political views and allegiance he is a Democrat.

On March 19, 1894, Mr. McClain was joined in marriage to Miss Betty Kilpatrick, daughter of William Kilpatrick, of Perry county. The union of Mr. and Mrs. McClain has been blessed with ten children, all living and all at home except the eldest daughter, Jennie, who is now the wife of Linton Maxwell and resides at Mount Pleasant, Maury county, Tennessee, and the youngest, who died March 8, 1913. In order of birth they are: William Thomas, Jennie, John Turley, Felix Martin, Capitola, Gladys, Alice, Medola. Lavona and Matthew.

GEORGE J. PIERCE.   The honored subject of this review is numbered among the progressive and representative agriculturists of Obion county, where he is the owner of a finely improved landed estate of five hundred acres, situated near the boundary line between Tennessee and Kentucky, Pierce Station being his postoffice address.   He is a scion of one of the old and influential families of northwestern Tennessee and through his character and achievement he has well upheld the prestige of the honored name which he bears and which has been closely identified with the civic and industrial activities of this section of the state for more than seventy years.

Mr. Pierce was born in Obion county, Tennessee, on the 8th of June, 1850, and is a son of Thomas M. and Margaret (Blacknell) Pierce, the former of whom was born in North Carolina, in 1810, and the latter of whom was several years his junior.   Thomas M. Pierce received excellent educational advantages and was a man of fine intellectuality and marked business acumen.   He was a successful teacher in the schools of Tennessee for a number of years and eventually became one of the prominent agriculturists and merchants of the northwestern part of the state, both he and his wife having passed the closing years of their lives in Obion county and both having held the unqualified esteem of all who knew them.   Thomas M. Pierce came to Tennessee in the year 1842 and first located in Dresden, Weakley county, whence he later removed to Obion county.   He became the owner of a fine landed estate of eight hundred acres, which he operated with slave labor prior to the Civil war, most of this property having been confiscated at the close of the war, though he had been a stanch supporter of the cause of the Union and had ably opposed the secession of the Southern states.   Notwithstanding his personal atttitude at this climacteric period in the history of the nation, three of his sons—Thomas D., Henry H. and Rice A.—espoused the cause of the Confederate government and were valiant soldiers in the Southern service during the great fratracidal conflict.   Mr. Pierce was a man of specially progressive ideas and policies, and he developed an extensive merchandise business, in connection with which he had well equipped general stores at Jacksonville, Union City, and Pierce, Tennessee, and at Fulton, Kentucky.

Pierce Station was named for Thomas M. Pierce, who built the first station house himself, and was the first station master. He was also the first postmaster and held both offices until a short time before his death when he resigned.   He was a Democrat but held the postoffice through the Republican administration.

Both Mr. Pierce and his wife held membership in the Methodist church, their lives having been ordered in harmony with the faith which they professed.   Mrs. Pierce was graduated in one of the excellent educational institutions of her native state, Virginia, and was a woman of exceptional culture and refinement.   She was a successful and popular teacher in the schools of Tennessee prior to her marriage and she ever held the affectionate regard of all who came within the sphere of her gracious and gentle influence. The names of the children, with respective years of birth are here noted: Harriet, 1834; William B., 1836; T. Devereaux, 1838; Henry H., 1840; Rice A., 1842; Lawrence, 1844; and George J., 1850. The four eldest were born in North Carolina and the remainder in Weakley county, this state, except George J., who is the subject of this review and the youngest of the number, he having been born in what is now Obion county, as previously noted. Of his brothers, Rice A., is now living.

George J. Pierce was reared on the old homestead plantation and in connection therewith he gained practical discipline, the while he had the gracious environment and influences of a refined and hospitable home,— one representing the best of the fine old Southern regime. After availing himself of the advantages of the common schools he identified himself actively with agricultural pursuits, and during the long intervening years he has never severed his allegiance to this great basic industry, through the medium of which he has attained to substantial success and prosperity. His present beautiful and productive landed estate comprises five hundred acres and is one of the model farms of northwestern Tennessee. It is principally devoted to the raising of tobacco, cotton, wheat and corn, and in carrying on the work Mr. Pierce employs many negroes, having about seven families on the estate and some of the number having been with the family since the days before the Civil war.

Mr. Pierce is not only one of the progressive and enterprising agriculturists of Obion county but is also a citizen of marked loyalty and public spirit. He gives his co-operation in support of measures projected for the general good of the community and he holds secure vantage ground in the confidence and high regard of the people of his native county. He is a stanch supporter of the cause of the Democratic party and both he and his wife are zealous members of the Presbyterian church, in which he held the office of elder for fully a quarter of century.

In the year 1882 was solemnized the marriage of Mr. Pierce to Miss Mary L. Gibbs, who was born in Mississippi, and who is a daughter of the late Judge Q. D. Gibbs, a representative citizen of his county, in Mississippi. Mr. and Mrs. Pierce became the parents of nine children, namely: Annie, Louise and Joseph, who are deceased; and William B., George J., Jr., Margaret Dorsey, Mamie, and Sherley. The attractive family home is known for its generous and gracious hospitality and Mr. Pierce and his family are popular facts in the social life of the community.

JOSEPH GOODWIN RICE. In political and mercantile circles, probably no man in Lewis county is more widely known than Joseph Good-

win Rice, the present genial and efficient county clerk. His grandfather, Jerry Rice, was a pioneer farmer of southern Illinois, where
his children were born, but before they grew to maturity he removed
to Dunklin county, Missouri. Here he passed the closing years of his
life engaged in agricultural pursuits. James B. Rice, the father of
the subject of this sketch, was born in Illinois in 1834, but went with
his parents in childhood to Missouri, where he was educated in the
common schools and became a minister in the Methodist Episcopal
church, South. He was also engaged in farming and merchandising
at Kennett, Dunklin county, Missouri. About the time he arrived at
man's estate, Samuel and Leona Wilburn removed from Tennessee to
Dunklin county and settled at Kennett. Their daughter, Sarah, who
was born in Perry county, Tennessee, in 1834, became the wife of Rev.
J. B. Rice, and of the seven children born to them the subject of this
review is the only one now living. J. B. Rice died in 1869 and his
widow subsequently married R. R. Johnson. With him and her children she removed to Tennessee, settling in Perry county, whither her
mother had gone some years before, after the death of Samuel Wilburn.

Joseph Goodwin Rice was born at Kennett, Dunklin county, Missouri, September 24, 1862. He attended the public schools of his
native county until the family removed to Tennessee, after which he
finished his education in the public schools of that county and at Beach
Grove Academy. His mother died in 1881, and about that time he
began his business career as a clerk in a store at Pleasantville. Later
he was similarly employed at Etna. In 1889 he was united in marriage with Miss Laura McClearen, daughter of A. C. McClearen, a
prominent farmer of Pleasantville, Tennessee. After his marriage Mr.
Rice removed to Hickman county, where for the next six years he followed farming, after which he was engaged in the mercantile business
at Kimmins, Lewis county, for about ten years. He still retains an
interest in this business, of which his son, Carl Rice, is manager. The
establishment has been organized as a stock company, known as the
Kimmins Mercantile Company, and has a large patronage among the
people of the town and the farmers of the surrounding country.

Ever since he became a voter Mr. Rice has been a consistent supporter of the Democratic party and its principles. His activity in
behalf of his party led to his nomination and election to the office of
county clerk in 1908, and under his administration the affairs of the
office were conducted with such skill and ability that he was honored
with a reelection in 1910. This indorsement by his fellow-citizens
speaks volumes for his efficiency and integrity, and is one of which
any man might feel justly proud.

Mr. Rice is a member and one of the board of stewards of the
Methodist Episcopal church, South. His fraternal relations are expressed by membership in George DeSmith Lodge, No. 182, Knights

of Pythias, of Hohenwald, and in both church and lodge he is an active and useful worker.

Mr. and Mrs. Rice are the parents of eight children—Carl, Herman, Bernard, Irene, Aubrey, Fred, Edward and Willadene. As previously stated, Carl is manager of the Kimmins Mercantile Company. The other children are at home with the parents, with the exception of Edward, who died in 1905 at the age of fifteen months.

As a matter of family history it is worthy of note that Mr. Rice's father was a lifelong Democrat and a member of the Masonic fraternity, and also that he served in the Confederate army under Gen. Sterling Price. He was captured and held a prisoner for some time, being finally exchanged at Vicksburg.

FRED L. SCHUBERT. It is noteworthy that many of the sturdy and useful citizens of the United States either came from Germany or are of German extraction. Moritz Schubert, the father of Fred L., was born in Saxony, Germany, in 1824, and about 1845 left the Fatherland to seek his fortune in America. He located in Ohio, where he followed farming until 1880, when he removed with his family to Tennessee. In 1860 he married Miss Bertha Kiefer, a native of Baden-Baden, Germany, where she was born in 1833 and came with her parents to Ohio when she was eleven years of age. Moritz Schubert passed to the life beyond in 1892. His widow is still living. He was a stanch Democrat in his political belief and during President Cleveland's second administration served for four years as postmaster of Hohenwald, where he located upon coming to the state in 1880, and near which town he owned a fine farm. He also served as justice of the peace for six years and in the latter years of his life was interested in mercantile pursuits, as well as other business enterprises. His religious belief was expressed by membership in the German Lutheran church.

Fred L. Schubert, the fifth in a family of seven children born to Moritz and Bertha (Kiefer) Schubert, was born at Cincinnati, Ohio, May 3, 1873. His early education was acquired in the public schools of his native state and Tennessee. After completing the course in the public schools he prepared himself for the vocation of teacher and in 1889 began following that profession. While teaching he devoted his spare time to the study of law and in 1894 was admitted to the bar, shortly after he had reached the age of twenty-one years. Upon being admitted to practice he located in Hohenwald, where he has built up a satisfactory clientage and has won recognition as one of the able and successful attorneys of the county. He also owns a large farm in Lewis county, which he manages in connection with—or rather in addition to—his legal business. His agricultural instinct was doubtless inherited from his father, and in the management of his farm he has shown a skill that challenges the admiration of the community.

Mr. Schubert has also found time to devote to the public welfare as a member of the Tennessee legislature. In 1905 he was elected to represent the Twentieth senatorial district in the state senate, and after serving two years in that body was elected to the lower house from the Seventeenth district for a term of two years. He then declined further political honors to attend to his private affairs, though he still takes a keen interest in the fortunes of the Democratic party, with which he has been identified since he attained to his majority, and which so signally honored him by twice electing him to the general assembly.

In fraternal circles Mr. Schubert is well known, being a member and past master of Hohenwald Lodge No. 607, Free and Accepted Masons, Waynesboro Chapter, Royal Arch Masons, and George DeSmith Lodge No. 182, Knights of Pythias, of Hohenwald.

On October 18, 1900, Mr. Schubert married Miss Pearl DeHart, daughter of I. N. and Julia DeHart, of Nashville, Tennessee, and to this union has been born one daughter—Julia Bertha.

RAYMOND CRAWFORD HOOPER. A well-known and popular citizen of Hohenwald, Tennessee, was Raymond Crawford Hooper, who was twenty years in the service of the Nashville, Chattanooga & St. Louis Railway Company and for the last twelve years had charge of that company's interests at Hohenwald as station agent, during which time he so ordered his course as to win the high esteem of his acquaintances and to be accounted one of the sterling men of his community. He came from one of Tennessee's pioneer families and was a son of one of this state's loyal defenders of the Southern cause during the Civil war. The originator of the family in Tennessee was John Hooper, the great-grandfather of Raymond C., who came from North Carolina and settled on Sam's creek in Cheatham county, where he continued his occupation as a farmer. He had married before leaving North Carolina. One of his sons was Jesse Hooper, the grandfather of our subject, who spent his entire life in Cheatham county, Tennessee, and was one of its most prominent men. The latter also was a farmer and was an extensive slave holder. His son, Jesse Owen Hooper, the father of Raymond C., was born in Cheatham county, August 10, 1834, and grew to manhood in that county, receiving there his schooling. As a youth imbued with the loyal ardor so marked among the sons of Tennessee he ran away from home to join the Confederate ranks for service in the Civil war and became a member of Capt. Charles May's company in the Fiftieth Tennessee regiment. He served until near the close of the war and most of the time was a fifer in the fife and drum corps. After the war he returned to Cheatham county, was married there and shortly afterward removed to Dickson county, where he took up a farm in district No. 6, near Charlotte. Later he was engaged in the mercantile business at Charlotte for a number of years and spent his closing years there retired. He was a staunch Democrat in political views, and fraternally was a Mason. He was a member of the Christian church, while his wife was affiliated with the Methodist Episcopal church, south. The latter, who was Miss Mary Catherine Cullem as a maiden, was born in Cheatham county in 1836 and departed life in 1882. To these parents were born eight children, of whom our subject was second in birth and is the only one now living.

Raymond Crawford Hooper was born at Charlotte, Dickson county, Tennessee, August 20, 1869, and received his education in the public schools of that town and at the Dickson Normal school. He first took up responsible duties as a clerk at Dickson, Tennessee, but after two years of that employment he entered upon railroad work as a brakeman on the Centerville branch of the Nashville, Chattanooga & St. Louis Railroad. Some time later he took up telegraphy and after he had mastered it he was appointed agent at Kimmins, Tennessee. That was in 1899. After twenty-one months of service there he was transferred to Hohenwald, Tennessee, where he remained twelve years, the whole of his twenty years of railroad service having been for the same company. He was also interested in agriculture and owned a farm in Lewis county and also one in Wayne county, this state.

On January 15, 1903, Mr. Hooper was united in marriage to Miss Annie Laura Downing, daughter of S. W. Downing, who is engaged in farming and in the saw-mill business in Wayne county: To Mr. and Mrs. Hooper were born four children, Mary, Maggie, Jesse Owen and Raymond, the latter two of whom are deceased. Mr. Hooper was a loyal supporter of the Democratic party and an enthusiastic worker in its behalf. Fraternally he was a member of Dickson Lodge, No. 468, Free and Accepted Masons, and of Nashville Consistory No. 21 of Scottish Rite Masons, and was a charter member and past chancellor commander of George D. Smith Lodge No. 182, Knights of Pythias, at Hohenwald. He was a member of the Methodist Episcopal church, South, as is also his wife, and in its faith he passed away January 4, 1913.

John P. Dabbs, M. D. Among the immigrants to Tennessee from the state of North Carolina was Vincent S. Dabbs, who was born in the latter state in 1815, and who came with his brothers and sisters to Tennesssee at an early date. They settled in Perry, Wayne and Lewis counties. Vincent S. Dabbs was a successful farmer and stock dealer. He was twice married. His first wife was a Miss Grinder, by whom he had two sons and two daughters, and after her death he married Ellen Elizabeth Lancaster, who bore him eight children, four of whom are still living, Dr. John P. Dabbs being the fourth in order of birth. Vincent S. Dabbs died in 1880, and his second wife, who was born in Missouri in 1835, passed away in 1911. He was a Whig until after that party was disbanded, and from that time until his death he affiliated with the Democratic party. He was a member of the Presbyterian church and his wife was a Primitive Baptist.

Dr. John P. Dabbs was born in Farmers' Valley, Perry county, Tennessee, April 21, 1856. He received his early educational training in the public schools of his native county, after which he took a course in the Bryant & Stratton Business College at Nashville. He then taught in the public schools of Perry county for two years, at the end of which time he began the study of medicine. After suitable preparation, he entered the medical department of the University of Nashville, where he received the degree of M. D. in 1878, and took another course of lectures in 1882. He began practice at Farmers' Valley, but in 1890 removed to Linden and was actively engaged in practice until he located at Hohenwald in 1909. He is a member of the Tennessee State Medical Society and the Perry County Medical Society, and although more than a third of a century has elapsed since he first received his degree, he has not permitted himself to fall behind in the march of medical progress. In keeping up with the procession, however, he knows how to be conservative without being non-progressive, and is never in a hurry to abandon a remedy that has been tried for the realm of experiment or empiricism. In addition to his professional work, he has been also extensively interested in farming in Perry county, and has dealt in real estate to some extent.

For many years Dr. Dabbs has been recognized as one of the leaders of the Democratic party in his county and district. In 1896 he was elected to the state senate from the Twentieth senatorial district, composed of Maury, Perry and Lewis counties, and served for two years. He served as chairman of the Democratic executive committee of Perry county for some time, and is now the secretary of the executive committee of Lewis county. In 1904 he was appointed by Judge Woods to fill out an unexpired term as clerk of the circuit court of Perry county, and in whatever official position he has been called to serve he has given a good account of his stewardship.

Fraternally Dr. Dabbs is a member of the camp of Woodmen of the World at Linden, the Masonic Lodge, No. 256, at Linden, and the Royal Arch chapter at Jackson, Tennessee. He and his wife are members of the Christian church.

On August 21, 1877, Dr. Dabbs was united in marriage with Miss Sarah L. Randel, daughter of Dr. A. P. Randel, of Oregon county, Missouri. To this union were born seven children, five of whom are still living, viz: Mollie May, Commodore Olna, Ethel, Cleveland R. and Sadie Matt. Mollie married Samuel Lomax of Linden, Tennessee; Ethel is the wife of Joseph Tucker, a well known resident of Perry county; Sadie married C. H. Cude and lives in Texas; and the two sons are engaged in the conduct of a large mercantile concern at Hohenwald, under the firm name of J. P. Dabbs & Sons.

WILLIAM TAYLOR DANIEL. It is an interesting and gratifying fact, so much has the restless, nomadic spirit grown in America, that among the representative men of Tennessee there is a remarkable percentage of native sons, men who have found in the locality of their nativity ample opportunity for successful professional, industrial and business careers. One of these is William Taylor Daniel, of Hohenwald, who since 1904, has been a resident and business man of Lewis county and previous to that was a well known and prominent citizen of his native county of Perry. The Daniel family has been established on Tennessee soil for full a century and its members have ever held worthy and useful places in society. It originated here with John W. Daniel, the grandfather of William T., who came into Tennessee from North Carolina about the beginning of the last century and settled on Yellow Creek. He married Elizabeth Taylor. William Taylor Daniel, Sr., one of their seven children, was born in Dickson county, Tennessee, June 24, 1822, but was yet a youth when the family removed to Perry county, where he grew up and concluded a common school education. Taking up farming, he followed that occupation the most of his life, but in his later years he engaged in the mercantile business at Tom's Creek, Perry county and was one of the best known and most highly respected citizens of that county. In political sentiment he was a Democrat and was a magistrate of the fourth district in Perry county for forty years. In a fraternal way he was identified with the Masonic order, and in religious faith and church membership he was affiliated with the Christian denomination. He passed away in Perry county on July 18, 1910. There he was wedded in 1852 to Margaret Anne O'Guin, who was born in Perry county, August 23, 1833, and is let living. She is also a member of the Christian church.

Eleven children were born to this union and of this family William Taylor Daniel, Jr., our subject, was second in birth and is one of four children yet living. He was reared in Perry county, was educated in its public schools, and when he came of responsible age he took up farming there, following it until 1904, though in the meantime he was also engaged in the mercantile business at Tom's Creek fourteen years. He then removed to Lewis county and entered the lumber business at Hohenwald as a lumber buyer for the firm of Fair & Ketter at Pittsburg, Tennessee, continuing thus engaged four years. During the last four years he has been associated with Samuel H. Hinson in the lumber business at Hohenwald. While a resident of Perry county he served as county judge from 1894 to 1902 and previous to that he had served as county surveyor five years and had been a magistrate of the fourth district of that county six years. Politically he has always been aligned with the Democratic party. Fraternally he is affiliated as a member of Hohenwald Lodge No. 607, Free and Accepted Masons, with George D. Smith Lodge No. 182, Knights of Pythias and with Camp No. 215 of the Woodmen of the World.

On February 16, 1875, Mr. Daniel was united in marriage to Miss Mary Elizabeth Dyer, a daughter of C. C. Dyer, a well known farmer citizen of Perry county. Eight children have blessed this union and all are living. In order of birth they are: Lillie May, now Mrs. J. E. Burns, of Perry county, Tennessee; Nora L., now Mrs. R. T. Campbell, and Chester Arthur Daniel, both residents of Hohenwald; Ethel, who is the wife of J. R. Downey and resides at Etna, Tennessee; E. A. Daniel, Maude, now Mrs. W. J. Beasley, and Gertrude, the wife of T. C. Allison, all of whom reside in Hohenwald; and Samuel L. Daniel. Mr. Daniel and his family are all members of the Christian church.

WILLIAM BARNABAS TUCKER, M. D. Well established in the successful practice of his profession in the thriving town of Hohenwald, Dr. William Barnabas Tucker is numbered among the representative physicians of Lewis county and prior to his locating at Hohenwald in 1907, was one of the best known members of the medical profession in the adjoining county of Perry, where he was a medical practitioner thirty-four years. He is a scion of one of the old pioneer families of this commonwealth, one that was established here very shortly after Tennessee was admitted to statehood and whose members in the interim of a century or more have always been identified with the most worthy order of citizenship in this state.

A native of Perry county, Tennessee, William Barnabas Tucker was born near Linden, December 13, 1852, a son of Robert P. Tucker. The latter also was a native of Perry county, where he was born in 1818. Joseph Tucker, father of Robert P., was the founder of the family in Tennessee and came to this state in 1799 from North Carolina, where he was born in 1769, and where he was subsequently married to a Miss Glass. On coming to Tennessee he located in Perry county, where he spent the remainder of his life in the vocation of a farmer, passing away there in 1873. He helped General Jackson demonstrate the order of American soldiery at the battle of New Orleans in 1815 and sustained a severe wound in that engagement with the British. Of the eight children of his family, Robert was the third in birth. After receiving a common school education, Robert also became a tiller of the soil and followed agricultural pursuits very successfully throughout his life. In political sentiment he was a staunch Democrat and in a fraternal way he was affiliated with the Masonic order. His death occurred in 1870. He was married in Perry county, Tennessee, to Mary A. Peach, who was born in Williamson county, this state, in 1826 and is yet living. Two children were born to these parents: Dr. Tucker, of this review and John R. Tucker, now living in Perry county.

Dr. Tucker was educated in the Perry county public schools and in the medical department of the University of Nashville and of the University of Tennessee, attending the former institution two terms and the latter one term. He took the degree of Doctor of Medicine in each, in the University of Nashville in 1872, and in 1886, he took additional work in the University of Tennessee, receiving again the degree the M. D. In fact, throughout his whole medical career, Dr. Tucker has kept abreast with every advance made in the science and practice of medicine and while no longer representing the younger generation of the profession, he retains the keenest interest in the discoveries and progress of this science and has besides the invaluable knowledge gained from his own long experience. He began the practice of medicine at Linden, Perry county in 1873 and continued there thirty-four years, or until 1907, when he changed his location to Hohenwald, Lewis county. He is a general practitioner and while located in Perry county was a member of the Perry County Medical Society. He has always been more or less interested in agriculture and still owns a farm. Politically he is an adherent of the Democratic party.

In 1876, Dr. Tucker was married to Miss Louisa Jane Beasley, daughter of Beverly Beasley, of Perry county. To Dr. and Mrs. Tucker have been born four children, namely: James Thompson Tucker, now of Chicago, Illinois; Maude, who became the wife of O. J. Baars and resides in Perry county, Tennessee; Eve, who is at the home of her parents; and William Homer, now a resident of Fort Dodge, Iowa.

DR. JAMES FRANKLIN WHITWELL. One of the representative professional men and highly esteemed citizens of Lewis county, Tennessee, is Dr. James Franklin Whitwell, who has been a medical practitioner in that county for thirty years and has also become well known there through considerable county official service. The family to which Dr. Whitwell belongs is one of the old connections of Tennessee, as it was established here considerably more than a century ago, and he is of the third generation native to the soil of this state. Different of its members have held prominent places in the public life of this section and the father of Dr. Whitwell gave up his life at the battle of Franklin as a loyal defender of his state and the Confederacy during the Civil war. The family originated in America with Robert Whitwell, the great-grandfather of Dr. Whitwell, who emigrated from England and located in Tennessee, settling in Hickman county, where he reared a large family. Rev. Pleasant Whitwell, one of his sons, was born in Hickman county in 1803, but after he reached man's estate he removed to Perry county, this state, where afterward remained his home and where in an industrial way he followed farming. Entering the ministry of the Primitive Baptist church, he attained considerable note in this connection and in his day was one of the strongest believers and exhorters of that faith in this country. He was a Democrat in political belief and served as clerk of the Perry county court eight years. A son of his, Thomas Whitwell, was judge of Perry county sixteen years. Rev. Pleasant

Whitwell married Margaret Anderson, who bore him five children, one of whom was Elijah H. Whitwell, the father of Dr. Whitwell. Elijah H. Whitwell was born in Perry county, Tennessee, in 1832 and grew to manhood there, receiving a public school education. He followed farming until the opening of the Civil war, when he enlisted in Hulmes' company, formed at Linden, Perry county, and assigned to the Forty-eighth Tennessee regiment, with which he served until he gave up his life on the bloody battlefield of Franklin on November 30, 1864. In 1851 he was married to Angeline Randall, who was born in Perry county January 10, 1834, and died April 13, 1913. To this union were born five children, of whom Dr. Whitwell was second in birth and is the eldest of four that reached maturity and are yet living. The mother was married later to Joseph Dabbs, a farmer of Perry county.

James Franklin Whitwell was born near Linden, Perry county, Tennessee, May 9, 1854, and was but a lad of eight years when the father's sacrifice to the cause of the Southland deprived him of the provident care of that parent. He grew up in the vicinity of his birth and attended the public schools of the locality, later becoming a teacher. After being engaged in that manner in Perry and Lewis counties for some years he began to prepare for the profession he had determined should be his permanent line of endeavor and to that purpose began the study of medicine under Dr. T. S. Evans in the medical department of Vanderbilt University, Nashville, concluding his training in the medical department of the University of Tennessee. Beginning the active practice of medicine at Riverside, Tennessee, in 1882, he continued there until 1896, when he came to his present location at Hohenwald, where he is now well established in practice. Politically he is a staunch Democrat and served as registrar of Lewis county twelve years, or from 1898 to 1910; was secretary of the executive committee of the county for several years and has also served as its health officer for a number of years. He is much interested in truck gardening and horticulture and keeps in touch with and applies the most advanced ideas in regard to each of these lines of cultivation.

In 1873 Dr. Whitwell was united in marriage to Miss Sophia Grinder, daughter of John Grinder, a former citizen of Lewis county, Tennessee. To Dr. and Mrs. Whitwell were born two daughters: Nora, who became the wife of C. M. Paxton and died in 1909, at the age of thirty-three, and Cora, whose husband is Andrew Raspbury, an interested principal in the mercantile firm of Rasbury & Warren at Hohenwald. Dr. and Mrs. Whitwell are both members of the Christian church and the former is an elder of that denomination.

WALKER W. O'GUIN. For three generations at least the O'Guin family has been identified with the fortunes and affairs of Hickman county, Tennessee. Thomas O'Guin, the grandfather of the subject of this sketch, was born in the county, there grew to manhood, married, and became a prominent farmer. When the Civil war broke out he cast his lot with the Southern Confederacy and entered the army as a private soldier. Exposure and hardship incident to military life so impaired his health that he died of tuberculosis soon after being discharged from the service, leaving two sons, the younger of which, Sidney L. O'Guin, was born near Whitfield, Hickman county, in April, 1863. In 1884, S. L. O'Guin and Sarah Coble were united in marriage in Lewis county, Tennessee, though she is a native of Hickman county, where she was born in 1856. Three children have been born of this union—Walker W., Alden and Marvin—the first named in Lewis county and the other two in Hickman county. In early life S. L. O'Guin followed the vocation of a farmer, but later engaged in mercantile pursuits. He is now the proprietor of a shoe and gents' furnishing store at Centerville. Politically he is a Democrat, and both he and his wife are members of the Christian church.

Walker W. O'Guin, the eldest of the three children born to his parents, was born in Lewis county, Tennessee, February 1, 1886, but removed with his parents to Hickman county in his early childhood. He was educated in the Hickman county schools and at the Murray Institute, Murray, Kentucky, and until 1909, was engaged in teaching in the public schools of Lewis and Hickman counties. In 1909 he entered the field of journalism as owner and editor of the *Hohenwald Herald*. On August 18, 1912, the office and equipment of the paper were destroyed by fire, and soon after that Mr. O'Guin removed to Centerville, where he became the editor of the *Hickman County Citizen*. This paper has the largest circulation of any newspaper in the county. In national politics it is a supporter of Democratic principles, but in state and local affairs it is independent. Although Mr. O'Guin has been in charge of its editorial columns but a comparatively short time, he has demonstrated his grasp of public questions and his ability as a writer. His long residence in Hickman county and his familiarity with conditions peculiarly qualify him for the position he occupies. He knows the needs of the county and is always ready to further any measure for the social and material uplift of her citizens.

In his political affiliations Mr. O'Guin is an unswerving Democrat. His fraternal relations are with Hohenwald Camp No. 215, Woodmen of the World; Sam Davis Lodge No. 158, K. of P., located at Centerville; and Centerville Camp M. W. A. In all these orders he is popular because of his genial disposition and good fellowship.

In 1907 Mr. O'Guin married Miss Ruby Poore, daughter of J. W. Poore, a well known resident of Hickman county. Two children have come to bless this union—Harriet Jane and Sydney Lamar. Mr. and Mrs. O'Guin are members of the Christian church and take a commendable interest in promoting its good works.

BEN B. GILLESPIE. The career of Ben B. Gillespie, of Gallatin, Tennessee, presents a striking example of enterprise, industry and integrity, conducing to eminent success. Reared to the work of the farm, he has continued his operations along agricultural lines to such good effect that today he is the owner of a handsome property in Sumner county, and is known as one of the leading Hereford cattle breeders in the state. Mr. Gillespie was born in Sumner county, Tennessee, February 1, 1860, and is a son of Richard G. and Susan C. (Harris) Gillespie.

The Gillespie family was founded in America during the middle of the eighteenth century by one James Gillespie, who came to this county from Scotland. From him descended Jacob Gillespie, the grandfather of Ben B., who was born in North Carolina, and came to Tennessee at an early date. He served in the War of 1812, under General Jackson, was known as a mighty hunter, and eventually entered land from the government and spent the rest of his life in farming in Tennessee, dying full of years and in the possession of a handsome competency. Richard G. Gillespie was born in Sumner county in 1826, and spent his entire life in agricultural pursuits, being exceedingly successful in his operations and accumulating 1,400 acres of land. He was one of the founders of the First National Bank of Gallatin, and a director for years, and all movements of a progressive nature could depend upon his support. He was an enthusiastic member of the A. F. & A. M., and in his political views was a stalwart Democrat. His death occurred in March, 1903. Mr. Gillespie married Susan C. Harris, who was born in Sumner county in 1833, daughter of Bright and Sallie (Walton) Harris, natives of North Carolina. Mr. Harris was a stone mason by trade, and made his way to Kentucky, and thence to Tennessee, with a kit of tools on his shoulder, but lived to attain to eminent success. Mrs. Gillespie survives her husband and lives with her son, Ben B., who was the fourth of her six children. She is a woman of many Christian virtues, and has been a member of the Methodist Episcopal church all of her life.

Ben B. Gillespie received his education in the public schools of Sumner county, following which he attended the University of Tennessee, at Knoxville. On his return to the home farm he resumed agricultural pursuits, which he has followed ever since, and is now the owner of a well-cultivated property of 300 acres. Mr. Gillespie has given his attention during late years to the breeding of thoroughbred Hereford cattle, making a specialty of traveling all over the fair circuit. The year 1912 was a most successful one, as he returned to his farm without an animal, whereas he had started out with a large herd. His animals bring top prices, and a long list of ribbons testify eloquently to their success as prize winners. About forty head are raised annually, all pure breed, and many of these are disposed of through mail orders. Mr. Gillespie is known as an excellent judge of stock, and his advice is often sought, and freely given, in matters pertaining thereto. During a long experience, he has come in contact with men in every walk of life, and the high esteem in which he is universally held, gives evidence of his integrity in business matters.

In November, 1887, Mr. Gillespie was united in marriage with Anna Lou McGabock, daughter of John McGabock, a retired farmer of Scotch-Irish descent, who is now living in Nashville. Mr. and Mrs. Gillespie have had two children: Nellie and Frank W., both living at home. Mrs. Gillespie is a member of the Methodist Episcopal church. Mr. Gillespie has shown some interest in fraternal work, being a member of the Loyal Order of Moose. In his political belief he is a Democrat. He is at this time steward in the Methodist Episcopal church, and for more than a quarter of a century has served as superintendent of the Sunday school.

FRANK H. DUNKLIN, M. D. During a practice in medicine of more than a quarter of a century, most of which has been passed in Sumner county, Dr. Dunklin has utilized many opportunities for devoted public service, and at the same time has been held in the high esteem of his fellow citizens. His home for many years has been in the country near Gallatin, on Rural Route No. 3, and his practice has been very largely among the rural communities. His professional associates regard him as one of the best doctors in Sumner county, and this appreciation was borne out by the success which has always attended his efforts.

Dr. Dunklin was born in Lowndes county, Alabama, May 24, 1863, the son of Thomas W. and Martha (Crumpton) Dunklin. On the maternal side the family was from Virginia, and most of its members were identified with the service of the church, a brother of Dr. Dunklin's mother, having been one of the most prominent divines in Alabama. The paternal grandfather, William Dunklin, was born in North Carolina, whence he moved into Alabama and there lived and died. The family was originally from England.

Thomas W. Dunklin, the father, was born in South Carolina in 1812, and his death occurred 1877. His wife was born in Alabama in 1818, and died in 1881. From South Carolina the father, when a youth, accompanied his parents to Alabama, where he became a successful planter. He owned a great deal of wealth in slaves and other property, and at the time of the war invested in quantities of the Confederate bonds. The outcome of the war resulted disastrously to his financial standing, though he always provided well for his children. He and his wife were the parents of ten children, of whom the doctor was the youngest. William James, the oldest child, served four years as a Confederate soldier, and the test of his gallant service was the five different wounds he received. The parents were very interested members of the Missionary Baptist church, in which the father was deacon for years. He was a member of the Masonic order, and in politics a Democrat.

Dr. Frank H. Dunklin attended the common schools of Alabama and the preparatory school of Greenville in that state. In 1884 he entered the University of Tennessee, from which he was graduated M. D. in 1886. The same year he entered upon active practice in this state, then spent two years in Alabama, and since 1889 has made his permanent home in Sumner county. He was a poor man when his professional career began in this county, and he has been so fortunate as to acquire a position of substantial comfort and affluence. He is owner of a fine farm of three hundred acres besides considerable bank stock.

In October, 1887, occurred his marriage to Miss Mary Bell, daughter of John W. Bell. Her father was born and reared in Sumner county, where during his active career he came to own an estate of five hundred acres and was known as one of the most successful farmers and stockmen of the county. The doctor and wife are the parents of two children: F. B., who is studying medicine in Vanderbilt University at Nashville; and K. B., who is manager on his father's farm. Dr. Dunklin and wife are members of the Methodist church South. He is a Democrat in politics, has been a member of the county Democratic executive committee, and has served as chairman of the county board of education. He is a member of the county and state medical societies, and the American Medical Association. He has been president of the county medical society, and at the present time is president of the Sumner County Health League.

ROBERT W. CALDWELL, of Gallatin, has now served a decade as circuit clerk of Sumner county and has proved a most capable and efficient official, the length of his service being indicative of his standing in the public estimation of this county both as an official and as a citizen. Here he has maintained his home from the time of his nativity and always has been identified with the best citizenship of the county, his own sterling qualities adding prominence to a name that has been known and respected in this locality for more than a century. The family originated in this state with Hardy Caldwell, a native of North Carolina, who came into the state in a very early day. His son, William, born October 10, 1807, in Sumner county, became a well-to-do farmer and reared a large family. Hardy Caldwell, son of William and the father of our subject, was born June 1, 1831, and passed away January 15, 1912, in the locality in which he had lived for a little more than four score years. His whole active career was spent as a farmer and he was very successful in that vocation, leaving to his children at his death, an estate of several hundred acres. He was numbered among Tennessee's gallant defenders in the Civil war and as a member of the Twentieth Tennessee Regiment, he fought at Mill Springs, Shiloh, Murfreesboro and Chickamauga, being wounded in his foot at the battle of Shiloh. He served from 1861 until his capture at the battle of Chickamauga in

1863, and from that time until the close of the war he was held a captive in the Federal prison at Rock Island, Illinois. On being released he returned to his home in Sumner county, Tennessee, and began life anew, resuming his occupation of farming. His entire life was marked by the deeds of a patriotic, public-spirited citizen and he so lived as to hold a secure place in the confidence and esteem of his community. He was a member of the Masonic fraternity and in politics was a stalwart Democrat. A valued member of the Methodist Episcopal church, he was one of its most energetic workers in this county, having served for years as a Sunday school superintendent and also having served as trustee and steward in the church of his membership. He wedded Miss Frances Markcum, a native daughter of Tennessee, who was born January 19, 1844, and yet survives her husband. She, too, is an earnest and devout member of the Methodist Episcopal church. There were six children born to this union. Robert W., the eldest and one of five now living, was born in Sumner county, April 29, 1867. Educated first in the public schools of his native county and then in a private boarding school at Willette, Macon county, Mr. Caldwell began independent activity as a teacher and taught in public schools for seventeen years. In 1902 he was elected clerk of the circuit court and has served in that office continuously and acceptably to all concerned to the present time.

On October 12, 1898, Mr. Caldwell was joined in marriage to Miss Willie Barnes, whose father is William Barnes, a native and a well known and successful farmer of Sumner county. This union has been blessed with seven children, named: Rowena F., Ruel A., Stella M., Alleen, William B., Robert W., and Joseph A., the first four of whom are now attending school. Mr. and Mrs. Caldwell are members of the Methodist Episcopal church, South, and he unites fraternally with the Woodmen of the World, of which order he now is council commander in his local lodge. As a Democrat he has long taken an active part in the local political affairs of his party. He owns a good farm in this county and also owns town property. As teacher, official and agriculturist he has put energy and intelligence into his efforts and in each line of endeavor has attained definite success.

HENRY CLAY RICHARDSON. The profession of law and the realm of politics are substantially represented in Dickson by Hon. Henry Clay Richardson, who is a native of this county and whose progenitors have for three preceding generations been associated with this part of Tennessee. They have constituted a family line notable for military vigor and other strong characteristics.

Austin Richardson (the great-grandfather of our subject) joined the Revolutionary army when a mere boy, following his father and five uncles to the exciting scenes of that conflict. They had gone thither from their home at Culpepper Courthouse, Virginia, but only Austin

Richardson returned, for the others had fallen in battle or died from other ills of war, and only this youth and one brother were left to represent the family. In spite of the fact that he had taken part in the great war and had served under Washington, he was then but an orphan boy and was "bound out" until he reached the years of his majority. When he became his own master, he left Virginia and came to Tennessee in 1793, first settling at Greenville. Here he married a Miss Johnson and three years later they removed to the part of the state which is now Dickson county, selecting as their home one of the highest points in the county and one near a large spring. His was a large family, one of his sons being Louis Richardson, born in 1807 in Dickson county. He became a prominent farmer and married Miss Vina Walker of Hickman county. Their son, W. Turner Richardson (the father of H. C. Richardson) was born in Hickman county, in 1843, and early displayed a thirst for adventure and action. At the age of seventeen years he ran away from home and joined the Confederate Army, serving in Company K, of the Eleventh Tennessee Infantry. He served under Johnson and Hood in all engagements; was captured at Missionary Ridge; was held prisoner at Rock Island prison in Illinois; was exchanged at Greensborough, North Carolina; and after the close of the war returned to the occupation of peace. He was a farmer and a dealer in lumber and lime, conducting a large kiln and managing a large business in that line. In 1866 he married Miss Emily Catherine Alspaugh, who was a native of North Carolina, born in 1841; her mother was the youngest daughter of Colonel Josiah Clifton, a large land owner and colonel in the Revolutionary war. He was at Yorktown with Washington when Cornwallis surrendered. To Emily C. Alspaugh Richardson and W. T. Richardson were born twelve children, eight of whom lived to the years of maturity. The eldest of these was H. C. Richardson, who was born in the town of Burns, in Dickson county, Tennessee, on the twenty-first day of March, 1867.

Henry Clay Richardson early evinced an intellectual keenness suggestive of that of his distinguished namesake. He was educated in Edgewood College, and then fared forth upon the professional pathway of teaching. Like many other young men of ability, he found it possible to give due attention to his pedagogical labors and in his hours of leisure to broaden his own mind by carrying on independent study. The line which Mr. Richardson chose for further mental development and advancement in life was that of law. Meanwhile, however, he became an authority on county educational matters and his personal standing was such that for two years his services were required as superintendent of public instruction for Dickson county.

In 1891 Mr. Richardson wrote his bar examinations and was admitted to practice in Tennessee. The quality of his professional activity may be readily guessed from the fact that recognition of his ability was indicated by his district in sending him to the state legislature in 1894. Hon. Richardson served for four years as a representative and then turned to his home and practiced in Dickson. He is a stanch Democrat and has been very active in the affairs of his party.

Numerous fraternal organizations count Mr. Richardson a valued member. He is a member of the Ancient Free and Accepted Masons; of the Independent Order of Odd Fellows; of the Knights of Pythias; and of the Improved Order of Red Men. Mr. Richardson is socially popular as well as professionally successful.

N. W. TRUE. Both prominent and efficient as an abstract attorney and as county surveyor, N. W. True enjoys a wide measure of popularity among the citizens of Springfield and of Robertson county in general. This young man is a lifelong resident of the county, his birth having occurred here on November 14, 1879; of his parents, F. M. and Harriet (Bigbee) True, extended account is given in the biographical sketch of H. C. True, appearing elsewhere in these pages.

The public schools of Robertson county provided the mental equipment of N. W. True, so far as formal school training may accomplish that end. He turned to definite purpose all such opportunities, also taking advantage of all other intellectual material that came in his way. To such a youth openings are ever at hand, and Mr. True first occupied himself as a self-supporting young man, with the duties of deputy court clerk.

Mr. True's specialty is that of abstracts and titles, in relation to which his accurate legal knowledge is of great value to his clients. His office practice is very large and his business in connection therewith makes it necessary that he investigate estates at considerable distance from Springfield. He is therefore thoroughly familiar with Robertson county and with the surrounding counties as well.

In 1912 Mr. True was honored with election to the office of surveyor for Robertson county, a position which he is well qualified to fill, and the duties of which he discharges with competent ability.

The Democratic party is that of Mr. True's allegiance and its fortunes are a matter of great moment to him. His activities in behalf of the great political camp of Democracy are particularly enthusiastic at the periods of campaign movements, his party work taking him into all parts of the state. Political leaders look to Mr. True as one of the strong coming men in civic work.

In addition to the interests of his profession and political work, N. W. True is one of the leading members of the secret societies of Springfield. The Independent Order of Odd Fellows and the Knights of Pythias share his fraternal affiliations. He is tireless in his attention to both his public and personal business operations. Mr. True has thus far been the creator of his own success and bids fair to be one of the makers of "The New South." He was married in 1912 to Miss Maud Tipps, of Tullohoma, Tennessee.

MAYOR PITT HENSLEE. Not only is Hon. Pitt Henslee variously prominent in financial affairs in Dickson, but he is the present incumbent of the highest local office in the gift of the city, an honor which he well deserves for his many services to the municipality.

Mayor Henslee is a son of Dr. J. T. Henslee (1838-1895), the latter a Kentuckian by birth, a graduate in medicine at Vanderbilt University, a practitioner at Hollow Rock, Tennessee, and in Dickson county, besides three years' professional activity in Texas. He was a Baptist, a Mason and a Democrat and had served in youth as a Confererate soldier under General Forrest. He married in 1870, Miss Mary Lipe (1852-1873), a native of Carroll county. They were the parents of but one child—the son of whom we now write as Mayor Henslee. Dr. Henslee's second marriage was with Miss Dora Pickler of Hollow Rock, and three children have in the succeeding years been born to them.

It was on August 18, 1871, that Pitt Henslee was born in Carroll county, Tennessee. After his elementary education in the public schools of Dickson, he studied in Bethel College at McKenzie, and for one year —because of troublesome eyesight—was a student in the School for the Blind, at Nashville.

Mr. Henslee is possessed of a gift for mercantile and other commercial operations. He is the president of the Henslee Dry Goods Company; he is a director of the Cumberland Valley National Bank of Nashville; he is associated with the S. G. Holland Stove Company of that city. But his greatest financial achievements have been in connection with the First National Bank of Dickson, of which he was first president and founder. Its capital is rated at $50,000; its surplus at $11,000; and its average deposits at $250,000.

Another line in which he has shown his unusual ability is that of publishing a local newspaper. As president and manager of the *Dickson County Herald,* he has been responsible for the virile character of that eight-page sheet of news and editorial exposition. Mr. Henslee is a Democrat in politics and has been honored by his constituency with election to the Tennessee legislature, the date of his period of service being from 1899 to 1912. During his incumbency special chancery and circuit courts were established in Dickson. It was on September 12, of the latter year that his townspeople evinced their confidence in him and their esteem for him by electing him the next mayor of Dickson.

The mayor's home is graced by the presence of Susie Spencer Henslee, his wife. Mrs. Henslee is a daughter of the Reverend Samuel Spencer of Spencer Mill. The date of her marriage to Pitt Henslee was 1899. In the ensuing years a small son, named Lipe, has been born to them.

Geo Dahucke.

The Baptist church is the religious denomination with which the mayor and his wife are formally connected and to which they give their special support, Mr. Henslee being one of the trustees of this church. The members of four different secret societies also claim his fraternal interest; these are the Independent Order of Odd Fellows—Harmony Lodge; the Ancient, Free and Accepted Masons—Number 468 Dickson; the Modern Woodmen of America and the Junior Order of United American Mechanics. No citizen of Dickson, public or private, is the object of greater esteem or warmer friendship than the successful, but kindly and genial Pitt Henslee.

GEORGE DAHNKE. In Union City, Dahnke enterprise and energy has become so intimately intertwined with the business and civic activities within the last two decades that the most casual review of the business life of the city would be incomplete without reference to the Dahnke brothers.

George Dahnke started out to make his own way when thirteen years old without money, and came a stranger to Union City as a journeyman baker, and has worked his way up until today he is at the head of about all the important industries of the county, and by big odds is the most prominent and active business man of the state.

Mr. Dahnke is a native of Nashville, Illinois. He was born September 29, 1866, a son of H. F. and Katherine (Benner) Dahnke. His youthful days he spent in clerking in his native town, and from clerking he turned his attention to the bakery business. This he followed at Nashville until 1887, and landed in Union City, October 8, of that year, a journeyman baker. He worked three months; at the end of which time he bought out the establishment where he had been employed, opening a restaurant and bakery. In 1888, he added a confectionery department to his growing business, which has kept pace with the progress of the times, and the Dahnke cafe has a conspicuous place in the activities of Union City.

In 1900, when the Dahnke-Walker Milling Company was organized he was made its manager, and has since continued at the head of the firm with the result that at this writing the Dahnke-Walker Milling Company is not only the largest concern of its kind in Obion county, but it ranks among the largest in Tennessee. The plant covers about five acres on the Mobile and Ohio Railroad and has a capacity for turning out fourteen hundred barrels of flour and meal per day. The best and latest improved machinery is installed, a force of fifty hands are employed, a capital of fifty-thousand dollars is used in carrying on the business, and the company's trade extends to territory in the states of Tennessee, Mississippi, Alabama, Georgia, and in fact all of the southeastern states. An approximate estimate of the grain shipped by the plant would be about two thousand cars. In addition to this mill the company has another of equally large capacity where coarse feed is ground.

The ice company was organized in 1891 and operated at a loss, and came to the end of its resources in 1896. In that year the stock was sold to George Dahnke and brother for less than half its original value, and George Dahnke then became president and manager of the company, a position he has since retained. This ice plant has a capacity of two thousand tons storage, and manufactures fifteen tons of ice per day. The present company is known as the Union City Ice & Coal Company, several years ago dealing in coal. The plant covers an area of two acres.

Another important industry which Mr. Dahnke promoted is the Union City Cotton Gin, which was established in 1908, and is doing a prosperous business. A conspicuous fact about Mr. Dahnke is his ability as a reorganizer. He has taken a number of concerns in this vicinity, recognized as complete failures, and has injected life and vitality into them, until they have all become very successful under his direction. Mr. Dahnke is a director in Union City Canning Company, the Third National Bank of Union City, the Obion Land & Improvement Company, and the Obion County Fair Association.

A year ago at the meeting of the Business Men's Club, Mr. Dahnke proposed that they get an expert soil doctor to increase the average yield of grain per acre. He was appointed a committee of one to organize the proposition, which he did, as more fully explained in later paragraphs, was made president of the resulting organization, wrote to all the leading agricultural colleges in the United States, and finally succeeded in getting an expert to take charge of the technical end of the business. This was the first county in the state of Tennessee to have such an organization, and Mr. Dahnke was the man whose original enterprise accomplished the deed. He is the leading factor and director of the Obion River Drainage Company, formed for the purpose of reclaiming about fifty-seven thousand acres of the most fertile land in Obion county, by a system of leveeing and drainage, the undertaking including the straightening the channel of Obion river. One of the drainage districts has been organized, its bonds sold, and the work well toward prosperous completion.

Socially Mr. Dahnke affiliates with the Masonic order, the Independent Order of Odd Fellows, and the Knights of Pythias, and the Benevolent and Protective Order of Elks. He is, as already mentioned, one of the influential members of the Business Men's Club of Union City, and is at the present time its president. His religious creed is that of the Lutheran church, and in politics he is a Democrat, but has never assented to become a candidate for office. Mr. Dahnke was married November 25, 1891, to Miss Eleanor Hoffman. They are the parents of eight children, namely: Catherine, Louise, Mary, Helen, Nellie, Ruth, Marjorie, and George Jr., all of whom are at home.

From the preceding paragraphs it will be understood that Mr. Dahnke is a man of very exceptional ability. He is one of those who possess "life and leading" and whose services are indispensable in twentieth century progress. As an addition to the somewhat formal biography already written, the value of this article will be enhanced by the following estimate of his work and influence, written by one who has observed the career of Mr. Dahnke and his public spirited activity, and is thus in a position to judge and appreciate this forceful business leader.

Mr. Dahnke comes of stout old German stock, and he possesses in his make-up and general character the many notable qualities that have made Germans potent factors in the history of civilization. We note that Mr. Dahnke is what he is. He is frankness personified. We do not believe there is a particle of insincerity or hypocrisy in him. Because of this and because of his veracity, his unusual, we might truthfully say, his extraordinary determination of character, he is recognized as the soul and center of Union City's business interest. He is presiding officer of the Business Men's Club, and has been for several years. He enjoys the profoundest confidence of the business man. He is constantly revolving in his mind some worthy plan for benefitting Union City and Obion county. He is big and broad enough to work not only for Union City, but for all of Obion county. He is a self-made man. He came to Union City a few years ago, a penniless young stranger. His favorite saying is that a man's business is no bigger than the man himself. He established a bakery and cafe. Humble as this business was, he gave it prestige and honor and dignity, and gave Union City an institution that is one of its brightest and most successful ornaments— the justly famous Dahnke Cafe.

He acquired a majority of the stock in a run-down, dilapidated ice factory, and he overhauled and revamped it, stamped it with the stamp of success, and fine executive ability and made it, too, one of the leading institutions of Union City. He next bought a leading interest in an unsuccessful flouring mill proposition. He overhauled this business, he made a patient, exhaustive, laborious analysis of what had caused its failure. He modernized the machinery, he made a practical study of grain, and the Dahnke-Walker Milling Company is the product of his labor, one of the most successful milling enterprises in the middle west or in the south.

Mr. Dahnke, as the president of the Business Men's Club, was the first to suggest the advisability and the possibility of "curing" the "sick" soil of Obion county. He it was who was first heard to mention the constantly increasing yield of wheat and corn year by year. It was Mr. Dahnke who made the call for the farmers to meet and effect organization and secure funds for the employment of a soil doctor. The meeting of farmers was held in the court house of Obion county, and the organization was made the Obion County Agricultural Improvement Association. Mr. Dahnke in recognition of the deep interest he had shown in soil improvement was by the farmers assembled, elected president of the association. Mr. Dahnke put his shoulder to the wheel and used his personal influence to bear upon the concern, inducing the farmers to assist in getting up the needful funds. He also came into touch with the great national organization that had been effected to bring about soil improvements, and increased crop production. All his efforts were crowned with success. The money was made up, the agricultural expert secured, and Obion county put in line with the foremost and most aggressive counties in the United States. Mr. Dahnke secured a visit from the famous D. Ward King, and as a result of Mr. King's teachings the compulsory use of the King Road-drag has been incorporated into the road law of Obion county.

But, perhaps, Mr. Dahnke's greatest work was the part he took in the creation of several drainage districts in Obion county, in Obion river valley. When others doubted and quibbled and found fault, Mr. Dahnke with serene confidence and unwavering faith and fidelity held firmly to the absolute feasibility of the draining plan. This enterprise, too, has been crowned with success, the bonds have been negotiated, and work will at an early date begin on the drainage of one district, the forerunner of other drainage districts, whose reclaiming will add millions of dollars to the resources of Tennessee. This brief sketch will, we believe, fully suffice to show that Mr. Dahnke is not only a live-wire as a business proposition, but a broad, useful, public spirited citizen.

CAPT. CHAS. SANDERS DOUGLASS, A. B., A. M. Prominent among the educators of Tennessee is Capt. Chas. Sanders Douglass, who for twenty-five years has been superintendent of the city schools of Gallatin and in various other relations has been a prominent and influential factor in the educational affairs of this state for over forty years. This long identification alone is ample evidence of his efficiency in educational work and of his character and standing as a man. The Douglass family trace their lineage to the bold, sturdy Scotch-Irish stock. Firm and dauntless, loyal, conservative and honorable, are the characteristics that marked this race in the mother country, traits that were not lost by emigration and residence in this land of freedom and adventure. Back in the colonial period three brothers emigrated from their native Scotland to the United States, one locating in middle Tennessee, another in Virginia, while the third settled in North Carolina. Stephen A. Douglas, the American statesman and politician, was descended from this connection. From the North Carolina ancestor was descended James Douglass, born in North Carolina in 1762, who was the grandfather of

Capt. C. S. Douglass of this review. In young manhood he came to . Tennessee, where he married in 17—. He passed away in this state in 1851 at the venerable age of eighty-nine years. His son, Col. Young Douglass, was born in Sumner county, Tennessee, in 1805 and followed farming up to his marriage in 1834 to Benetta Rawlings, after which he took up merchandising. Later he returned to agricultural pursuits and was quite successful in that line of endeavor until his death in 1865. He was captain of one of the first military companies organized in Sumner county and it was from this connection that he received his familiar appellation of Colonel Douglass. Benetta (Rawlings) Douglass was born in Sumner county, Tennessee, in 1813, a daughter of Dr. Benjamin Rawlings, who was a pioneer physician in middle Tennessee. She passed away in 1849, the mother of six children, the third of whom is Capt. C. S. Douglass of this review. After her death Colonel Douglass married Mrs. D. Killebrew, nee Green.

. Capt. Chas. S. Douglass was born in Sumner county in 1839. His preliminary education was received in the country schools of this county and his collegiate training was received at Central University, Danville, Kentucky, from which institution he was graduated in 1860 as a Bachelor of Arts. The degree of Master of Arts was conferred on him by the same institution in 1884. After completing his literary education he took up the study of law, but soon discontinued it, however, for at the opening of the war between the states at about that time his fealty to the South was promptly evinced. He was one of the organizers of Company H of the Thirtieth Tennessee Infantry, and in the beginning was at once commissioned adjutant, with the title of first-lieutenant. At the battle of Fort Donelson in February, 1862, he was captured and taken to Camp Chase, from whence he was later transferred to Johnson's island, being held as a prisoner seven months. On his release he returned to the Confederate service as captain of Company H of the Thirtieth Tennessee Regiment, Army of Tennessee, and having lost most of his company was afterward appointed an adjutant general, in which capacity he served during the remainder of the war. Besides the action at Fort Donelson, he participated at Jackson and Raymond, Mississippi; at Chickamauga and Missionary Ridge in Tennessee; at Resaca, Georgia, and in all the other engagements of the Western army under Hood and Johnston. At the battle of Jonesboro he was wounded in the left arm and had a horse shot from under him. Throughout the whole of his service he exhibited the highest of soldierly qualities. At the close of the war he returned to Sumner county, where on July 23, 1865, he wedded Susan Graham, who was born in Sumner county in 1846 and is a daughter of Dr. Alexander Graham. The two children of their union are: Ada, who became the wife of Dr. C. W. Meguiar, now president of the Kentucky examining board in dentistry, and Charles Clair Douglass, who resides in California.

In 1871 Captain Douglass, together with Prof. C. W. Callender, organized the Sumner high school in Hendersonville, Tennessee, but two years later Prof. Callender was elected superintendent of public instruction in Sumner county and for seven years thereafter Captain Douglass continued alone as principal of the school. During that time he also filled the unexpired term of another instructor in a male seminary at Gallatin. In 1880 he was elected superintendent of public instruction in Sumner county, and in 1884 and 1885 he was also principal of the normal school at Gallatin. He was yet serving as county superintendent when he was elected superintendent of the city schools of Gallatin in 1888, a position that he has now held continuously for twenty-five years. Further mention of his position in public esteem in Gallatin is barely necessary in this connection, for this long service alone speaks more eloquently than words in this respect. He is a member of the Tennessee State Teachers Association, has served as its vice-president and as a member of its executive committee, and in 1883 was president of that body. He has served nineteen years as a member of the state board of education, was president of the board one term, and was a member of the committee that adopted the first uniform text books for the state; he also was the first president of the Teachers and Officers Association of Tennessee. He was for twenty years conductor of State Institutes.

In political sentiment he is a staunch Democrat, and in 1878 was a candidate for the state legislature but was defeated by eighteen votes. As a Confederate veteran he became a charter member of Donaldson Bivouac, of Gallatin; was its president one term, and has been its secretary seventeen years. He and his wife are members of the Methodist Episcopal church, south, at Gallatin, and he is now serving his second year as president of the County Sunday Schools. As a citizen, soldier and educator he has lived up to high ideals and his life and services have been those of one of the most worthy of Tennesseeans.

THOMAS W. HUNTER. Superintendent of public instruction in Sumner county, Thomas W. Hunter is an educator who upholds the highest standards of efficiency in the school service of the county. To gain his own education he went in debt, and he advanced to a place of influence in relation to the public welfare through his own vigorous efforts. It has been his endeavor in his present work to guide the young people of the county to the channels of state education, the facilities which in his own boyhood, he was so painfully in want of. Mr. Hunter is one of the leading educators of northern Tennessee.

A native of Sumner county, he was born on a farm September 3, 1875, a son of Thomas M. and Ellen (Wallace) Hunter, both of whom were natives of Sumner county, the father born here in 1853 and the mother in 1856. Both families have been long identified with this section of the state. The maternal grandfather, whose name was Duncan Wallace, was born in Sumner county. On the paternal side, the founder of the Hunter family in Tennessee, was the great-grandfather of the present superintendent of public instruction. His name was Lewis Hunter, a native of Virginia, who when a young man came into Tennessee and thus established the family in this locality. His opposition to slavery caused him to leave his slaves behind in Virginia, they being turned over to his brother. A son of Lewis Hunter was also named Thomas M., who was born in Sumner county and spent all his life there on a farm. Two of his sons, named Frank and Lewis, were soldiers in the Civil war, and Frank rose to the rank of brigadier-general. Thomas Miller Hunter, the father, was reared and educated in Sumner county, where he and his wife have spent all their lives, and their home is now on the old farm in the Eleventh district, where his grandfather settled on first coming from Virginia. Farming as a vocation has been reasonably successful to him and along with a fair degree of material prosperity he has also enjoyed the thorough esteem of his fellow citizens He and his wife were the parents of five children, four of whom are now living, and Thomas W. is the oldest. Both parents are members of the Methodist church, the father being a Democrat, and they have lived quiet and unassuming lives, taking a considerable interest in church affairs, but otherwise not participating largely in the public affairs of their community.

Thomas W. Hunter was educated in the Tullatuskee College at Beth Page, Tennessee, and he continued his studies at Hartsville, this state. His career as teacher had already begun before he finished college. His first school was at Gumwood, Macon county, where he taught for a time, then was engaged by the directors in Sumner county, where he taught five months in the year and spent five months in furthering his own education. In 1910 occurred his election to the office of superintendent of public instruction for the county, and during the past two years he has made a notable record in improving methods and securing the systematic cooperation of all parties concerned, which is a factor of the greatest importance in facilitating the perfect service of local schools.

Mr. Hunter has also been known to the citizens of this county as a merchant, having been associated with his brother in 1903-9 in a store. but in the latter year he sold his interest to his brother Though starting his career in debt for his education he has long since put himself even on that score and has acquired from year to year a gratifying increase of material prosperity.

Mr. Hunter was married December 28, 1897, to Miss Ollie Smithson, a daughter of M. Smithson, a farmer of Sumner county. Mrs. Hunter died in 1906, leaving one son named Dewey, now in school. In 1909 Mr. Hunter was united in marriage with Mary L. Montgomery, a daughter of James Montgomery, a native of Sumner county and in former years a lawyer, and also a soldier during the Civil war. Mr. and Mrs. Hunter are the parents of one child, William Hutchison, now two years of age. Mrs. Hunter is a member of the Cumberland Presbyterian church, and he belongs to the Methodist church. His fraternal affiliations are with the Masonic order, belonging to Beach Camp Lodge No. 240, A. F. & A. M., at Shackle Island, Tennessee. In politics he is a Democrat.

EDWARD ALBRIGHT, lawyer and editor of the *Sumner County News* at Gallatin, represents two of the old and respected family connections of Sumner county, Tennessee, the Albrights and the Guthries, both of which have been established here well toward a century and have given to Tennessee men and women of sterling worth. The Albright family originated here with Thomas Albright, a native of North Carolina who removed from there to Kentucky, thence to Tennessee, and finally became a resident of Illinois, where he passed away. One of his sons is John W. Albright, the father of Edward, a Confederate veteran of the Civil war and a well known farmer citizen of Sumner county. John W. Albright was born in Kentucky in 1843 and came to Sumner county, Tennessee, when a child. He was but a youth in his teens at the opening of the Civil war, nevertheless he spent four years fighting bravely for the Southern cause, and as a member of Company I of the Twenty-fourth Tennessee Regiment he served in the battles of Shiloh, Perryville, Murfreesboro and all of the principal engagements of the Tennessee campaigns, but was never wounded or captured. After the close of the war he returned to Sumner county and took up the vocation of farming, which he has since followed, residing on the farm which has been in the family since 1796. In fraternal associations he is a Mason and has served as master of his lodge. Politically he is a stanch Democrat, and in an official way has served as a justice of the peace. He wedded Caldonia Guthrie, who was born in Sumner county, Tennessee, in 1850 and is a daughter of James I. Guthrie, a native of North Carolina and one of the early settlers in Sumner county, Tennessee. She is a member of the Presbyterian church. John W. and Caldonia (Guthrie) Albright have three children living, namely: Edward Albright of this review; Oscar Albright, who assists in the management of the home farm; and Clemmie, who is now Mrs. Luther Franklin and resides in Sumner county.

Edward Albright, a native of Sumner county, was born August 18, 1873. He was educated at Cumberland University, Lebanon, Tennessee, from which institution he was graduated in law in 1898. For eight years thereafter he was an active practitioner at the Gallatin bar and still continues in that line of professional labor, but since 1907, at which time he purchased the *Sumner County News*, he has given the major portion of his attention to the management of this publication and to his editorial duties in connection therewith. As a writer of considerable ability, he is exceptionally well qualified for this line of professional activity, and in this connection it may be mentioned that he is the author of Early History of Middle Tennessee, that is considered a work of much merit and has been well received. The *Sumner County News* was established in 1897, is a weekly publication and is now circulated to about 2,000 subscribers, being one of the most successful papers of Sumner county. Democratic in politics, under the able management of its editor it wields a strong influence in the political affairs of Sumner county, but while Mr. Albright thus gives stanch support to his Democratic friends he has never himself been a candidate for official honors. He is a member of the Knights of Pythias and has been chancellor commander of his lodge for the last four years.

RUFUS L. ROCHELL. In a work of this character, it is eminently proper that due notice be given to those men who, beginning life with small capital and under adverse circumstances, build for themselves a business and a reputation as men of sterling worth through the exercise of their talents and industry. Instead of waiting and wishing for opportunities, they accepted conditions as they arose, overcame obstacles and won success, and their examples are worthy of emulation by the young men of the present and future generations. Rufus L. Rochell, one of the leading grocers of Troy, Obion county, is a native son of Tennessee, having been born in Weakley county in 1853, and is the fifth of six children born to James H. and Nancy (King) Rochell, both members of old Tennessee families. James H. Rochell was a farmer in Weakley county prior to the Civil war. When that great conflict began he cast his lot with the South and served for the greater part of the contest as a soldier in the Confederate army. The exposure and hardship incident to military life so undermined his health that he died soon after leaving the army, and the subject of this sketch was called upon to contribute to the support of the widowed mother and the other members of the family. He managed to secure the rudiments of a good English education, but the greatest assets of his life have been a strong physical constitution and a determined will, both of which have been of incalculable benefit to him in the great battle of life.

Mr. Rochell first started in business for himself in Jackson, Tennessee, but in 1890 he removed to Troy, where he took charge of his brother's business and purchased same the following year. Here he has built up a large patronage and established a reputation as one of the leading grocers of the busy little city and is now the oldest one in the town. His stock consists of a full line of staple and fancy groceries —the best and freshest that the market affords—and the people of Troy have a belief that if an article cannot be found at Rochell's, they will probably have to go to some other city to procure it. February 9, 1910.

Mr. Rochell's place of business was completely destroyed by fire, causing him a loss of about $6,000. He laughed at his disaster, however, and within a short time reëstablished himself in his present quarters, where he has a room 24 by 70 feet well stocked with everything the good housewife is likely to need in her domestic economy. Good goods, full weight and correct business methods have ever been the principles that Mr. Rochell has applied to the management of his store, and the result is "once a customer, always a customer."

Mr. Rochell is a member of the Masonic fraternity and also of the Methodist church. In his church and lodge, as well as in business and social life, he is a man whom it is well to know and one whose word can always be relied on in every particular. Mr. Rochell is unmarried.

JAMES F. FINLAY, son of James Finlay and Elizabeth Jane Finlay. Born at Greenville, S. C., September 4, 1882. Awarded B. A. degree at the University of the South, Sewanee, Tenn., in 1906, and LL. D. at the University of Virginia, Charlottesville, Va., in 1908. Now engaged in the practice of law at Chattanooga, Tenn.

JOSEPH WINFIELD SCOTT. Since 1897 a member of the Harriman bar, Mr. Scott is regarded as one of the ablest lawyers of Roane county, and is a special authority on the branch of real estate and land-titles law. He is senior member of the firm of Scott, Chandler & Anderson, the several members of which represent special ability and success in all branches of the law.

J. W. Scott was born in Morgan county, Tennessee, and his family have been well known and prominent in the state for upwards of a century. His parents were John L. and Perlesia (Holloway) Scott, both of whom were natives of Morgan county, the former born in 1832 and died in 1907, and the mother born in 1834 and now living, in her seventy-ninth year. One of the first settlers in Morgan county, Tennessee, in 1821, was the great-grandfather, Samuel Scott, who came to this state from Kentucky. He had formerly lived in Virginia and in North Carolina, had served in the Revolutionary war and was in the battle of Kings Mountain. He was a colonel in the War of 1812, his common title in his community in later years being "colonel." Grandfather Russell Scott was born in Kentucky, and was very young when the family moved to Morgan county, Tennessee. He was a substantial farmer in Morgan county during the remainder of his life. Russell Scott was a brother of Julian F. Scott, a very prominent politician in Morgan county, and who is said to have furnished the character for the Colonel Sellers, made famous in Mark Twain's book under the title "The Gilded Age." Grandfather Joseph Holloway was a soldier in the War of 1812.

The late John L. Scott, the father, was a farmer by occupation, and spent many years of his career in the public service. He was clerk of the county court, and also county register, holding office altogether for twenty years. As a Democrat in politics, and a man who was accounted a good liver, he was very popular and genial among all his friends and associates. He was a member of the Baptist church in which he took much interest, and his wife has been a Presbyterian all her life. Of their nine children, six are still living.

J. W. Scott had to work for his support and advancement, and was identified with different occupations before he took up his profession. His early education was obtained in the common schools of Morgan county, and later he read law under able preceptors, being admitted to the bar in 1897. He at once located in Harriman, and has since built up a large general practice.

In 1878 Mr. Scott married Miss Dillie Long, of North Carolina, and they were the parents of one child, Lawrence, who is now in the insurance business in Harriman. Mrs. Scott died in 1881, and her husband afterwards married Sarah J. Smith, of Post Oak Springs. The children of their marriage are: Clay, who is manager of the picture show in Harriman; Mabel, the wife of Thomas N. Smith, of Maysville, Kentucky; and Lloyd, at home. Mr. and Mrs. Scott are members of the Christian church, and fraternally Mr. Scott is a Chapter Mason, and has served as master of the Masonic lodge two terms, and is a member of the Junior Order of United American Mechanics. He is a Democrat, and for two terms was clerk of the circuit court in Morgan county. In 1897-99 he was mayor of Harriman.

WALTER H. ANDERSON, the junior member of the well known law firm at Harriman of Scott, Chandler & Anderson, has been in practice at Harriman since 1910, and has already attained recognition as one of the rising young attorneys of the east Tennessee bar. Mr. Anderson educated himself, and while growing up contributed to the support of other members of the family, so that he is in every sense of the word a self-made man.

Walter H. Anderson was born in Wayne county, Kentucky, May 29, 1886, a son of Luke and Jane (Young) Anderson. The paternal grandfather was Jacob Anderson, a native of Whitley county, Kentucky, a farmer by occupation, and during the war was a member of the home guards. The maternal grandfather was James Young, born in Wayne county, Kentucky, and for many years a school teacher and farmer. Luke Anderson was born in Whitley county, Kentucky, June 8, 1853, and his wife was born in the same county in 1854. Both are still living, and during the earlier years the father followed the vocation of farming. Latterly he has been in the coal mining industry. They are both members of the Baptist church, and he is a Republican in politics, and a member of the Junior Order of United American Mechanics. The six children in the family are mentioned as follows: John Marion, of Kentucky, Mary D., wife of J. L. Wilson of Chattanooga; Walter H.; Benjamin H., of Scott county, Tennessee; Edna, wife of Clarence Ramsey of Kentucky; and Eva, unmarried and living at home.

Walter H. Anderson attended the public schools of Scott county,

Tennessee, afterwards had a course in the Williamsburg Institute in Kentucky, and in 1902, took a business course in the Knoxville Business College. For several years he was employed in clerical and other lines of work and in that way obtained the means to put him through law school. In 1908 he graduated in law from the Cumberland University at Lebanon, and started to practice in Scott county, Tennessee. In 1910 he moved to Harriman, and there joined forces with Mr. J. W. Scott, one of the best known lawyers of east Tennessee.

On November 11, 1905, Mr. Anderson married Miss Emma Bowling, a daughter of William Bowling, who was born in Virginia, and came to Tennessee in 1866. He had previously served as a soldier in the Confederate army, and was twice captured, being confined in the Federal prison in Ohio for a time, and for a time in New Jersey. The children born to Mr. and Mrs. Anderson are: Stephen Arnold Douglas, aged seven; Gus Carr, aged four; and Walter H. Jr., born in 1913. Mrs. Anderson is a member of the Methodist Church South. Fraternally Mr. Anderson is affiliated with the Junior Order of United American Mechanics, the Knights of Pythias and the Masons, being past master of John Frizzell Lodge No. 592, A. F. & A. M., in Scott county. In politics he is Republican, but gives all his time to his legal profession, in which he is winning a worthy success.

WILLIS F. ARNOLD. The present postmaster of the city of Jackson, the judicial center of Madison county, is not only giving an able administration of the affairs of this office, but has also achieved prominence and distinction as one of the representative younger members of the bar of this county, besides which he has been an influential figure in the councils of the Republican party in this section of the state. His character and ability have admirably measured up to the requirements of the metewand of popular approbation, and his circle of friends is unmistakably coincident with that of his acquaintances, the while he is recognized as one of the progressive and public-spirited citizens of Madison county.

Willis Fillmore Arnold is a scion of one of the old and honored families of Tennessee and was born in Henderson county, this state, on the 10th of December, 1882. He is a son of Dr. John Martin Arnold and Laura Frances (Dodds) Arnold, both of whom were likewise born in Tennessee, their present home being in the city of Jackson. Dr. Arnold was graduated in the medical department of Vanderbilt University, as a member of the class of 1877, and was for thirty years engaged in the successful practice of his profession in Henderson county, whence he removed to Jackson in 1907. He is a man of high intellectual and professional attainments and has long been recognized as one of the representative physicians and surgeons of Tennessee. He is a stalwart Republican in his political proclivities and his wife holds membership in the Baptist church.

ʻThe present postmaster of Jackson gained his early educational discipline in his native county, and after attending the Georgia Robertson Christian College, at Henderson, he finally decided to prepare himself for the legal profession. With this end in view he was matriculated in what is now Union University, at Jackson, in the law department of which institution he was graduated as a member of the class of 1902 and from which he received the degree of Bachelor of Laws, with incidental admission to the bar of his native state. In 1904 he engaged in the active practice of his profession in Jackson, where he soon gained secure vantage ground as an able advocate and well fortified counselor. He built up a substantial practice and continued to give his attention to the same until he was appointed postmaster of Jackson, on the 16th of April, 1911. From 1905 until 1911 he also served as deputy clerk of the United States district court.

Mr. Arnold has taken a specially deep interest in political affairs in his native state and has been prominently identified with the manœuvering of political forces in his home county. That he is here a leader in the ranks of the Republican party needs no further voucher than the statement that he has served consecutively as chairman of the Republican committee of Madison county since 1906, and that his ability in directing the affairs of the local party contingent has been proved in a most effective way, the while he has created the minimum of antagonism and has gained the confidence and good will of the representative members of the opposing party as well as of those of his own party. His term as chairman of the committee will expire in 1914. He is affiliated with the Modern Woodmen of America and the Tribe of Ben Hur, as well as other representative civic organizations in his home city, and both he and his wife hold membership in the Baptist church. It has consistently been said that Mr. Arnold is ''a man of large views and conservative and dependable judgment.''

On the 24th of April, 1904, was solemnized the marriage of Mr. Arnold to Miss Johnnie Johnston, daughter of John N. Johnston, a prominent citizen of Jackson, and she is a popular factor in the social activities of her home city. They have one son, Willis E.

ROBERT LEE BYNUM. Another prominent educator of the state of Tennessee is Superintendent Robert Lee Bynum, now of Jackson. He has given generous service to the public schools of the state, both in the capacity of a teacher and as a superintendent. Both in county and city educational offices, he has done high credit to himself and to the collegiate institutions of which he is an alumnus.

Robert Lee Bynum is a native of this state, but a son of Kentucky parents. His father, William J. Bynum, and his mother, Theresa Gilbert Bynum, were living in Union City, Tennessee, where the former was a merchant and agriculturist, when the son was born whom they named

Robert Lee. The date of his birth was September 28, 1867. William J. Bynum died in 1874, but the mother of our subject is still living, in Jackson.

In the rural schools of the vicinity of Union City, Robert L. Bynum received his elementary education. He later became a student in the Vanderbilt Training School at Union City and subsequently entered Bethel College at McKenzie, from which he was graduated with the degree of Bachelor of **Philosophy.**

The young Ph. B. gained his first teaching experience at Ashland, Mississippi. Returning thereafter to Tennessee, he held positions in schools in Obion county, gathering such experience and developing such ability that in 1897 he was elected superintendent of public instruction in Obion county. To this position he was successively re-elected, serving in his office until October of 1901, at which time he entered upon the duties of the principalship which he had accepted from the Jackson Board of Education, serving two years as principal of the intermediate department and two years as principal of the high school. At the end of that period his fitness for county superintendency again led to his election to such office. He therefore took charge of the school system of Madison county and devoted his time and thought to supervising the schools and examining and directing the teachers of this county until tendered the superintendency of the Jackson schools. This latest position came to him on June 14, 1912, and he entered upon its duties August 1, 1912. The many interested and appreciative patrons of the Jackson public schools view with confidence the future of the city's most important enterprise—the education of her youth.

Superintendent Bynum is very well known throughout the state of Tennessee in all educational movements. From 1907 to 1909 he served as president of the Tennessee Public School Officers' Association. He is president of the Tennessee State Teachers' Association. In both the Tennessee State Board of Education and the National Educational Association he is an energetic member, as well as a prominent co-worker with his brother officials in the department of superintendents.

Mr. Bynum is a logical thinker along political lines. And while his political alignment is consistent with the famous name his parents bestowed upon him, his civic theories are nevertheless based upon carefully reasoned premises. His religious convictions are of the modern practical type that conceives morality as the highest *raison d'etre* of religion; he respects, therefore, all sects that aim for a high ethical standard and has a vigorous sympathy for each. His church membership is with the Jackson First Presbyterian church, U. S. A., of which Mrs. Bynum is also a member.

In her girlhood Mrs. Bynum was Miss Fanny Allen, her native home being Mississippi. The Allen-Bynum marriage took place in 1894. In the subsequent years three children have completed the family, and have been named as follows: William Jennings, Gattye Louise and Robert L. Bynum, Jr. The Bynum family has been counted a most desirable acquisition to the life of Jackson. Superintendent Bynum is noted as a man of genuine cordiality as well as of great executive ability. He is a member of the Masonic order, in Jackson lodge No. 332.

ROBERT GATES. Colonel Gates—by which name the subject of this review is affectionately known through all Tennessee and in many other Southern states—has lived a life that is not only eventful but full of valuable achievement for his state. Distinguished as a Confederate veteran, effective as an editor of prominence and influence, notably successful as a promoter of many movements for the economic and industrial upbuilding of Tennessee, his sum of human effort has been remarkable in kind and in result.

Though a native of Tennessee, the genealogical origin of Robert Gates is Virginian. His father, Benjamin Franklin Gates, was born in Chesterfield county of the Old Dominion state, but came at the age of twelve—with other members of his father's family—to Henry county, Tennessee. There he grew up, adopted the occupation of farming, married and reared his family; in Hayward county of this same state he died, at the home of his daughter, in 1898, having reached his eighty-third year. His wife was Elizabeth Jackson Roper, also a Virginian, and born near Lynchburg, Virginia; her mother was a member of the noted Lewis family, which produced such men as Gen. Andrew Lewis and Col. Charles Lewis, of Revolutionary fame. Elizabeth Jackson Roper Gates passed from mortal life when her son, our subject, was sixteen years of age. His birth had occurred at the Henry county home of the above-named parents on May 5, 1840.

In the rural schools of his native vicinity, Robert Gates gleaned his preliminary education. He later pursued courses in West Tennessee College, which subsequently became Southwestern Baptist University and is now called Union University.

Having scarcely attained his majority at the outbreak of the Civil war, the young man nevertheless eagerly answered the call to arms on behalf of the South, and throughout his military experience he constantly maintained an attitude of courageous loyalty and of martial initiative. He enlisted as a private, his regiment being the Sixth Tennessee Infantry; when the Southern congress passed a law promoting members of this division to the rank of officers, he was made a lieutenant in the regular Confederate army. In this capacity he served in the Light Artillery, first with Smith's battery and subsequently with Eldridge's. With the latter, Lieutenant Gates continued until the battle of Murphysboro. After serving a period on the staff of Col. A. W. Campbell on special duty he then came west with General Forrest, carrying advance orders that the independent forces organized in west-

ern Tennessee assemble at Jackson. There the general organized his
army, which he commanded until the close of the war. After the organization at Jackson General Forrest conducted his famous march through
the Federal lines with five thousand unarmed men. As he took his men
to northern Mississippi, which was the scene of his exploits for the
remainder of the war, that locality was the scene of Mr. Gates's service
thereafter during the conflict, being in command of a detachment of
scouts. After the battle of Jack's Creek, Col. D. M. Williams submitted
recommendations that for conspicuous gallantry on the field, Lieutenant
Gates receive promotion to higher rank. This was so near the close of the
war, however, that the promised promotion had not time to materialize.
His war record was none the less an honorable and honored one, for his
specific acts of bravery have been well known and frequently mentioned.
One of these was undertaken on the need of General Forrest for more
pistols than his army required; Lieutenant Gates made his way to Ok-
olona, Mississippi, and escorted six hundred pistols back to the army. He
remained with General Forrest until the surrender, being one of those
who shared that melancholy experience with their leader on the field.
Since those years Robert Gates has, by the general consent of all who
know him, been everywhere spoken of as Colonel Gates; and the title,
thus informally bestowed, has never been given to one who better deserved
its complimentary significance.

The war being over, the first enterprise to which General Gates turned
his attention was the very important work of a railroad contractor.
The many railroads that had been destroyed during the war were rebuilt as rapidly as possible and Colonel Gates did much toward supplying the demand for ties, wood and cross timbers. This work he continued for about three years and, as the need of it lessened, he entered
other lines of activity.

Being a man of decided convictions on many public matters of importance during the reconstruction period, Colonel Gates found the
press a congenial outlet for his endeavors. He had, furthermore, a personal interest in *The Whig*—one of the oldest newspapers in the South,
and long edited by his uncle, W. W. Gates; the latter was during his
activity the best-known newspaper man in the South and his political
career was a noted one. The Colonel remained with *The Whig* for some
time, passing from its offices to a newspaper establishment of his own;
for, in conjunction with the Honorable B. A. Enslow, he founded the
Jackson Sun, a combination of *The Whig* and *The Tribune*. For ten
years Colonel Gates continued to be a proprietor and editor of the *Sun*.
Those ten years were the most strenuous in the history of southern politics and Colonel Gates' influence in this capacity proved to be decidedly
salutary. He was one of those who finally brought about the Fifty and
Three Compromise, of Gov. W. B. Bates' administration.

Another important phase of progress present required Colonel Gates' assistance. In order to engage in it he resigned service with the news-paper above mentioned. This new work was that of right-of-way and subscription agent for the Ohio Valley Railway Company, in Tennessee and Kentucky. He later became right-of-way and subscription agent for the Tennessee Midland. This road—which has since become part of the Louisville & Nashville system—was given remarkable impetus through the colonel's efforts. He made many railway speeches and se-cured a large subscription list for his company.

The business ability of Colonel Gates made him a very desirable secretary and manager for the Commercial Club at Memphis. This office he accepted and held for about five years. During that time he had an exceedingly active existence, successfully locating in the city of Memphis many important new enterprises. He was eventually in-duced to take up a broader field of promotive work, and in order to do so, he resigned his office with the Memphis commercial organization.

It was at this time that movements were on foot for the Tennessee Centennial. Colonel Gates was made one of the officials of the first or-ganization and was in charge of the preliminary field work. When the exposition opened, he was again prominent as the head of the Shelby county and Memphis building.

At the close of the Centennial, a new responsibility came to the colo-nel, who had now established an unusual reputation for success as a promoter of public enterprises. The Louisville & Nashville Railway sought his services as a special industrial and immigration agent. In this connection his wide acquaintance throughout the state led to his service in connection with the railroad legislation of Tennessee, during the legislative sessions. He has at times been special representative in Washington, while Congress was in session, for railroads of Tennessee. For sixteen years he has been thus occupied; and although this period has been one of great upheavals, injuriously affecting many railroads, no adverse legislation has been passed in Tennessee against roads of the state. This immunity has been attributed largely to the efforts of Colo-nel Gates.

In combination with these definite employments above named, the colonel has done much writing and public speaking along lines relating to industrial and agricultural movements in Tennessee. Numerous ar-ticles from his pen have been published by the Tennessee department of state and its department of agriculture; many others have appeared in the newspapers of the state. When in the early 'eighties he was particu-larly interested in immigration to Tennessee, Colonel Gates delivered a number of addresses to that end, in various parts of Iowa and Illinois. He organized two excursions of prospective immigrants from the north-west; one train of these visitors went through western Tennessee and the other through middle Tennessee, the residents of both sections enter-taining them as guests. This was followed by a series of agricultural and industrial conventions, attended by persons from Illinois, Kentucky, Mississippi and Tennessee, and held in Jackson, Tennessee. All of these were conducted by Colonel Gates, who gave numerous addresses on improved methods of farming, on conditions of labor and on immigration. He has always been deeply interested in agriculture and during his period of editorship he had devoted much space and attention to diversified farming, as a result of which the present system of small fruit and truck farming in the central counties of West Tennessee was given the needed impetus. The good results of all this activity for the general good of the state and its people is constantly noted in many ways by the people of this region. He is, furthermore, one of the founders of the Farmers' Institute of Tennessee; these associations meet annually at Knoxville, Nashville and Jackson and during these annual meetings for fourteen years, Colonel Gates has been one of the program of speakers.

Another interesting achievement of the colonel's eloquence is the Confederate monument that stands at Jackson, Tennessee. For some years a plan has been on foot for erecting such a tribute to the Southern soldiers. It was not easy, however, to raise the required funds, although the leaders in the movement were assisted by a ladies' auxiliary. For two years the enterprise lived, but lagged. Finally, on a Memorial Day, Colonel Gates, with the same powerful initiative he had shown throughout his career, addressed the crowds from the cemetery and raised $1,700. The work was at once set in motion, with Judge H. W. McCorry, the late Frank B. Hamilton and Colonel Gates as the committee with full powers for erecting the monument.

It is unnecessary to say that Colonel Gates is decidedly a Democrat. His religious convictions are Episcopalian, as are those of all his family.

The colonel's life as a man of family has extended throughout the busy years of his activity since 1867. In that year he was united in marriage to Miss Caledonia Jane Jester of Jackson, Tennessee, descendant of the Scotch families of Tait, Sutherland and Sinclair. His two children are a daughter, named Emma; and a son, named Robert M. The former is Mrs. C. A. Folk, of Nashville; and the latter is well known as a newspaper man, at present the Washington correspondent for the *Commercial Appeal* of Memphis. Colonel Gates has four grandchildren in the Folk family and one in that of his son, R. M. Gates. May he live long to enjoy a ripe old age as one of the best loved men in Jackson, and one who is appreciated throughout the state as one of the makers of modern west central Tennessee.

MILES SCOTT. M. D. For a good score and a half of years Dr. Miles Scott has held an important place in this community of Robertson county as a medical practitioner of extensive and successful patronage. This county was the home of his mother's family, for his grandfather, Thomas Gunn, was an early settler here and was well known as a Baptist preacher and one who was fortunate in the possession of a large tract of land, made the more valuable because of the numerous slaves who called him master. Thomas Gunn's granddaughter, Martha Gunn, was born in Robertson county in 1822 and here spent her entire life, which closed in 1905. The paternal line of our subject's ancestry was Virginian. In the Old Dominion state in 1812 was born H. S. Scott, who came with his parents to Tennessee when he was a child. Here he married Martha Gunn and became a leading physician in this part of the state, where he practiced for forty years. He was conspicuously a Democrat and the church relations of the family were of the Methodist denomination, Martha Gunn Scott being a faithful member of that church. They were the parents of eight children, of whom three are yet living. Seventh in order of birth in his generation of the family was Miles Scott, to whom this brief review is dedicated. His earthly existence began on April 7, 1854, in Robertson county, Tennessee.

The Robertson county public schools gave Miles Scott his intellectual start in life. It was under the parental roof, however, that his ambitions were best nourished. He looked to a career in the same profession as that distinguished by his father, and a medical course was therefore his educational goal. He entered the College of Medicine of Vanderbilt University, in Nashville, Tennessee, and in 1878 received his degree as a doctor of medicine.

Dr. Scott began his medical practice at Barren Plains and has since conducted those activities in this locality. His professional endeavors cover a wide range of territory and has been one of genuine success in its healing offices. Dr. Scott has met with sincere appreciations for his ministrations and his financial returns have been of a gratifying status.

An attractive and productive farm of three hundred and fifty acres provides the doctor's favorite diversion, for under his supervision excellent crops of tobacco are raised. His chief interest is, of course, his professional practice. He is a member of the county and state medical societies. Of religious organizations, his personal connection is with the Methodist church, South, to which the other members of his family also belong.

As a daughter of Anderson Holman, Mrs. Scott has formerly been well known, both as Miss Dora L. Holman and later as Mrs. Taylor. Additional data regarding her family will be found in the sketch of C. G. Holman elsewhere to be found in these pages. It was in July of 1890 that Dora Holman Taylor became Mrs. Scott. She and the doctor are the parents of one child, a son named George Robert, who resides at the parental home. The doctor's family is valued as one of wholesome influence as well as of notable service to humanity.

EDGAR GREEN PARISH. In the varied and tangible evidences of man's creative and constructive ability, none commands more universal respect than that class of work which evolves the many types of human habitation.   Ordinary though the uses of buildings may be, through them a city or town takes on its visual character.   Thus it is that no slight credit accrues to carpenter, architect or contractor, whose organizing ability makes possible those structures which combine usefulness, durability and harmony of outline.   Edgar Green Parish might be one of those who, adapting the old saying, exclaim: "Let me erect the buildings of the city, and I care not who makes its laws."   As a matter of fact, Mr. Parish is concerned with both the building and the law-making in Jackson, Tennessee.

Mr. Parish's genealogy is Virginian, his birthplace in Milan, Gibson county, Tennessee, the date of his nativity the 11th of July, 1868. His parents were Nehemiah Parish, an undertaker of that town, and Lucinda Poole Parish, his wife.   The former lived until 1884, but the latter's demise occurred in 1878, when Edgar Green Parish, the son, was ten years of age.

Leaving Tennessee at the age of twelve and going to Clinton, Kentucky, for residence, Edgar G. Parish received his final education in Marvin College, of that place.   After his five years of life in Kentucky, he returned to Tennessee, settling at Jackson, where for two years he engaged in the work of a carpenter.   In 1887, he turned his knowledge of construction to account in taking up the contracting business for himself.   This line of activity Mr. Parish has ever since continued, his contracts becoming more and more numerous and important.   He has supervised the erection of some of the most modern buildings in Jackson, and, in fact, in this entire section of the state.   The structures for which he is responsible as contractor include, among others, the First National Bank, the new high school, the Elks' building, and the Southern Hotel. He is also notable for handsome and up-to-date private residences.

Jackson has honored Mr. Parish with civic office.   In 1904 he was placed on the board of aldermen and has ever since continued to serve in that capacity.   He had before that time for six years made one of the Madison county court.   In both offices his judgment and his sanity of viewpoint have been such as to win respect and appreciation.

Mr. Parish's large circle of friends includes many brothers of fraternal orders, in which the contractor has taken high honors.   The Benevolent and Protective Order of Elks claims his membership in lodge No. 192; the Knights of Pythias in Lancelot lodge No. 13, in which he has held every office except that of chancellor commander; and the Order of Moose, in which he is also an important member.

In 1891 Mr. Parish was married to Miss L. Moss, who died in 1899. His second marriage was solemnized in 1904, when Miss Edna Patton Wheeler, of Henderson, Tennessee, became Mrs. Parish.   The two children of the family are both sons and are called Edgar Moss Parish and Robert Harvey Parish.   The family are valued members of the Cum-

berland Presbyterian church. In political affiliation, Mr. Parish is a
Democrat.

REV. HERBERT WHITING VIRGIN. A name of distinction among Baptist clergymen, among leaders in social reforms and philanthropies, and among theologians of his denomination, is that of the Rev. Herbert Whiting Virgin, D. D., now of Jackson, Tennessee. His vigorous personality and mind have stimulated religious and moral enthusiasm in many cities and in numerous states, for his guidance has been sought by churches and educational institutions in Kentucky, in Louisiana and in Missouri, as well as in Tennessee. Before noting the successive steps of his broad and unusually efficient service, we shall first briefly outline the main facts of his birth and education, although it must here be said that Dr. Virgin is one of those rare men who never cease to study—who look to eternity itself as the infinitely splendid post-graduate opportunity of the soul.

Louisiana is the state of his birth. At Mandeville, in that commonwealth, a summer home was maintained by Edwin Forrest Virgin, a wholesale seed merchant of New Orleans; here he came from time to time, with his wife, Helen Caruthers Virgin, a lady of South Carolina parentage; and here, in 1872, occurred the birth of their son, who was christened Herbert Whiting.

The public school system of New Orleans was that which provided the early foundations of Herbert Whiting Virgin's education. From there he passed to Georgetown College. That step completed, he sought the class-rooms of the greatest of Baptist institutions—the University of Chicago. There he pursued courses in theology and history—as well as at the Southern Baptist Theological Seminary of Louisville, Kentucky. Thus equipped with the scholarly material fitting him for his chosen vocation, he was ready for his era of service, looking nevertheless to further study at later periods.

In 1895 Reverend Virgin began his pastoral work, locating at Nicholsville, Kentucky. With this ministerial responsibility he combined professorial duties in Jessamine Institute, where he taught graduate courses. This he continued for two and one-half years. When, at the end of that time, he was called to Lake Charles, Louisiana, to take charge of the First Baptist church of that place, he not only fulfilled the duties of his pastorate there, but organized three other Baptist churches in adjoining towns. This climate proved to be a difficult one for his young wife and child; he therefore removed, for their healths' sake, to La Grange, Kentucky. He became the pastor of the DeHaven Baptist Memorial church at La Grange, and at the same time pursued theological studies in the Baptist Theological Seminary located in Louisville, Kentucky.

When four years had passed, Reverend Virgin left La Grange, Kentucky, to assume the spiritual leadership of the First Baptist church of Nevada, Missouri. After continuing there for nearly five years, he was called to the Benton Boulevard Baptist church of Kansas City.

In the meantime the name of Herbert Whiting Virgin had become more and more widely significant of clear-sighted sincerity and of vital strength in the work of his denomination and related lines of spiritual advancement. These qualities, in addition to his rich theological erudition, led to the conferring upon him, by two institutions, of the doctor's degree which he now holds by double right. In 1908, Georgetown College of Georgetown, Kentucky, awarded him the degree of Doctor of Divinity; and in the same year he was similarly honored as Doctor of Divinity by Union University of Jackson, Tennessee.

While engaged in the city pastorate at Kansas City, Dr. Virgin's work had grown extraordinarily full of varied responsibilities. Its multiplicity of service included his association with the Word and Way Publishing Company, of which he was secretary and to which he also gave editorial assistance in the capacity of book reviewer. At the same time he was president of the Sunday Observance League and vice-president of the Sunday School Board, for Missouri, being also a member of the executive committee of the State Board and of the locating committee of the City Mission Board. During the years he had spent in Missouri, Reverend Virgin had also organized the Young People's Assembly of that state, which has since assumed large proportions.

It was in 1908 that Dr. Virgin accepted the call to become pastor of the First Baptist church of Jackson, Tennessee. While thus officiating, he has also held for two years the chair of Sunday School Pedagogy of Union University. He has in the meantime inspired the interest that has led to the erection of the present $100,000 church edifice in which his people worship.

Dr. Virgin's aid and advice are sought by many organizations whose purpose is religious and educational advancement. He is a member of the State Mission Board of Tennessee; of the Education Commission of Tennessee; and of the District Board of Education. His human interests are by no means confined within the limits of his church organization, but broadly touch all civic and other public causes. The political stand which Doctor Virgin takes is independent, although his economic convictions are of the Democratic cast.

In the year 1897 Reverend Virgin was united in marriage to Miss Isabel Josephine Goff. Mrs. Virgin is a daughter of C. C. Goff of New Orleans. She and Doctor Virgin are the parents of four children. The daughters are named Ruth, Bessie, Mary Helen and Isabelle Josephine; the young son bears his father's name—Herbert Whiting.

To Doctor Virgin the church of the South owes no slight measure of appreciation for the vigor which he adds to church life and to the principles for which all churches are striving. His is a name that stands for spiritual strength and progress. The fact that Doctor Virgin is as yet barely forty years of age is a cause for thankfulness to many whose hopes loom large for a nobler future for humanity. Realizing what such work as his can signify, it is good to anticipate his further aid, with that of his consecrated comrades, toward the gradual accomplishment of the soul's dream that the divine will may indeed one day be done in a mundane world as it is upon the celestial heights.

RUFUS FARMER LONG. Among the public spirited citizens of any community are often found prominent those who have been reared amid influences which tend to the higher development of the race in general— physical conditions such as the farm offers, with its pure air, water, sunshine and plenty of healthful exercise, which permit free play to the best instincts of man. One of these substantial citizens is R. F. Long, a banker of Hendersonville, who has combined agricultural pursuits with a business career, and thus enjoys the broad freedom of the independent life in the country.

John R. Long, father of the subject of this sketch, was born in 1830, in Robertson county, Tennessee, where he has engaged in farming all his life, which occupation he has pursued with much success. For a considerable period of time a member of the Methodist Episcopal church, he has been steward for years, and politically he is affiliated with the Democratic party, favoring prohibition. His service in the Civil war extended over a period of seven months. The birth of Lucinda A. (Batts) Long, wife of John R. Long, occurred in Robertson county also, in 1835, she being a daughter of Jeremiah Batts, an early settler of the county and a prosperous farmer.

Born April 4, 1869, in the county which is the birthplace of his father, after his school days were spent and he had completed a business course at Nashville, R. F. Long began his career on the farm, to the management of which he has applied his business ability with unusual success, being the owner of 711 acres of land. Integrity, business acumen, foresight and wisdom are recognized qualities in this man, and in 1910 he was elected cashier and vice-president of the Bank of Hendersonville, the capital stock of which is $5,000, surplus and undivided profits $2,000, with average deposits of $35,000. He is also a member of the board of directors of this bank, and has served as school director, is a Democrat in politics, a member of the Methodist Episcopal church and belongs to the Elks, Nashville Lodge No. 72.

Mr. Long was married in 1890 to Mary Woodard, daughter of Judge John Woodard, for years judge of the county court of Robertson county and also an eminently successful business man of Nashville. Four children have been born to Mr. and Mrs. Long: John W., a bookkeeper living in Nashville; Nellie, wife of O. E. Davis, with Foster & Parks Company, Nashville; Albert W. and Rufus H., fourteen and eleven years of age respectively.

WALTER S. DOTSON, M. D. A specialist in eye, ear, nose and throat diseases, Dr. Dotson has had a very successful career both in general medicine and in his special work. A few years after taking his medical degree and beginning practice, his inclination and the trend of his abilities led him to specialize. His training is a product of some of the best clinics and hospitals in the country, and he is rapidly acquiring a position of exceptional distinction.

Walter S. Dotson was born in Macon county, Tennessee, December 13, 1878, a son of Hiram J. and Alice (Cornwell) Dotson. James Dotson, the grandfather, was a native of middle Tennessee and spent his life as a farmer. The maternal grandfather, T. J. Cornwell, a native of this state, had a prosperous career as farmer and merchant, and is now living in Macon county past eighty. He is a man of fine intelligence and education, and gave much attention to the sciences of astronomy and mathematics. Both Hiram J. Dotson and his wife were natives of Macon county, the former born in 1850 and the latter in 1859. The father served during the last year of the war, though only fifteen, and was one of the youngest soldiers of the Union army. While on the road to Nashville a piece of artillery was overthrown and injured him. After the war he became a Macon county farmer, where he still owns a large estate, but is now living in Sumner county. He was the father of eight children, the doctor being the oldest, and educated them all for professional careers with the exception of the youngest, who is still a school boy. The father is a member of the Christian church, is affiliated with the Grand Army, and is Republican in politics though never taking an active part.

Dr. Dotson is a graduate of the University of Tennessee and the University of Nashville, having graduated in the medical department of the former in 1898 and taking his medical degree from the latter in 1901. He began practice at Kempville in Smith county in 1898, and continued there until 1906. He then prepared himself for his favorite lines of work, and studied and had clinical experience in New York, Philadelphia and Chicago, being in three of the leading hospitals of New York City, and in hospitals of the other cities. With this training for specializing he opened his office at Gallatin in 1908.

Dr. Dotson married, in 1897, Miss Anna Dennis. Her father, the Rev. J. M. Dennis, whose home is at Franklin, Kentucky, is a minister of the Christian church, an evangelist whose work takes him to all parts of the United States. The Doctor and wife have two children, Mabel, now in school, and Walter S., Jr., four years old.

He and his wife are members of the Christian church. He is a chapter Mason, is past master and now senior warden, and is grand lecturer for the order in the fourth congressional district. He also holds the office of president in the order of the Lions, and is prelate in the Loyal Order of Moose. He is a past worthy patron in the Eastern Star. In politics a Republican, he is now serving as alderman in Gallatin. Dr. Dotson is a popular member of his profession, is secretary and treasurer of the Sumner County Medical Society, a member of the Upper Cumberland and Middle Tennessee Medical Society, is medical councilor in the fourth congressional district for the State Medical Society, and a member of the American Medical Association. Since the above was compiled the doctor has been re-elected to each of the above offices.

JOHN R. PARKER, M. D. For twenty years Dr. Parker has practiced his profession in Sumner county, has devoted his ability and skill to a large circle of patients. A native of the county, he represents a family which has been identified with this part of Tennessee since pioneer days, and its individual members have always borne names synonymous with solid worth and integrity.

John R. Parker was born in Sumner county, December 29, 1871. Washington T. Parker, his grandfather, was also a native of the same county, which places the settlement of the family in this vicinity at a very early date. He attained to a successful position as a lawyer, finally moved out of the state into Texas, where he died.

John R. Parker, Sr., father of the doctor, was born in Sumner county in 1831 and his death occurred in 1871. Educated in his native county, when he was a young man he accompanied his parents to Texas, where he remained only a few years, then returned to Tennessee, and during the war served in Company J of the Second Tennessee Infantry, Confederate army. His military experience covered the four years of the war, carrying the musket of a private, and he fought at Shiloh, Chickamauga and other noted battles. After the war his years were passed in the quiet pursuits of the farm. He married Susan Brown, a daughter of George T. and Amanda C. Brown, both natives of Albemarle county, Virginia, where they were married, and thence came into Tennessee on horseback, becoming early settlers of Sumner county, where they were well-to-do people. Susan (Brown) Parker was born in Sumner county in 1839 and died in 1892. She was the mother of three children: Clare, who is unmarried and resides on the old home place; Washington T., also a farmer; and Dr. John R.

The common schools and the training of the home farm gave Doctor Parker his early preparation for a life of usefulness. He then entered the medical department of the University of Louisville, where he was graduated M. D. in 1893. The first twelve years of his practice were passed at Bethpage in Sumner county, and since 1905 he has had his office and residence in the county seat. He gives all his time to his profession. He is a member of the Sumner County, the State, the Middle Tennessee Medical Societies, and the American Medical Association, and has been president of the county society. He is the owner of farm property in this vicinity.

LEWIS M. WOODSON, M. D. Since his graduation as an honor man from the University of Louisville Medical College in 1885, Doctor Woodson has been practicing his profession at Gallatin. He is one of the ablest surgeons in this part of the state, and enjoys the prestige of successful achievement and the esteem of his associates in the medical fraternity. He is a son of the late Dr. Thomas M. Woodson, who in his time ranked second to none among the best physicians of Tennessee.

Lewis M. Woodson was born in Sumner county, April 1, 1864. His grandfather, also named Lewis M., was a native of Cheatham county, this state, representing one of the early families, later moved to Sumner county, where most of his career was passed. He was a large farmer and slave owner, a minister in the Methodist church, and a man of much ability and influence.

The late Dr. Thomas M. Woodson, who was born in Sumner county in 1830 and died in 1906, was a practicing physician in this county for fifty-two years and stood in the front rank of Tennessee physicians. He accumulated a large estate, was a chapter Mason and a Democrat in politics, and he and his wife took an active part in the Methodist church. He married Amelia Allen, who was born in Allen county, Kentucky, in 1835, and now resides in Gallatin. Her father, Luke P. Allen, was a native of Kentucky. Dr. Thomas Woodson and wife had seven children, four now living, as follows: E. A. Woodson, a Sumner county farmer; John C., a farmer and stockman also in this county; Dr. Lewis M.; and Tennessee, who lives with her mother.

Lewis M. Woodson attended the Gallatin public schools and also had private tutoring. In 1883 he entered the University of Louisville Medical College, where he was graduated with honors in 1885. Since that date his office has been regularly maintained in Gallatin, and with a large general practice he has combined a great deal of surgery, which is his specialty. Since 1887 he has been surgeon for the Louisville & Nashville Railroad. He has membership in the Sumner County and State Medical Societies, and the American Medical Association, and has been a very active worker in the county society.

Dr. Woodson was married in 1890 to Miss Eva Brown, daughter of W. H. Brown, who for a number of years was one of Gallatin's merchants. They have two children: Catherine B., a graduate of Howard College at Gallatin; and Amelia A., aged five years. Mrs. Woodson is a member of the Presbyterian church, while the Doctor is a Methodist. He is affiliated with the lodge and chapter Masonry, with the Odd Fellows, Knights of Pythias, and the Loyal Order of Moose. He has been master of his Masonic lodge, is a past chancellor commander of the Knights of Pythias, and is trustee and physician for the order of Moose.

XAVIER B. HAYNIE, M. D. For thirty years a physician in Gallatin and forty years in the state, Doctor Haynie has given such services to his fellow men as only a good doctor can, and his record in profession and citizenship deserves all the honor which his associates and friends have bestowed. In a sense he inherited his profession, for his father was a medical practitioner in Smith county for more than half a century. The Haynie family is one of the oldest in Tennessee, and its members have always been citizens of more than ordinary ability and position in their respective spheres.

Xavier B. Haynie was born in Smith county, June 8, 1848. Taking up some of the history of his family, his great-grandfather, William Haynie, a native of North Carolina, was a soldier in the patriot army during the Revolution, and later crossed the mountains to the west and became one of the first settlers to locate in Smith county. His son, Elijah Haynie, the grandfather, was a soldier under Jackson at the battle of New Orleans, was a substantial farmer citizen of Smith county, where his death occurred.

Dr. Henry B. Haynie, the father, was born in Smith county in 1816 and died in 1881, having spent nearly all his life in that county. He continued the military record of the family by serving first in the Seminole war, and later was a captain in the Twenty-third Tennessee Regiment of the Confederate army. He was wounded at Shiloh, and was afterwards transferred to Morgan's noted cavalry as surgeon of the Ninth Tennessee Cavalry, and as such served until May, 1865. He was again wounded in one of Morgan's skirmishes in Ohio. In 1844 he had graduated from the Louisville Medical College, and with the exception of the period in the army was identified with the medical profession of Smith county all his career. He was in active work as a physician for fifty-five years, and his was the largest practice accorded to any one physician in the county. In politics he was a Democrat and just before his death had completed his second term as a member of the state legislature. He married Sarah Bradley, who was born in Smith county in 1822 and died in 1891. Her father, John Bradley, a native of Virginia, came in an early day to Smith county, where he spent the rest of his life. Mrs. Sarah Haynie was for sixty years an active member of the Methodist church, and her husband was a member for twenty years. Their five children are all living, and Dr. Xavier is the oldest.

After leaving the common schools of Smith county, Dr. Haynie entered the University of Nashville as a student of medicine, and received his degree in 1873, being valedictorian of his class. The first ten years of his practice were in his native county, and in 1882 he located at Gallatin, where he has devoted himself unsparingly to the needs of his large clientage. He is a member of the Sumner County, the State and the Mississippi Valley Medical Societies.

Doctor Haynie married, in 1874, Miss Belle Bradley, who died in

1877. In 1883 he was united in marriage with Miss Fannie Allen, daughter of Van H. Allen, who was a native of Smith county and a prosperous farmer there for many years. Of the four children born to the Doctor and his present wife, two are living, namely: Lucy V., the wife of Lieutenant-Commander Stafford Doyle of the United States Navy; and Xavia, the wife of William R. Sturtevant, of Texas. Mrs. Haynie is a member of the Presbyterian church. The Doctor affiliates with the Independent Order of Odd Fellows, the Knights of Pythias and the Knights of Honor, and in politics is a Democrat.

ALBERT C. DOBBINS. One of the oldest officials of Sumner county, Tennessee, both in points of age and service, is Albert C. Dobbins, county registrar, who is a native of Robertson county and is a scion of a family that was established in this vicinity about a quarter of a century before Tennessee attained its statehood in 1796. He therefore represents one of the oldest connections of the state and is of the second generation native to its soil. The original progenitor of the family in this county was John Dobbins, the grandfather of our subject, who was a native of Ireland and came to America as a young man prior to the Revolution. Here he espoused the patriot cause and fought for American independence. After his service in the Revolution he located in Sumner county, Tennessee, being one of this county's earliest settlers. Three of his sons, Alexander B., Carson and Robert, followed his example of patriotism and valor and served in the War of 1812. Alexander B. Dobbins, the father of Albert C., was born in Sumner county, Tennessee, in 1781, and spent his whole life in this state, passing away in 1844. He was a farmer and tobacco planter and was quite successful in a business way. In the second war for independence he fought with General Jackson in the battle at New Orleans and also in the engagements in Alabama. He wedded Lovina C. Brigance, who was born in Sumner county in 1803, a daughter of James Brigance. Mr. Brigance, a native of North Carolina and a wood worker by trade, came into Tennessee when a young man and married in 1799. He located in Sumner county and there spent the remainder of his life. Alexander B. and Lovina C. (Brigance) Dobbins were the parents of eight children, of whom Albert C. is now the only survivor. Both parents were members of the Baptist church.

Albert C. Dobbins was born in Robertson county, Tennessee, October 8, 1841. He grew up a farmer boy and attended the rural schools of his vicinity. With the martial spirit of his ancestors and with loyalty to the state of his birth he promptly entered the Confederate service at the opening of the Civil war and served from 1861 to 1865 as a member of Company E, of the Thirtieth Tennessee Regiment of Infantry. He·fought at Fort Donelson, where he was captured and then was held prisoner in Northern camps seven months. On his release he returned to the Confederate army and fought at Jackson and Raymond, Mississippi; and Chickamauga, Tennessee; and at Dalton and Atlanta, Georgia, as well as in a number of engagements of lesser note. At Atlanta he was again captured and was held nine months, being a prisoner at the time the war closed. On his return home he learned the carpenter trade and followed it for a number of years. He also taught school for about fifteen years. In 1898 he was elected registrar of Sumner county and has been successively re-elected to that office to the present time, now having served nearly fifteen years. This is a very convincing testimony of his standing in Sumner county as an upright, reliable and honorable citizen. As an official he has been faithful, prompt and capable.

Mr. Dobbins has been twice married. In 1871 he married Miss Jinsie Love. She was a daughter of Solomon Love, who was born in Sumner county and was a farmer and blacksmith. She died in 1875, leaving a daughter, Lena L., now the widow of Robert Maddox. On December 25, 1897, Mr. Dobbins took as his second wife, Miss Susie Armstrong, daughter of Josiah Armstrong, who was born in Sumner county and was a wagon maker and wheelwright. Mr. and Mrs. Dobbins are members of the Christian church. He is a member of the Masonic order and has been secretary of his local lodge for a number of years. Politically his faith is founded upon the tenets of the Democratic party and he has long been an active participant in the local affairs of his party.

JAMES D. G. MORTON. One of the most influential Tennesseeans in Democratic politics is James D. G. Morton, of Gallatin, chairman of the state Democratic committee. Mr. Morton has a keen and almost natural ability as a·political organizer. During his fifteen years' residence in Sumner county he has been very active in public affairs. He is a practicing lawyer at Gallatin, and for some years has been clerk and master of the chancery court.

At Washington, Indiana, Mr. Morton was born September 15, 1874, a son of J. H. and Josephine (Neal) Morton, mention of whose families appears in later paragraphs. Early in his career he learned the printing trade, and by that vocation supported himself through the period of his advanced education, which was obtained in Bethel College at Russellville, Kentucky.

Admitted to the bar in 1894, he began practice in Granada, Mississippi, where he remained until the spring of 1897, at which date he came to Tennessee, and a few months later located at Gallatin, where he has since been one of the enterprising members of the bar. In 1906 came his appointment as clerk and master of the chancery court.

Mr. Morton, in 1896 at Holly Springs, Mississippi, was secretary of the congressional committee, before age permitted him the privilege of voting. He was manager of Judge B. D. Bell's campaign against Judge Landon, Richardson and Henderson, for the supreme bench of Tennessee, and secured the triumph of his candidate. In 1910 he was a member and secretary of the state Democratic committee, and was chosen chairman of the committee for 1912. Mr. Morton has come into a position of influence through his own energies and ability, and has been a hard worker all his life. His church is the Presbyterian, and his affiliations are with the Knights of Pythias and the Sigma Nu College fraternity.

The father of the state chairman of the Democratic committee is the Rev. J. H. Morton, a retired minister of the Presbyterian faith, and now a resident at Gallatin. He was born in Logan county, Kentucky, November 17, 1833, a son of Joseph and Louisa (Davidson) Morton. His paternal grandparents were William and Martha (Pryor) Morton, both natives of Virginia, and in an early day came over the mountains into Kentucky, where they spent the rest of their lives. Joseph Morton was born in Virginia in 1790 and died in 1846. He was a soldier in the War of 1812 and sometime after that war came into Kentucky and settled on a farm in Logan county, where he spent the rest of his active career as a farmer. His wife, Louisa (Davidson) Morton, was born in Virginia in 1803 and died in 1898, coming to Kentucky when a young girl. Her parents were James H. and Harriet (Smith) Davidson, and the latter's father, Jonathan Smith, was in the Revolutionary army, serving as a fifer.

Of the ten children in the Morton family six are still living. J. H. Morton, the fifth of the children, attended the common schools of Logan county, Kentucky, where he was subsequently for eight years superintendent of the county schools. At the beginning of the war he was a student in Cumberland University, preparing himself for the ministry of the Presbyterian church. For eighteen months he was also a pupil in the private school of Professor William Mariner.

His first charge in the ministry was at Union Grove, Kentucky, and he was located at many places in that state, also for a time at Washington, Indiana, was pastor of a church near Memphis two years, preached three years at Oakland, Mississippi, and for one year in Marshall county, Tennessee. His active ministry continued from 1864 to 1902, a period of nearly forty years, at the end of which he retired and has since resided chiefly in Gallatin, where he found employment for his energies in the deputy clerkship under his son.

Fraternally he is a chapter Mason, and in politics is a Democrat. On May 1, 1865, he was married to Miss Mary Dean Gleaves, a daughter of William and Mary Gleaves, of Davidson county, Tennessee. She lived only about a year after their marriage. On May 15, 1867, was solemnized his second marriage, when Josephine Neal became his wife. Her parents were Rev. William and Sarah (Green) Neal, her father having been a minister of the Cumberland Presbyterian faith. The four children born of this second union are: Minor, a resident of New York state; J. D. G., of Gallatin; Mary Dean, the wife of A. C. Bigger, of

Dallas, Texas; and Fannie, who married H. P. Crume and resides in Hamilton, Ohio.

HENRY S. COLLIER. After more than a century of statehood and a much longer period of settlement the population of Tennessee is one that is largely native born. The family of which this successful Gallatin lawyer is a member is one that has been identified with Tennessee nearly a century and has been well represented in the legal profession of this state, his father and grandfather both having devoted the active years of their lives to the practice of law. Henry S. Collier is a lawyer of ability and strength and has well upheld the prestige of the family name for professional attainment.

Born near Gallatin, Sumner county, Tennessee, September 4, 1877, he is a son of Henry C. Collier. The latter was a native of Dickson county and spent almost the whole of his professional career in his native county as a practitioner at Charlotte, the county seat of that county, having served during that time as a clerk of the court and for a number of years as a master in chancery. He was deceased in 1881 and was a member of the Presbyterian church. Miss Nannie Woodard, who became his wife, was born in Sumner county, Tennessee, in 1859. Two children came to their union and of these only Henry S. Collier survives. John C. Collier, the paternal grandfather of our subject, was a native of Dickson county, this state, and gave the whole of his active career to the practice of law at Charlotte. Felix G. Woodard, the maternal grandfather, was born in Davidson county but moved to Sumner county when a young man and there spent the remainder of his life as a successful farmer.

Mr. Collier was reared in Sumner county and after obtaining a public school education he entered Cumberland University, Lebanon, Tennessee, where he was graduated from the law course in 1898. He began the practice of his profession at Gallatin and continued alone until 1905, when he formed a partnership with J. T. Baskerville, which association has continued to the present. Mr. Collier has attained distinction as an able, hardworking and far-seeing practitioner, is admitted to practice in all the courts of the state, and is recognized as one of the foremost members of the Sumner county bar. The bar has long seemed a stepping stone to political preferment under our American system. In 1912 Mr. Collier, who has always given unswerving allegiance to the principles of the Democratic party, was nominated and elected a Democratic representative from Sumner county to the Tennessee state legislature.

In religious faith and church membership he is a Presbyterian, and fraternally he is a member of the Knights of Pythias, in which connection he has served as chancellor commander of Rowena Lodge No. 21 at Gallatin. Mr. Collier has largely made his own way in life and is numbered among the forceful, progressive and worthy citizens of Gallatin.

HARRY SWANEY. For ten years postmaster of Gallatin, Mr. Swaney was head of the Sumner county Republican organization for a number of years, and is one of the most popular men in the public life of this county. His career has been one of self-advancement, and by efficient service and ability to get things done has risen to a place among the men of mark in this section of the state.

Harry Swaney was born in the county of his present residence on the 31st of March, 1872, a son of Bailey P. and Susan (Belote) Swaney. Both parents were natives of Sumner county, and the family has long been identified with this section of Tennessee. His mother passed away in 1872, while the father, who has long been a substantial farmer and was a soldier during the Civil war, now lives on his home farm in this county. There was only one child in the family of the parents. The mother was a member of the Methodist church. In politics the father was an independent Democrat.

During his boyhood Mr. Swaney attended the rural academy where he was graduated and also had a special course of instruction under Capt. J. H. Bate. His practical career began on a farm, and he has always been more or less actively identified with farming. At the present time he owns a farm of three hundred acres in this county, and has improved it and made it an excellent evidence of his business prosperity. Some years ago he moved his residence into Gallatin, where he became connected with the federal service in the capacity of assistant postmaster, and from that position was appointed to the office of postmaster April 1, 1902. His appointment has been reconfirmed under the successive administrations so that he has now served for more than eleven years. During that time many notable changes have been made in the service, and he will be particularly remembered in the history of the local post office as having been the incumbent during the development of the rural free delivery service and also at the installation of the new parcel post and city delivery.

Mr. Swaney in early life became connected with the local organization of the Republican party, and for a number of years was chairman of the county committee. From this position of influence in the local organization he was promoted to the present office as postmaster.

Mr. Swaney was married to Miss Alfa W. Angle, daughter of William Angle, who was a farmer and mechanic, who spent many years in Sumner county, where he was known as a solid and substantial man of business and a public-spirited citizen. Mr. and Mrs. Swaney are the parents of three children: Rufus, who is now in school, and Harry and Miller W. Mrs. Swaney is an active member of the Christian church.

Yours truly

W. F. Roberts

WM. F. ROBERTS, M. D. Perhaps the old adage, ''There is always room at the top,'' applies with more force to the medical profession than to any other calling, though it is measurably true of all occupations, and the more obstacles encountered in the climb the more room will be found when the top is reached. The man who is satisfied with mediocrity rarely ever rises above that state, while the man of true merit, inherent strength of character and laudable ambition pushes on toward a higher ideal. Years may elapse before his real worth and sterling qualifications become generally known, but when once seen are sure to be appreciated.

The Roberts family, which is of English origin, is one of the old families of Tennessee. The great-grandparents of Doctor Roberts were natives of North Carolina and were among those who came from that state and settled in Tennessee at an early date. Their son, William D. Roberts, the grandfather of the subject of this sketch, was one of the prominent and influential citizens in his day, a large land and slave owner, and was for some years prior to the Civil war engaged in the tobacco and cotton business. When the trouble between the North and South came on, he remained loyal to the Union, and this attitude drew forth the hatred and enmity of his neighbors who sympathized with the Confederacy. Consequently he lost the greater part of his property and was reduced to rather straightened circumstances financially, but he never sacrificed his principles and remained true to the government established by our forefathers. He married Martha Brown, a native of South Carolina, and they became the parents of eight children. Alonzo L. Roberts, the doctor's father, was a prosperous and successful farmer of Henry county, Tennessee, and was a man of strong intellectual ability. He married Miss Emma Wimberly, daughter of Lewis and Matheny (Western) Wimberly, and a member of a well known Tennessee family. To this union were born two children.

Dr. W. F. Roberts, the elder son, was born in Henry county, July 11, 1869. He matriculated in the University of Tennessee, where he was graduated as a member of the class of 1894, and then took a postgraduate course in Chicago Polyclinic in 1901. The same year he located at Troy, Obion county, where he has since practiced his profession and has won the reputation of being one of the leading physicians in that section of the state. Commencement day at his Alma Mater was really a commencement with him, for he has never ceased to be a student—both of books and men—and he has kept fully abreast of the new discoveries pertaining to his chosen field of effort. Being a firm believer in the effectiveness of organization and association with his brother practitioners, he is a member of the American and the Tennessee State Medical Associations, the Tri-State and the West Tennessee Medical Associations, and of the Obion County Medical Society. Through the interchange of ideas among the members of these organiza-

Yours truly
W. F. B.

…ing to a wide field of commerce and

…mother, is a daughter of Col. Richard …er came from England and settled …, this original ancestor, had a son …came to Sumner county, Tennessee, …re he married Lettie Carey. They …C. Sanders. Col. Sanders at the …as elected lieutenant-colonel of the …and served with distinction for …Following the war he represented …after taking up his residence in …n this county to the legislature. …such commanded a large practice …ennessee.

…ition has been to make the best …y and at the same time to do …ared in his native county, and …University of Lebanon, attend- …ls in that institution. From …has enjoyed a liberal share …county, and at the same time …the field of practical politics. …0, and in 1902 was elected …re-elected to this office. As …he stood for the Democratic …though he ran a good race …Mr. Faulkner is not mar- …the Christian denomination, …er of Odd Fellows and the …ce he has a prominent place …ion Bank & Trust Company

…y has furnished Wilson county, …ee generations. The first repre- …was Dr. Andrew Eskew, a native …section with the early tide of immi- …and was one of the first physicians …reafter continued to practice until his …kew, one of the best known and esteemed …en a successful medical practitioner in this …period of fifty-one years, and his grandson …s this review and who in every respect …

tions, he has gained many useful and practical hints concerning the treatment of diseases, and he has ever been willing to impart information gained through his own large and constantly growing practice. This course has marked him as a skillful and progressive physician— one who alike commands the respect and confidence of the members of the profession and the general public. Doctor Roberts is a member of the Masonic fraternity and of the Christian church, in which he holds the office of elder. In both lodge and church work he takes a lively interest and is deservedly popular because of his genial disposition, his open-handed charity and his general good fellowship. He believes in good government and the election of honest and capable men to office, but has never taken an active part in political affairs, preferring to devote his time and talents to the work of his profession and in behalf of his patients. On November 25, 1897, Doctor Roberts married Miss Sallie J. Redditt, a native of Louisiana and daughter of LaFayette and Sallie J. (Dunagan) Redditt, both natives of Tennessee, farming people. The former served in the Confederate army.

OLIVER DUVAL MOORE, clerk of the court in Sumner county, Tennessee, was one of that county's successful business men prior to taking up his official duties as clerk, and in both relations he has proved his capability and efficiency. He is a representative of some of the oldest and most prominent family connections of Sumner county and in his own career has followed their example for useful, honorable and worthy citizenship.

He is a son of Dr. William P. Moore, who was born in Sumner county in 1829 and passed away in 1901 in the vicinity where he has spent over forty years in the sacrificing labor of a physician. Doctor Moore was reared in Sumner county, received his earlier schooling here, and for some time he followed the profession of teaching. His preparation for the medical profession was made in the Vanderbilt College of Medicine, Nashville, Tennessee, and the Louisville Medical College, Louisville, Kentucky. Locating at Portland, Tennessee, he there began the labors of a medical practitioner and continued them for over forty years, one of the best beloved and honored of his profession in Sumner county. He was not only an able physician and one of long experience, but he possessed the personal qualities of gentleness, sympathy and painstaking care. While he was very successful in his practice and accumulated a fair estate, no mercenary motive was allowed to influence his services. His aim was to do all that could be done for his patient, whether that patient lived in a palatial residence or in a cabin, and to satisfy the dictates of his own kind and unselfish heart. He also did noble service among the Southern soldiery during the Civil war. Doctor Moore was twice married. His first wife was Amanda Dickey and to this union were born: W. P. Moore, Jr., now a physician at Portland, Tennessee; R. D.

Moore, cashier of the Portland Bank; and G. S. Moore, a resident of Springfield, Tennessee. His second wife was Mary Duval, a daughter of Dr. O. H. P. Duval, a very able and skilled physician and cultured gentleman who was one of the early members of his profession in Sumner county. To this second union were born three children, two of whom are living: O. D. Moore and H. M. Moore, twins, the former of whom is our subject and the latter of whom is a merchant at Portland, Tennessee. The paternal grandfather of Mr. Moore was Richard D. Moore, a Virginian by birth, who migrated to Sumner county, Tennessee, in an early day and taught school here for a number of years. He served as one of the early registrars of Sumner county.

Oliver D. Moore, our subject, was born November 20, 1867, and received his education in the rural schools of his native county of Sumner. He began business life as a merchant and followed the mercantile business twenty-two years, or until his election as county clerk in 1910. This was a contest that drew the attention of the whole state, as his opponent was H. Brown, who had served in that office for twenty-four years. As a man of sterling principles and integrity Mr. Moore has very capably and acceptably performed the duties of his office and is numbered among the popular officials of the county.

On December 26, 1894, was solemnized the marriage of Mr. Moore and Miss Jennie Moss, who was born in Sumner county and is a daughter of W. F. Moss, a well known and successful farmer of this county who passed away in February, 1912. He was a Confederate veteran of the Civil war and in that conflict served under Gen. John H. Morgan of Kentucky. Mr. and Mrs. Moore have three children: Charles D., Mary and W. F., aged respectively seventeen, twelve and four years. Charles D. and Mary are now attending school. Mr. Moore is a member of the Methodist Episcopal church, South, and in political faith is aligned with the Democratic party. He was a prosperous business man when active along that line and owns a comfortable home in Gallatin.

GEORGE W. BODDIE. Notably successful as a lawyer and a former clerk and master of the chancery court of Sumner county, George W. Boddie has been a member of the Gallatin bar for a quarter century. His own career has been chiefly passed in Sumner county, of which he is a native, and his family is one that has been identified with the state for a century or more.

He was born in Sumner county, January 14, 1852, a son of Charles E. and Evalina (Douglas) Boddie. His paternal grandparents were Elijah and Maria (Elliott) Boddie. The former, a native of Nash county, North Carolina, crossed the mountains into Tennessee early in the last century, and spent most of his life in Sumner county. He was a soldier of the War of 1812, and fought with General Jackson at New Orleans.

Charles E. Boddie, the father, was born in Sumner county in 1818, and his death occurred in 1896. His active years were spent in farming, and his homestead was located six miles from Gallatin. His first wife, Evalina Douglas, was a daughter of James Douglas, who gives special distinction to this family history as having been the first male white child born in Sumner county, where he spent all the rest of his life. Evalina Boddie died in 1856, the mother of seven children, of whom three are still living, including George W., who was the second in the family. Charles E. Boddie married for his second wife Susan A. Maney, and they had six children, of whom four are living. The father was a member of the Methodist church, South, was an Odd Fellow, and a Democrat in politics.

George W. Boddie spent his early life on the farm, and was graduated in law from the Cumberland University in 1875. In 1887 he located at Gallatin, and during the subsequent twenty-five years has enjoyed a liberal share in the legal business of the local courts and office practice. From 1894 to 1906 he was clerk and master in the chancery court. Politically he is a Democrat. Mr. Boddie has been prominent in Odd-fellowship, having passed the chairs of his local lodge, and has served as delegate to the state Grand lodge. His church is the Methodist South.

He was married February 25, 1875, to Miss Alice Davis of Wilson county, Tennessee. Six years later she passed away, in 1881. Of her three children one is living, Mina. In 1885 Mr. Boddie married Miss Willie Davis, daughter of W. C. Davis, a Wilson county farmer. Five children have blessed this union, and the four living are: James B., of Columbia; and Rufus F., Sarah and Portia, all at home.

WALTER SANDERS FAULKNER. A candidate at the primaries in 1912 for the Democratic nomination for governor of Tennessee, Mr. Faulkner has become one of the state's public leaders. He possesses many of the qualities that are most valued in political life, and his popularity and capacity for services are not likely to become less. By profession he is a lawyer and has gained distinction in the bar of his home county, and has twice been honored with the district attorney generalship. He worthily upholds the prestige of a family which has been prominent in Tennessee for several generations.

Walter Sanders Faulkner is a native of Lebanon, Wilson county, Tennessee, a son of J. J. and Nora (Sanders) Faulkner. The Faulkner family was originally from Scotland, coming to America in a very early day and locating in the colony of Virginia. Grandfather Asa Faulkner spent the activities of his honorable career in Warren county, Tennessee, where he was quite a wealthy manufacturer. He owned and operated several cotton and woolen factories before and after the Civil war. He was much interested in public affairs, and represented Warren county in the state senate several times. J. J. Faulkner, the father, was a business man, and had considerabe genius as an investor, his enterprises usually being successful and extending to a wide field of commerce and industry.

Nora (Sanders) Faulkner, the mother, is a daughter of Col. Richard C. Sanders, whose great-grandfather came from England and settled in North Carolina. James Sanders, this original ancestor, had a son also named James, who in his time came to Sumner county, Tennessee, locating near Castalian Springs, where he married Lettie Carey. They became the parents of Col. Richard C. Sanders. Col. Sanders at the beginning of the Civil war enlisted, was elected lieutenant-colonel of the Twenty-eighth Tennessee Regiment, and served with distinction for the full four years of the struggle. Following the war he represented Smith county in the legislature, and after taking up his residence in Wilson county repeatedly was sent from this county to the legislature. By profession he was a lawyer, and as such commanded a large practice over several of the counties of middle Tennessee.

Walter Sanders Faulkner, whose ambition has been to make the best of his own talents and individual ability and at the same time to do credit to his honored forefathers, was reared in his native county, and was chiefly educated at the Cumberland University of Lebanon, attending both the literary and the law schools in that institution. From almost the beginning of his practice he has enjoyed a liberal share of the legal business in the courts of this county, and at the same time his personal popularity soon led him into the field of practical politics. He served as Democratic elector in 1900, and in 1902 was elected district attorney general. In 1910 he was re-elected to this office. As already stated, in the campaign of 1912 he stood for the Democratic nomination for governor of Tennessee, and though he ran a good race in the field of candidates he was defeated. Mr. Faulkner is not married. He has his church membership in the Christian denomination, and is affiliated with the Independent Order of Odd Fellows and the Knights of Pythias. Besides his law practice he has a prominent place in business affairs, as president of the Union Bank & Trust Company of Lebanon.

A. OSCAR ESKEW. The Eskew family has furnished Wilson county, Tennessee, prominent physicians for three generations. The first representative of the family in Tennessee was Dr. Andrew Eskew, a native of North Carolina, who came to this section with the early tide of immigration from the old North State and was one of the first physicians in Wilson county, where he thereafter continued to practice until his death. His son, Dr. John C. Eskew, one of the best known and esteemed men of Wilson county, has been a successful medical practitioner in this county for the remarkable period of fifty-one years, and his grandson is he whose name initiates this review and who in every respect is most worthily upholding the honor and professional prestige of the name he bears.

Dr. John C. Eskew, above mentioned, was born in Wilson county, Tennessee, in March, 1841, and during the more than half-century of his professional labors and his long life as a citizen of this community has so ordered his course as to command a secure place in the esteem of his fellowmen and to permit his name to go down in history supported by all the attributes of a well spent life and an honorable career. He has always enjoyed a large practice and is a member of both the Wilson county and the Tennessee state medical societies. At the opening of the Civil war he was appointed regimental surgeon for the Forty-fifth Tennessee Infantry and served in that position and with that command throughout that long struggle. He is staunch Democrat in political belief. He wedded Martha C. Rogers, who was born in Wilson county, Tennessee, in 1846, a daughter of James Rogers, an early settler of Wilson county and during the remainder of his career one of its extensive and successful farmers. Both Dr. and Mrs. Eskew, residents of Lebanon, are members of the Christian church. Five children came to their union and of this family Dr. A. O. Eskew is third in birth and is one of three yet living.

Dr. A. Oscar Eskew was reared in Lebanon and received his first collegiate training in Cumberland University, graduating from that institution with the class of 1893. He then entered the University of Tennessee, where his progress was most rapid, speedily developing those qualities of mental acquisition and retention so essential to a broad and comprehensive knowledge of the profession he had chosen. So well did he apply himself in this direction that he was graduated from the medical department of that institution in 1897 as salutatorian of his class, as a reward for which high honors he was given charge of the Davidson county asylum for one year. At an early age he had developed those qualities of cool judgment, kindness of heart and strength of mind so essential to the success of a good physician and having now completed his professional training he entered upon the active practice of medicine in Lebanon in connection with his father. This association was continued two years and since then our subject has practiced independently, rising steadily in professional prestige and becoming recognized as an able, conscientious and in every respect reliable practitioner, with a large and increasing clientèle.

In 1904 Dr. Eskew was married to Miss Carrie Harris, daughter of Joseph Harris, a native and well known farmer citizen of Wilson county who is also a Confederate veteran of the Civil war. Mrs. Eskew died in 1908. She was a most estimable lady and was a consistent member of the Presbyterian church. Dr. Eskew affiliates with the Christian denomination. In politics he is a Democrat. He has served four years as assistant city health officer of Lebanon and keeps abreast with the advances of his profession as a member of the Wilson county and Tennessee state medical societies and the American Medical Association.

EDWARD E. BEARD. A prominent citizen and financier of Lebanon, Tennessee, and one of the leading and older members of the Wilson county bar, Edward E. Beard bears further distinction as a scion of two of Tennessee's worthy pioneer families. He has devoted over forty years to law with that success that has won him rank among the best legal talent of the state, and as president of the American National Bank of Lebanon and in other financial relations he is well known in the business circles of this section of Tennessee, where he is recognized as a shrewd and forceful business man. He has been a member of the Tennessee state legislature, and as a warm and earnest advocate of the church, of liberal education and of general public advancement he has rendered valuable services in these different directions.

Edward E. Beard was born at Princeton, Kentucky, August 27, 1850, his parents being Rev. Richard and Cynthia E. (Castleman) Beard, both of whom were natives of Tennessee, the former born in Sumner county and the latter in Davidson county. The Beard family originated in this state with John Beard, the grandfather of Edward E., who was a North Carolinian by birth and migrated to Tennessee in an early day, settling in Sumner county, where he spent a number of years as a school teacher. He finally moved to Arkansas and passed away in that state. The Castlemans were of Virginia stock, the founder of the family in Tennessee being Andrew Castleman, the father of Mrs. Beard, who came to Tennessee from the Old Dominion with General James Robertson, of pioneer fame in this state, and became a well-to-do farmer and the owner of 640 acres of land near Nashville. He was one of the well-known men of Tennessee in his day. Rev. Richard Beard, the father of our subject, received his earlier educational discipline in Tennessee and was a schoolmate of J. C. Jones, the great Whig governor of this state. He was well educated and took up the profession of teaching, with which line of endeavor he was thereafter prominently identified for over fifty years. After teaching in West Tennessee for a time he went to Princeton, Kentucky, to add collegiate training to his qualifications, and was graduated from Cumberland College there. Later he became president of that institution, and from there he came to Lebanon, Tennessee, to become an instructor in the theological department of Cumberland University. He was also a minister of the Cumberland Presbyterian church for a number of years and was one of the foremost leaders in the work of this denomination in Tennessee, his learning and ability, superior mind and unbending integrity making him an effective power in the direction of church work and of advancing and uplifting society. He was first a Whig and then later a Democrat in his political allegiance. Death closed his useful career in 1880. Rev. Richard and Cynthia E. (Castleman)

Beard reared six children, of which family Edward E. was the youngest in birth and is one of three yet living. Both in the arts and in law Edward received the excellent educational advantages of Cumberland University and was graduated from the literary department of that institution in 1870 and from the law department in 1871. He began the practice of law at Lebanon. Fitted by natural gifts and education for the profession of his choice, he soon displayed marked aptitude and ability in this direction, rose rapidly at the bar and early acquired a large and lucrative practice. Each succeeding year has but strengthened his legal reputation and he is admitted to practice before all the courts. He is no less able as a business man than as a lawyer, and as president of the American National Bank at Lebanon that institution has the services of a very wise and capable directive head. For twenty-five years he has also been treasurer and a trustee of Cumberland University. In political views he is a Democrat and in 1885 gave public service as the representative of Wilson county in the state legislature, the duties of which honorable office he discharged with ability and with fidelity to his constituents. Fraternally he is identified with the Knights of Pythias and is a past chancellor commander of his lodge.

In 1876, in a house built by Andrew Jackson and near his old home, The Hermitage, Mr. Beard was joined in marriage to Miss Sarah Livingston, a daughter of James Livingston, who was a prosperous merchant of Nashville. To this happy union were born three daughters: Mary E., now Mrs. Thomas Pierce, of St. Louis, Missouri; Emma, who became the wife of B. R. McKinnie, a wholesale merchant at Nashville, Tennessee; and Edna, who is now Mrs. Wever Harris, and also resides in Nashville.

Both Mr. and Mrs. Beard are active members of the Presbyterian church and Mr. Beard served as a member of the committee that in 1906 effected the union of the Cumberland Presbyterian branch and the mother church. Mr. Beard's life has been a useful and worthy one. Not alone in his profession and business relations has he proved himself one of the world's useful workers, but his upright, intelligent, conservative and consistent course as a citizen, both in public and in private life, has made him worthy of recognition as one of the representative men of Tennessee.

CLAUDE V. YOUNG, M. D. Well established in the successful practice of his profession in the old and beautiful little college city of Lebanon, Dr. Young takes rank among the leading physicians of this section of the state, and for his useful services in behalf of suffering mankind and as a native son of this commonwealth, he is well deserving of mention among the representative citizens of Tennessee.

Born in Wilson county on June 16, 1867, he is the only son and is the eldest of four children of William H. and Bettie (Vivrette) Young, now residents of East Nashville, Tennessee, but formerly well known and highly respected farmer residents of Wilson county. Both parents are natives of Wilson county, where the father's birth occurred in 1842 and where the mother was born in 1847, and both have long been faithful members of the Baptist church. William H. Young followed the pursuit of farming in Wilson county a number of years but subsequently removed to Nashville, where he engaged in the hardware business for a time. He is now residing in East Nashville, retired. He is a Confederate veteran of the Civil war and throughout that conflict fought as a member of Company I of the Seventh Tennessee Regiment. This regiment, one of marked bravery, saw long active and hard service in Virginia and fought under "Stonewall" Jackson from the battle of Seven Pines in 1862 to the fall of that brave general. With the Seventh Tennessee Mr. Young participated in many of the hardest fought battles of the eastern campaign, as well as in many of less importance, among the severer engagements being that of Sharpsburg, Fredericksburg, Chancellorsville, Gettysburg and the battles of the Wilderness campaign. At Fredericksburg he was severely wounded, suffering wounds also in two later battles, and shortly before the war closed he was captured. Returning to his home in Tennessee he began life anew and became a successful man in business. His father, William L. Young, had been a farmer of considerable competence up to the time of the war, but suffered heavy financial losses during that conflict. The latter was a native of London and had immigrated to this country shortly after attaining his majority, settling in Wilson county, Tennessee, where he continued a resident until his death. He was well known in this county, having served as chairman of the county court for over twenty years, and he lived to be nearly ninety years old. Mrs. Bettie (Vivrette) Young, the mother of Dr. Young, is a daughter of Buchanan Vivrette, who was born in Tennessee and spent his life at Greenhill, Wilson county, as a successful farmer and trader. The sisters of Dr. Young are Ruby Lee, who now resides in Los Angeles, California, and whose husband, H. E. Herrin, is a hardware merchant there and also has similar interests at Nashville, Tennessee; Floy Belle, now Mrs. Jesse W. Rives, of East Nashville, Tennessee, whose husband is a bookkeeper; and Nancy Elizabeth, who became the wife of Eugene Johns, a theatre manager at Nashville.

Dr. Claude V. Young spent his boyhood in Wilson county and there was prepared for his entrance in the college at Santa Fe, Maury county. At the conclusion of his collegiate studies he matriculated at Vanderbilt University, Nashville, to prepare for the profession of medicine, and was graduated as a Doctor of Medicine in 1893. He began the practice of medicine in the country in Wilson county, continuing thus until 1906, when he removed to Lebanon, where he has since steadily built up a representative and profitable practice and has become recognized as one of the most successful representatives of his profession in Wilson county. His professional interest is indicated further by his membership in the

Wilson County Medical Society, the Tennessee State Medical Society and the American Medical Association. Dr. Young has good business ability as well as medical skill and his financial accomplishments have paralleled his professional success.

In 1898 he was joined in marriage to Elizabeth, daughter of Rev. James M. Donnell, a Presbyterian minister who has followed his honorable calling many years and is yet living, a resident of Lebanon and in advanced years. Rev. Robert Donnell, the grandfather of Mrs. Young, and a pioneer clergyman of the Presbyterian church in Tennessee, built the first church in Lebanon and was one of the leaders in the founding of the Cumberland Presbyterian branch of this denomination, his ministerial labors also covering a long period of years. Mrs. Young is affiliated with this denomination, while Dr. Young sustains membership in the Baptist church. They have one son, William D. Young, now attending school at the Castle Heights Training School, Lebanon. In politics Dr. Young has identified himself with the Democratic party.

HOUSTON F. STRATTON. It is most gratifying to note by means of the personal reviews appearing in this publication that a very representative percentage of the native sons of Tennessee who are accorded recognition have found in this commonwealth ample opportunities for the achieving of success along the various lines of business, professional, official and industrial endeavor, and that through their character and services they are honoring the fine old state which they may well be proud to designate as their native heath. Such an one is Mr. Stratton, the efficient and popular incumbent of the office of circuit court clerk of Wilson county, and one of the highly esteemed and progressive citizens of Lebanon, the judicial center of his native county.

A scion of one of the sterling pioneer families of southeastern Tennessee, Houston F. Stratton was born at Lebanon, Wilson county, on the 20th of December, 1866, and is a son of S. G. and Alice (Fisher) Stratton, of whose two children he is the elder; the younger son, Frank C., is the incumbent of an executive position in the Lebanon National Bank. S. G. Stratton was born in Wilson county, on the 30th of January, 1844, and here passed his entire life, his death having occurred in 1909. On the 9th of November, 1865, was solemnized his marriage to Miss Alice Fisher, who likewise was born in Wilson county and who was a daughter of Houston and Ann C. Fisher, who also were natives of this state and representatives of families that were here founded in the early territorial epoch, the subject of this review having been named in honor of his maternal grandfather. Mrs. Alice (Fisher) Stratton was summoned to the life eternal in October, 1877, and in August, 1879, S. G. Stratton wedded Miss Leila Owen, who survives him and still maintains her home in Lebanon. Three children were born of this union, all daughters and married. The father of the subject of this sketch was long numbered among the prominent business men and influential citizens of Wilson county and so ordered his life in all its relations as to retain the inviolable confidence and esteem of all who knew him. He was for many years identified with the banking business and was one of the organizers of the Bank of Lebanon, which was eventually merged into the present Lebanon National Bank. He was one of the substantial capitalists of his native county, was the owner of valuable farming property and city realty, and was specially influential in public affairs of a local order. He was called upon to serve in nearly all of the various county offices and also represented his county in the state legislature. He was a zealous member of the Methodist Episcopal church, South, as were also his first and his second wives; was a prominent and appreciative member of the Masonic fraternity, and also was affiliated with the Lebanon lodge of Knights of Pythias. He gave unqualified allegiance to the Democratic party and was prominent in its local councils and activities. At the time of the Civil war he was in the Confederate service for a short period, and two of his brothers likewise gave valiant service as soldiers of the Confederacy, both having been wounded in action. S. G. Stratton was a son of Thomas Jefferson Stratton and Caroline (Golladay) Stratton, the former of whom was born in Sumner county, this state, on the 5th of August, 1817. Thomas J. Stratton was one of the representative citizens of Wilson county, where he was a pioneer banker and merchant of Lebanon and the founder of one of the first banks in the county. He owned also a large landed estate and a number of slaves, was a stalwart in the camp of the Democratic party and continued as one of the leading men of Wilson county until his death. The brief data here incorporated show that the name of the Stratton family has been most conspicuously and worthily identified with the civic and material development and upbuilding of this county, and he who figures as the immediate subject of this sketch may well take pride in the ancestral record.

Houston Fisher Stratton is indebted to the public schools of Lebanon for his early educational discipline and at the age of twenty-one years he began reading law under effective private preceptorship. He made substantial and rapid advancement in his absorption of legal lore and was admitted to the bar, at Lebanon, in 1888. He has since proved himself most resourceful and successful in the practical work of his profession and has presented causes in the various courts of the state, including the supreme court and those of Federal establishment. He has served as circuit court clerk for his native county since 1910, and he gives a most careful and acceptable administration of his official duties, besides controlling a substantial and representative law practice with prestige as one of the able and popular members of the bar of Wilson county. In both political and religious lines he has not deviated from the ancestral faith, as he is a staunch Democrat and a member of the

Methodist Episcopal church, South; his wife being a member of the Cumberland Presbyterian church.

On the 11th of July, 1902, was solemnized the marriage of Mr. Stratton to Miss Emma McCauley, daughter of the late Broderick Mc-Cauley, a representative agriculturist and honored citizen of Houston county, this state. Mr. and Mrs. Stratton have one child, Samuel G., who was born on the 22nd of September, 1904, and who is now attending the public schools of Lebanon.

ROBERT COX. Capable, energetic and progressive, Robert Cox, post-master at Lebanon, Tennessee, is a young man who stands high in the regard of his fellow men in his native county of Wilson and is a very worthy representative of its best citizenship. As a business man he is resourceful and accomplishing, and to his duties as an official and citizen he gives of his highest order of endeavor.

Born at Greenvale, Wilson county, Tennessee, September 7, 1877, he grew to young manhood in the vicinity of his birth and during that time obtained a good education, his earlier discipline received in the public schools of Wilson county and at Watertown Academy being supple-mented by about two years of study in the University of Tennessee. When entering upon independent activity in the business world he did so as a farmer, but shortly afterward, or in 1898, he came to Lebanon to take up the duties of assistant postmaster, in which position he con-tinued to serve six years. He severed his connection with the postoffice in 1904 by resignation and engaged in the laundry business in Lebanon, continuing that business identification until 1910, and in the meantime serving as business manager of the Lebanon College a year and a half, or until it burned in 1909. In 1910 he was appointed postmaster at Lebanon and at that time took up the duties with which he was already familiar and which he has since performed in the most acceptable man-ner. He is a Republican in political sentiment and adherency. The parents of Robert Cox, who are James A. and Ann S. (Grimmet) Cox, well known and highly respected citizens of Wilson county now residing at Watertown, are both natives of this county, the former's birth having occurred at Statesville in 1843, and the birth of the latter having occurred at the village of Greenvale in 1841. The elder Mr. Cox fol-lowed merchandising successfully for a number of years, or until 1908, when he assumed the duties of postmaster and served in that office until 1912. He is now living retired. In his political belief he is a Repub-lican, but while he has always taken an active part in the local political affairs of his party he never ran for office and his one request for official position was granted him. He has served as a member of the county committee for fifty years. This branch of the Cox family originated in Tennessee with A. W. Cox, the father of James A., who was a native of North Carolina and came into this state early in the last century. A tailor by trade, he came here alone at the age of seventeen and settled in Statesville, Wilson county, in 1835. Mrs. Ann S. (Grimmet) Cox is a daughter of William H. Grimmet, who also was an early settler in Tennessee and became well known throughout this section of the state through his services as a Baptist minister. He was a native Virginian and came to Tennessee on horseback in 1830 as a young man. He was engaged in spreading and teaching his religious faith until his sudden death at Statesville, Tennessee. To James A. and Ann S. (Grimmet) Cox were born three children, two of whom are living: Mary, now Mrs. Thomas J. McAdoo, of Memphis, Tennessee, and Robert of this review

In 1905 Mr. Cox was married to Miss May Belle Wilson, daughter of Mr. and Mrs. J. M. Wilson, residents of Rome, Tennessee, and prosperous farmer citizens of that community. William Bell, the maternal grandfather of Mrs. Cox, gave true and manly service in defense of the Confederacy during the Civil war, but was captured early during that struggle and served as a prisoner of war at Staten Island three and a half years. Yet surviving at the remarkable age of ninety-nine years, he resides at Rome, Tennessee, and is well and prominently known throughout the state. He is a cousin of John Paul Jones, the naval hero of the Revolution. Mrs. Cox is a member of the Presbyterian church. Mr. Cox affiliates fraternally with the Masonic order and the Knights of Pythias, and is a past chancellor commander of the latter order.

L. B. WALTON, M. D. The name of Dr. L. B. Walton connects both a distinguished family and a notable career in the medical profession, in which he has been prominent for considerably more than a half century. In both paternal and maternal lines has his ancestry been of distinction. To a leading Virginia family belonged Martyn Walton, physician and land owner, his grandfather; and of a similar class came his paternal grandmother, who was a sister of Gen. Joseph E. Johnston. They came from Louisa county, Virginia, to Robertson county, where their son T. J. Walton, was born. Through the latter the families of Walton and Bartlett were joined. Thomas Bartlett (the maternal grandfather of our subject), was a native of Louisiana and a very wealthy man, an extensive portion of whose estate was left to his daughter. She, Martha Bartlett, was born in Robertson county, Tennessee, and here married T. J. Walton, referred to above. He it was who became, in his day, Robertson county's most noted physician, practicing here for sixty-four years. He was also a land owner of extensive property and a slave holder as well. Martha Bartlett Walton, his wife, was a devoted member of the Methodist Episcopal church and carefully reared the four children who were born to her and Dr. T. J. Walton; of these three are yet living. The first born child of his parents was L. B. Walton, whose name forms the caption of this biographical account.

Born in Robertson county on December 27, 1827, T. J. Walton in his earlier years was given such educational advantages as were obtainable in the common schools of the period. He fitted himself for entrance into the medical college at Louisville, Kentucky, from which institution he was graduated in 1848. He immediately entered upon his medical practice, locating at Crossplains, where he has ever since remained, gradually increasing his usefulness and his reputation through his more active years. His services have been in great demand, his professional errands of mercy have been many and arduous, and he has frequently ridden on horseback such distances as from Goodletsville to Adairsville. He has lived a life not only of usefulness, but also of thrift. The Civil war left him without property, the estate his wife had brought into the family having been swept away by the fortunes of war. But the doctor's tireless toil and his wise care have established a gratifying financial status. He is the owner of five hundred and fifty acres of land and has been prominently connected with the Crossplains bank, of which he was president for one year.

Not the least of the good doctor's achievements, nor the least considerable phase of his good fortune is his family. On December 18, 1854, he was united in marriage to Miss Mildred H. French, the daughter of Thomas J. French, who was a native of Montgomery county, Tennessee, and a member of a rich and prominent family of that region. The doctor and his wife are the parents of four sons and two daughters. The eldest, christened Mattie, is Mrs. George Bradford, of Nashville; T. J. Walton, the elder son, is also a resident of that same capital city; Fannie Walton became Mrs. W. S. Simmons and lives in Springfield; Martin—the junior Dr. Walton—continues the family line of physicians and now relieves Dr. L. B. Walton of much of his practice. The mother of these sons and daughters passed to the invisible life in May of 1905, remembered for her noble qualities as a mother and a Christian. The family church connection is that of the Baptist denomination. The fraternal affiliation of Dr. L. B. Walton is Masonic; he has been a member of the organization for sixty years and is also a chapter Mason. Few men of the estimable doctor's age can look back upon years of greater usefulness.

JOHN CALVIN GEURIN, M. D. There is perhaps no field of modern practical science in which more notable progress is being made than in that of medicine. The conservation of human resources, the symmetrical development and care of body, nerves and brain, the amazing possibilities life holds, not only for the strong, but for those heretofore defrauded of their birthright of health—these are receiving from the up-to-date physician more constructive study than ever before. The present-day physician is no mere drug-dispenser; he is also apostle of sane living. He takes pride not only in the cure, but in the prevention of disease; he prescribes not only antidotes in bottle form, but also intelligent rules for his patient to follow; he understands not only materia medica, but also psychotherapy; he not only mends the battered human structure, but also builds up a higher, finer development. His mission is not only of today, but of tomorrow. It is said that, financially, the physicians of today are losing out, for the multitude who pay willingly for bottled nostrums, grudge payment for the wise advice which accompanies or takes its place. But the conscientious doctor toils on, looking to a day when medical practice may be institutionalized and each practitioner justly remunerated by a system as advanced and efficient as that of his own science.

One who may live to see that day is the talented young physician of Slayden, Tennessee, Dr. John Calvin Geurin. Tennessee is this young physician's native place, as it is also that of his parents. His father's family were formerly of North Carolina residence, Henry Geurin, his grandfather, having spent his latter days in Tennessee, where H. K. Geurin, the doctor's father, was born. Cumberland Furnace was the birthplace and March 29, 1851, the date of birth of H. K. Geurin, who married Miss Dona Martha Slayton, born in 1852, in the ninth district of Dickson county. They lived in that same locality, where they possessed a farm of 101 acres. H. K. Geurin was at one time connected with the fraternal society The Wheelers, an organization which no longer exists. Politically he is a Democrat. Both he and his wife are still living.

In the parental home, located as above noted, John Calvin Geurin and five other children were born, three of whom are now living. The subject of this review was the first-born, the date of his birth being December 11, 1878. The second in line was Augusta, now Mrs. L. C. O'Hara, of Princeton, Kentucky; and the third, William Geurin, now a resident of Dogwood, Tennessee. Dr. Geurin's early education was pursued in the south side public schools and his professional preparation was accomplished in the University of Nashville, where in the medical department he studied the prescribed courses, and having completed his period of research, received his license to practice medicine in the year 1906.

Dr. Geurin gained his initial experience in medical practice at Pardue, Tennessee, where he located immediately for practice. From there he removed to Ellis Mills, where he remained until 1908, the date of his coming to Slayden. Here he has ever since been in practice with a steadily growing patronage and with an increasing reputation for thorough reliability.

The Montgomery County Medical Society and the State Medical Society include Dr. Geurin as one of their most enthusiastic members. Of non-professional organizations, he is a member of the Independent Order of Odd Fellows, in Slayden lodge, No. 469, and of the Masonic Camp, lodge No. 445, Slayden. His political alignment is with the Democratic party.

HARRY E. DOWLEN of Montgomery county, Tennessee, not content with the ordinary successes that greet any hard working farmer who does not have a run of hard luck, has followed the trend of the times toward specialization, and by devoting all of his energies toward raising certain products, has become one of the most prosperous farmers in Montgomery county. He is a native of the state of Tennessee and is descended from parents and grandparents who were citizens of this state, so his interest and activity in her behalf are necessarily strong.

Harry E. Dowlen was born in Robertson county, Tennessee, on the 13th of March, 1883. His parents were both born in Tennessee, his father having been born in 1852 and his mother in 1853. He is a son of Cicero Dowlen, whose wife was Sallie W. Thompson before her marriage. Cicero Dowlen is the son of John Dowlen, who was an early settler in the state of Tennessee. The maternal grandfather of Harry E. Dowlen, William R. Thompson, was a native of Virginia, and also settled in the state at an early date, becoming a successful farmer and tobacco merchant. Both of Mr. Dowlen's grandparents were large slaveholders and the owners of fine plantations in Montgomery and Robertson counties. Cicero Dowlen was reared and educated in Robertson county, and after completing his own education he became a school teacher and for a number of years taught quite successfully. On giving up pedagogy as a profession he turned to farming and the remainder of his life has been spent in this occupation. He has been very successful and owns one of the best producing farms in Montgomery county. In politics Cicero Dowlen is a member of the Democratic party, and for twenty-five years he has been magistrate in district No. 5. He is a member of the Independent Order of Odd Fellows and takes much interest in all the interests that he has in addition to his farming. A brother of Cicero Dowlen, Harris by name, served through the Civil war as a member of the Confederate army, but he was too young to enlist. Five children were born to Cicero Dowlen and his wife, namely, Harry; R. E., who owns part of the farm which Harry Dowlen operates; John S., who lives with his father; Coma, who also lives at the old homestead, and Erma, who is dead. Mrs. Dowlen died in 1904. She was a member and active worker in the Methodist Episcopal church, South.

Harry Dowlen was educated at the schools in Montgomery county, attending two terms of school at Murfreesboro. He began work for his living on his father's farm and in 1905 he saved enough money to buy some land for himself. This property in which he owned a one-third interest was one hundred and twelve acres in extent. After a time he sold this land and went to east Tennessee, where he bought a one-third interest in four hundred acres. He only remained in that part of the

state for a year, and on his return to Montgomery county he purchased his present farm of one hundred and thirty-four acres. In the August after his return he was elected magistrate, and now sixty-six years in this office have been rounded out by the men of his family, for his father and grandfather held the office before him. Mr. Dowlen has served the public in other capacities, at the age of twenty-one being elected constable, an office which he held for four years. Wheat and tobacco are his principal crops and he has met with great success in the cultivation of both commodities. This year he has forty-six acres planted in tobacco. Mr. Dowlen has never cared to take a very active part in fraternal affairs, but he is a member of the Benevolent and Protective Order of Elks, affiliating with the Clarksville chapter, No. 601.

On the 13th of February, 1911, Mr. Dowlen was married to Ruth Marshall, of Tullahoma, Tennessee. Mrs. Dowlen is a daughter of W. A. Marshall, who is a wealthy and prominent resident of Tullahoma, having been mayor of that city for twenty years.

JOHN HORATIO CLAGETT. Probably no member of the Hickman county bar is better or more favorably known than he whose name introduces this review. His grandfather came from the state of Maryland in 1817 and settled on Lick creek in Hickman county, where he was one of the first white men to enter land. After a residence of a few years there he removed to Bedford county, but some years later returned to Hickman county, where he was engaged in agricultural pursuits until his death in 1867. His son, Horatio Clagett, the father of the subject of this sketch, was born in District No. 2, Hickman county, January 18, 1819, and was one of a family of seven children. He was educated in the common schools of Hickman and Bedford counties and upon arriving at manhood formed a partnership with his brother and engaged in merchandising under the firm name of W. G. & H. Clagett at Centerville. This association lasted for almost fifty years. In 1847 Horatio Clagett and Elizabeth Montgomery were united in marriage. She was born at Charlotte, Dickson county, Tennessee, in 1827. Of the seven children born to this marriage, five are still living. When the First National Bank was organized at Centerville in 1885, Horatio Clagett was elected the first president of the institution, which he held until the time of his death, December, 1912. About 1890 he disposed of his mercantile interests, and thereafter lived retired until his death. In his early years he was identified with the old Whig party, and after that organization was discontinued he affiliated with the Democratic party. His church relationship was with the Methodist Episcopal denomination, South, of which his wife was also a member until her death in February, 1908, and he was a Mason.

John Horatio Clagett, the fifth child of his parents, was born at Centerville, June 4, 1859, and received his elementary education in the schools of his native county. He then attended Vanderbilt University at Nashville, Tennessee, for two years, after which he entered the law department of the University at Lebanon, Tennessee, from which institution he received the degree of LL. B. in 1881. The same year he was admitted to practice at Centerville and formed a partnership with J. A. Bates, which association lasted until 1890, when Mr. Clagett removed to Union City. Three years later he returned to Centerville, where he practiced alone for some time and then formed a partnership with W. B. Flowers, now of Nashville, Tennessee. In 1912 the present firm of Knight & Clagett was formed and it occupies a prominent place in the legal affairs of Hickman and adjoining counties. For more than thirty years Mr. Clagett has been engaged in the practice of his chosen profession in his native state. His university training gave him the groundwork for a thorough understanding of the law, and his studies since leaving college have placed him among the well equipped attorneys of Tennessee. Conscientious in looking after the interests of his clients, careful in the preparation of his cases, and energetic in all matters pertaining to his business, he has achieved a measurable success in a practice that has covered practically all branches of the law.

Mr. Clagett is a Democrat in his political views, a member of the Methodist Episcopal church, South, and belongs to Sam Davis Lodge, No. 158, Knights of Pythias, of Centerville. In political, church and fraternal circles he has made many friends by his courteous demeanor and genial disposition.

JOSEPH E. JUSTICE. Whatever the vocation or calling, it is efficiency that finally determines the question of success. The profession of law requires a strong mentality and a keen discriminative ability, but it is only when such native talents are combined with patient study, investigation, training in reasoning and with a large capacity for the most laborious attention to detail that the lawyer attains a distinctive position in his profession. Well qualified in these different directions for the profession of his choice, Joseph E. Justice, of Ashland City, Tennessee, has won a foremost place at the Cheatham county bar. He is not only an able lawyer but is a representative of the native talent of Tennessee and of his own immediate vicinity, for he was born in the 13th civil district of Cheatham county, the date of his birth being May 17, 1866. He is also a representative of pioneer connections in this vicinity of Tennessee and on the paternal side is a scion of Virginia ancestry, while his mother's people, the Hilands, were originally North Carolinians. The first of the Justice family here were the grandparents of Joseph E., both of whom were Virginians by birth and migrated to Tennessee in an early day. Their son James E., the father of our subject, became one of the prominent and well known men of Cheatham county. He was born in Coopertown, Robertson county, Tennessee, in 1834, and spent many years in the profession of teaching, being superintendent of public instruction in Cheatham county at the time of his death in 1869. In political faith he was first a Whig, but on the breaking up of that party he became aligned with the Republican party. He wedded Ann J. Hiland, who was born in Cheatham county, Tennessee, in 1832, and survived her husband many years, passing away in 1905 at the age of seventy-three. She was a member of the Presbyterian church, while Mr. Justice affiliated with the Missionary Baptist church. They became the parents of four children, three of whom are yet living, namely: Mrs. Effie Carroll, who resides in Dickson county, Tennessee; Joseph E. Justice, of this review; and Mrs. Jennie Cooley, whose home is near Union City, Tennessee. The parents of Mrs. Justice were George W. and Martha A. (Morris) Hiland, the former of whom was a native of North Carolina and came to Robertson county, Tennessee, as a pioneer, becoming an extensive farmer and large slave holder there. Mrs. Hiland was born in Robertson county, this state.

Joseph E. Justice grew up in Cheatham county, receiving his literary education at Ashland City and Dickson and his preparation for law at Cumberland University, Lebanon, Tennessee, from which institution he was graduated in 1904. He began the practice of law at Ashland City as a partner of J. C. Wilson, but later the firm dissolved and since 1906 Mr. Justice has continued his professional labors there alone. He is admitted to practice in all the courts and has demonstrated that ability as a lawyer that places him among the leading members of the Cheatham county bar. He is the legal representative of the Ayer & Lord Tie Company, which is very extensively engaged in the timber business in this section, and he was one of the organizers and one of the first directors of the Ashland City Bank & Trust Company, in which he yet retains an interest. Mr. Justice has been largely dependent upon his own resources in making his way in life and has employed them to that advantage that today he is a man of competence, as well as a lawyer of well established reputation and practice. In political views he is a Democrat and a staunch supporter of his party, and at one time was the Democratic candidate for the office of attorney-general of the ninth judicial district. Fraternally he is a member of the Knights of Pythias and the Independent Order of Odd Fellows and has filled the executive offices in the local lodge of each of these orders.

In November, 1897, was solemnized the marriage of Mr. Justice and Miss Lula Lenox, daughter of Judge J. J. Lenox, who was a prominent member of the Cheatham county bar for many years and was also a wealthy farmer. Mrs. Justice, who was a devoted and consistent member of the Methodist Episcopal church, South, died in December, 1904, leaving three children: Kathleen, James E., and Mary A., all of whom are now attending school. Mr. Justice also is a member of the Methodist Episcopal church, South.

REV. JAMES T. BAGBY. No matter to what denomination ministers of the Gospel may belong, nor how much they may differ as to the fundamental principles and theories of theology, there is one point upon which they agree and one end for which they are working—and that is the elevation of the general moral tone of the whole people. The influence of their teaching is felt far beyond the immediate confines of their respective congregations. It is reflected in the probity of the citizen, the loyalty of the soldier, the sanctity of the home, the education of the young, and in many other ways in all walks of life, even upon those who never attend church and who claim to doubt many of the precepts taught by the followers of the Master. For the work of the pastor Rev. J. T. Bagby is well qualified by natural disposition, training and experience, and although one of the youngest ministers of the Methodist Episcopal church, South, in the state, he has made a reputation that for one of his years is rarely equaled.

Mr. Bagby was born in Decatur county, Tennessee, May 14, 1879, and is a descendant of one of the state's pioneer families, his paternal grandfather and grandmother having come from North Carolina at an early date. He is the seventh in a family of ten children born to James L. and Martha (Rushing) Bagby, both natives of Tennessee. One of his brothers is also a Methodist minister. He was educated in the common schools while being brought up on his father's farm in Henderson county, Tennessee, and afterward attended Scott's Hill Normal Institute at Scott's Hill, graduating with honors, and the McTyeire Institute at McKenzie, Tennessee, graduating with great honors as a debater and as a linguist with no superiors. In 1906 he was made a deacon in the church, at that time becoming a member, in full connection, of the Memphis conference, and in 1908 was ordained an elder. His first charge was Bethel and Selmer, a double station in the Lexington district, where he served his congregation with zeal and fidelity until he was called to Columbus, Kentucky, three years later, where he added to his reputation as a conscientious, intelligent and faithful worker in the vineyard. In 1911 he was assigned to his present pastorate at Obion, Tennessee, after a four-years' pastorate at Columbus. Mr. Bagby is a diligent student of all questions relating to his profession. He has an extensive vocabulary and a faultless enunciation; his sentences are well rounded and complete, and his manner of presentation of a subject is both instructive and entertaining. Outside of his pulpit he is a genial gentleman and sympathetic pastor, and among his brother clergymen he has attained to a high position through his eloquent and scholarly sermons and his earnest work in behalf of the church along all lines. His church at Obion has over two hundred members and under his administration this number is constantly increasing. Those who know him best predict for him still greater charges and more onerous duties in the future.

In 1905 Mr. Bagby was united in marriage with Miss Daisy Steadman, daughter of John H. Steadman, and to this union has been born one son—Thomas S. Mrs. Bagby is well fitted for the duties of a pastor's wife and co-operates with her husband in all his efforts for the advancement of the church and Sunday school.

It is worthy of more than passing mention in connection with the history of this family, that Levi Bagby, an uncle of Rev. J. T. Bagby, was a valiant soldier in the Federal army during the great Civil war and rose to the rank of brigadier general, thus giving the name a permanent place in history as belonging to a loyal citizen in the dark days when the Union was threatened with disruption.

ADAM DIEHL. A citizen of worth and ability, Adam Diehl of the firm. of Diehl & Lord has been prominently identified with the business interests of Nashville for almost half a century, and during the time has won for himself a fine reputation as one who deserves for himself the confidence and trust of his fellow men. A son of Peter Diehl, he was born October 12, 1846, in Louisville, Kentucky, of thrifty German ancestry.

Born in Bavaria, Germany, where his parents were lifelong residents, Peter Diehl attended school regularly until sixteen years of age, when he came with two of his brothers, Adam Diehl and Jacob Diehl, to the United States, locating in Cincinnati, Ohio. Learning the tailor's trade, he resided in that city six years. Going then to Louisville, Kentucky, he established himself as a merchant tailor, and there carried on a good business until his death, at the age of seventy-seven years. He married Margaret Schwartz, who was born in Westmoreland county, Pennsylvania, where her father, John Schwartz, located as a farmer on coming to this country from Westphalia, Germany, his native place. She died at the age of sixty-seven years. Fourteen children were born of their marriage, a family of which the parents were justly proud.

In the city of his birth Adam Diehl acquired a practical education in the different branches there taught. Leaving school at the age of eighteen years, he was there employed as a bookkeeper for three years. On attaining his majority Mr. Diehl located in Nashville, Tennessee, where he established his present business, which is both extensive and remunerative. Since taking up his residence in Nashville, Mr. Diehl has ever evinced an active interest in municipal affairs, and his influence and assistance are always sought in behalf of undertakings for the public good, and for the advancement of the best interests of the community.

Mr. Diehl is married and has six children, namely: Edward, Margaret, Jack B., Walter, Frank and Ruth. Fraternally Mr. Diehl is a member of the Ancient Free and Accepted Order of Masons; of the Benevolent and Protective Order of Elks; of the Improved Order of Red Men and of the Order of Moose. He is an ex-member of the city council and during his connection therewith he did effective work for the city.

LEE ELLIOTT. An able citizen of Montgomery county and a lifelong resident of the community is Lee Elliott, who efficiently combines the time-honored occupation of farming with the useful services of dentistry. His is a capable individuality, made up of interestingly blended ancestral elements. North Carolina had been the home of his maternal grandparents, Garaldus and Mary (Marshall) Pickering, who early settled in Tennessee; here was born their daughter, Judith Pickering, her birthplace being in this county and about one and one-half miles distant from the present Elliott home. Near the time of the Pickerings' removal to Tennessee, this state had also become the home of David Elliott and Sallie (Cook) Elliott, his wife—the former a native of Pennsylvania and the latter of Ireland. To them was born in Port Royal on March 22, 1819, a son whom they named George H. This boy and the little girl, Judith Pickering, grew up together as childhood sweethearts and in 1840 they were married. Of the ten children born to them Lee Elliott was the fifth, his brothers and sisters being as follows: John A., who is deceased; David G., a resident of Port Royal; William S. Elliott, M. D., now deceased; Stonewall Jackson Elliott, who lives with Dr. Lee Elliott; Jacqueline, deceased; Marinda, widow of C. Gardner of Clarksville; Henrie, the third daughter, who is now Mrs. T. G. Ezelle, of Woodford; Alice, who is Mrs. A. D. Rhinehardt of Port Royal; and Sallie, deceased.

The Elliott home, during the childhood of George Elliott's children, was the farm on which Dr. Elliott now lives; for the father of the family had given up his inherited occupation in order to give his attention to farming. There it was that on February 14, 1867, Lee Elliott was born.

After a general education in the public schools, a professional course was sought by the young man, Lee Elliott. He entered the College of Dentistry of Vanderbilt University, where he pursued the prescribed study, and was graduated in 1898, receiving the degree of Doctor of Dental Surgery.

Resuming his location on his attractive rural property, Dr. Elliott proceeded to engage in the activities of his profession. He has established a large country practice, for his skilled services are in considerable demand. He also supervises the work on his farm of 225 acres, which has been extended to that size from the one hundred acres which had been owned by his father. His land produces very satisfactory crops of such useful products as wheat, corn and tobacco.

Dr. Elliott is a Democrat in politics, as was his father, and is also, like the latter, a prominent member of the order of Ancient Free and Accepted Masons. The Independent Order of Odd Fellows is another secret organization which claims the doctor's membership.

MILTON S. ELKIN, a prominent factor in the business circles of Gallatin, is a young man who well represents the younger generation of energetic and enterprising business talent of Tennessee, and of his native city of Gallatin. He was born May 12, 1884, to Milton S. and Mattie (Moore) Elkin. The senior Milton S. Elkin, born in Scott county, Kentucky, October 9, 1840, was educated in Pennsylvania and took up law as his life pursuit. The field of his professional practice was at Gallatin and at Nashville, Tennessee, and he became both successful and prominent as a lawyer. In 1865 he married Mattie Moore, born in 1845 in Kentucky, a daughter of Joseph and Mary S. (Herndon) Moore. Mr. and Mrs. Moore were natives respectively of North Carolina and Virginia, but after their marriage they became residents of Kentucky and remained there until their deaths. Mr. Moore farmed extensively and owned a large number of slaves. He was a prominent man in his community and served for many years as a justice of the peace. Mrs. Elkin was educated in the female college at Hopkinsville, Kentucky. She is yet living and divides her home between Gallatin and Lebanon.

Milton S. Elkin, the immediate subject of this sketch, has spent practically his whole life in Gallatin. After receiving his education in Cumberland University, Lebanon, Tennessee, he entered upon an independent and active business career as a dry goods merchant at Gallatin, in which line of activity he continued four years. Subsequently several years were spent in the insurance business, and then in 1909 he bought a livery business in Gallatin, to which he has since given his attention. The possessor of naturally keen business acumen and a good stock of energy and industry, he has made each of his ventures a profitable one and in a comparatively brief period has become recognized as one of the forceful business men of the city. He is a stanch supporter of the Democratic party in political affairs and is now serving as a councilman of Gallatin. In a fraternal way he is affiliated with the Masonic order, the Woodmen of the World and the Loyal Order of Moose. In religious faith and church membership he is identified with the Baptist denomination. He is highly regarded as one of Gallatin's honorable business men and exemplary young citizens and his congenial and pleasant disposition make him a popular member of the circles, business, church and social, in which he mingles.

SMITH FAMILY OF SUMNER COUNTY. In Sumner county is the famous family seat, Rock Castle, now a century and a quarter old, and through many generations the home and center of family associations and memories of the Smith family and its related branches. The present owner of this historic estate is Mrs. Horatio Berry of Hendersonville, and one of the descendants of this old home. The founder of this branch of the Smith family was Henry Smith, who came from England and first settled in Maryland, and later moved to Stafford county, Virginia. He married Sarah Crosby, and one of their children was Gen. Daniel Smith, the founder of the family in Tennessee, and the builder of Rock Castle.

Daniel Smith was born in Stafford county, Virginia, on October 29, 1748, and died at his home in Rock Castle in Sumner county. He was educated at William and Mary College, and, like many of the young men of talent of his day, became a surveyor. In 1771 he married Sarah Michie, of the eastern shore of Maryland, and soon afterwards settled upon the western waters. He was appointed deputy surveyor of Augusta county in 1773. At that time Augusta county embraced nearly all of southwestern Virginia. Mr. Smith settled in that part of the county which later formed Botetourt, then Fincastle, then Washington and finally Russell county. His place was on Clinch river, twelve miles below Blackmore's Fort at Maxwell's Hill. It was known as Smith's Station, though the fort was called Fort Christian. This was in the advance guard of settlement thrown across the Alleghenies, previous to the Revolution, and which had remarkable results in holding all the central west as far as the Mississippi river within the possessions of the American colonies after the Revolutionary war.

As early as 1774 Mr. Smith was captain in the colonial troops, and was one of the most active company commanders in Dunmore's war. The correspondence which passed between him and his superior officers shows him to be a man of education beyond most men of his day. He participated in the crucial battle of Point Pleasant on the Ohio river in October, 1774, this engagement being regarded by his friends as one of the most important fought on the western slope of the Alleghenies during the eighteenth century. He was also active in many engagements with the Indians throughout this country. During the Revolution his station was on the frontier, guarding against the combined attacks of Indians and British. He was a member of the committee of safety for Fincastle county in 1775, and of a committee that sent resolutions to the Continental Congress July 15, 1775, in which they declared that they would "never surrender their inestimable privileges to any power on earth but at the expense of their lives."

When Washington county was organized, Captain Smith was appointed one of the justices of the peace by Governor Patrick Henry. December 21, 1776. On the same day he was appointed major of Washington county militia. In 1780 he was appointed sheriff of Washington county, and the next year, upon the reorganization of the militia, he was commissioned colonel in the second battalion. In 1779 he was appointed with Dr. Thomas Walker to extend the line between Virginia and North Carolina, which line had been run by Jefferson and others. He was in the battle of King's Mountain, and soon after the close of the war in 1783, with the Bledsoes, Shelbys, Blackmores, Neeleys and others came to Tennessee.

As one of the pioneers of Tennessee, Major Smith located a large body of valuable land near the present town of Hendersonvillé in Sumner county. In 1784 he began the building of Rock Castle, but owing to the depredations of the Indians, the house was seven years in being completed. It is constructed of cut stone, has seven large rooms, and is as sound today as when built and has been "the roof tree" of five generations, and is now the property of Mrs. Horatio Berry, a great-great-granddaughter of General Smith. Two carpenters engaged in the construction of the house left work one Saturday afternoon to fish in Drake's creek nearby and were killed by the Indians. Two youths, one a son of Col. Anthony Bledsoe, and the other a son of his brother, Isaac Bledsoe, were living at General Smith's and attending school at Hendersonville, and were killed by prowling Indians. Samuel Donelson, who was General Jackson's law partner, married General Smith's only daughter. He died of pneumonia while on a visit to the Hermitage.

In 1790 General Smith was appointed by President Washington secretary of the ceded territory south of the Ohio. He was elected by the first legislature of Tennessee, one of the four presidential electors. In 1798 he succeeded Andrew Jackson in the senate of the United States, and was again elected in 1805 and served until 1809. In 1793, in the absence of Governor Blount, he acted as governor of the territory. He was a member of the constitutional convention of 1796. He made the first map of Tennessee, published by Carey of Philadelphia, and used by Imlay in 1794. Michaux, a French botanist and noted traveler, who passed through this section of the country in 1802, and after his return to France, published an interesting book of travel, speaks of his visit to General Smith, of the beautiful fields of cotton and corn which surrounded his house, of the translations of foreign works his library contained, and of the quiet studious and exemplary life led by a retired public servant. Living at a time when many public men were justly or unjustly the object, not only of censure, but of official accusation, it is worth while to publish the following from Jefferson's paper: "Daniel Smith was a practical surveyor whose work never needed correction. For intelligence, well cultivated talents, for integrity and usefulness, in soundness of judgment, in the practice of virtue, and in shunning vice, he was equalled by few men and in the purity of motive excelled by none."

Smith county in Tennessee was named in honor of General Smith, and he was easily one of the foremost among Tennessee's distinguished citizens during the making and founding of this state.

The only daughter of General Smith and wife was Mary, familiarly known as Polly. Samuel Donelson, the son of a neighbor, was the object of her affections, but there were parental objections to the successful culmination of their romance. The story of how they overcame the difficulties in the pathway of love is about as follows. One night in 1797, when Polly was in her sixteenth year, her suitor Donelson and Andrew Jackson, afterwards president of the United States, placed a sapling ladder beneath her window. In this manner she quietly left Rock Castle, and got up behind Jackson on horseback and the party crossed the river below Rock Castle, and went to what was known as the Hunter's Hill neighborhood where the marriage was performed. Polly Donelson never returned to Rock Castle, until after her husband's death, and she was left a widow with three children. These children were: John, who served in the Creek war and died soon afterward; Andrew Jackson; and Daniel Smith. Andrew J. Donelson became a protege of President Andrew Jackson, and under the influence of that great political leader, received many. promotions in public life. Daniel S. Donelson, the third son of Polly built and lived in the brick house which is now the home of Mrs. Horatio Berry.

This sketch cannot be properly brought to an end, without the insertion of a document which contains much interesting reminiscence and statement of facts concerning some of Tennessee's most noted characters. It is the statement of Mrs. Daniel Smith, the widow of General Daniel Smith, and it is quoted practically without change as follows:

"As well as I remember Mr. Smith and myself settled here in the year 1784. At that period, or shortly after that, Mrs. Donelson and family were among the families who came and settled on the south side of Cumberland river, where though they were but a few miles from me, yet in consequence of the river running between us, and the danger of visiting in those days, I did not become acquainted with them for two or three years after. The family, however, were universally spoken of as one of the most respectable and worthy of the whole country. The first time I ever saw Mrs. Jackson, then Mrs. Robards, was at the station of Colonel Mansker. One of her brothers had not long before brought her from Kentucky, where she and Mr. Robards had married and settled. The cause of her return to Tennessee was then attributed to the cruel and unjust treatment of her husband, who was spoken of everywhere as a man of irregular habits and much given to jealous suspicions. About two years after I first saw Mrs. Robards, I learned that Robards had arrived in this country and by the assistance of the family of his wife, that their differences had been reconciled and that they were again living together at Mrs. Donelson's. They were not long together, however, before the same unhappy apprehensions seized the mind of Robards, the consequence of which. was another separation, and as it soon appeared, a final one. All the circumstances attending this rupture, I cannot attempt to state at this late day, but it is hardly possible, considering the free and unreserved intercourse that prevailed among all the respectable classes of people here, that an incident of this kind should occur without being fully and generally known and that every person should concur in the same upon

its character, without the best reasons. In this transaction, Mr. Robards alone was censured and I never heard a respectable man or woman intimate that his wife differed from the most virtuous and prudent female. General Jackson boarded at the time in the home of Mrs. Donelson, and it was the general belief that his character and standing, added to his engaging and sprightly manners, were enough to influence the mind of poor Robards, addicted as he was to vicious habits and the most childish suspicions. Mr. Robards had not long been gone from Tennessee, when information was received here that he had obtained a divorce from his wife. Whether the information came by a letter or by a newspaper from Virginia addressed to my husband, I cannot say with certainty, but think by the latter. It was after this information came that General Jackson married Mrs. Robards and I recollect well the observation of the Rev. Mr. Craighead in relation to the marriage. It was, that it was a happy change for Mrs. Robards and highly creditable to General Jackson, who by this act of his life evinced his own magnanimity, as well as the purity and innocence of Mrs. Robards. And such was the sentiment of all my acquaintances. Since this period, I have lived in a few miles of Mrs. Jackson and have never been acquainted with a lady more exemplary in deportment or one to whom a greater share of the respect and regard of friends and acquaintances can be awarded.

"Given at my plantation in Sumner county, State of Tennessee, on the sixteenth day of December, 1826—Sally Smith."

MARTIN V. BRUCE. Fortune ofttimes seems a capricious goddess, smiling at one time and frowning at another, but in the end she seldom refuses her favors to those who have proved worthy of them, who with grit and determination refuse to succumb to adverse circumstances or to countenance failure but with undaunted courage overcome the difficulties that beset them and steadily but firmly press forward toward the goal of success. In taking account of the men who have been contributors to the progress of Tennessee we take pleasure in presenting a brief review of the career of Martin V. Bruce, of Bruces Switch, Obion county, who by what he has accomplished has demonstrated that success is largely a matter of character; that while education, influence and capital are invaluable aids to him who knows how to use them, the young man who has not been favored by these aids but who possesses native ability, pluck and resolution may be an equally forceful factor in society.

Martin V. Bruce began life in Perry county, Tennessee, on September 24, 1848. He had no educational advantages, no financial aid from parent or friends, and had but his own native resources on which to rely in getting a start in life and for waging his contest for success in life. Today he is the owner of eight hundred acres of land in Obion county, seven hundred acres of which is under cultivation and produce large crops of cotton, corn and wheat, being also the owner of other valuable business interests. His eight hundred acre tract lies in a body, with nine tenant houses and from sixty-five to seventy people. He rents it to tenants. He also has a store at Bruces Switch which he manages in connection with his farm and saw mill. He began as a farmer, in a very modest way at first, experiencing the varying successes and failures incident to that vocation but steadily gaining the while until he had accumulated the capital which warranted more independent and larger agricultural operations. In 1900 he also entered into the manufacture of lumber at Bruce's Crossing, Obion county, and is yet identified with that business. His mill is run by steam and is lighted by electricity generated at the mill and his force averages sixteen workmen. All of this represents years of untiring industry on the part of Mr. Bruce and native business genius well applied.

In 1867 he was joined in marriage to Miss Sarah A. Taylor, born in Obion county, Tennessee. To their union were born twelve children, eight of whom grew to maturity and six of whom are now living. Three died young, James J. died at the age of sixteen and of those who grew to maturity, Laura is the wife of C. T. Arnold, of Kenton, Tennessee; Ella married Ed Prunington and died at about twenty-seven years of age; George W. is a farmer of this county; Nevada is the wife of A. J. McNeely, of this county; Elbert R., of St. Louis, Missouri, is connected with a loan and trust company; Martin V., Jr., is a farmer at Amson, Texas; John A., is a farmer in this county; and Lexie married E. L. Peoples, and died January 6, 1913. Mr. Bruce is a son of James and Pearly (Hooper) Bruce, who came to Tennessee from South Carolina and of whose eight children he is third in birth. Both he and his wife are members of the Baptist church, and he is a Democrat in his political views, but would never accept office.

JESSE ALLEN. While Tennessee may well be proud of her statesmen and her soldiers, and freely acknowledge her indebtedness to them, yet she is equally indebted to those captains of industry who have been contributors in advancing her commercial prestige. In the following lines is presented a brief outline of the career of Jesse Allen, a retired capitalist of Burns, Tennessee, who both as a soldier and as a business man has honored the state that gave him birth. He was one of thousands of Southern young men left at the close of the Civil war with nothing but those resources within themselves with which to wage their contest for success in life. Today Mr. Allen is one of the wealthy men of Dickson county. He began under the spur of necessity, but he had courage and integrity, a large capacity for business, and was willing to strike hard blows; such men seldom fail of the merited reward of their labors.

Born in Henry county, Tennessee, May 15, 1840, his life was spent on the paternal farm until the opening of hostilities between the states in 1861, when he enlisted in Company D, of the Tenth Tennessee Regiment of mounted infantry, of which N. N. Cox, of Franklin, was colonel. He served throughout the war and participated in many of the hardest fought battles of that conflict but escaped being wounded or captured. Hardships and privation had been the common lot of the soldiery of the South during the latter part of the war. At its close young Allen went to Nashville, where at the home of an uncle he was clothed and fed, and for some time he was employed there with these necessities as his only remuneration, though at that time they were luxuries to him. Later he became an employe in the A. H. Hurley mercantile establishment, where he remained three years and by his ability and fidelity to his employers' interests won promotion to the position of foreman. Following that he clerked for a time for D. Weil & Company, a Jew, and then went to Murfreesboro, where he sold goods at auction and also peddled goods through the country. Later he opened a store at Murfreesboro but it was burned after a few years and then Mr. Allen went into business again, opening a first-class drygoods store in the heart of the business section. After several years at Murfreesboro he went to Greenville, Mississippi, but he only remained a short time and then returned to Nashville, Tennessee, where he became a traveling salesman for a wholesale house in Nashville. After ten years spent in this line of activity he, in partnership with the wholesale firm he represented, bought a large quarry and lime kiln in Dickson county for $15,000. Of this Mr. Allen became manager and from time to time he added to his interests in the establishment until finally he became its sole owner. This he has developed until its present capacity is four cars of lime per day. It is one of the largest plants of its kind in the state, has its own spurs and railroad sidings, and is valued at $100,000. It pays the heaviest taxes of any business concern in Dickson county and employs on an average of fifty men, though frequently it has double that force in its service.

Richard H. Allen, the father of our subject, was born January 1, 1807, in Halifax, Virginia, and came to Williamson county, Tennessee, with his parents when he was sixteen years of age. He served a three years' apprenticeship at carpentry at Franklin, Tennessee, and from there in 1831 went to Paris, Tennessee, then a new town, where he acted as foreman in the construction of many of the early buildings of that place. There he was married in 1833 to Elizabeth Parker, who was born in North Carolina, in 1814, and was a daughter of James Parker, a large slave owner in this state. Of the fourteen children born to this union, Jesse is seventh in birth and is one of five now living. After his marriage Richard H. Allen took up farming in Henry county and continued in that occupation until his death, he too being a large slave holder. His first wife died in March, 1874, and he afterwards married Mrs. Annie Caldwell, widow of Preston Caldwell. In politics he was a Whig and in religious faith both he and the mother of our subject were devout Baptists. He was a son of Lawson Allen, a soldier in the War of 1812, who settled in Williamson county of this state about 1823.

While a resident of Murfreesboro Mr. Allen, our subject, was married in 1871 to Miss America Smith, of Murfreesboro, and to their union two children were born: John R. and Jesse A. John R., whose birth occurred in 1872, died in 1897. Jessie A., became the wife of Andrew D. Clark, now manager of the Jesse Allen Lime Kiln. Mrs. Allen died December 2, 1876, at Nashville, and in 1882, Mr. Allen wedded Adelia Ware, daughter of John W. Ware, of Cannon county, Tennessee. Both Mr. and Mrs. Allen are members of the Methodist Episcopal church, South. Mr. Allen gives his political allegiance to the Democratic party but is a stanch believer in prohibition and has labored zealously to promote prohibition in Tennessee. Imbued with the spirit of charity, he gives liberally of his means to relieve the needy. Mr. Allen is now retired from active business and is enjoying the leisure well deserved as the reward of years of energetic and fruitful endeavor. Mr. and Mrs. Allen now usually spend their winters in Orlando, Florida, where they have a handsome home.

JESSE KENT SPARKS is a representative of the younger native legal talent of Tennessee and has chosen his native county of Perry as the immediate field of his endeavors in carving out a legal career. Though he has been before the bar but a little more than three years and has yet had barely time to prove his merits as a lawyer, he has given evidence of that ability and that ambition and energetic spirit which presages that he will steadily progress successward. His name is a familiar one in this locality as he is the third in line of descent to bear it here, and his great-grandfather, also named Jesse, was for many years a resident of the adjoining county of Hickman. The family originated in Tennessee with the latter, who came here from his native state of Georgia and settled in Hickman county, passing the remainder of his career in that locality as a farmer. His son Jesse grew to manhood in Hickman county but subsequently removed to Perry county, where at the age of forty-five he was united in marriage to Mrs. Polly Horner. He became one of the prominent farmers of that county and passed away there at the age of eighty. In politics he was a stanch Democrat. To his marriage was born one son, Jesse, who is the father of our subject. Jesse Sparks was born at Lick Creek, Perry county, Tennessee, in 1862, and has spent his whole life in his native county. He was educated in the public schools in the vicinity of his birth and at McKenzie and Centerville, Tennessee, and began his independent career as an agriculturist, locating on the Lick Creek farm of his father. As years have passed he has become one of the well known and prominent men of Perry county and was its representative in the Tennessee state legislature in 1909 and 1910. Politically he is an adherent of the Democratic party. He is a director of the First National Bank at Linden. In 1886 he wedded Miss Minerva Ledbetter, a native of Perry county and a daughter of H. M. Ledbetter, a well-known farmer of Perry county. Two children came to this union: Jesse Kent Sparks of this review, and Ammah, who is now Mrs. D. E. Starbuck and resides at Linden.

Jesse Kent Sparks, born July 17, 1888, first pursued his educational training in the Branham and Hughes school at Spring Hill, Tennessee, later becoming a student in Cumberland University, Lebanon, Tennessee, from which institution he was graduated in 1908 with the degree of LL. B. As he was then but twenty years old and not of legal age he was not admitted to the bar until the following year of 1909. He then took up the practice of law at Linden, Perry county, where he has continued to the present time. Full of the vigor of young manhood, able, energetic and well prepared in technical training, we feel safe in predicting that in due time he will be numbered among the foremost members of the Perry county bar and as one of the most forceful men of that community. He is also at the present time the postmaster at Linden, Tennessee, and editor of the *Perry County News*. He is an enthusiastic Democrat and an active and efficient worker in behalf of his party. Fraternally he is affiliated with Linden Lodge No. 210, Free and Accepted Masons, and with Chapter No. 156, Royal Arch Masons, and is also a member of the Methodist Episcopal church, South. He is unmarried.

JAMES EDWARD SMITH. One of the prominent and highly respected citizens of Linden, Perry county, Tennessee, is James Edward Smith, cashier of the First National Bank of Linden, who has formed a wide acquaintance during his twelve years or more of residence there and who by his force, probity of character and honorable business methods has become recognized as a business man of worth and a citizen of high principles.

He was born near Wartrace, Bedford county, Tennessee, January 26, 1876, and represents a family that was established there full a century ago. After completing his educational studies in the Brandon Training School at Wartrace, Tennessee, he entered the Bedford County Bank at Wartrace, as bookkeeper, and from there he came to Linden, Tennessee, in 1899, to take up the duties of cashier in the Perry County Bank, of which he became also a stockholder and director. In 1912 the bank was reorganized as the First National Bank of Linden, in which Mr. Smith still continues to hold the responsible position of cashier. As a financier he is conservative, yet progressive, and is deeply interested in furthering the prosperity of his community. The First National Bank of Linden has a capital of $25,000, a surplus of $8,000, with deposits averaging $75,000, and has won a large confidence and patronage in this community. Mr. Smith also holds farming interests in Perry county.

The first of the family in Tennessee was James Edward Smith, the grandfather of our subject, who located in Bedford county. He was well educated and taught school there for many years, but later in life turned his attention to farming. He married a Miss Stokes, who bore him four children, the eldest of whom was Jasper Newton Smith, the father of our subject. The grandfather and his brothers joined the emigration to California in 1849, but the former died on the way. His brothers continued on to California and located there. Jasper Newton Smith, born November 28, 1828, in Bedford county, Tennessee, remained in his native county, where he became a prominent and well-to-do farmer. He married Sarah Elizabeth Caruthers, also a native of Bedford county, and to their union were born twelve children, of which family James Edward Smith of this review is next to the youngest and is one of the eight children now living. Jasper Newton Smith passed away in Bedford county in March, 1912, at the advanced age of eighty-four years, and had been preceded in death many years by his wife, whose demise occurred in 1888. He was a Democrat in politics and served as a Confederate soldier during the Civil war. Both he and his wife were consistent members of the Baptist church.

James Edward Smith was married in 1900 to Miss Addie Starbuck, daughter of the late Daniel Starbuck, of Linden, Tennessee. They have five children, named: Leila, Elizabeth, Lena, James Edward, Jr., and Ben Daniel. Both Mr. and Mrs. Smith are members of the Christian church, and in political sentiment and allegiance Mr. Smith is a Democrat. He is prominently affiliated with the Masonic order as a member of Linden Lodge No. 210, Linden Chapter No. 156, Jackson Council, and of Tennessee Consistory No. 1, at Memphis, in which he has attained the thirty-second degree of the Scottish Rite.

DANIEL EUGENE STARBUCK. A young and energetic figure in the business circles of Linden, Tennessee, is Daniel Eugene Starbuck, assistant cashier of the First National Bank of Linden and a representative of one of the wealthy and prominent business families of Perry county. Paternally the family is of Irish lineage and originated in this country with the grandfather of Daniel Eugene Starbuck, who emigrated from Ireland along in the forepart of the last century and settled in Tennessee, where his attention was given to farming. Daniel Starbuck, his son and the father of our subject, was born in Perry county, this state, in 1853. He grew up here and received such educational advantages as the public school of the time afforded, but he was ambitious for a better knowledge than he could thus obtain and by self-instruction and extensive reading he sought diligently to correct those deficiencies, finally becoming by those means a well educated and informed man. He engaged in the lumber business in Perry county and became a well known and prominent business man in this connection, being very successful in his operations and accumulating a large estate. He passed away here in 1906 and at the time of his death was president of the Perry County Bank at Linden. His political tenets were those of the Republican party and in a fraternal way he was identified with the Masonic order. In 1881, at Linden, Tennessee, he was joined in marriage to Frances Eugenia Harris, who was born in Perry county in 1859 and preceded her husband in death, her demise having occurred in 1901. Seven children came to their union, as follows: Ethel, now Mrs. E. J. Ayers; Addie, the wife of J. E. Smith, who receives individual mention in this work; Bessie, who is now Mrs. C. W. Brown; John E., Sam H. and Daniel E., the three sons; and Lena, deceased. Both parents were members of the Christian church. After the death of his first wife, Daniel Starbuck, the father, wedded Eureka Hufstedler, of Perry county, and to this union was born a son, Thomas Reed Starbuck.

Daniel Eugene Starbuck was born at Linden, Tennessee, June 28, 1891, was educated at Branham & Hughes Preparatory School at Spring Hill, Tennessee, and entered upon his business career as a bookkeeper for the Nashville Trust Company, at Nashville. He continued in that position until 1910, when he came to Linden to take up the duties of assistant cashier in the First National Bank of Linden, his present position. He is also a stockholder in that institution. In political affairs his allegiance is given to the Republican party.

In 1910 he was married to Miss Ammah Sparks, daughter of Jesse Sparks, a prominent farmer and capitalist of Perry county and a representative in the state legislature in 1909 and 1910. Mr. and Mrs. Starbuck are both members of the Methodist Episcopal church, South, and are numbered among the most estimable young people of Linden.

D. A. PAYNE. Of a high personal status in both the real-estate and insurance business; of a family noted in both lines as one of substantial worth; of prominent church and lodge connections and of good social standing, the life of D. A. Payne is one to which should be accorded a biography as full as our data will permit.

The maternal line of Mr. Payne's progenitors was that of the Virginia family of Darden. David Darden (grandfather of D. A. Payne) was born in the Old Dominion State, whence he came in an early period to Robertson county, Tennessee, settling in Springfield and becoming the proprietor of the first inn ever conducted at that place. He was the father of Susan T. Darden (who later became Mrs. Payne and the mother of our subject) and also of George W.. Darden, well known as one of the best financiers not only of Tennessee, but of the entire South, also being, at the time of his death, one of the members of the Nashville Board of Control. George W. Darden was most highly honored by the Independent Order of Odd Fellows, who joined with the Nashville city council in making his burial one of great pomp and the most largely attended ceremony ever held in Springfield, a chartered train of ten. cars from the capitol city being paid for by the civic bodies mentioned. No less estimable than the Darden family was that of Warren Payne, also of Virginia, and also of early settlement in Robertson county, Tennessee. Warren Payne was one of the patriots of the War of 1812 and was the father of Perry Payne (1817-1889). The latter was a farmer for some years and also gave public duty as county register for three terms; he later entered the mercantile business in Springfield in company with Milton Green, and was engaged in that vocation up to the time of his death. He and his wife, the above-mentioned Susan Darden Payne (1828-1873) were among the best-known and highly respected people of the county. She was a member of the Cumberland Presbyterian church and he of the Primitive Baptist, but in later years he attended the former church with his wife. Perry Payne was known as a successful man, for he had great ability and the work of his hands prospered. But his was a heart too generous for a self-seeking world; never, it is said, did he ever turn a deaf ear to any request for charitable assistance, and such requests, repeatedly granted, resulted in the dissolving of his pecuniary resources. Bereft of fortune though he was, he died rich in affection.

Of the four children born to Perry and Susan Payne, two besides our subject are still living. George W. Payne, born in 1851, now lives in Nashville. Thomas H. Payne, born in 1854, is a resident of Oregon. D. A. Payne, to whom this brief review is dedicated, first saw the light of day on November 18, 1855, in Springfield, Robertson county, Tennessee.

After gleaning a useful sum of knowledge from the public schools of this locality, young D. A. Payne began life in a self-supporting capacity as a clerk and salesman in his father's mercantile establishment. After a time he became interested in the railway postal service and after successfully passing the government examinations he acted in the capacity of a mail clerk for five years. Mr. Payne showed remarkable ability in this exacting work, earning the distinction of being called one of the best clerks in the fifth division of the postoffice department, only two others in his division being considered his equals in the swift and accurate performance of duty. After a time Mr. Payne entered another line of traveling activities, one for which his mercantile experience and his years of traveling gave him peculiar fitness; this was the occupation of a traveling salesman, in which work he also secured gratifying results. This, too, was a temporary vocation for D. A. Payne, who resigned that itinerant service in 1894 in order to take up a line of business permitting a more definitely localized residence.

In the year named, Mr. Payne entered—as the pioneer of this community in that business—the work of a real estate agent. He has combined with it the activities of an insurance underwriter and has formed a partnership with H. H. Mason. Mr. Payne conducts a large amount of business both in Tennessee and in Kentucky and his labors meet with most favorable results.

As a citizen of Springfield Mr. Payne is both prominent and highly esteemed. Like his father and his uncle, George W. Darden, he holds a distinguished place in the Independent Order of Odd Fellows, having passed all chairs and being incumbent of the office of treasurer, which he has held for many years. Politically he is an independent Democrat and takes a very deep and active interest in civic affairs, in both local and national movements. He and his family are connected with the Presbyterian church, U. S. A.

Mrs. Payne, as Miss Emma Funk, was in her girlhood well known in Lebanon and Danville, Kentucky, where her father, Madison Funk, was prominent as a landholder. Her marriage to Mr. Payne was solemnized on November 18, 1903, and during the ensuing years they have become the parents of two children, Hattie S. Payne and Madison P. Payne, both of whom are still at home. Mrs. Payne holds an imprtant place in Springfield's social life, especially in those phases of it that are ethically purposive along lines of public welfare. She has for many years been the president of the local organization of the Woman's Christian Temperance Union, which office she still ably fills.

EDWARD L. ANDERSON. A banker, tobacco manufacturer and one of the leading business men of Gallatin, Mr. Anderson is now foremost in influence and position in the affairs of Sumner county. However, he began his career as a poor boy, educating himself, and the success he has won and the influence he has acquired have all been the result of a notable career of self-achievement.

Edward L. Anderson, who represents one of the old families of Tennessee, was born at Livingston, Overton county, Tennessee, December 30, 1879. His parents were Byrd and Geneva (Draper) Anderson. The paternal great-grandparents were Caleb Anderson and wife, who were early settlers of Jackson county. Edward B. Draper, the maternal grandfather, was also an early settler in the same county, where he lived and died, being an extensive farmer and the owner of a number of slaves. He also had a tannery and made shoes. The results of the war broke him up in business.

The founder of the Anderson family in Tennessee was the great-grandfather of the Anderson now in business at Gallatin. He was Caleb Anderson, who came from Virginia to Jackson county, Tennessee, at a time when most of the country was still public domain, and he took up a large quantity of land, including some splendid water power. The water power was developed for the operation of a mill, which this pioneer settler erected on his land. The land and mill property which this pioneer established in Tennessee were passed on to his descendants, and the land is still held in the name of members of the Anderson family, while the mill is being conducted by one of his grandsons.

William Carroll Anderson, the grandfather, was born in Jackson county, Tennessee, where he spent all his life as a prosperous farmer and miller, being connected with the business which had been established by his father. During the Civil war, when he was in his old age, some soldiers from the Union army captured him and compelled him to ride a horse bareback to Gallatin. This was an experience which almost killed him, and he never entirely recovered from the effects of that ride. One of his sons, named John, was a soldier of the war and was killed at Fisher Creek.

Byrd Anderson, father of the Gallatin business man, was born in Jackson county in 1851, and is now a resident of Sumner county. Farming has been his occupation throughout practically all his life. His wife, Geneva (Draper) Anderson, was born in Overton county in 1856. Of the six living children, Edward L., is the oldest. The father is a Democrat. He is a member of the Methodist church, while the mother is a member of the Christian church.

Reared on the home farm, Edward L. Anderson was educated principally in Burritt College at Spencer, Tennessee, where he graduated in 1897. This education was the result of money which he had himself earned. For a number of years he has been connected with the manufacturing of tobacco, and this has in fact been his principal business ever since he was a boy. He has a large factory at Gallatin, and has made it the source of a very prosperous income.

Mr. Anderson has for three years been superintendent of the Electric Light & Water Company at Gallatin. He is vice-president of the Sumner County Bank & Trust Company, and is a director and stockholder in the First National Bank. He also has interests in farming, and is one of the most substantial men in business circles of his home city.

In 1905 he married Miss Jamie P. Anderson, a daughter of James Anderson, who for a number of years was judge of the county court of Sumner county and a prominent man in local affairs. The two children of their marriage are: Walter L., and Edward L., Jr. Mr. Anderson and his family are members of the Christian church. In politics he is an independent Democrat, and has served as an alderman of Gallatin.

WILLIAM G. SCHAMBERGER. The successful career of William G. Schamberger, one of the prominent financiers and business men of Sumner county, Tennessee, affords added proof that opportunity exists in the older as well as in the newer sections of our country and that opportunity is as much a matter of character as of favorable conditions in the outside world. The direct descendant of German forebears, he has exhibited to a strong degree those traits of thrift, industry and energetic endeavor universally accredited to the German people, and he knows how to make money make more money, which is the secret of wealth.

William G. Schamberger was born in Vanderburgh county, Indiana, December 6, 1859, a son of John G. and Helena B. Schamberger, both natives of Germany and now deceased. The father came to America when a young man and was married to Helena B. Schwab, then Mrs. Schroeder, a widow, near Evansville, Indiana. He was a carpenter by trade and did considerable carpentering at Princeton, Indiana, finally moving to Spencer county, that state, and from there to Mount Vernon, Indiana, where he engaged in the mercantile business for a number of years. Then in 1873 he changed his location to Gallatin, Tennessee, where he purchased a small farm and continued to operate it until his death, at which time he was also in the coal business at Gallatin. Of the three children of these parents, two are now living: William G. of this review, and Dora, now Mrs. W. Winn, of Sumner county, Tennessee. Both parents were brought up in the Lutheran faith but became identified with the Methodist Episcopal church, South, after their removal to Tennessee. The father was a member of the Independent Order of Odd Fellows, and in political views.was a Democrat, serving at one time as alderman of Mount Vernon, Indiana.

William G. spent his earlier youth in Indiana and began his educational training in the city schools of Mount Vernon, that state, completing it in the country schools of Sumner county, Tennessee. He began business life as the proprietor of a store in Gallatin and continued thus identified nearly fourteen years, being also engaged in the milling business a little more than eight years and being quite successful in both lines of business activity. In 1905 he organized the Sumner County Bank and Trust Company, of which he became president and has since officiated in that station. This institution is capitalized at $25,000, has average deposits of $100,000, and has taken a place among the prosperous financial institutions of the county. The same year, 1905, Mr. Schamberger also entered the real estate and loan business and in this line also he has been very successful, operating mostly on a commission basis. His personal holdings include a fine farm of 550 acres in Sumner county, the entire east side of the public square (with the exception of one store building) of Gallatin, besides considerable other valuable city realty. He started with but little money, but he had business acumen of a high order and was endowed with that faculty of indomitable will and energy which conquers all things. From the foregoing lines it will be seen that he is not of the standstill class of men, but is a man of push and energy who not only advances his own material interests but thereby promotes the prosperity and advancement of his town and county as well, which, in turn, adds to the commercial prestige of the whole commonwealth of Tennessee.

On September 5, 1882, was solemnized the marriage of Mr. Schamberger and Miss Mary W. Harrison. She is a daughter of Dr. J. W. Harrison, a native of Sumner county, Tennessee, and a well-known country physician here for many years, whose people were among the earliest settlers in Sumner county. The three children born to Mr. and Mrs. Schamberger are: Freddie M., who married Emmett McCullock, now secretary of a large saddlery company at Nashville, Tennessee; Harrold L., with Anderson & Company at Gallatin, Tennessee; and Helena, now a student in school.

Mr. Schamberger is an adherent of the Democratic party in political views. Deeply interested in community affairs, he has given hearty co-operation to many movements for the general good, and has served as mayor of Gallatin two years and as an alderman twenty years. Both he and his wife are valued members of the Methodist Episcopal church, South, and Mr. Schamberger is affiliated fraternally with the Independent Order of Odd Fellows and the Knights of Pythias, of which latter order he is a past chancellor commander. He always delights in doing for the good of Gallatin what to some seems impossible, as he has been tested by his raising money for schools, seminaries, etc.

JAMES M. VENTERS, M. D. The medical profession of Sumner county is represented by some of the most skilled and learned men of this calling to be found in the state, who have devoted themselves, their time, their energies and their lives to the preservation of public health and the alleviation of human ills. Theirs is no easy task, nor is it always remunerated as befits their high standing and undoubted great work, and yet they cheerfully accept the disadvantages, content in the knowledge of useful careers. The training of the modern physician is remarkably rigid and embraces not only a college course, but extended subsequent study, the constant changes and developments in the profession demanding the practitioner's closest attention, while the country physician has the added labor of covering a wide territory, always being compelled to hold himself in readiness to answer a call, irrespective of time or weather. One of the representative physicians of

Sumner county, whose devotion to duty, professional skill and kindly
sympathy has won him a high place in the esteem of the people of his
community is James M. Venters, M. D., of Portland, a man fitted by
nature and training for his honored calling. Dr. Venters is a native
of southwestern Virginia, and was born February 5, 1873, a son of G.
M. and Rhoda (Branham) Venters.

John Venters, the paternal great-grandfather of Dr. Venters, was a
native of England, from which country he emigrated to the United
States, settling first in South Carolina and subsequently removing to
Virginia, where he was engaged in agricultural pursuits until his
death. His son, James Venters, was born in Virginia and was a successful farmer, but late in life met with financial reverses. He served as
a soldier during the war between the states and is now making his home
in Kentucky, being eighty-seven years of age. On the maternal side,
Dr. Venters' grandfather was Martin Branham, a native of what is
now West Virginia, whose people came from South Carolina. As a
young man he moved to Virginia, there taking up four thousand acres
of land from the government, and this property he left to his estate at
the time of his death. G. M. Venters, father of the doctor, was born in
1846, in Virginia, and in 1884 accompanied his parents to Kentucky,
where he located in farming. He also followed horse trading, buying
as many as five hundred animals at a time and taking them to Georgia,
and this business he continued to follow until his death, which occurred
in 1895. He was married to Rhoda Branham, who was born in 1848,
and she died in 1882, having been the mother of seven children, of
whom six are now living, Dr. Venters being the third in order of
birth. The mother was a member of the Baptist church, and Mr.
Venters was a prominent member of the Masonic fraternity.

James M. Venters received his early education in the public schools,
following which he attended Lexington State College, where he remained
two years. He next was a student in Hospital College of Medicine, of
Louisville, which he attended from 1901 to 1904, in the latter year
being graduated with the degree of Doctor of Medicine. Following this
he was engaged in practice for two years in southeastern Kentucky, but
in 1906 came to Portland and established himself in a country practice, now having a large and representative clientele. In addition to
the onerous duties of a large practice, Dr. Venters also manages his
175-acre farm, which is in an excellent state of cultivation, and on which
he raises tobacco, wheat, corn and hay. He is well-deserving of the title
of self-made man, having started out in life on his own account at the
tender age of ten years, since which time he has received no financial
help whatever. His sturdy independence, tireless industry and commendable ambition have gained him the respect of all who know him,
and Sumner county has no more popular young professional man.
Fraternally, the doctor is affiliated with the I. O. O. F. and the Loyal

TENNESSEE AND TENNESSEANS

Order of Moose. He is a member of the Sumner County Medical Society, the Tennessee Medical Society and the American Medical Association, and takes an active interest in the work of these organizations, and his political proclivities cause him to support the principles and candidates of the Democratic party.

WILLIAM POLK MOORE, JR., M. D. Thirty years devoted to the practice of his profession is the record of Dr. W. P. Moore, Jr., of Portland, Tennessee, thirty years of faithful service in the alleviation of the ills of his fellow men. During this time he has risen to an enviable position among the medical men of his state, but his energies have not been confined to the duties of his calling, for he has been engaged successfully also in various lines of business, and has shown equal skill along commercial lines. A striking example of the benefits to be gained through the practice of constant industry, integrity and sobriety, he has been the architect of his own fortunes, and a record of his career will be read with interest by those who appreciate self-made manhood.

William P. Moore was born in Sumner county, Tennessee, June 15, 1857, and is a son of Dr. W. P. and Amanda (Dickey) Moore. He lost his mother when he was still a child, but was given a good training in his youth, and his early education was secured in the Portland public schools. Subsequently he entered Vanderbilt Medical College, from which famous institution he was graduated in 1882, and the following year received his degree from the University of Nashville. Immediately after completing his studies he entered upon the practice of his profession in Portland, where he has since continued, and he is at this time one of the best known and most highly valued physicians in this part of the state. Dr. Moore entered upon professional life with but little capital, and his earlier years were attended by many trying struggles, but perseverance, a love for his chosen calling and inherent ability eventually brought recognition and appreciation and the financial emoluments that go therewith. In the field of business he has likewise succeeded, being the proprietor of a large dry-goods, ladies' furnishings and millinery establishment, located in his own building, in addition to which he is the owner of another business building and a well-cultivated farm. As the proprietor of a tobacco business, he is the only independent dealer in Portland.

On June 22, 1890, Dr. Moore was united in marriage with Miss Ella Goostree, daughter of Watson W. and Fannie (Gimlin) Goostree, the former a native of Tennessee and the latter of Kentucky. Mr. Goostree was for some years a farmer, but in his later years entered the mercantile field. Dr. and Mrs. Moore have one daughter: Belle, who married, June 22, 1910, J. E. Derryberry, who is engaged in a general merchandise business in Portland. Mr. and Mrs. Derryberry have a little boy, William Spur Derryberry, born March 28, 1911. The family is connected with the Church of Christ, and in political matters Dr. Moore is a Democrat, but takes only a good citizen's interest in affairs of a public nature. His life has been an active and useful one, and his connection with various movements of a progressive nature have aided materially in advancing the interests of Portland.

PAT W. KERR. There is no more urgent problem in America today than the problem of educational reform. The success of the democratic experiment, the preservation of our free institutions, is dependent primarily upon its successful solution. Vocational education and citizenship training must be developed. Besides these broad considerations are new problems, those of health regulation and the social care of backward children, the development of schools as civic and social centers—problems of the most practical kind. To this work some of the most earnest and public-spirited citizens of Tennessee are today devoting their energies, and prominent in this class stands Pat W. Kerr, superintendent of schools of Portland, and a man whose whole active career has been spent in educational work. Mr. Kerr was born January 2, 1879, in Trousdale county, Tennessee, and is a son of Joe M. and Martha A. (Carey) Kerr.

Levi E. Kerr, the paternal grandfather of Pat W. Kerr, was born in Tennessee, whence his parents had come from North Carolina, at an early date. They settled on a farm in White county, and there spent the remainder of their lives, Levi E. inheriting their property and adding thereto, and also being a tiller of the soil throughout his career. John G. Carey, the maternal grandfather of Mr. Kerr, spent his life in farming in Trousdale county, and there died advanced in years and with a handsome competence. Joe M. Kerr was born in White county, Tennessee, in 1848, was there educated in the district schools, and remained in his native neighborhood until reaching the age of eighteen years. At that time he removed to Trousdale county, where he was married in 1868 to Martha A. Carey, who was born in this county in 1852, and they had a family of four children, Pat W. being the third in order of birth. Some time after his marriage Mr. Kerr went back to White county, but eventually returned to Trousdale county, where his death occurred in 1896, his widow surviving until 1911. They were members of the Methodist Episcopal church, and in political matters Mr. Kerr was a Democrat.

Pat W. Kerr received his education in the Masonic Institute at Hartsville, and in 1895 began his career as an educator, teaching public school for one year. The next two or three years were passed in farm labor, when he again took up teaching, and has so continued to the present time, gaining success and popularity in his chosen calling. He taught White Sulphur Springs school at Rome, Tennessee, where he remained four years, and was also at D. A. Duke College, at Difficult, Tennessee, and after two years came to Portland, where in 1907 he took charge of the high school. Since then he has acted in the capacity of superintendent of schools, and his administration has been featured by numerous innovations and much needed reforms. Mr. Kerr has given his office conscientious service, and his ability in his profession has never been questioned. A scholarly man and deep thinker, he is an omnivorous reader and is well informed on all live issues of the day.

In 1904 Mr. Kerr was married to Miss Lydia Lipscomb, daughter of John R. Lipscomb, living at Hartsville, Trousdale county, successful farming people. Two children have been born to this union: Gladys L. and Harold, both being deceased. Mrs. Kerr is a member of the Christian church and her husband of the Methodist Episcopal denomination. He is a member of the Modern Woodmen of America, in which he has held the chair of advisor, but the greater part of his time is devoted to educational work, and he is a valued member of the Middle Tennessee Educators Association. In politics he is a Democrat. Mr. Kerr also has some farming interests, and is a stockholder of the Farmers Bank of Portland and a member of the directing board of that institution.

EDGAR F. PEDEN, M. D. Bringing to his practice thorough scholastic training, innate soundness and accuracy of judgment, and a cheerful disposition, Dr. E. F. Peden has maintained a high position among the disciples of Æsculapius in Tennessee. The greater part of his professional life has been spent in Portland, where since 1904 he has ministered to the sick and built up a large and representative practice, and he has also been successful along commercial lines, owning a flourishing drug business and being part owner in a large business block. Dr. Peden bears the added distinction of being a native son of Tennessee, having been born in Sumner county, August 4, 1872. His paternal grandfather, Hosie Peden, was born in Virginia and accompanied his parents to Tennessee as a lad, passing the remainder of his life here in agricultural pursuits. On the maternal side, Dr. Peden's grandfather was also a Virginian, but was reared in Kentucky, where he became a successful farmer and merchant. J. W. Peden, father of the doctor, was born in 1838, in Sumner county, Tennessee, and as a young man enlisted in the Thirtieth Regiment, Tennessee Infantry, in the Confederate service, fighting with that organization until his capture by the Union troops. At that time he was confined at Fort Donelson, and continued to remain a prisoner for ten months. On receiving his honorable discharge, he returned to the duties of peace, taking up his residence on the old home farm, where he still resides, and which he owns. He has developed a handsome, valuable property, and is considered one of the substantial men of his community. In politics he is a Democrat, and his religious belief is that of the Methodist Episcopal church. He was married to Mary Anderson, who was born in Scottsville, Kentucky, in 1843, and she died in October, 1911, having been the mother of two children: W. H., who makes his home with his father on the old homestead; and Dr. E. F.

E. F. Peden received his early education in the public schools of Sumner county, following which he became a student in the Portland high school. In 1896 he entered the medical department of the University of Nashville, where he was graduated in May, 1899, with his degree, and first settled himself in practice at Mitchellville, Tennessee. Dr. Peden came to Portland in 1904, and here he has continued to reside to the present time. He has an excellent practice, drawn to him by his undoubted ability, his deep sympathy and his kindness of heart, and holds a high place in the esteem of his fellow practitioners. Not long after establishing himself in Portland, Dr. Peden opened a pharmacy, which he has continued to maintain, and in partnership with Dr. W. P. Moore is the owner of a business block.

Dr. Peden was married in 1901 to Lena Wright, daughter of G. T. Wright, a retired farmer of Portland. Dr. Peden is a valued member of the Odd Fellows and the Masons, and in his political proclivities is an independent Democrat. His religious convictions make him a Baptist, while his wife is a member of the Methodist Episcopal church, South, and both have numerous friends in religious and social circles of the city.

JAMES O. GAMBILL. One of Saundersville's successful men in the mercantile business is J. O. Gambill, who has displayed his business ability both in the management of his store and in the operation of his farm. Born in Robertson county, August 9, 1859, he is the only son of B. F. and Caroline (Brewer) Gambill.

The settlement of Mr. Gambill's ancestors in Robertson county dates back to the time of his grandparents, Benjamin Gambill and John M. Brewer, pioneers in the county and very well known and prosperous men of their time, the former being a farmer, also engaged in the milling business and for years a magistrate, and the latter the owner of many slaves and a believer in the Union, in the army of which he had one son in service.

Mercantile pursuits for years claimed the time and attention of the father of J. O. Gambill, he being successfully engaged in business at Erin, Tennessee, where he is one of the leading citizens. He belongs to the Methodist Episcopal church, South, and is a Democrat in politics. He was born in Robertson county; his wife was born in Sumner county.

After his boyhood days in school were spent, J. O. Gambill began life in the milling business and was thus engaged until he received a position as clerk in a store. Subsequently he became railroad agent at Erin, in which capacity he was engaged for twelve years. The following ten years were spent in the mercantile business at Erin, and in 1901 came to Sumner county where he farmed for ten years. April 1, 1911, he opened up the general store at Saundersville, where he is at present located and where he is doing a prosperous business.

The union of Mr. Gambill and Susan Gray, to whom he was married in 1893, has resulted in three children: William O., Houston, who attends high school at Gallatin, and Walton, five years old. Mrs. Gambill's father, long one of Sumner county's leading farmers and highly respected men, lives at Gallatin.

In his political views, Mr. Gambill is a Democrat, and fraternally he is a member of the Knights of Pythias, being past chancellor commander. He is one of Saundersville's foremost citizens, having been postmaster since January, 1912. He carries a nice stock of merchandise in his store and is the owner of a large farm.

Throughout the career of Mr. Gambill, both in his mercantile and agricultural pursuits, have been evident the persevering endeavors and the industriousness and activity which have crowned his efforts with success and brought him to the forefront among his fellowmen.

JOHN C. REVELL. The above-named gentleman is one of the well known and much respected planters of Obion county, where he has extensive property; and one of the prominent citizens of the thriving little city of Obion, where he maintains his residence, one of the several fine houses which he possesses here.

Tennessee has been Mr. Revell's home since 1834 and Obion county for about forty-seven years. His birthplace was in North Carolina, where his parents spent a large portion of their lives. They were Axim Revell and Martha (Norvill) Revell and were the parents of ten children, of whom the sixth in line was J. C. Revell, the subject of this biographical review. The date of his birth was March 16, 1828.

As a boy, Mr. Revell's first interest in Tennessee began when in 1834 his parents removed from North Carolina to the part of Tennessee which was then known as Hayward county. He early turned his attention to agricultural pursuits and in this pursuit he has succeeded beyond his most sanguine expectations.

In 1852 Mr. Revell was united in marriage with Miss Mary Jones, of Crockett. With the passing of the years their home was brightened by the coming of seven children, of whom three are yet living. They are Mrs. Odela Cunningham of Obion; Mr. Guy Revell, a farmer of this county, district 14, and Mr. Milton Revell, also a farmer of district 14.

The second marriage of J. C. Revell took place in 1903, at which time he was united to Mrs. Mary Allsadine (Fairleigh) Seabolt. The Church of the Disciples, or Christian Church, is that of the religious

JOHN C. REVELL

affiliation of Mr. Revell and his family. He has long been associated with leading fraternal societies, having belonged to the Independent Order of Odd Fellows since the year 1854, and being also prominently connected with the Ancient Free and Accepted Masons since 1867.

Mr. Revell's agricultural property consist of nearly four hundred acres of fertile land. Three hundred acres of this is now under cultivation, its chief grain product being corn. Pastures for the feeding of stock also comprise a part of its extent. Mr. Revell is an experienced planter and his farming operations also have the advantage of being conducted by means of the best machinery of modern and most approved construction. Not only is J. C. Revell very successful as an agriculturist, but also is he held in high personal esteem by all who know him. He is now probably the oldest citizen in the village of Obion. Being a cripple, he could not serve in the war, but his sympathies were with the South. He would never accept office and is still active and hale and hearty.

CHARLES ANDREW DERRYBERRY. In this era of the practical, education is keenly alive to the need for the purposive; and "vocational training" is the watchery of the majority of educators, as well as of those parents who would anticipate lives of definite usefulness for their children. America is one of the most businesslike of nations and her commercial leaders are demanding an ever better preparation of those who would enter the arena of business life. In lieu of this need, much credit is due the men who conduct and supervise institutions for thorough training in both educational foundations and the practical superstructure of business courses.

Among these we note Charles Andrew Derryberry, who is personally responsible for the present School of Business in Jackson, the first institution of its kind ever organized in this place. Of its originator and head, not only professional data, but also genealogical and biographical information of a personal kind will be of interest.

In Uptonville, Madison county, Tennessee, Charles A. Derryberry was born on May 9, 1870. His parents were William Jordan Derryberry and Narcissa Weathers Derryberry. On the parental farm which was his birthplace and his father's lifetime residence, Charles Derryberry spent his juvenile days, attending the rural schools of his vicinity. From these he passed to the high schools of Hayward county. On completing this period of his education, he entered professional life, deferring special and more advanced courses until a later time.

The schools of Madison county were the first field for Mr. Derryberry's activities as a teacher. After his service in that region, he followed the same line of work in Henry county. Having thus served his own state for a goodly term of years, he then accepted positions in the high schools of Graves county, Kentucky. Altogether his period of public school teaching continued until 1901.

In the year mentioned Mr. Derryberry became a student in the Southwestern Baptist University in Jackson, where he carried full courses for two years. At the end of that time he was tendered, in recognition of his proficiency and his pedagogical acumen, the position of principal of the Stenographic Department in this same institution. In 1905 the university authorities deemed it best to confine the college curricula to classical, literary and scientific lines, leaving the commercial training to independent outside enterprises. This gave Professor Derryberry an excellent opportunity to further define his own work along individual lines.

He therefore established the Jackson School of Business in that same. year of 1905. This was the first school of business ever established in the city of Jackson. It has flourished in gratifying degree and still continues its important work, with Mr. Derryberry as its head.

Professor Derryberry has become identified with many of the prominent movements of Jackson. He has numerous fraternal associations, including the following: The Free and Accepted Masons, Lodge 45; the Knights of Pythias, Lancelot Lodge 13, of which he is a past chancellor; and the Woodmen of the World, in Lodge 469. He is an intelligent political thinker, adhering to the main doctrines of the Democratic party. The religious connections of the Derryberry family are with the Baptist church.

The home of Charles Andrew Derryberry was established in 1892, on which date he was united in marriage to Miss Pearl Birge Graves, of Grundy Center, Iowa. Mr. and Mrs. Derryberry are the parents of two children, named Voris Graves and Flo. S. Derryberry. The family is one of both intellectual and social importance in Jackson.

JAMES DALE MCMURRY. Among the younger attorneys of Trousdale county, Tennessee, the subject of this review occupies a commanding position. He is a lawyer to the manor born, his father, John S. McMurry, having been a prominent and successful attorney of Hartsville for nearly half a century. John S. McMurry was born in Trousdale county in 1843, and continued to reside in that county all his life. He married Miss Caroline Duncan McLain, daughter of Dr. Jesse McLain, a native of Tennessee, where he practiced medicine for many years and died in the city of Nashville at the age of eighty years. John S. McMurry read law with Judge Andrew McLain, his wife's uncle, and in 1865 was admitted to the bar. From that time until his death on April 23, 1909, he practiced his profession in Hartsville, a fine example of the old school lawyer, courteous and dignified, but persistent and energetic in protecting the interests of his clients. He enjoyed a lucrative practice, but through his liberality gave away a large portion of his

income, and never accumulated much of an estate. He was a Democrat in his politics and was an active participant in political campaigns in behalf of that party. In 1905 he was elected to the state senate and served one term in that body, where he made a record of which his constituents might justly feel proud. His fraternal relations were with the Masonic fraternity. His father, Charles McMurry, was born in Tennessee while that state was a part of North Carolina and lived there all his life as a farmer. He was also a justice of the peace for many years and was an influential citizen. Caroline Duncan McMurry was born in Maury county, Tennessee, in 1855, and died in December, 1900. She and her husband were the parents of nine children, seven of whom are now living. She was a member of the Methodist Episcopal church, a faithful wife and a devoted and loving mother.

James Dale McMurry, the third child of the family, was born in Trousdale county, Tennessee, April 13, 1873. In his boyhood he attended the public schools and in 1897 was graduated at the Hartsville Masonic Institute. He then entered his father's law office as a student and prosecuted his studies with such assiduity that in November, 1898, he was admitted to the bar. Immediately upon his admission he began practice in Hartsville, where he has built up a large clientage, his practice extending to all the state and Federal courts. The thorough training he received under the preceptorship of his father, together with his subsequent study and experience, gave him all the essential qualifications of the successful lawyer—one who commands alike the respect of the bench, bar and general public. Like his father, he is a Democrat, and has served as county attorney.

On January 1, 1899, Mr. McMurray married Miss Laura Puryear, daughter of William L. Puryear, a native of Trousdale county, where he was a wealthy and successful farmer. To this union have been born four children—three sons and a daughter. John P. and Jesse S. are attending school, and Cecil P. and Elizabeth are at home. Mrs. McMurry is a Baptist in her religious faith, and her husbnd is a member of the Presbyterian church.

FINLEY MARBOROUGH DORRIS is a fine representative of the active and substantial citizens of Nashville. He is a partner of George A. Karsch and is one of the leading undertakers in the city, and being thoroughly skilled in all branches of his profession, his services are much sought in this community.

A son of Rev. William G. and Elzira (Ruth) Dorris, he was born in Clarksville, Tennessee, February 15, 1863. The family in 1865 moved to Sumner county, Tennessee, where Finley M. Dorris was educated, principally under the tutelage of Prof. C. B. Tate, a noted educator of Virginia. In 1880, at the age of seventeen years, he entered the employment of his uncle, William R. Cornelius, an undertaker of Nashville, and during the twenty-two years that he was associated with him he became familiar with the details of all branches of the profession. In 1902 Mr. Dorris engaged in business in Nashville on his own account, continuing alone until 1907 when he formed a partnership with George A. Karsch. In 1911 these gentlemen, who have met with eminent success in their work, erected their present establishment, which is considered by many as being the most beautiful and well adapted of its kind anywhere to be found.

Mr. Dorris is a member of various fraternal and social organizations. He belongs to the Ancient Free and Accepted Order of Masons, in which he has taken the 32nd degree, and is also a Shriner. For twenty-nine years he has been a member of the Knights of Pythias. He is also a member of the Country Club and the local Board of Trade; a member of McKendree Church, and has been an official in the Methodist church for more than twenty-five years. In 1912 he was asked to become a candidate for member of the County Court, and out of the sixty odd candidates he led the field without having a card printed or asking a man for his vote.

Mr. Dorris was married January 7, 1885, to Miss Mattie Carter, (who was born at Greenhill, Tennessee,) a daughter of Charles and Elizabeth (Stevenson) Carter, natives of this state. Two children have been born to Mr. and Mrs. Dorris: Finley Carter and Frances Elizabeth, who is now one of the young schoolgirl set. On March 13, 1912, Carter Dorris married Miss Margaret Barnett of Pikeville, Tennessee, a daughter of Dr. James and Gertrude (Rankin) Barnett. To them one child has been born: Margaret Dorris.

The Dorris Family—In tracing the origin of the Dorris family, we find that the name "Dorris" is a Greek name. It was first spelled Doris, and we have been able to trace it back to the Greek city of Doris. In this city the first Doric column was built, and was built by one of the Doris family. It was first called the Doris column, and afterwards changed to the Doric column. We also find that Hellenus gave the name of Hellenes to the Greeks, and that he had three sons. The second son was Dorus. The country that Dorus inherited was named by him "Doris," and from this country came the family name "Dorris." (Hollins' Ancient History.)

In the Roman Army under Julius Caesar fought a Greek general by name of General Josef Dorris. After the conquest of Great Britain he was awarded by Caesar the county of Downs, Ireland, for meritorious service rendered. This was about the years 54 and 55 B. C. (Caesar's Commentaries.)

Josef Dorris, a lineal descendant of Gen. Josef Dorris, and a native of the County of Downs, Ireland, had nine sons, seven of which emigrated to America in the early part of 1700, locating first near Baltimore, Maryland. After a short period, William, Isaac and John went to Amhurst county, Virginia, and located. While here William married, and a son from this marriage by name of Josef Dorris migrated to Mecklenburg, North Carolina, and became a noted Baptist minister. He married Cynthia Irwin, and from this union there were two sons, John Irwin and Thomas. After her death, he married Mary Williams and by her had ten sons and three daughters, among whom were: George P., Stephen, Isaac, William, Rolland, etc. Several of these sons were with General Francis Marion, who led the North Carolina forces in the Revolutionary war, and made efficient soldiers.

William and Isaac married two sisters by name of Frost from Frostburg, Maryland. The Frost family being a prominent family, the town was named for their father, who owned a body of land on which was discovered one of the first coal mines in America.

William, Isaac, and their half brother, John Irwin, came South prospecting, and while on the trip they met with Peter Demombreun; together with him they came on his keelboat down the Holston river to the Tennessee river and down the Tennessee river on to the village of Nashville. Peter Demombreun afterwards located in Nashville, and William, Isaac and John went to Fort Hamilton, now known as Tyree Springs. After locating at Fort Hamilton, William and Isaac went back for their families in Maryland, returning by wagon to Fort Hamilton, where they secured land and settled. Later on came their brothers— Stephen, who became the chaplain in General Jackson's army at New Orleans; George P., who went to St. Louis, and Roland, who located in Sumner county.

John Irwin married Elizabeth Menees near Springfield, Tennessee, and had one son and two daughters: The son, Dr. William Dawson Dorris of Nashville, a noted physician in his day, and one of the first to advocate the germ theory when the cholera was so bad in Nashville in 1869.

William Dorris married Katherine Frost, and from this union there were two sons and six daughters: Samuel Frost, Betsy, Rebecca, Kate, William D., Tobitha, Drusilla and Levina. Samuel Frost, Betsy, Rebecca and Kate were born in Baltimore, Maryland, before the family moved and located at Fort Hamilton. After locating at that place William D., Tobitha, Drusilla and Levina were born. Samuel Frost married Susanna Pitt of Cottontown, Tennessee. Betsy Dorris married John Hudson. Rebecca married Samuel Hendricks. Kate married Drew Edwards. William D. married and went to Illinois to live; his wife's name is unknown to the writer. Tobitha married John P. Hendricks. Drusilla married James Hendricks. Levina married Pleasant Mays.

After Samuel Frost Dorris and Susanna Pitt married they moved near Fountain Head, Tennessee, on Stroughters branch, and here made their home for many years. From this union there were eight sons and four daughters: Henry, William Gibbs, Jeremiah, James, Isaac G.,

Daniel W., Benjamin F., George B., Katherine, Zilpha, Susan and Martha. Katherine Dorris married Richard Shaffer. Zilpha married John Calvin Shivers. Susan married Robert Ruth. Martha married William R. Cornelius.

Samuel Frost Dorris, father of these children was born in Baltimore, Maryland, November 20, 1787, and died at Nashville, Tennessee, October 16, 1878. Susanna Pitt, mother of these children, was born in Cottontown, Tennessee, April 23, 1794, and died at Nashville August 24, 1870. Samuel Frost Dorris, while living at Fountain Head, Tennessee, was engaged in transporting goods by teams from Nashville, which was the distributing point for all merchandise for miles around, including nearly the whole of Tennessee and Southern Kentucky into the interior. Nashville was then a small hamlet with scant promise of its present size and prosperity. Mr. Shelby owned the land lying on the East Side of the river, which is now known as "East Nashville." Mr. Dorris had a fine saddle horse which Mr. Shelby was so anxious to possess that he offered to exchange all of that large tract of land for the animal. In those days there was no sale for the land, and as Mr. Dorris had use for the horse he refused to trade. Mr. Dorris in 1825 removed from Fountain Head, Tennessee, to Nashville, where he spent his closing days, dying at the venerable age of ninety-one years, and was laid to rest in the old City Cemetery beside his wife, Susanna Pitt.

The true "Dorris" type is light hair, blue eyes, fair complexion, a mechanical turn of mind, very active and of quiet disposition.

In tracing the history of the Dorris family from its early beginning the writer was not able to find or learn of any one by the name of Dorris with but one exception who. ever possessed any great amount of wealth. They all seem to be content with living quiet and peaceful lives.

Rev. William Gibbs Dorris, son of Samuel Frost and Susanna Pitt Dorris, and father of Finley M. Dorris, was born near Fountain Head, Tennessee, on Stroughters branch, May 6, 1815. In 1825 the family moved to Nashville by wagons, coming over the Nashville and Gallatin dirt road, there being no pikes in those days. Arriving at the Cumberland river on the East Side, they had to cross in flat boats. The family located on North Front street, just below the site of the old Methodist Publishing House. He relates that General LaFayette had just made his visit to Nashville by boat up the Cumberland river.

After moving to Nashville he went to school for a short period, after which he for a time served as apprentice to a tailor. In 1832 he went to Jackson, Tennessee, engaging in the tinner's business with his brother, Henry, and from there he went to Bolivar, Tennessee, and while in Bolivar he relates the witnessing of the scene of the falling of the stars, which was in 1833. After two years spent at Jackson and Bolivar, Tennessee, he went to Huntsville, Alabama, and engaged in cattle trading. He did not follow this occupation very long, as it did not suit him, but secured a position in the jewelry house of Thomas Cain. While working for him, in the year 1834, he married his daughter, Charlotte, and from this union they had two children: Thomas and Sarah. Shortly after his marriage he and his brother-in-law, James Cain, went into the dry goods business at Decatur, Alabama. They were very successful in their business venture, but they concluded to speculate in cotton, which broke them up.

William G. Dorris had now joined the Masons, and a brother Mason and chum of his, Charlie Lane, went into the dry goods business with him, and he was again very successful. They continued this business until the death of his wife, which occurred in 1846. Charlie Lane often told him he had no business behind a counter selling goods, and often suggested to him that he would make a good preacher. Neither of these young men were members of the church at that time, but a few years later they both joined the Methodist church, and both made good and useful preachers. Charlie Lane joined the Texas Conference and W. G. Dorris the Tennessee Conference in October, 1849, which at that time comprised the whole of Middle Tennessee and North Alabama. The Conference sent him to his first charge as a Junior Preacher to the Lime Stone Circuit, Alabama. Two years later, in October, 1851, he was sent to his first station at Shelbyville, Tennessee. While here he met Miss Elzira Ruth, daughter of George W. Ruth, a jeweler, whom he married on October 27, 1853. From this union were born twelve children, three dying in infancy and nine coming to maturity: William Murphy, who married Fanny Oden of Rutherford county, Tennessee; George Benjamin, who died in infancy; Florence Eugenia, who never married; Blanche Gibson, who married Charles W. Bedford of Bourbon county, Kentucky; Charles Westley, who died in infancy; Finley Marborough, who married Mattie Carter of Nashville, Tennessee; Henry Beaumont, who married Nettie Comfort of Warren county, Kentucky; Virgie Abston, who died at the age of twenty-three; Martha Summers, who married Lindsley Bender of Sumner county, Tennessee; Annie Ruth, who married Maudaut Patterson of Robertson county, Tennessee; Birdie Frazier, who died in infancy; Robert Pane, known as Bishop, who married Kate Stroude of Wilson county.

In October, 1855, William G. Dorris was sent to Murfreesboro, Tennessee, and in 1857 to McKendree Church. He also served the churches of Columbia, Tennessee, Andrew Charge, which is now known as Elm Street, and Hobson's Chapel. About this time he bought out the Eclipse Foundry and made Eclipse stoves, and had his warehouse at 56 Broad Street. For a while he had as a partner a man by name of "Kitch," but he soon bought him out and ran it alone until the Civil war came on and forced him to give it up. In October, 1861, he was sent to Clarksville, Tennessee, remaining there during the Civil war. In 1865 he was sent to Columbia, Tennessee. The country at that time was in a torn up condition and he found it impossible to secure a home for his family, so he decided to buy a farm, which he did in Sumner county, near Saundersville, moving his family on it the latter part of October, 1865. From here on he served various charges until 1880, when D. C. Kelly, the Station Pastor at Gallatin, Tennessee, concluded to make the race for prohibition governor and W. G. Dorris was sent there to fill out his unexpired term. In October, 1880, he was sent as presiding elder to the Lebanon District, and in October, 1882, was sent as presiding elder to the Murfreesboro District for four years, which concluded his work as an active member of the Conference, and he was placed on the superannuated list and retired to his farm, where he lived until his death, which occurred on April 8, 1900.

Of the many things that were written and spoken of him, the following written by his life long friend, Dr. J. D. Barbee, expresses more fully from every viewpoint the power, the character and the esteem in which he was held by those with whom he came in contact:

"William G. Dorris was born in Kentucky, May 6, 1815, and died at his home near Nashville, Tennessee, April 8, 1900. In his early manhood he was a model for the artist, being tall and symmetrically proportioned, and withal possessing a strikingly handsome face. To a dignified mien he added an easy, graceful carriage, and a stranger passing him on the street would involuntarily turn for a second look and mentally inquire: 'Who is it?' A full, round, sonorous voice, with tender, persuasive tone, and his benignant eye ever impressed those with whom he conversed that he was a man of loving heart and kind spirit. In character he was integrity personified. I would at any time have been willing to subscribe an unqualified endorsement of him in this regard, and that was the general estimate. An incident in his early life illustrates his reputation with those who knew him well. He and another young man had formed a copartnership to enter into the dry goods business at Decatur, Alabama, and young Dorris had gone to Philadelphia to purchase the first stock of goods for the firm. There he met a friend who was retiring from business at Huntsville, Alabama, who introduced him to a wholesale house, saying: 'Sell this man all the goods he wants.' This endorsement was never dishonored, of course, and it is a noteworthy fact that after years of successful business the two young partners became each an itinerant Methodist preacher, one of them finally dying a member of the Texas Conference, and the other, at an advanced age, falling asleep in Jesus, a superannuated member of the Tennessee Conference.

"William G. Dorris never enjoyed the advantages of thorough college training, but he was nevertheless an educated man. His mind was disciplined to think, and that is education. He was a self-made man, as every man is who is made at all or amounts to anything worth the mention. It is application, not genius, which makes the difference between men intellectually. This good man applied himself and learned from all sources. He gathered great store from books and had the gift of absorbing much from persons with whom he associated; and even in his old age he conversed and preached out of the fullness of his mind to the delight and edification of his hearers. A wealth of incidents, anecdotes, and facts of life made him a charming fireside companion and a peculiarly interesting public speaker.

"Common sense and intelligent judgment were conspicuous qualities of his mind; hence it was not possible for him even to have bordered on fanaticism, or to have viewed any object so intensely as to have seen it exclusively or disproportionately to other objects with which it stood related; therefore he always acted with sound wisdom and discretion. Hence he was a safe counselor, and one could scarcely have gone wrong in following his advice. He was an exemplification of the proverb: 'Moderation is the daughter of wisdom and the mother of power.'

"Justice and Charity blended in his judgment of others, and he beheld the scales in equipoise even when weighing an enemy. With a judicial mind and a warm, sympathetic heart, none had cause for apprehension in his hands. As a friend he was sincere, true and courageous; in nothing was his individuality more distinctly and intensely marked. He was not the friend of the sunshine who 'when winter comes is flown.' Though all men might forsake his friend, he stood by him unmoved and immovable.

"As a Christian he was simple and sincere, and being very modest, he professed little but exemplified much. Like the sun which does not fire a cannon to announce his rising but simply shines, so he reflected Christ in his life, and every one took knowledge of him that he had been with Jesus. He illustrated Paul's definition of the gospel, 'It is the power of God unto salvation to every one that believeth;' and his highest claim was that he was a sinner saved by grace. He who claims more is self-righteous and puffed up, and is sure to behave himself unseemly.

"As a preacher he was perspicuous and strong, instructive and edifying, therefore eminently useful. Having joined the Tennessee Conference in October, 1849, he preached his semicentennial sermon to his brethren of that body in session at Columbia, Tennessee, in October, 1899. It was a memorable discourse, reminiscential and spiritual and sounded like the trumpet blast of a superannuated captain urging his younger brethren on to the battle from which he was retiring to receive his crown, for the crowning day was at hand. During the half century of his itinerant career he filled all grades of appointments, from the humblest to the highest, and ever acquitted himself like a man; and at the great age of eighty-five years he peacefully fell asleep in Jesus."

A copy of his semi-centennial sermon, preached to the members of the Tennessee Annual Conference (in session October, 1899), at Columbia, Tennessee, is on file in the archives of Vanderbilt University, Nashville.

RUTH FAMILY: Having been repeatedly asked by the immediate members of his own, as well as other branches of the family, to place in convenient form his knowledge of the family history, the writer has endeavored to outline briefly, such facts as may satisfy those who are interested.

A little more than a century has elapsed since our country took its place among the nations; that period may mark the beginning of a family history as well as the birth of a nation. While our knowledge of those ancestors who existed before the first mentioned names, or of the ante-revolutionary period, has not come to us so complete as to be authentic, being only traditional, enough is known to say in truth, they were of respectability, with them, like those who succeeded them, "The post of honor is the private station."

Of the record here made the writer has received much from his own parents; also from Mrs. Margaret Walsh, of Murfreesboro, daughter of James Ruth, now in the seventy-second year of her age. Some information, also, some interesting tradition, was obtained from the late Robert Ruth, who was a son of David Ruth, first mentioned. Robert Ruth was born in Raleigh, North Carolina. When a young man he came to Nashville, and died there at an advanced age. He was a man of much strength of character, and by extensive reading and study he attained a high literary culture. For some of the facts here stated, as well as a verification of his own knowledge, the writer is indebted to his sister, Mrs. W. G. Dorris, of Avondale, Sumner county, Tennessee.

David Ruth, with whom this record begins, was the son of James Ruth and Sarah Tenne Ruth, who came to Pennsylvania from Scotland with the tide of emigration to the Middle and Southern colonies, that began about the middle of the eighteenth century. David Ruth was a native of Philadelphia, Pennsylvania, was born about the year 1761. His ancestry were of Presbyterian faith. At the age of sixteen he was draughted into the service of the Continental Army, and was engaged in the battle of the Brandywine, September 11, 1777. He was married a few years subsequent to that period to Mary McGlochlin, the daughter of Joshua McGlochlin, a Presbyterian minister, who lived near the city of Wilmington, N. C. Soon after his marriage he removed to Granville county, North Carolina.

His immediate descendants were James, David, Sarah, Elizabeth and George Washington Ruth, the last named, being born October 6, 1799, was the youngest and father of the writer. There is a well authenticated tradition that he was honored with the name of "George Washington" by reason of the following circumstances:—General Washington, during the month of November, 1799, made a tour of North

Carolina and passed near the residence of David Ruth, the babe being a few weeks of age and unnamed, he was held a few moments in the arms of the first President. It is an historical fact that General Washington died of pneumonia contracted by reason of undue exposure on his return from his tour, his death occurring the following month. About the year 1802 David Ruth removed to Raleigh, then coming into prominence as the capital of the state. At the age of seventeen George W. Ruth was apprenticed to Mr. Jehu Scott, the "Jeweler and Silversmith" of Raleigh, who was reputed to be one of the most skillful and thorough of his craft, having mastered his trade in the mother country. At the end if his apprenticeship he was discharged with full recommendations as to his skill as a workman, and as a "young man worthy of confidence." With his discharge, he received a set of tools, some of which had been "much used but serviceable." With these and a limited wardrobe, a bundle of modest weight, he left Raleigh, determined to establish himself in some of the rapidly developing states of the southwest. Leaving Raleigh, he traveled mostly on foot, passing through the states of South Carolina and Georgia, he at length reached Mobile, at that time the most prominent point in the territory of Alabama. Finding the field occupied, he directed his course to St. Stephens, then the territorial capital and land office. The town he described as being filled up with land speculators, adventurers and gamblers. While successful in his trade, he fell a victim to chills and finally a severe attack of fever. After a residence of near five months, he left St. Stephens in search of more healthful location. The town, from its unhealthy location, subsequently fell into decay, and is now only known as a steamboat landing of little importance.

Leaving St. Stephens, he visited Tuscaloosa, and then Huntsville, and stopping in the latter place, he worked a brief period for Thos. Cain, the pioneer "watch maker and silversmith" of that place. From thence he went to Fayetteville, Tennessee, where he engaged to work for E. M. Ringo. His stay there was brief. He arrived in Shelbyville in the summer of 1822, and here he found he had been preceded by Daniel Turrentine, who was somewhat his senior, having immigrated from Hillsboro, North Carolina, a short time previous, and had already established himself. He, having had the advantage of a thorough master, Mr. Turrentine gave him employment, which position he retained for more than four years. On the 30th day of May, 1824, he was united in marriage to Miss Anne Downs, who was born in the state of Maryland, near Baltimore, her father being James Downs, whose immediate ancestors were residents of Virginia, and members of the Church of England, her mother being Anne Shilcut, whose family were of Scotch origin, and of the Society of Friends (or Quakers). Her father died prior to her birth. Her mother died in giving her birth and she was given to her maternal grandmother.

When about six years of age she was taken from her grandmother by relations of her father. She remembered crossing a large body of water in a boat, which was probably Chesapeake bay, her destination some distance from the opposite shore. She did not remain long, as an uncle Peter Shilcut, whom she quickly recognized, rode up to an orchard fence, where she was playing with other children, she was taken upon the horse before him and carried away, he being on the road to Tennessee, where he settled. She was never informed as to the reasons that prompted either of those parties in their conduct to her, her uncle although treating her with great kindness and even consideration, gave her no intimation beyond expressing his purpose to give her means. He did give her a substantial and comfortable home. But his death occurred soon after and no deed was given. He died intestate, being carried away after a few hours of illness of cholera in July, 1833. He was a pioneer merchant of Shelbyville, coming to that place soon after James Deery, who arrived with the first stock of merchandise in 1811. Peter Shilcut is described by those who knew him to be an upright merchant, of a taciturn manner, yet of a kindly nature. In appearance he was of medium height, a swarthy face, black eyes and dark hair, his place of business was a two-story building of hewn cedar logs, and stood on the spot now occupied by the Farmers Bank building, on the southwest corner of the public square.

George W. Ruth after being in the employ of Mr. Turrentine for several years, at length entered into a partnership, the style of the firm being, Turrentine & Ruth. On the 30th of May, 1830. a destructive cyclone swept over the business portion of Shelbyville, destroying totally their building, causing a serious loss in goods and material. This building stood on the spot now occupied by S. K. Brantley, and owned by him. It was a small frame one-story, and was rebuilt on the same place with a work shop and forge in the rear, and stood until removed to Depot street during the year 1855 or 1856, and torn away by Moses Marshall, Esq., giving place to his present brick building.

Soon after the storm he was induced to remove to Lebanon, Tennessee, by Dr. Frazer, a leading citizen of that place. Not being satisfied with the outlook, he returned to Shelbyville after an absence of nearly one year, again entering into business with Mr. Turrentine, which partnership continued until January 29, 1833, when they dissolved by mutual consent, Mr. Turrentine remaining in the original stand. The following July cholera broke out in Shelbyville, Mr. Turrentine falling a victim to the great scourge.

George W. Ruth lost by cholera three children within three days, Mary, the eldest, being eight years of age on the 3d of July, and Paulina aged six years, and David aged fifteen months on the 5th of July.

Mr. Turrentine was a man of slight form, medium height, genial temperament, of strict integrity and great piety. The writer has been informed by Richard Foreman, Esq., that he visited him in company with his father, Richard Foreman, Sr., while on his death bed, his residence being on the spot now occupied by the residence of O. Cowan, Esq.

In 1837, George W. Ruth removed to Nashville, and entered the employ of Paul Negrin, a leading jeweler and silversmith, whose place of business was on what is now the corner of College and Deaderick streets. He remained with Mr. Negrin only about a year and a few months, when he returned to Shelbyville and resumed business at the old stand of Turrentine and Ruth. John M. Seahorn, Esq., a jeweler and silversmith, came to Shelbyville from East Tennessee in 1842, and entered into a partnership with George W. Ruth, but the firm was of limited duration, no date having been preserved. His failing health determined him to engage in a more active business. In 1849 he formed a partnership with the Hon. James Mullins, the firm being Ruth & Mullins, their stock being family groceries exclusively, this being the first firm to engage in that business in Shelbyville, such goods having been sold in all stores with other merchandise. They continued business several years. He then resumed his former business as jeweler, and up to the time of his death, occupied a building that stood on Depot street nearly opposite the store-rooms owned by Moses Marshall, Esq.

George W. Ruth died on Friday morning, August 20, 1858. He was reared by Presbyterian parents, being early after his conversion or profession of religion associated with Methodists, he continued a thoroughly consistent member of that connection until his death. He was long a member of the Masonic fraternity, was mayor of Shelbyville, served many years as a magistrate, a steward in the church and filled other positions of trust in the community whose confidence he retained to the fullest extent.

The following extract from his obituary written by the Rev. Welborne Mooney, who was his pastor, will show in strong light his character as a churchman:

"His life of unblemished holiness was indeed a living comment on the religion he professed; a comment known and read of all who knew him. He was a reading intelligent christian; well informed as to the doctrines of his church; in fact, he was one of the best theologians we ever met among the laity of any church. At different times in his history he filled the offices of class leader and steward, and filled them too with credit to himself and usefulness to his brethren. The death of such a man is a public calamity."

The following is an extract from the notice of his death in the *Shelbyville Expositor:*

"There was perhaps, no man, in the community more beloved and respected than the deceased. No one knew him but to love him."

The following is a note to the writer from Joseph H. Thompson, Esq., who, in his early life, was engaged in business with him:

"I knew George W. Ruth from my boyhood, but began to know him best when I entered his employ in 1846. He was then one of the merchants of Shelbyville. I remained with him until he went out of business, but my intimacy with him continued until his death in 1858. Mr. Ruth was a man of strong individuality. He was full of sympathy for humanity; always a friend to the poor and the unfortunate. He was a man of nerve and courage; and open, frank and manly; hated sham; despised intrigue and corruption. Although born and reared by Presbyterian parents, his early associations led him into the fold of Methodism. Mr. Ruth was a student, and to him the writings of the fathers of the church were familiar subjects. While a strong churchman, he never closed his eyes to the good that was in others. He was a good citizen, faithful in all the relations of life."

The descendants of David Ruth were: David, who married Martha Woodard. Born 1790, died 1863. James, who married Elizabeth Nutt. Born 1789, died 1837. Sarah, who married —— Miller. Elizabeth, who married —— Barbour. George W., who married Anne Downs.

The descendants of George W. Ruth were: Jane Maria, born February 11, 1828. Married Maj. Thos. J. McQuiddy, February 24, 1847. Elzira Stone, born October 26, 1829. Married Rev. William G. Dorris, October 27, 1853. Died, February 1, 1911. John Wesley, born February 27, 1839. Married Fannie E. Newton, March 26, 1865. Died, 1906. Charles Leonidas, born January 17, 1841. Married Julie T. Hardwick, July 16, 1867. George Anne, born October 20, 1844. Married Robert Wright, October 31, 1872. Died March 8, 1880. Ambrose Driskell, born January 12, 1845. Married Jennie S. Newton, September 24, 1867. Samuel Moody, born March 30, 1848. Married Sophia Winfred, October 24, 1871.

SLOSS D. BAXTER. Although heredity and environment have, mayhap, played some part in fashioning the life of Sloss D. Baxter, a successful attorney of Nashville, the development of his natural talents, his mental attainments, and his untiring devotion to the duties of his profession, have won him a high reputation for legal knowledge and ability. A son of the late Edmund D. Baxter, and grandson of Judge Nathaniel Baxter, he was born, September 6, 1880, in Nashville, Tennessee, which he has always proudly claimed as home.

Scholarly in his tastes, and an ambitious student, Mr. Baxter acquired his early education under private tutors, and at Saint Albans, Radford, Virginia. In 1901, he was graduated from the law department of the Vanderbilt University, and since that time has been actively and prosperously engaged in the practice of law in Nashville, where he has built up a large and lucrative clientele.

Mr. Baxter married in February, 1900, Miss Corneille Lindsey, a daughter of A. V. S. Lindsey, of Nashville.

Ed. Baxter

COL. WILLIAM PARSONS WASHBURN. For nearly half a century, the late Colonel Washburn was a member of the bar of Knoxville and east Tennessee. During that time he was associated with the most prominent men of his day, and himself became one of the most eminent in the group of lawyers who were the recognized leaders of the bar and as men of affairs in this section of the state. A successful lawyer, he was also identified with larger business and had a large influence and place in public affairs. Colonel Washburn was a most wholesome type of citizen, clean in both private and public life, conscientious to a fault, and one whose ideals were high and who sought to live on a high plane.

William Parsons Washburn came from distinguished ancestry, and of an old New England family. He was born in the old scholastic center at Amherst, Massachusetts, April 15, 1830. His parents were Rev. Royal and Harriet (Parsons) Washburn, natives respectively of Vermont and Massachusetts. The mother was the daughter of a minister, Rev. David Parsons, and her grandfather of the same name was one of the most noted ministers of the New England states. Rev. Royal Washburn was a clergyman of the Congregational church at Amherst, where his death occurred in 1833.

The late Colonel Washburn was reared in Massachusetts, and received a collegiate education as a matter of course, being graduated from Amherst College in 1851. For several years he served as a tutor at Culpepper, Virginia, and in 1856, at the instance of Horace Maynard, came to Knoxville to prepare himself for the practice of law. He was at the beginning of his professional career when the Civil war broke out, and he espoused the cause of his adopted state, entering the Confederate army, and making a brave and patriotic record. After the war he returned to this city, and entered upon the practice of his profession with zeal and ability and success rewarded his efforts from the state. He formed a partnership with Mr. Horace Maynard who was for many years one of the leaders of the Knoxville bar, and their association through a long period brought the young lawyer into contact with the most prominent men of the day and rapidly promoted him to professional distinction. Throughout his career as a lawyer, Colonel Washburn gave particular attention to equity causes, and ranked second to none as an equity lawyer. His fairness and honesty with his colleagues, his great respect for the law, and all who interpreted it, his fidelity to his clients, made him one of the most popular members of the Knoxville bar. After the dissolution of his partnership with Mr. Maynard he became associated with General G. W. Pickle, and the firm of Washburn, Pickle & Turner continued for a number of years. About three years before his death, the firm dissolved and Colonel Washburn soon afterwards took into his office his nephew, James Maynard, and the firm of Washburn & Maynard continued until the death of Mr. Washburn.

Colonel Washburn was a Democrat in politics and took a prominent part in public life. He was many times named as special judge to serve in the lower courts, and was also at different times a special judge of the supreme court. One of the esteemed members of the Local Bar Association, and for his felicity of utterance he was often designated by the other members of the bar to speak on memorial occasions, and was equally popular as a speaker in social events. As a business man he was vice-president of the Knoxville Gas Company, was secretary of the Knoxville Car & Wheel Company, and was a director in the Mechanics National Bank. Colonel Washburn was prominent as a church man, was elder for a number of years in the Second Presbyterian church at Knoxville, and for twenty years or more was superintendent of the Sunday school in that church.

Colonel Washburn was twice married. In 1864 he married Mrs. Minnie (Brown) Leonard, who died in 1877. His second wife was Mrs. Eliza Maynard, daughter of Robert Harper. Mrs. T. O. Baker of Brooklyn, New York, was an adopted daughter by his first marriage. The two children born to the second marriage were a daughter who died in infancy, and a son, William P. Washburn, who is mentioned in a succeeding paragraph. Mrs. Washburn and her son still reside at the old Washburn residence west of the city on the Kingston Pike, this home being considered one of the most beautiful in east Tennessee.

William P. Washburn, Jr., son of the late Colonel Washburn, and one of the rising attorneys of Knoxville, was born in this city on August 30, 1885. From the public schools he entered the University of Tennessee, where he graduated in 1906, then became a student at Princeton University where he graduated with the class of 1907, and was subsequently a student of the Harvard College of Law and spent one year in travel and study in Europe. His admission to the Knoxville bar occurred in 1909 and since then he has been rising rapidly to professional distinction. His office is in the Holston National Bank building, and he resides with his mother on the Kingston Pike.

JOSIAH C. DUNCAN. In the death of Josiah C. Duncan on August 1, 1911, Knoxville lost one of its most interesting and most highly esteemed citizens. In an age of electrical invention and usage, the career of Mr. Duncan was that of a pioneer. He belonged to the old-time telegraphers, having been an operator during the war, and soon after the conflict taking charge of the telegraph office at Knoxville. He later identified himself with the newer application of electricity to the phonetic telephone, and his name deserves remembrance for his connection both with telegraphy and telephony in this city.

Josiah C. Duncan was born in Cumberland county, Virginia, in 1840. He had only moderate advantages at school, but early in life manifested a practical energy, which carried him successfully through life. When he was eighteen years of age he began to learn the science of telegraphy, which at that time was still crude and only about thirteen years old. He made himself expert as an operator, and when the Civil war came on he was taken into the service with the Army of Tennessee as an operator, and gave a soldier's part in a position of special useful- ness in military operation. The year following the close of the war, in 1866, he came to Knoxville to take charge of the Western Union Tele- graph Company, and continued in that service for a number of years. Throughout most of his active lifetime he was a student and experi- menter in electrical and phonetic science, and was one of the first men in Tennessee to assume practical direction of the new invention, the telephone. The invention of the telephone and its first practical demon- stration occurred in 1876, and four years later in 1880 Mr. Duncan organ- ized the East Tennessee Telephone Company at Knoxville. It was under his direction that the first telephone was introduced into use in that city, and he had the management of the local exchanges during their growth into general popularity. He became president and treasurer of the People's Telephone and Telegraph Company, and held that position during the latter years of his life. Mr. Duncan married Miss Fannie J. Brooks, a daughter of Gen. Joseph A. Brooks, who was prominent as a farmer, and a member of the State Guards during the war. His death occurred in 1879. Mr. and Mrs. Duncan were the parents of four sons. The late Mr. Duncan had an ideally happy home and in his social rela- tions was a man of many kindly qualities and numbered his friends by the score. As a business man he was thorough and possessed of an energy which gave him a successful place among his contemporaries. He was ready at all times to assist in the upbuilding of his home city, and its advancement along civic and material lines. His family now reside at 1500 Cumberland avenue.

ROBERT M. JONES. Among the attorneys of Knoxville, Tennessee, a high place is given to Robert M. Jones, of the firm of Wright and Jones. He is considered one of the most brilliant members of the Knoxville bar and added to his mental powers he has the capacity for hard work and close application. He is not only an able lawyer, he is also an honest one, and his personality has won him wide popularity.

Robert M. Jones was born in Roane county, Tennessee, on the 3d of September, 1870. His father is the Rev. Henry B. Jones, and his mother was Mary (Hudson) Jones. The Rev. Henry B. Jones was born in the state of Virginia and became a minister of the Methodist Episcopal church. He became in time a widely known and very influential minis- ter, and is still living, his wife having died in 1890.

Robert M. Jones was one of seven children and after having passed through the public schools the question as to any further education pre- sented rather a blank face. He had always been brought up with the realization that an education was the most valuable weapon a man could

possess in his battle with life and therefore many sacrifices were made
that he might be well equipped along these lines, for ministers do not
receive munificent salaries.   He attended Roane College and later
became a student at a university, from which he was graduated in 1892.

Having determined to become a lawyer the young man now entered
the offices of T. Asbury Wright in Rockwood, and after four years of
study, was admitted to the bar.   This was in 1896 and immediately after
his admission he began to practice in Roane county, where he resided
until June 1, 1911, when he moved to Knoxville and formed a partnership with Mr. Wright, and this association has continued ever since,
and is considered one of the reliable firms of Knoxville.

Mr. Jones is a member of the Republican party and belongs to the
Ancient Free and Accepted Masons and to the Knights of Pythias.   He
is also a member of the Cumberland Club, and Cherokee Country Club.

HON. M. L. ROSS.   The wholesale grocery house of M. L. Ross &
Company at Knoxville was founded and built up on the solid elements
of commercial integrity, straightforward methods, and an almost unique
energy of its chief executive officers.   This company, starting on a small
scale, finally came to possess a trade over half a dozen states, and was one
of the commercial enterprises which gave character and stability to the
city of Knoxville.

The founder and for many years the head of this company whose
death occurred May 30, 1899, easily ranked as one of Knoxville's most
prominent business men, and by his connection with the larger affairs of
the city was equally useful and influential as a citizen.   The late M. L.
Ross was born in Anderson county, Tennessee, and was one of three children born to James and Mary (Martin) Ross.   The father, a native of
Virginia, and of Scottish descent, was first married to a Miss Slover, by
whom he had five children.   He later married Miss Mary Martin.   James
Ross attained official distinction as a soldier under General Kirkpatrick
during the War of 1812, and subsequently was engaged in merchandising
for upwards of fifty years.   His death occurred in 1869.   During the
first half of the nineteenth century, he was one of the leading men of
the state and had a large circle of influential friends, including such
men as John Bell, General Zollicoffer, James K. Polk and Andrew Johnson.

The late Martin L. Ross was reared in a good home, and in an atmosphere of refinement and culture endowed by the many associations with
such men as have already been named, and was a student at Emory &
Henry College in Virginia when the death of his father occurred in 1869.
That event caused him to leave college, and he returned home to take
charge of a store in Anderson county.   After managing this successfully for a time he sought out a larger field for his enterprise and in
1871 came to Knoxville.   Here he formed a co-partnership with Major

D. A. Carpenter, for the purpose of conducting a wholesale grocery business. The first name of the undertaking was Carpenter & Ross, and this continued until 1879. Mr. Ross in the meantime had become the chief executive of the concern and the firm name was then changed to M. L. Ross & Company. Under this title it came to possess a foremost position as a wholesale grocery, and extended its trade to five or six of the adjoining states.

In 1870 Mr. Ross married Miss Helen Carey, a daughter of Hon. William Carey, of Careyville, in Campbell county. Three children were born to their union, and the two now living are Mary Martin and William Carey Ross. Mrs. Ross and her family have a very attractive and beautiful residence at 1415 Laurel avenue in Knoxville.

ROBERT H. HARALSON. The life of Robert H. Haralson, of Lebanon, affords an excellent illustration of what independence, self-confidence and persistent effort can accomplish in a material way for an individual. The men of that stamp are also usually those that a community numbers as the leaders in the different phases of community affairs. This is true of Mr. Haralson, for besides demonstrating substantial business abilities as a farmer and stockman he has also given very efficient service in an official way and is now serving his third term as sheriff of Wilson county.

This is his native county, for he was born here June 18, 1866, a son of James and Annie (Young) Haralson. Both parents also were natives of Wilson county, the father's birth having occurred in 1832 and that of the mother in 1834, and both departed life there, the former having passed away in 1886 and the demise of the latter having occurred in 1894. Nine children came to their union and of this family six are now living, Robert H. being the third of those surviving. Both parents were members of the Methodist Episcopal church, South. James Haralson spent his life as a farmer and directed his efforts in that vocation with that intelligence that brought gratifying rewards and established him as a successful man. He was a member of the time-honored Masonic fraternity and of the Independent Order of Odd Fellows, and in the exercise of his franchise the Democratic party received his unswerving support. When the long sectional quarrel flamed out at last into civil war he ranged himself with his native state on the side of the South and served three years in support of the Southern cause as a member of Hatton's Regiment. During the siege of Murfreesboro in 1864 he was wounded and was then discharged from the service on account of disability. He suffered heavily from the ravages of the war, having lost over forty mules, besides other property, but after the conflict closed he started out anew and at the time of his death had acquired a very comfortable estate. His father was Zara Haralson, a Virginian by birth who came into Tennessee in an early day and settled on a farm in Wilson county, where he spent the remainder of his years. His estate comprised some seven hundred acres of fine land and he was also a large slave owner. Annie Young Haralson, the mother of Robert H., was a daughter of William Young, a native of England, who after his immigration to this country was located first in Pennsylvania but later removed from there to Wilson county, Tennessee. He was a farmer, a man of competence and was one of the best known citizens of Wilson county, where he served forty-two years as a justice of the peace.

Robert H. Haralson grew up a farmer boy in Wilson county and received in the meantime a public school education. He began independent labor as a farm hand at twenty-five cents per day, and later took employment at sawing logs, for which labor he received forty cents per day and provided his own dinner. At the time of his marriage in 1891 he had a cash capital of $7.50 and was in debt $140, but he was young and had health, energy and pluck, assets that were worth more to him than unlimited inheritance. He bought a farm and put his best abilities into play to pay for it. This he had accomplished by the end of the second year and he yet owns this farm of eighty-two acres. He has dealt considerably in stock and has been quite successful in that line of business venture. His entrance into official life was made when he was elected constable. This was before he had attained his majority and he had to wait seven months to reach legal age and to be able to qualify for the office. After serving six years as a constable in Wilson county he took up similar duties for a time in Fannin county, Texas, as a special deputy sheriff, but later he returned to his former home in Tennessee. In 1908 he was elected sheriff of Wilson county and has been twice re-elected, which fact gives conclusive evidence of the satisfaction he has given the citizens of his county in his service as sheriff and his conduct as a man.

Mrs. Haralson was Miss Florence Martin prior to her marriage, a daughter of J. F. Martin, a well-known and successful farmer of Wilson county. Mr. and Mrs. Haralson have three children: Annie, at home; Perry, who is attending school, and Robert, now three years old. Mrs. Haralson is a member of the Baptist church. Mr. Haralson sustains fraternal associations as a member of Magnolia lodge, Independent Order of Odd Fellows at Lebanon, and as a member of the Modern Woodmen of America, in both of which orders he has held the highest office of his lodges. Politically he gives stanch allegiance to the Democratic party.

J. LEWIS SADLER, M. D., has been active in his profession since 1897, having seen service in Cuba as hospital steward in the Fourth Tennessee Volunteers, after which he located in Nashville, Tennessee, continuing there until the time when he located in Johnsonville, in 1905. Since that time Dr. Sadler has been prominently identified with the medical profession in this city, where he has a well established practice, and an enviable reputation in his profession.

Born in Colbert county, Alabama, on August 7, 1875, Dr. Sadler is the son of William George and Sarah E. (Sadler) Sadler, the mother being a distant relative of her husband. The father was born in Alabama in 1848 and was a son of Lewis Hubbard Sadler, one of the pioneer physicians of northern Alabama, himself the son of George Twyman Sadler, a civil engineer of the early days in Alabama. Lewis Hubbard Sadler came with his family into Tennessee about 1878, and engaged in the practice of his profession in Nashville, there dying in 1880. His son, William G., early identified himself with business interests and activities in that city, and for several years was engaged as a traveling salesman. He eventually became interested in the manufacture of fertilizers, and the first ton of acid phosphate made from the Tennessee phosphate rock of Hickman and Maury counties was manufactured by him. Mr. Sadler is now secretary of The National Fertilizer Association, and is established in Nashville in a business way, although he maintains his home at Monterey, where he has a fine residence. He is also interested to some extent in farming in Humphreys county, and is prominent and prosperous, taking an important place among the leading business men of this section of the state. He is an Independent Democrat and a member of the Methodist Episcopal church, South. Fraternally, he is a charter member of Reynolds Lodge No. 33, of the Knights of Pythias, in which he is past grand chancellor. He is a Mason of the thirty-second degree, a Knight Templar, and is affiliated with the Ancient Arabic Order of the Nobles of the Mystic Shrine, Al Menah Temple of Nashville. Mr. Sadler served in the Confederate army in an Alabama regiment, as did also his honored father. The mother of Dr. Sadler was born in Robertson county, Tennessee, at Sadlersville, and was married on December 25, 1869. They became the parents of five children, four of whom are living: Edna L., married to Richard Preuit, of Leighton, Alabama; Mary Lizzie, the wife of L. L. Haygood, of Humphreys county; Vashti Louise, married to W. W. Wilhoite, of Monterey, Tennessee; and Dr. J. Lewis of this review.

J. Lewis Sadler was educated in the public schools of Nashville, followed by a season in which he was placed in the hands of private tutors. He then entered the Vanderbilt University at Nashville and there pursued a medical course, graduating from that institution in 1897 with the degree of Doctor of Medicine. Dr. Sadler began the practice of his profession in Mount Pleasant, Tennessee, where he continued for the space of a year, after which he entered the army as hospital steward in the Fourth Tennessee Volunteers. Following his army service, Dr. Sadler located in Nashville, where he remained in practice until 1905, when he came to Johnsonville, and here he has been busily engaged in medical practice ever since. He has built up a representative and ever growing practice in the years that have passed, and is occupying a leading place in the medical fraternity in this section of the state, where his ability is recognized and acknowledged.

Dr. Sadler is a stanch Democrat, and his fraternal relations are represented by his membership in the Knights of Pythias.

On November 9, 1911, Dr. Sadler was united in marriage with Miss Annie C. Parker, the daughter of Mr. and Mrs. James E. Parker, well-known residents of Johnsonville, in Humphreys county. The marriage took place at Johnsonville, Tennessee.

DR. ANDREW B. MARTIN. In reviewing the career of Dr. Andrew B. Martin, it is interesting to note one highly important factor—heredity. Entirely a self-made man, still the stock from which he sprung gave him the impetus and patience to meet destiny more than half way and conquer it. Dr. Martin is yet another portrait in the gallery of poor boys who have gained a measure of distinction. Dr. Martin is the son of Matthew M. and Matilda (Crow) Martin. The father was born in Albemarle county, Virginia, was a physician who for a number of years conducted a practice in Smith county, and moved to Paris, Texas, with his family, where he died in 1849. He was a Mason and a member of the Presbyterian church. The mother was born in the north of Ireland in 1802 and died in Tennessee in 1876. Thus in the ancestry of Dr. Martin is to be found the good old blood of Virginia and that of Ireland. Peter Martin, his grandfather, left Virginia, his native state, in 1792, and emigrated to Kentucky, where he lived the balance of his life in the vicinity of Bowling Green. A farmer, the stubborn soil yielded to his intrepid nature, and this not inconsiderable trait contributed to the physical capital of his grandson. On the other hand does he possess that rare asset, humor—so felicitous in easing the obstacles of the workaday world—for his maternal grandfather was a loyal son of Erin, who was born and died in his native land.

Dr. Martin was born in Smith county, Tennessee, on December 9, 1836. From the common schools he went to the law school of Cumberland, from which he was graduated in 1858, after which he immediately began the practice of law, pursuing that calling until 1878, when he was elected professor of law in the Lebanon law school. He has been a member of the board of trustees of Cumberland University for forty-five years, and president of that board for more than thirty years. His life has been filled with big interests, not alone that of his profession, but politics and business of various natures. Notwithstanding his professional prominence and activities, he has served the Democratic party in many capacities. He was at one time a presidential elector-at-large on Hancock's ticket, and he has represented state interests in the legislature, of which he was a member from 1871 to 1872, acting in that time

And^w B. Martin

as chairman of the judiciary committee. The degree LL.D. was conferred upon him by Lincoln University of Illinois in 1883.

Dr. Martin is a member of the Presbyterian church, and in addition to his interests there, his fraternal relations include such organizations as the Masons and the Knights of Pythias, and in the latter order he has served as chancellor commander, and as master in the former. He is also a member of the Knights of Honor.

In 1868 Dr. Martin married Alice Ready, daughter of Charles Ready, of Murfreesboro, Tennessee. She, like her husband, was a member of the Presbyterian church and active in its work. Seven children were born to them, four of whom are living. Mary, Martha, Helen and Andrea are the four surviving ones. The three first named are widowed, while Andrea is the wife of Ira J. Partlow, and lives in West Virginia. In 1890 Mrs. Martin died, and three years later Dr. Martin married Sue Brittain, of Georgia.

Dr. Martin maintains his home in Lebanon, Tennessee, and he is recognized as one of the most successful educators in his subject in the state. Aside from his professorship in the law school, he is financially interested in a number of industrial and manufacturing plants in the community, and is enjoying a degree of prosperity which is commensurate with the efforts he has expended in life thus far.

DR. PHILIP N. MATLOCK, a successful physician and a prominent and influential citizen of Obion county, Tennessee, whose residence is at Masonhall, is a man of intrinsic merit as a man, a citizen and a physician, and as supporting evidence of this statement is his record of forty-three years of continuous service there in a professional capacity and the fact that he has held the highest position in the Masonic order in Tennessee that the Free and Accepted Masons of the state could confer upon him. He comes of Revolutionary stock and is himself a Confederate veteran of the Civil war.

Philip N. Matlock was born in Davidson county, Tennessee, January 9, 1844, and was the only son in a family of five children born to Simpson and Maria (Shumate) Matlock, both of whom were natives of Davidson county. Simpson Matlock owned a farm of five hundred acres and was a citizen of prominence there. Philip N. grew up on the home farm and after pursuing the usual studies in the common schools of that locality he completed a course in Franklin College. It was about this time that the storm of civil war lowering finally burst over the country. In 1861 young Matlock, then but a youth of seventeen years, entered the Confederate service as a private in Harding's Artillery, being subsequently transferred by the war department to Carter's Scouts with the commission of first lieutenant, which rank he held until the close of the war. He was thrice wounded, the first time at Stone's River on December 31, 1862, when his right shoulder was injured. He was next wounded in his left thigh at Sulphur Branch Trestle, Alabama, September 2, 1862, and on April 3, 1865, at Tuscaloosa, a few days before he surrendered, he received a wound in his right leg. Being paroled shortly afterward, he returned to his home in Tennessee and at once took up a course of medical study at Nashville College. Graduated in 1867 he began the practice of medicine, locating first at Fredonia, Kentucky, but removing in 1869 to Masonhall, Obion county, Tennessee, where he has since continued and where he is now the only representative of his profession. In line with the interest of his life work he sustains membership in the Obion County Medical Society, the Tri-State Medical Society, the Tennessee State Medical Society and the American Medical Association.

On June 18, 1865, was solemnized his marriage to Miss Mary J. Jetton, and to this union were born six children, three of whom are yet living, viz.: Philip E., and Preston C. and Presley (twins).

Dr. Matlock has also literary gifts of considerable merit, and in a fraternal way is prominently affiliated with the Masonic order as a member of the blue lodge, chapter and commandery. In 1896 he served as grand master of the Masonic Grand Lodge of Tennessee, is a past grand worthy patron of the Order of the Eastern Star of Tennessee, and is now (1912) grand sojourner of the Grand Chapter of Tennessee.

The Matlock family originated in Tennessee with William Matlock, the grandfather of Dr. Matlock, who came to this state from North Carolina in 1789. He was a soldier of the Revolution and was captured at Charleston by the British. His wife was Mary Simpson, who alone of her family survived from a murderous attack by Indians near Nashville, Tennessee. Simpson, the father of Dr. Matlock, was the youngest of ten children born to William and Mary (Simpson) Matlock.

WALTER M. CASTILE, agent for the Nashville, Chattanooga & St. Louis Railroad Company at Johnsonville, Tennessee, was born in Camden, Benton county, Tennessee, on the 18th day of March, 1882, and is the son of James Monroe and Amy Jane (Cole) Castile, both born in Benton county. The parents were both left orphans at an early age, and no records were preserved of their families so that it is impossible to give in this connection any further information concerning their ancestry. They were married in Benton county on September 23, 1867, and they became the parents of eight children, five of which number are yet living. Walter M., of this review, was the only son. The father was educated in the common schools of Benton county and in the Benton Seminary at Camden, Tennessee. After leaving school he taught in the public schools for a number of years, and later was superintendent of the public schools of Benton county for a number of years. Later on he engaged in the milling and mercantile business. In 1910 he located in

Johnsonville and is now making his home in this city. He served throughout the war in the Confederate army, and received seven wounds in the battle of Atlanta. He saw much active service, participating in many battles and was taken prisoner at Island No. 10 on the Mississippi river and spent several weary months in the prison at Chicago, Illinois. Mr. Castile is a Democrat, and has taken a prominent part in the politics of the state, serving in the state legislature from the 26th senatorial district. He and his wife are both members of the Methodist Episcopal church, and Mr. Castile is a member of the Masonic fraternity, affiliating with Camden Lodge No. 179.

Walter M. Castile was educated in the public schools of Camden, and on leaving school he took up the study of telegraphy, at the age of twenty-two becoming active in the railroad service in the capacity of telegrapher. He was engaged in that work in the Camden office for five years, after which he was appointed agent at the Denver, Tennessee, office, where he continued for a period of nine months. His next appointment was that of agent at the Johnsonville office of the Nashville, Chattanooga & St. Louis, which position he has ably and efficiently filled since 1908.

Mr. Castile, like his father, is a Democrat, and a member of the Methodist Episcopal church, South, as is also his wife. He is a member of the Masonic fraternity, Caldwell Lodge, No. 273, and of the Independent Order of Odd Fellows, Lodge No. 606, at Denver.

Mr. Castile was united in marriage in 1905 with Miss Bamma Garrett, the daughter of Mr. and Mrs. John W. Garrett of Camden. They have no children.

WILLIAM THOMAS McGLOTHLIN. The really useful men of a community are those in whom their fellow citizens can rely in affairs of public importance; to whom they can come for assistance in seasons of financial distress; men who have won this confidence by the wisdom of their own investments and by the honorable lives they have led on every field of effort and as neighbors and friends. Very often, in prosperous towns, these men are retired farmers and merchants, frequently they are bankers, and in not a few cases it will be found that they are veterans of that great struggle which makes the war between the states yet fresh after the passage of a half a century of time. Such a one in every particular is W. T. McGlothlin, president of the Farmers' Bank of Portland, a citizen whose entire career has been one of industry, integrity and upright living. Mr. McGlothlin was born in Sumner county, Tennessee, August 4, 1837, and is a son of James and Lucinda (Beard) McGlothlin.

Joseph McGlothlin, the paternal grandfather of W. T. McGlothlin, was born in Ireland, and he and wife and one child emigrated to the United States in 1800, settling in Sumner county, Tennessee, where he reared a family and spent the rest of his life in agricultural pursuits. On the maternal side, Mr. McGlothlin's grandfather was David Beard, who was born in Sumner county, and there spent his entire life in tilling the soil. James McGlothlin was born in Sumner county, October 21, 1804, was reared on his father's farm, and eventually engaged in agricultural pursuits on his own account, accumulating a tract of 300 acres and becoming one of his community's prominent citizens. He was a Democrat in politics, a devout Christian, and a member of the Presbyterian church, in the faith of which he died November 3, 1856. He married Lucinda Beard, who was born in Sumner county, March 3, 1807, and she passed away August 15, 1853, having been the mother of six children, of whom four are still living, W. T. being the second in order of birth.

W. T. McGlothlin received his education in the schools of Sumner county and Western Tennessee, and when the war between the states broke out was a student in Cumberland University. Abandoning his studies, he enlisted for service in Company B, Thirtieth Regiment, Tennessee Volunteer Infantry, in the Confederate army, with which organization he served first as private, and after the reorganization as ordinance sergeant. He fought at Fort Donelson, where he was captured by the Union troops, but eventually, after seven months, managed to secure his exchange at Vicksburg, Mississippi, and at once rejoined his regiment, participating in the battles at Chickamauga, Missionary Ridge, from Dalton to Atlanta, Franklin and Nashville, and then participated in his last battle, at Benton, North Carolina, April 26, 1865. A brave and cheerful soldier, he was respected alike by officers and men, and faithfully performed whatever duties fell to his lot, and when he returned to private life, he just as faithfully performed the duties of peace. On his return, he began life on a farm and taught school for several years, but in 1868 entered the mercantile business, in which he continued for ten years. Being industrious and thrifty, he wisely invested his earnings in farm land, which he disposed of several years ago to enter the Portland Bank. He was connected with that institution until 1911, when he became one of the organizers of the Farmers' Bank of Portland, of which he has since been made president. This institution is considered one of the solid and substantial banking houses of this part of the state, and is capitalized at $20,000, with $60,000 deposits. Mr. McGlothlin's connection with the house has stimulated public confidence, and his wise and shrewd administration of its affairs has served to popularize its coffers.

In September, 1874, Mr. McGlothlin was married to Miss M. C. West, daughter of David and Mary (Wright) West, natives of Robertson, Tennessee, where they spent their lives in agricultural pursuits. Mr. and Mrs. McGlothlin are members of the Methodist Episcopal church. He is a Master and Royal Arch Mason and a Democrat in politics.

JAMES THOMAS BASKERVILLE. Prominent among the legal talent of Sumner county, Tennessee, is James T. Baskerville, of Gallatin, a former state senator from this district, who is not only one of the best lawyers of Gallatin but is of high standing as a citizen and business man. He springs from Revolutionary ancestry on the paternal side and is of Irish lineage by maternal descent, and both the Baskervilles and his mother's people, the McGlothlins, are numbered among the oldest and m)st respected connections of Sumner county, the former having been established here as early as 1801. The Revolutionary ancestor referred to was Richard Baskerville, the great-grandfather of James T., who fought in the Revolution as a Virginia patriot and whose son, Thomas, born in the Old Dominion state, came to Tennessee as a settler in 1801. Thomas located on a farm in Sumner county, where he spent his remaining years as an agriculturist. His son, Abner, the father of James T., was born in Sumner county, Tennessee, in 1838 and is yet living. As a loyal soldier of the South he served the cause of the Confederacy during the Civil war as a member of the Thirtieth Tennessee Regiment and participated in all of the principal engagements in Tennessee up to and including the battle of Chickamauga, where he was severely wounded. He was detained in the hospital several months but upon his discharge was unable for further military service and returned to his home in Sumner county. He took up farming as his vocation, and in later years has filled different public offices of responsibility, having served as tax assessor of Sumner county from 1892 to 1896, and as a county trustee from 1900 to 1906. In political affairs he has always been a stanch adherent of the Democratic party, and in church membership he is identified with the Christian denomination. He owns a good farm in this county and now devotes all of his time to its management. In this county he wedded Nancy J. McGlothlin, who was born in Sumner county in 1840 and passed away at the old homestead here in 1907, a devoted member of the Methodist Episcopal church, South.' Her father was James McGlothlin, an early settler of Sumner county, who continued his residence here until his death. His father, Joseph, immigrated to this country from Ireland. Of the children born to Abner and Nancy (McGlothlin) Baskerville, five are living and are as follows: James T., of this review; R. H., a Sumner county farmer; J. A., a bookkeeper in the comptroller's office at Nashville, Tennessee; Sallie, who is a teacher and resides at Portland, Tennessee; and J. E., who also is a resident at Portland, Tennessee.

James T. Baskerville was educated in the common schools of Sumner county and in the Franklin training school, Franklin, Kentucky, and was prepared for law at Cumberland University, Lebanon, Tennessee, where he was graduated in 1896. Shortly thereafter he began the active practice of his chosen profession at Gallatin, where he rose rapidly at the bar and now stands at the fore among the best legal talent of Sumner county. He has a large clientage and is admitted to practice in all the courts of the state, his success being the reward of merit and untiring effort to make his professional efficiency that of the highest order. He has been city attorney of Gallatin eight years. Like his father, Mr. Baskerville is a stanch Democrat and is one of the strong and influential workers in Sumner county in behalf of his party. He was a member of the state Democratic executive committee 1906-1907. He was his party's successful candidate for the state senate in 1908 and sat in that body in 1909 and 1910, proving an exceptionally energetic and able member during his service. The high appreciation in which he was held by his colleagues was attested by his important committee duties and other responsible distinctions. He was chosen to serve on the judiciary committee, the committee on ways and means, as well as on several other committees, and was made chairman of the committee on constitutional amendment. He is a good business man as well as a good lawyer and holds a number of profitable investments in this vicinity. As a prominent member of the Independent Order of Odd Fellows in this state he is now serving as conductor in the Tennessee grand lodge of this order; and through his firm belief in its benevolent principles and his homiletic skill as an expositor of its teachings he has been of much service to the order in making addresses before its different lodges in this state and for years has been frequently called for this service. His religious faith is expressed by membership in the Christian church.

In April, 1901, Mr. Baskerville was happily married to Miss Lua King, a daughter of William H. and Mary E. (Harcourt) King. Mr. King was a native of Mississippi but removed to Sumner county, Tennessee when a young man and was agent for the Adams Express Company at Gallatin for many years. He passed away in Sumner county. Mr. and Mrs. Baskerville are the parents of three children, named: Marion, Nancy and Amelia, who are now aged respectively ten, seven and two years.

ROBERT EDWARD SAUNDERS, the well known live stock dealer of Sumner county, is one of the prosperous and substantial farmers of that county, where he was born February 14, 1859, a son of H. H. and Elizabeth M. (Bondurant) Saunders. The birth of H. H. Saunders occurred in the same county in October, 1819, while his wife was born in Davidson county in 1829. H. H. Saunders engaged in agricultural pursuits with much success, becoming the owner of over six hundred acres of land, and he and his brother, William, were the pioneer merchants of Saundersville, the former also having served in the Seminole Indian war. Of the eleven children born to him and his wife, four are now living, of whom the subject of this sketch is the sixth in number. Previously a Whig, after the war he became a Democrat, and he and his wife were enthusiastic workers in the Methodist Episcopal church. He died in 1879, she surviving until September, 1906.

One of the first preachers of the Methodist Episcopal denomination in Tennessee, Rev. Herbert Saunders, the paternal grandfather of R. E.

Saunders, came in 1798 from Culpeper county, Virginia, to Sumner county, Tennessee, where he built the first Methodist Episcopal church in the county—Saunders' chapel. He married a niece of Patrick Henry —Miss Russell, who had seven brothers in the Revolutionary war, one of whom was Robert Russell, a general of note under General Washington. The maternal grandfather of R. E. Saunders, Jacob Bondurant, settled early in Davidson county and engaged in farming, becoming the owner of a large estate and a large slave holder. Rev. Hubbard Saunders was a great lover of fine horses and imported some very valuable ones from Virginia. He raised Tenn, Oscar, Nell Saunders, and imported from Europe, Wonder, one of the greatest stallions in the South. Rev. Herbert Saunders and wife and also the father and mother of Robert E. Saunders, are buried in the Saunders cemetery on the old Saunders homestead.

After his common school education was completed, R. E. Saunders attended high school, being instructed by Capt. C. S. Douglas, who conducted a high school in Hendersonville. Farm life has appealed to Mr. Saunders from the beginning and he has never diverted his attention from this pursuit, being especially interested in live stock. He owns the good farm where he lives and where live also his brothers, W. B., Joseph E. and J. T. Saunders, together with whom he owns the homestead which has been in the family for over one hundred years. He is a heavy trader in all kinds of live stock. A magistrate for twelve years, he has been reelected for six years more, has been a school director for ten or twelve years, is a Democrat in politics, and a Mason, being past master of Saundersville lodge, No. 359. Mr. Saunders has never married.

JAMES W. BLACKMORE. One of the best known and most highly respected citizens of Sumner county, Tennessee, is James W. Blackmore, of Gallatin, prominent for years as one of the ablest members of its bar, as one of its leading financiers, and who as soldier and public official has performed that service that gives him recognition among Tennessee's honored men. He wore the "gray" four years in defense of the southland, and his service in a later period as state senator was marked by the same earnest effort and conscientious devotion to the interests and welfare of his state of Tennessee, while as president of the First National Bank of Gallatin he has long been a dominant factor in the financial circles of Sumner county. The name of Blackmore is a familiar one in Sumner county, for the family was established here more than a century ago and its members have ever maintained the name in high prestige for worth and attainment.

George D. Blackmore, the originator of the family here, born and reared in Maryland, ran away from home as a youth and after serving throughout the Revolution as a member of the patriot army, came to Tennessee. He settled on a farm in Sumner county and continued there until his death. He became a well known pioneer of this section, and as a major in the state troops took an active and leading part in driving the Indians from the state. His wife was Elizabeth Neely, a daughter of Capt. Alexander Neely, who was killed by the Indians. The career of William M. Blackmore, their son, and the father of James W. Blackmore, of this review, is a part of the Tennessee history of his time. He was born on the Sumner county homestead in February, 1803, was educated here and took up law as his profession, being admitted to the bar along in the '20s. Rising rapidly in his profession, he also became a prominent figure in the Democratic political circles of the state, and served as a member of the state legislature in 1848 and 1849. Previous to this he served as a soldier in the Mexican war, and was captain of Co. I, First Regiment, Tennessee Infantry. He was elected a brigadier of the state militia, and with his command participated in the battles of Monterey, Vera Cruz and Cerro Gordo. He was a prominent member of the Independent Order of Odd Fellows in this state, was a charter member of Howard lodge, No. 13, at Gallatin, and at one time served as grand master of the Tennessee grand lodge of this old and honored order. As a lawyer he excelled and for years maintained an extensive practice. He served as attorney general of this district at one time and was a clerk and master in chancery of the Sumner county court at the time of his death in November, 1853. No less able and successful as a financier, he left a large estate at his death. Rachel J. Barry, who became the wife of William M. Blackmore, was born in Sumner county, Tennessee, in June, 1812, and died in her native county in June, 1843, a consistent member of the Presbyterian church, and the mother of three children, of whom James W. Blackmore is now the only survivor. She was the daughter of Redmond D. Barry, who was born near Dublin, Ireland, and was educated in the University of Dublin. As a surgeon he took service in the English navy, but later he resigned on account of his sympathy and friendship for the American colonies, finally deciding to cast his fortunes with them. Locating first in North Carolina, he practiced medicine there a number of years, but subsequently took up the study of law under the father of John C. Breckenridge, and followed law in Tennessee for the remainder of his life, becoming a very wealthy man for his time. He died in Sumner county in 1821. He was a Catholic in religious faith but he married Jane Alexander, a daughter of William Alexander and a staunch Presbyterian, who reared her children in her own faith.

James W. Blackmore, the youngest child of his parents, was born in Sumner county, Tennessee, March 9, 1843. After pursuing the usual preliminary studies in the public schools of Gallatin he entered Central University, Danville, Kentucky, where he was a student in the sophomore class when the Civil war broke out. In this struggle he was in sympathy with the South, convincing evidence of which loyalty he gave by promptly enlisting in Company I of the Second Tennessee Infantry, with which he remained in service four years to a day. He participated in the first battle of Manassas, Virginia; the battles of Richmond and Perryville, Kentucky; Shiloh, Murfreesboro, Chickamauga, and Missionary Ridge, Tennessee; Dalton, Jonesboro and Atlanta, Georgia; and then served under General Hood to Nashville and on his retreat through Tennessee and into North Carolina, surrendering with the troops at Greensboro, North Carolina, on the day that closed his four years of service.

Resuming his interrupted studies, he completed his literary course and then took up the study of law with Judge Joseph C. Guild as his preceptor, subsequently completing his legal studies in Cumberland University, Lebanon, Tennessee, where he was graduated in law in 1867. On his admission to the bar immediately afterward, he began the practice of law with George B. Guild, continuing this association until 1871, since when Mr. Blackmore has labored independently, his practice extending to all the courts. He has always been a staunch Democrat and has always taken a prominent part in the local political councils of his party. As state senator representing Sumner, Robertson and Trousdale counties, he served in the Tennessee state legislature from 1883 to 1885 and at that time gave efficient service as a member of the bond committee that settled the state debt, serving also as chairman of the railroad committee. As a strong and able lawyer he has long stood among the fore in his profession in Sumner county, and has served as city attorney of Gallatin. He has shown no less strength as a business man and as president of the First National Bank of Gallatin he has directed the affairs of the bank with wisdom, fidelity and great financial ability. He also has heavy holdings in land and city property hereabout and ranks as one of the most substantial men of Sumner county.

In November, 1871, was solemnized the marriage of Mr. Blackmore and Miss Mariah L. Ewing, daughter of William B. Ewing, who was a successful farmer of Davidson county, Tennessee. She was an active and consistent member of the Methodist Episcopal church, South, and died in March, 1896. In 1900 Mr. Blackmore took as his second wife, Miss Lola Ezell, a native of Marshall county, Tennessee, and a daughter of J. B. Ezell, a prominent farmer of that county. Mr. and Mrs. Blackmore are both members of the Methodist Episcopal church, South, and Mr. Blackmore has been superintendent of the Sunday school of that denomination in Gallatin since 1877. He is a member of the Beta Theta Phi college fraternity. An able worker in his various avenues of activity, his life and services have been of that character which well entitles him to consideration in this history of Tennessee and Tennesseeans, for in every service he has honored the state that gave him birth.

MORRIS STRENG WILE. The ability to make a prosperous career from a beginning without capital and with only the resources of personal character has been well displayed in the life of Mr. Wile, who is head of the Gallatin Milling Company and otherwise prominently connected with local business affairs.

Mr. Wile is a native of Sumner county, where he was born August 13, 1868. His parents were L. and Jennie (Streng) Wile. The maternal grandparents were Joseph and Fannie Streng, both of whom were natives of Germany, and the former died in Mississippi of the yellow fever in 1878. He spent a number of his years as a merchant. Mr. L. Wile, the father, was born in Germany in 1824, and passed away in 1911. His wife was born in New York state in 1845. The father, coming to America a young 'man, met and married his wife at Louisville, Kentucky, in 1866. From that city he came to Gallatin, where he was a merchant, running a general store for a number of years. He accumulated a very good estate, although he had some severe business reverses during a portion of his career. Of his two children the only one now living is the Gallatin miller. The family were members of the Jewish faith, and the father was in politics a Democrat. During the Civil war he served as a soldier on the southern side, and from a wound received in service carried a bullet to his grave.

Morris S. Wile attended the common schools at Gallatin as the beginning of his education, but when he was thirteen years old his father failed in business, and from that time on he had to make his own way. It was with this handicap that he started in life, and has always been self-supporting. Up until he was about twenty-one years of age, he was employed chiefly in his father's store. At that time he began work in a mill, and milling has since been his principal occupation. He finally acquired the majority of the stock in the Gallatin Milling Company. The mill has a capacity of one hundred and fifty barrels of flour per day, is a modern and up-to-date institution, and its products are shipped throughout the state. At the present writing over sixty thousand bushels of wheat are stored ready for the grinding, besides a large amount of corn and other grains, these figures indicating the extent of the business. Mr. Wile is also a stockholder and director in the First National Bank of Gallatin.

He was married in January, 1899, to Bettie Abraham. She is a native of the state of Mississippi, and they are the parents of one child, named Simon A., now nine years old. The family are communicants of the Jewish church, while Mr. Wile is affiliated with the Masons and the Knights of Pythias, being past chancellor commander of the latter order and for some years has taken an active part in the work of the order. In politics he is a Democrat.

THOMAS Y. CARTER, M. D.   All of the efforts of Dr. Thomas Y. Carter are centered in the profession for which nature and education have fitted him—the practice of medicine. This concentration of effort has rendered his skill and ability unusually effective and has resulted in a high degree of efficiency in his work.

Dr. Carter was born in Sumner county, Tennessee, November 22, 1879, the only child of J. A. and Alice (McDole) Carter, both of whom are now living in that county. Born in Virginia in 1848, Dr. Carter's father in his early youth came with his parents to Tennessee, where he has been very successful in his agricultural pursuits. Politically, he is a Democrat, and has served as steward in the Methodist Episcopal church. Dr. Carter's mother was born in Sumner county in 1856.

A Virginian by birth, Thomas Carter, paternal grandfather of Dr. Carter, came to Tennessee about 1850, where he bought a large portion of land, and at the time of his death was the owner of six hundred or seven hundred acres. The maternal grandfather of Dr. Carter, F. A. J. McDole, was also a native of Virginia and a successful farmer, who came to Tennessee from Kentucky.

Choosing the medical profession as his life work, Dr. Carter pursued his studies at Bowling Green, Kentucky, and Vanderbilt University, Nashville, graduating from the latter institution in 1905. Since then he has been practicing medicine in Westmoreland, where he is held in the highest esteem and where the undivided attention he gives his work is much appreciated.

Dr. Carter's marriage to Lillian Foster occurred in June, 1910. She is a daughter of W. B. Foster, a lumberman of Allen county, Kentucky. One child, Annie Joe, fourteen months old, has been born to bless the union of Dr. and Mrs. Carter. The doctor and his wife are members of the Methodist Episcopal church, and he belongs to the I. O. O. F., M. W. A., and W. O. W., and is a member of the county, state, South Medical and American Medical associations.

Exclusively devoted to his chosen profession, Dr. Carter has been eminently successful from the beginning and enjoys a very large and lucrative practice. The attention he gives his patients is not a perfunctory service, but is characteristic of the whole hearted manner in which he applies himself to his work.

JOHN M. HODGES.   An important factor in any community is the banker. To him the patrons of his institution and others look for guidance in their financial affairs and upon the advice, which his investing experience enables him to offer, they often make decisions regarding their own problems. The stability of a bank is largely measured by the character and conservatism, the wisdom and experience of its officers and directors. As cashier of the Westmoreland Bank, Mr. Hodges stands for all that is most desirable in an institution of this kind, and conducts its affairs in a manner that gains the confidence of the people in general, who feel that he is a man whose judgment can be relied upon both in the investment of the funds of the bank and in assistance rendered its patrons. In the esteem of those with whom he has had direct business relations, he stands very high.

Born in Sumner county, Tennessee, November 20, 1875, Mr. Hodges is a son of C. W. and Sophia (Martin) Hodges, both of whom were born in that county, the former in 1853 and the latter in 1858. C. W. Hodges, like his ancestors, belongs to that class of tillers of the soil who have found in farming both a profitable and satisfying occupation. Well known in his community and very prosperous, he now lives on his farm in his native county, where he raises wheat, corn, oats and tobacco. To him and his wife were born three children: John M., the subject of this sketch; Belle, the wife of C. C. Brown, a farmer of Sumner county; and Thurman T., who died in 1912. C. W. Hodges is a member of the Methodist Episcopal church, and his fraternal affiliations are with the F. & A. M. and I. O. O. F., belonging to Bethpage Lodge, No. 521, F. & A. M. He is a Democrat in politics and has served as justice of the peace.

The Hodges were among the first settlers in Tennessee, coming from Virginia at a very early date, and the family is one of the oldest in the state. Samuel W. Hodges, father of C. W. Hodges and grandfather of John M. Hodges, was a well known and successful farmer and slave owner of Sumner county, who served under Jackson in the Seminole Indian war. In this county also John M. Hodges' maternal grandfather, Lewis L. Martin, was born and lived the life of a prosperous farmer.

John M. Hodges was educated in the public schools of his native county and later took a college course at Bethpage. The fourteen years of his pedagogical experience following fitted him well for the office he was to hold later, for in the study of human nature which teaching involves, he learned much of incalculable value in any business pursuit where insight is required.

In January, 1907, John M. Hodges was elected assistant cashier of the Westmoreland Bank, and in September of the same year cashier, which office he is holding at the present time. This bank has a capital of $8,000 and surplus and undivided profits of $1,000, and its average deposits amount to $50,000. In conducting the affairs of this bank, Mr. Hodges' prudence, insight and wisdom have been apparent on many occasions. He is justice of the peace and a member of the county Democratic executive committee, and has served as auditor of the county officers' books. Belonging to the Methodist Episcopal church, and in politics a Democrat, his fraternal affiliations are with the F. & A. M. as past master, the I. O. O. F. as past grand, the Jr. O. U. A. M. as past councillor and the M. W. of A. as deputy head consul, being also a member of the O. E. S.

The marriage of Mr. Hodges to Carrie Bradley occurred in September, 1898, she being a daughter of J. W. Bradley, a prosperous farmer

of Sumner county, now retired, who served for a period of four years
in the Confederate army. To the union of Mr. and Mrs. Hodges were
born five children: Joy and Virgil, Paul, Eve and Eva May, twins, in
school, and Wayne, the baby.

Mr. Hodges' resourcefulness and his ability to meet in a masterful
way every contingency which has arisen have marked him as a self-reliant
man. His business integrity, character, ability and personality have
made him most highly esteemed and respected among his fellow men.
He is a self-made man in every sense of the word.

, HON JAMES H. BATE. Former state senator from Sumner county, the
Hon. James H. Bate well upholds the prestige and dignity of a family
which has been notable in Tennessee history for the greater part of a
century. Men of this name have held many high posts in the local and
state affairs, one of them being governor and others distinguished in
military service. James H. Bate, himself, had a gallant record as a
soldier, and was the captain of his company during the Civil war. A
number of years he spent in Texas, but he has returned to Sumner
county to pass the declining years, of his life, and he now has a comfortable farmstead at Castalian Springs, the old homestead of the
family.

James H. Bate was born in Sumner county, Tennessee, October 16,
1841. He is a son of James and Amanda F. (Weathered) Bate. Grandfather Humphrey Bate was a native of North Carolina and he came to
Tennessee with his family and became one of the early settlers and
farmers of Sumner county, where he spent the remainder of his life.
Closely related to the Bate family is the Brimage family. They came
from England, and one of the family, Wm. Brimage, served as governor
of the Island of Bermuda under appointment from King George III
after which he settled in North Carolina.

James Bate, the father, was born in North Carolina, and during
young manhood came to Tennessee, where he died in 1842, having spent
many years in Sumner county. His business was that of farming, and he
owned a large acreage and managed his plantation with slave labor. He
was a captain in the Tennessee State Militia. His wife, Amanda Bate,
was a daughter of William Weathered, who was a Virginian, and came
from that commonwealth into Tennessee. He was one of the successful
farmers of this state in the early days. James Bate and wife were the
parents of four children, some of whom are distinguished. William B.
was formerly United States senator and also governor of Tennessee.
Capt. Humphrey Bate, the second son, was killed at the battle of Shiloh
while in the command of his company. Elizabeth P., the only daughter,
became the wife of Major E. P. Tyree, who was a major in the service
during the Civil war. The other is James H. Bate, the subject of this
sketch.

The last named received his education in the Rural Academy of Sumner county, after which he spent two years in Bethany College, of West Virginia, the famous old school in the Pan Handle of that state, established by Alexander Campbell, the founder of the Christian denomination. The outbreak of the Civil war found him in pursuit of knowledge at this institution and he at once entered the army as a private, but in 1863 was made captain. He was first under fire at Aquia Creek, also fought at the first battle of Manassas, and was in the first regiment to reenlist for service. As a veteran he participated in the battle of Chickamauga, the battle of Missionary Ridge and several other of the important engagements which marked the struggles of the northern and southern armies in the southern half of the Confederacy. His experience as a soldier continued for four years, during the entire period of the war.

After returning from the field of battle, his home for five years was in Memphis, where he was employed as a collector for one of the wealthy men of the city. This was followed by a farming experience, after which he went to El Paso, Texas, being a passenger on the first railroad train run into that city, which was in about 1881. He has the distinction of having constructed the first international street railroad in the state of Texas, and edited one of the first papers in the western part of that state. During his residence of five years in Texas he accumulated a good deal of money by his different ventures, and then returned to Sumner county, which has been his home to the present time. He is the owner of three hundred acres of land comprising the old Bate homestead near Castilian Springs. The old place where he was born and with which are connected so many family associations was built in 1840.

Mr. Bate was married in 1897 to Rebecca Allen, the daughter of Van Allen, who was one of the prosperous farmers of Sumner county. The two sons of their marriage are William B. and Francis X., both of whom are school boys. Mrs. Bate is a member of the Presbyterian church, while his church is the Baptist. Politically he is a Democrat, and in 1897 represented the county in the lower house of the legislature, and in 1898 was returned as a state senator.

HON. MARCUS D. RICKMAN, of Hartsville, farmer, miller and member of the state legislature, is a native son of Tennessee and a descendant of two of the state's most worthy pioneer families. His paternal grandfather, Mark Rickman, was a native of North Carolina. During the Revolutionary war he served under Gen. Nathaniel Greene, and at the close of that conflict received a grant of land in Tennessee for his military services. He removed to Tennessee in 1787, and his daughter, Nancy Rickman, was the first female white child born in the city of Nashville. His son, Samuel H., the father of Marcus D., was born in Sumner county, Tennessee, in 1805, and passed his life upon the farm where he was born, his death occurring in 1892. He was a successful man and at one time was the owner of about fifty negroes. He served as colonel in the state militia, was widely known, popular and well respected, was a Democrat in his political convictions, and a member of the Methodist Episcopal church. He married Frances E. Henry, a native of Sumner county, where she was born in 1829, a daughter of Jack H. Henry, also a native of that county, and a granddaughter of William Henry, who came to Tennessee from Virginia when the region now included in Sumner county was a wilderness. The only settlement of consequence in that section of the state at that time was the one at Castalian Springs. The Henry family is of Irish extraction. Jack H. Henry served in the Seminole war. He was a Methodist Episcopal minister for many years and died at the age of eighty-two years. Ten children were born to Samuel H. and Frances E. Rickman, five of whom are still living. The mother died in 1897. Like her husband and father, she was a devout member of the Methodist Episcopal church and was popular among her neighbors for her many little acts of Christian charity.

Marcus D. Rickman, the second child of the family, was born in Sumner county, Tennessee, August 18, 1849. He was educated in the public schools of his native county and began life on the farm. About 1880 he embarked in the sawmilling business, and in 1896 he built a model flour mill with a capacity of one hundred barrels of flour daily. In connection with this mill he also operates a corn mill and ships meal and flour to all the territory within reach of Hartsville. Notwithstanding his active operations as a miller, he has always retained his interest in agriculture. Although he is classed as a Democrat, he is rather inclined to be independent in his political views. Since he was twenty-two years of age he has served as a magistrate. In 1909 he was elected a member of the state legislature, and in 1912 was reelected. While in the legislature he served upon the important committees on agriculture, redistricting the state for members of the general assembly, and banking and commerce. To the office of legislator he brought the same careful methods that have distinguished him in his conduct of his private affairs, and the interests of his constituents were always faithfully guarded in the support of bills that would promote their general prosperity or the defeat of measures that he regarded as inimical to their welfare. Mr. Rickman is a member of the Masonic fraternity and has served his lodge as worshipful master. The teachings of this time-honored order form the basis of his ideals of good citizenship, and the tenets of brotherly love, relief and truth constitute a guide for his daily life and relations with his fellow men. He and his estimable wife are both members of the Methodist Episcopal church.

In 1873 Mr. Rickman married Miss Ella Mills, a daughter of Lewis G. Mills, a lifelong farmer of Sumner county. Two children have been born to this marriage. Mattie L. is now the wife of H. C. Smith, of Nashville, and Roy M. is associated with his father in the milling business.

NATHAN GREEN, LL.D. There is probably no better known name in the legal circles of the South than that of Judge Nathan Green, for fifty-seven years identified with the law department of Cumberland University, that illustrious institution where so many of America's most prominent men have received their legal education, his last twelve years' service being as dean of the law department. His father, for a number of years a professor of Cumberland University law department, and one of the most eminent jurists of Tennessee, was a supreme court judge twenty-five years, and was chancellor of this state for several years. Judge Grafton Green, only son of the subject of this sketch, is now one of the presiding judges on the supreme bench of Tennessee. For more than a half century Judge Nathan Green has had a large part in shaping the character of the legal talent of Tennessee, which is of an exceptionally high order, and for emulation he has given to the thousands of students that have come under his charge the example of an upright life, of talents employed to their fullest extent in useful, worthy and noble service for the advancement of humanity, and of a citizenship that in all its phases has marked him as one of America's noblemen. Now eighty-six years of age, the gloom of the deepening shadows of his life's twilight is dispelled by the consciousness of a life well spent and by the wealth of sincere and devoted friendships which are his.

The Greens come of Virginia Revolutionary stock and have borne a prominent part in the military life of our country as well as in law, having been represented in the Revolution, the second struggle for American independence, the Mexican war and the Civil war.

Judge Nathan Green was born in Franklin county, Tennessee, February 19, 1827, a son of Nathan and Mary (Feild) Green. The father, a Virginian by nativity, was born in 1792 and died in Lebanon, Tennessee, in 1866. The mother, born in North Carolina in 1792, was a daughter of James Field, a lifelong resident of North Carolina, and her death occurred in 1849. The senior Nathan Green grew to manhoood in Virginia and received his education there, including his preparation for the profession he followed throughout life and in which he became so eminent, that of law. He came to Tennessee in 1812 and it was not long afterward until he became chancellor of the state, subsequently serving from 1827 to 1852 as a judge of the supreme court of this state. He was yet filling that honorable position when he resigned to take a professorship in the law department of Cumberland University, with which institution he was thereafter identified until his death. He was first a Whig and then a Democrat in political sentiment, was identified fraternally with the Masonic order, and was a soldier in the war of 1812. He and his wife were both devoted members of the Cumberland Presbyterian church and he was also an elder of his church. Of the eight children that came to their union, our subject is the only one yet living. Their eldest son, one of the brave, aggressive and distinguished Confed-

erate soldiers of the Civil war, is mentioned in the Confederate Military History as follows:

"Brig.-Gen. Thomas Green, beloved and honored by everybody as a man, the chevalier of Texas soldiery, whose training as a soldier was commenced at San Jacinto and was perfected as captain of cavalry in Indian warfare and at Monterey in Mexico, and whose flag floated in the ascendant in every battle in Texas, Louisiana and New Mexico where his sword was drawn, determined to capture the enemy's gunboats on Red river. In the attempt at Blair's Landing, April 12, 1864, his valuable life was given to his country, on the banks of the river, while leading his men to the onset. His name had been a household word in Texas, and his fame is still cherished in memory throughout the state that he honored in his life." Major-General Banks, commanding the Federal army during that engagement, in his report to General Sherman, said: "General Green was killed by the fire of the gunboats of the 12th; he was the ablest officer in their service."

Thomas Green, the grandfather of him of whom we write, was also a native Virginian, a very wealthy planter of that state, and served in the patriot army during the Revolution.

Judge Nathan Green was educated in Cumberland University and was graduated from the liberal arts department in 1845, with high honors. In 1847 he was one of the first seven students to enter the law department of Cumberland University, this department being established Jan. 9, 1847, by Judge Abraham Caruthers, who resigned a seat on the State bench to accept the position. Judge Green graduated from the law school in 1849, and in 1845 his father, Judge N. Green, Sr., resigned a seat on the State bench and responded to an urgent call from Judge Caruthers to assist him with the work of the law department. Shortly thereafter in 1856 Lebanon's honored citizen was elected a professor of law in the law department, which position he has held continuously ever since, and today has the honor and distinction of being the oldest teachers in the state. The three gentlemen mentioned above continued as the faculty of the law department until the breaking out of the war in 1861.

Judge Green was among the first to respond to the call of arms, and a braver and more courageous man never shouldered a musket than was he, and his war record is one any man would be proud of. He soon distinguished himself by his bravery and daring, and won immediate recognition from his superiors in rank. He was made an adjutant general and staff officer under Gen. A. P. Stewart during the early part of the war. During the latter part of the war he served as superintendent of the engineering works and came through the entire conflict unscathed.

Immediately after the close of the war Judge Green came back to Lebanon and to his great sorrow found his alma mater in ashes. The fine college building located in the southern part of Lebanon in the center of a large campus was used during the war as barracks for the soldiers. A Confederate soldier, who had attended the college, became incensed at it being occupied by negroes, filled one room with cedar rails one night and applied the torch, destroying the entire property. Undaunted by the great disaster that had befallen his alma mater, Judge Green immediately set about to re-establish the school, which he succeeded in doing under great difficulties and got together about twenty students, all of whom were either Confederate or Federal soldiers, and among that number was Judge Horace Lurton and Capt. R. P. McClain, a prominent member of the Lebanon bar here.

In 1866 Judge Green, Sr., died and Hon. Henry Cooper succeeded to his position. Judge Cooper resigned in 1868 when Judge Robt. L. Caruthers was called to the position, and he, too, resigned a seat on the Supreme Bench. Judge Caruthers resigned in 1881 and died the following year and was succeeded to the professorship in the law school by Dr. Andrew B. Martin, and he, together with Judge Green, has conducted the school continuously ever since. Judge Green is the oldest teacher in the State of Tennessee and has the distinction and honor of having taught more law students than any other living man. In numerous instances has he taught both the father and in after years his son. Cumberland University has the honor of having had more men to graduate from its Law Department that have made themselves prominent and famous in the affairs of both Nation and State than any other institution in the country, and today its graduates are to be found in both branches of Congress and on the Supreme benches of Tennessee, Alabama, Florida, Texas, Arkansas, Missouri, North Carolina, Oregon and Montana. Judge Green was also chancellor of the university from 1873 until he resigned from the position in 1900. Nature was kind to him in her bestowal of a most vigorous intellect and that faculty which grasps as it were by intuition, the salient points of any subject presented for consideration. He has always been a man of liberal and broad views, of genial disposition and generous impulses, and of spotless integrity. In all the relations of life he has honorably and faithfully performed his duty. In political affairs he has always been an adherent of the Democratic party, and like his father, he has long been affiliated with the Masonic fraternity. He has also attained prominence as a litterateur through the authorship of two books, ''The Tall Man of Winton'' and ''Sparks from a Back Log,'' both of much literary merit and of large circulation.

Judge Green has been twice married. In 1850 he wedded Miss Betty McClain, daughter of J. S. McClain, and of the children of this union three are living: Ella, the wife of Judge W. Caldwell, of West

Tennessee; Mattie, who became Mrs. Reagan Houston, and resides in San Antonio, Texas; and Grafton Green, a graduate of Cumberland University, and who as judge of the supreme court of Tennessee is ably upholding the remarkable prestige of the family name for legal ability and attainment. The wife and mother died July 4, 1893. She was a valued member of the Cumberland Presbyterian church. In 1902 Judge Green married Miss Blanche Woodward, who passed away in 1910. He is a member of the Presbyterian church, U. S. A., and is an elder of his church at Lebanon.

Judge Green's old colonial home, one of the handsomest in Lebanon, was destroyed by fire several years ago, which came as a severe blow to him owing to the fact that many tender memories associated with the old building, which has since been replaced with a handsome modern brick bungalow. Judge Green is a lover of the beautiful, both in nature and life, and very fond of flowers, dahlias and sweet peas being his favorites, and his favorite pastime in the morning and afternoon is working his flowers in his flower garden near the house.

The 1912 graduating law class presented the university with life-size portraits of both Judge Green and Dr. Martin, which were hung on either side of the stage at Caruthers Hall and between which hangs a life-size portrait of Judge Abraham Caruthers, founder of the Lebanon Law School, presented to the university by Judge Green a number of years ago. The young men of the 1913 law class recently presented Judge Green with a handsome silver loving cup on the occasion of the celebration of his eighty-sixth birthday. On the same day the members of the Sunday school of the Presbyterian church surprised him with a delightful reception held in his honor in the main auditorium of the church.

Such is the brief review of one of the most eminent and respected of Tennessee's citizens. His life has been one of noble ambition and character, of superior intellect and education fittingly applied in all his endeavors and has made a deep impress for noble manhood and unfaltering integrity upon the annals of Tennessee. In conclusion is quoted a paragraph that recently appeared in a Tennessee paper:

Though Lebanon's most honored and revered citizen has already passed the eighty-sixth milestone in the path of life, yet to look at his erect and dignified bearing and manner both in public and private life, every movement of which bespeaks the refinement and bearing of a true Southern gentleman, one would easily judge him to be many years younger than he really is and for the past twenty years there has been no appreciable or noticeable lessening in his vigor and vitality, and his friends here and over the entire United States, who are legion, wish for him that the hourglass of life has yet many, many more years of life allotted him before it has run its course and that the days and hours of which may be filled with unalloyed happiness, pleasure and contentment, which he so richly deserves.

JOSEPH E. FAUST. A large number of the Tennessee pioneers came from Virginia. Among them were Joseph and Betsy Faust, who settled on a farm and there passed the remainder of their lives. They were of German extraction, industrious and frugal, and assisted in reclaiming the land from the wilderness. Their son, Joseph E. Faust, was born in Wilson county, Tennessee, August 5, 1824, received such an education as the schools of that early day afforded, and learned the trade of mill-wright. His life was passed in Wilson, Smith and Macon counties, where he was regarded as a useful citizen and a measurably successful man, though he suffered severe losses from floods in 1865 and 1882. He was a Democrat in his political belief and a member of the Masonic fraternity. His death occurred in Macon county in April, 1905. He married Mary Kearley, who was born in Smith county, Tennessee, in 1838, the daughter of William Kearley, a prominent physician and farmer and one of the well-to-do men of that day. She died in October, 1912, at Lafayette. Seven children born to Joseph E. and Mary (Kearley) Faust are still living, viz; John B., a miller at Lafayette; Ada, wife of W. L. Chamberlain, of Lafayette; Thos. E., an attorney of Lafayette; Nettie, wife of James Loftis, of Cookville; Dr. William D., who is practicing his profession at Ada, Oklahoma; Joseph E., the immediate subject of this review; Oscar L., who is engaged in the lumber business at Memphis.

Joseph E. Faust, son of Joseph E. and Mary Faust, was born in Smith county, Tennessee, January 18, 1868. After attending the common schools of Macon and Trousdale counties he matriculated in the law department of Cumberland University, where he was graduated with the class of 1890. Shortly after receiving his degree he began the practice of his profession at Hartsville, Tennessee, where he is still located. By close attention to his business and a conscientious discharge of his duties to his clients he has succeeded in building up a lucrative practice, which extends to all the state and Federal courts. While he has many friends among his brother attorneys, he has never formed a partnership with any one, preferring to conduct his cases in his own way. In this way he has developed a strong, self-reliant character that has placed him among the leading members of the local bar.

Mr. Faust is a firm believer in the principles and policies of the Democratic party, and in every campaign for several years he has rendered that party efficient service as a public speaker. He has served three terms in the state legislature, where he was always on the alert with regard to measures that would further the interests of his constituents, and he has also filled the position of clerk of the chancery court. But in whatever capacity he has been called to serve—as lawyer, legislator or public official—he has never shirked his duty. Beginning life with small means, without the aid of influential friends or favoritism in any way, he has achieved success through his own efforts and a careful consideration of the rights of his fellow men.

Mr. Faust's fraternal relations are with the Independent Order of Odd Fellows and the Knights of Pythias. In the latter order he has passed through the chairs and is a past chancellor. In church matters he has adopted the faith of his mother and holds membership in the Baptist church.

In February, 1891, Mr. Faust married Miss Fannie Allan, daughter of Arch. Allan, a prominent citizen of Trousdale county, where he was engaged in the livery business. He served several terms as sheriff of the county and as township trustee, and was also engaged as a mail contractor. Mr. and Mrs. Faust are the parents of the following children: Allan, Lizzie, Rupert, Ethel Frances and Mary H. All are attending· school except the eldest and youngest.

LYTLE DALTON. Back in the colonial days the English government gave a grant of land in Tennessee to Lord Dalton. This grant he transferred to his sons, who settled in what is now Sumner county, and they became the founders of the Dalton family in Tennessee. About the beginning of the nineteenth century a man named Ball came from Virginia to Tennessee with his family. His son, Lytle Ball, who was born at Hartsville in the year 1820, married Eliza Ann Holt, and this couple were the maternal grandparents of the subject of this sketch. Lytle Ball was a farmer all his life and for forty years held the office of constable. The paternal grandparents, R. C. and Mary S. (Carson) Dalton, were born in Tennessee. The grandmother is still living near Hartsville at the age of ninety-four years, and is active for one of her age. J. R. Dalton, the father of Lytle Dalton, was born and reared in Trousdale county, Tennessee. During the Civil war he served for three years as a member of General Forrest's celebrated cavalry command, being twice wounded while in the service. At the close of the war he returned home and resumed his vocation of farmer. He married Agnes Ball, a native of Trousdale county, and to this union were born twelve children, eleven of whom are still living. In 1905 the parents removed to Oklahoma, where they at present reside, retired from active business cares and enjoying the fruits of their labors of former years. J. R. Dalton has been a lifelong Democrat in his political opinions, but was never an aspirant for public honors. His wife is a member of the Methodist Episcopal church.

Lytle Dalton was born near Hartsville, Tennessee, March 4, 1869, the day President Grant was inaugurated for the first time. He was educated in the public schools and at the Hartsville Masonic Institute, after which he taught for six years in the public schools. His work as a teacher commended him to the authorities, and in 1900 he was elected county superintendent, which office he held for six years, when he resigned. By his own efforts he has achieved success in a financial way, and is universally recognized as "a man of affairs." He owns a fine farm of four hundred acres, as well as property in the city of Hartsville, holds stock in both the banks of that city, and is a director in the Bank of Hartsville.

Upon arriving at his majority Mr. Dalton adopted the political faith of his honored father and cast his lot with the Democratic party. His fidelity to Democratic principles and his activity in winning victories for his party marked him as a leader, and in 1906 he was elected to the office of county court clerk. It was this election that caused his resignation as county superintendent of schools. At the close of his first term as county clerk he was reelected and is now serving his second term. Whether as private citizen, teacher, superintendent of schools, or clerk of the court, Mr. Dalton has always been diligent and conscientious in the discharge of his duties, and his reelection was but the natural reward of his faithfulness and executive ability. Mr. Dalton is a Knight of Pythias and a past chancellor of his lodge.

In 1905 he married Miss Ada, daughter of Henry Dalton, a farmer of Trousdale county, and they have two children—Lillian and Lois. Mr. and Mrs. Dalton are both members of the Christian church.

EDWIN S. PAYNE. Shakespeare tells us that "Some men are born great, some achieve greatness, and some have greatness thrust upon them." Whatever degree of greatness or success that may have come to Edwin S. Payne has been the result of his own well directed efforts and the exercise of sound business judgment and sagacity. He was born in that part of Sumner county, Tennessee, which now constitutes Trousdale county, April 30, 1844, a son of Edwin L. and Sallie D. (McAllester) Payne. His father was born in Culpeper county, Virginia, in 1812, came with his parents to Tennessee in 1818 and passed the remainder of his life in that state, his death occurring in 1872. He was twice married. His first wife was a Miss Haynes, and to this union four children were born, all now deceased. After her death he married Sallie D. McAllester and this marriage was blessed with eight children, five of whom are yet living, the subject of this sketch being the second in the order of birth. The mother of these children was born in Smith county, Tennessee, and died in Trousdale county, Tennessee. Mr. Payne knows but very little regarding his paternal ancestry further than that his father was a lifelong Democrat in his political affiliations and for a number of years held the office of magistrate. He was a quiet, unostentatious farmer all his life, and a member of the Methodist Episcopal church, his second wife having been a Baptist. Garland McAllester, Mr. Payne's maternal grandfather, was an early settler of Tennessee. He married a Miss Flower. Both grandfathers were slaveholders prior to the Civil war.

Edwin S. Payne's early life was that of the average farmer's son. The summer months were passed in assisting in the farm work, and in the winter seasons he attended the country schools, where by close application to his studies he managed to acquire a good, practical education.

At the age of seventeen years he enlisted in Company D, Second Tennessee Confederate Cavalry, and served with that organization for nearly four years, taking part in the battles of Shiloh, Iuka, and a number of other engagements. He was paroled at Gainesville, Alabama, May 11, 1865, and returned home to build up his shattered fortunes. At that time his total capital consisted of $1.35, but with courage and determination he went to work upon the farm, where he continued for two years. He then accepted a position as clerk in a store and followed that occupation for two years, at the end of which time he went into a small store with his father. Here he laid the foundation of his fortune. From that time to the present he has been interested in mercantile pursuits, and for forty-three years he has occupied the same site at Castalian Springs, where he has a large and well assorted stock of general merchandise, and is regarded as one of the successful merchants of that section. He is also extensively interested in farming operations. His first purchase of land was that of one and three-fourths acres, but he now owns an excellent farm of 550 acres in one body, having recently sold two hundred acres. Mr. Payne was for several years president of the People's National Bank, and is now one of the directors of that institution. He holds stock in the Montgomery & Moore Company and the Armistead-McKinney Company, of Nashville, and is also one of the stockholders in the Willard Tobacco Company. In addition to these holdings he owns property in the city of Gallatin, Tennessee, and is considered by those who know him best to be one of the wealthiest men in Trousdale county. In the accumulation of his fortune he has been guided by principles of fairness and square dealing, believing that ''A good name is greater than great riches.''

Mr. Payne is a member of the Masonic fraternity and has been honored by being elected worshipful master of his lodge. He is a stanch supporter of the Democratic party and its principles, but has never been an aspirant for public office.

In 1872 Mr. Payne was united in marriage with Miss Ellen, daughter of Baxter Lipscom, one of the pioneers of Sumner county, Tennessee, and to this union were born four children, two of whom are yet living, Thomas S., residing in Nashville, and Henry C. in California. Mrs. Payne died November 27, 1897, and on April 24, 1900, Mr. Payne married for his second wife Mrs. John T. Reynolds, who was Miss Lizzie Martin, of Maury county, Tennessee. Three children have come to bless this second marriage. Allie May and Lewis Carr are attending school, and Frayola F., three years old, is the baby of the family. Mrs. Payne is a member of the Cumberland Presbyterian church.

HUMPHREY BATE, M. D. For a period of about forty-five years Sumner county has had the services in professional capacity of a father and son named Bate. The family name has many other distinctions to make it notable in local history, and in good citizenship, in business and military life the members of the family have always made good records. The present Dr. Bate well upholds the high standing of the family, and is one of the leadiig practitioners of medicine in the county.

Dr. Humphrey Bate was born in Sumner county, May 25, 1875, a son of Humphrey H. and Nancy (Simpson) Bate. The maternal grandfather Simpson came from his native state of North Carolina into Sumner county, Tennessee, as one of the early settlers. The paternal grandfather, Humphrey Bate, also came from North Carolina, and spent most of his active life on a farm in Sumner county. He had the distinction of being the first master of the Masonic lodge at Hartsville.

The education begun in the common schools of Sumner county, Dr. Bate continued in the University of Tennessee and was graduated in medicine from the University of Nashville in 1897. His medical practice began soon after, but in 1898, at the outbreak of the Spanish-American war, he entered the United States army as surgeon and continued until the close of the war. All his time is devoted to the demands of a large and lucrative practice. He is a member of the county and state medical societies, and has a nice farm property near his residence at Castalian Springs.

Dr. Bate was married in 1898 to Miss Gertrude Brown, a daughter of C. H. Brown, who is a retired farmer now living in Gallatin. Dr. Bate by his first wife had two children, namely: Nell and Edna, both of whom live in Gallatin. Mrs. Bate, the mother of these daughters, died in 1909. She was a member of the Christian church. In June, 1910, Dr. Bate was united in marriage with Miss Ethel Hesson, a daughter of Harvey Hesson, who was born in Smith county, this state. By this marriage there is one child, Alcyone. Mrs. Bate has membership with the Baptist church. Dr. Bate is a Democrat, but takes no active part in politics.

ANDREW J. SPARKMAN. The organizer of the Farmers & Merchants Bank of Bethpage, of which he is now cashier, Mr. Sparkman is one of the vigorous and enterprising business men of Sumner county. He has been farmer, banker and public official, and his career up to middle life contains all the elements of substantial success.

On the paternal side the Sparkman family originated in Ireland, where the great-grandfather of the Bethpage banker was born. Coming from that country, he settled first in North Carolina and then in Tennessee. The grandfather, whose name was George Sparkman, was born in North Carolina, whence he came to Tennessee with his parents and spent his life in this state as a farmer. During his time and among his contemporaries, he was one of the wealthiest men in Van Buren county. The largest slave owner in his section, he used their labor in the cultivation of his broad estate of a thousand acres. Besides raising all the crops of the fields, he specialized in stock. His family consisted of ten or twelve children, and to each of them as they grew up he gave a fine estate, so that each one was comfortably fixed at the beginning of his career. On the maternal side the grandfather was Solomon Sparkman, of North Carolina, whence he came to Tennessee at an early day, and the maiden name of his wife was Goddard. She attained to the great age of one hundred and two years.

The father of Mr. Sparkman was long a successful farmer in Van Buren county. His name was Solomon Sparkman, and he was born in Van Buren county in 1842, and died in 1904. His wife, Martha Jane (Sparkman) Sparkman, was born in 1844 and died in 1907. During the Civil war he favored the Confederate cause, but instead of going to the front on actual military duty he remained at home and assisted in the manufacture of ammunition, which was just as necessary to the service as that of carrying a musket. He and his wife were parents of eight children, four of whom are now living, named: Moses, Andrew, George and Wiley. The old homestead in Van Buren county is still owned by three of these sons, who bought out the other heirs. The parents were both members of the Baptist church, and in politics the father was an independent.

Andrew J. Sparkman was born in Van Buren county, Tennessee, March 20, 1872. Reared in the country, at an early age he determined to acquire a better than ordinary education. In order to pay his way through Burritt College at Spencer, where he was graduated in 1897, he worked for some time as janitor, this service paying his tuition there. He also taught school for four years, and then for a year was at work on a farm. His next promotion in life was his election to the office of county court clerk of Van Buren county, a position in which he rendered efficient service for eight years. From this state he then moved out to California, from there came back as far as Oklahoma, where he bought a farm. Then in 1909, locating at Gallatin, he purchased the Judge B. D. Bell place. In the same year he bought the old James Head farm, which he sold in 1910. The latter year he undertook the organization at Bethpage of the Farmers & Merchants Bank, of which he has since been cashier. This is one of the solid institutions of Sumner county, and has had a very prosperous career during its first two or three years existence. There is at the present time a surplus of $10,000 with profits of $2,500, and the deposits amount to more than $40,000. During his residence in East Tennessee Mr. Sparkman dealt to a considerable extent in coal lands, and his career has been a money-making one in nearly every venture which he has taken up.

He is active in Democratic politics, although he is at the present time not an aspirant for any official honors. His fraternal affiliation is with the Independent Order of Odd Fellows, while he and his wife are members of the Baptist church.

In 1900 occurred his marriage to Miss Myra Safley, a daughter of

Lawson Safley, who was a farmer of Warren county for many years and in connection with his agriculture was a minister of the Baptist church.

RICHARD C. OWEN. One of the representative business men of Hartsville is Richard C. Owen, who is the proprietor of a large tobacco manufactory and an active public spirited citizen. He is one of the fourth generation to reside in Tennessee, his great-grandfather having come from North Carolina at an early date and settled in Williamson county. His grandfather, Richard C. Owen, for whom he was named, and his father, Robert Owen, were both born in Tennessee and there passed their entire lives. Robert Owen was born in Williamson county in 1840. He was wounded at the battle of Shiloh and after some time in the hospital returned to his farm in Rutherford county, where he became interested in the tobacco business. He was successful in his business ventures and left an estate valued at some $50,000 upon his death in 1909. He married Miss Powell Dobson, a daughter of Baker Dobson, both she and her father having been born in Williamson county, Tennessee, and to this union were born five children, two deceased, the subject of this sketch being the second in order of birth. Henrietta married Robert Brown and lives in Rutherford county, Tennessee, and Mary married Condon Covington and resides in Williamson county. The mother of these children is a member of the Baptist church, to which her husband also belonged during his lifetime. He was also a member of the Masonic fraternity.

Richard C. Owen was born in Rutherford county, Tennessee, July 28, 1870. He was educated at Eagleville, Tennessee, and upon arriving at manhood embarked in the tobacco business, which he has successfully followed from that time to the present. The Owen family is of Welsh descent, and from his Welsh ancestors Mr. Owen has inherited those traits of industry and foresight which have contributed in no small degree to his financial success. For several years he was at the head of a tobacco company at Eagleville, but in 1904 he removed to Hartsville, where he established his present factory. Here he uses from four hundred thousand to five hundred thousand pounds of leaf tobacco every year and places upon the market eight different brands of manufactured tobacco. Every process of manufacture is constantly under his personal supervision and great care is exercised to see that his goods are kept up to the proper standard. The result of this policy is a large number of satisfied customers and a steadily increasing patronage. Mr. Owen classes himself as an independent Democrat politically, though he has never been an active political worker. He keeps himself well informed, however, on all questions relating to public policies, and always does his duty, as he sees it, on election day. His fraternal relations are with the Knights of Pythias and he is a member of the Baptist church.

In 1895 Mr. Owen married Miss Anna Bell, daughter of Leonidas D. Bell, a successful farmer of Williamson county and a veteran of the great Civil war. To this union have been born six children—Robert, Hainey, Carter, Dean, Roy and Ralph—all at home with their parents or attending school. Mrs. Owen holds membership in the Christian church.

JOHN E. EDGERTON. It has fallen to the lot of John E. Edgerton to carry on the business of the establishment founded by his brother, Dr. H. K. Edgerton, in Lebanon, Tennessee, in 1909, and he is conducting the activities of the plant of the Lebanon Woolen Mills with a progressiveness and enterprise that bids fair to make it one of the solid and substantial manufacturing concerns of the South. Mr. Edgerton is a native North Carolinian, born in Johnston county, on October 2, 1879, and is the son of Gabriel G. and Harriet (Copeland) Edgerton, both of whom were born in North Carolina.

Mr. G. G. Edgerton was born in 1842, and passed his life in that state, where he was all his days occupied with farming interests and there died in 1897. He was a son of William Edgerton, also a native of the state of North Carolina, and a Quaker, who was interested in the manufacture of cotton and in farming, and was a man of some position in his time. Gabriel and Harriet Edgerton reared a family of nine children, of which number seven are yet living.

As a boy in the home of his parents, John E. Edgerton attended the common schools of North Carolina, and later entered Vanderbilt University, where he took his B. A. degree in 1902 and his master's degree in 1903. Thereafter he taught one year at Castle Heights, in Lebanon, after which he went to Memphis, and taught one year in the University school at that place. His next move took him to Columbia, where he founded the Columbia Military Academy at that place, and there he remained for seven years. His brother, Dr. Edgerton, had in 1909 founded the Lebanon Woolen Mills, with a capital stock of $100,000, and was the first president of that concern, and, indeed, its only president thus far, for he still maintains that important relation to the plant. In 1912 Mr. Edgerton was called from his work in Columbia Military Academy to assume the duties of secretary, treasurer and general manager of the new and flourishing enterprise, and he is now the incumbent of those offices. The concern has experienced a steady and luxuriant growth in the short time of its existence thus far, and gives promise of taking a high rank in manufacturing circles in the South, at its present rate of development. Its trade comes from all sections of the United States, and the output of the factory is being constantly increased to meet the demands of the woolen blanket market.

Mr. Edgerton and his wife are members of the Methodist Episcopal church South. He is a member of his college fraternity, the Kappa

Sigma, and is also affiliated with the Masonic order. He is a Democrat, but finds little time to devote to the politics of the county, the demands of the business of which he is so important a factor making drafts upon his time and energies that permit of no dallying with outside interests.

On December 15, 1909, Mr. Edgerton was united in marriage with Miss Harriet Figuers, the daughter of T. N. Figuers, a successful merchant of Columbia, Tennessee, and one of the more prominent men of that city.

JAMES H. FERGUSON. Among the fine country homesteads in Montgomery county, up near the Kentucky line, is that of James H. Ferguson, who for thirty years or more has been one of the prosperous producers of the staple crops of this locality and a citizen of standing and influence in his community.

Mr. Ferguson was born in Todd county, Kentucky, August 5, 1850, a son of John D. and Nancy M. (Meriwether) Ferguson. Both the Fergusons and Meriwethers have been families of distinction and worth in Todd county for many years. Robert Ferguson, the paternal grandfather, who married a Miss Babcock, was a native of Scotland, who early in the last century came to America and lived in Massachusetts and Virginia and finally in Kentucky, where he died. He was a minister of the Christian church, and his family have furnished several valued servants to that denomination. One of his sons, Jesse B. Ferguson, gained a reputation throughout the South for his power as a preacher. John D. Ferguson, the father, was also a minister of the Christian church. He was born in Massachusetts in 1816, accompanied his parents to Virginia, where he was liberally educated in the William and Mary College, and then took up the work of the church, to which he gave most of his years until his death. He also conducted a farm during his residence in Todd county. His first wife, Nancy Meriwether, was a daughter of Charles N. Meriwether, a Virginian who spent most of his active life in Todd county, Kentucky, where he was a wealthy farmer and stock-raiser. Nancy Ferguson had two children, James H. and Carrie D., who married Douglas Meriwether, and resides in Kentucky. The father's second marriage was to L. Vaughn, and of their three children only one is living, R. V. Ferguson, of Todd county. John D. Ferguson died in 1892, and his first wife passed away in 1857.

After getting the fundamentals of an education in the common schools of his native county, James H. Ferguson took up farming as a regular vocation, and as he has made it a business and devoted the best energies of his lifetime to it his success has been more than ordinary. In 1880 he moved to Montgomery county, Tennessee, where he acquired five hundred and twenty acres. Every year since then his tobacco, corn, wheat and hogs have been no small contribution to the productive resources of this county and have brought him a regular revenue.

In 1877 Mr. Ferguson married Miss Parthena Kimbrough. Her father, Garth Kimbrough, a native of Virginia, settled in Tennessee many years ago, and was one of the successful farmers of the state up to the time of his death. Mr. Ferguson and wife have four children: Mildred C., at home; John D., a resident of Nebraska; Kittie, the wife of T. M. Anderson, who lives on Mr. Ferguson's farm; and James, a daughter, living at home. Mr. and Mrs. Ferguson are members of the Christian church, and he is affiliated with the Elks Lodge No. 601. He has always taken an active interest in local Democratic politics, but has never sought any official honors for herself.

WILLIAM EDGAR JOHNSON. One of the live, wide-awake and progressive business men of Lewis county, Tennessee, is William Edgar Johnson, of Hohenwald, mayor of the town and a successful contractor and builder there who is a worthy representative of Tennessee's energetic younger generation of business men and industrial workers. He was born in Perry county, this state, June 23, 1878, and received his public school education in Maury and Hickman counties, later attending the Dickson Normal College. Since entering upon his independent business career he has been identified with various enterprises, was engaged for a time in the mercantile business at Hohenwald and also in the planing mill business at the same place, and the while was engaged more or less in building and contracting, to which line of business endeavor he now gives his whole attention. He is interested in his work from a personal business standpoint and also because he takes a real pride in what is accomplished in that manner toward the material upbuilding and development of his town and community and he very loyally claims that Hohenwald is one of the livest, most progressive towns of Tennessee. This same spirit is evinced in his activities as mayor of Hohenwald, to which office he was elected in July, 1912, for any project that means the progress and prosperity of the town receives his cordial and hearty support. Mr. Johnson himself owns several fine buildings in Hohenwald, among them being a fine concrete business block, and he is also heavily interested in real estate in Lewis county.

He comes from an energetic and enterprising family that has held a worthy place in the business and industrial circles of this section of Tennessee for upwards of a century. Andrew Jackson Johnson came into Tennessee from his native North Carolina about 1820 and located in Maury county, where he married Median Cook. He was a tanner by trade and had a farm and tan yard in Maury county, from whence he later removed to Hickman county, continuing in the latter location to be extensively engaged in tanning. He was a Confederate soldier during the Civil war and while in that service was captured by the Federals and held a prisoner for some time. After his discharge as a prisoner he went to Arkansas to investigate some properties he owned there and while in that state, which was in 1865, he died of pneumonia at the age of sixty. He and his wife were the parents of four children, the youngest of whom was William Brantly Johnson, the father of William Edgar, born in Maury county, Tennessee in 1850. William Brantly Johnson grew to manhood in Maury county, receiving there but limited educational opportunities as the public school advantages of that day were not such as are afforded the present youth of Tennessee. After his marriage he was engaged in the mercantile business at Sawdust Valley and at Beardston, Perry county, later removing to West Tennessee, where he continued in the same line of business. From there he went to Texas and took up farming, but subsequently returned to Tennessee and passed away in Hohenwald in 1900, at the age of fifty. Politically he was a Democrat, and fraternally he was affiliated with the Masonic order. Both he and his wife were members of the Methodist Episcopal church South. The latter, who was Miss Martha Pipkin before her marriage, was born in Maury county, September 9, 1858, and is yet living, being now a resident of Texas. To these parents were born six children, of whom William Edgar was second in birth and the eldest son and of whom five are now living, namely: William Edgar, our subject; Howard, now a resident of Texas; Jesse, who is located at Hohenwald; Burton, now residing in California; and Maude, whose home is in Texas.

William Edgar Johnson was married September 10, 1902, to Miss Lillian Williams, a daughter of Sep Williams, of Montgomery county, Tennessee. To this union have been born three sons, Malcolm, Edward and Philip. Mr. Johnson is a Democrat in political views, and in a fraternal way is associated as a member of the Hohenwald Lodge No. 607 Free and Accepted Masons and of Hohenwald Lodge No. 293 Independent Order of Odd Fellows.

DR. HOWARD K. EDGERTON, of Lebanon, Tennessee, one of the most prominent and popular physicians of Wilson county, is a native of North Carolina but has spent full twenty years in Lebanon in the useful and noble work of his profession. His value to his community is not limited to that of his medical ability, however, for he is also identified with the commercial life of Lebanon and is recognized as one of the town's most public-spirited and useful citizens. On the side of his paternal progenitors Dr. Edgerton is of English lineage and is descended from May-flower ancestry, three of the Edgertons having been passengers on that famous ship. With the other colonists these immigrants first settled in Massachusetts but later removed to Connecticut, and from thence members of the family migrated South and established the North Carolina branch of the family.

Dr. Edgerton was born in North Carolina on October 22, 1865, a son of Gabriel G. and Harriett (Copeland) Edgerton. The father, born in North Carolina in 1842, passed his life in Johnson county, that state, as a farmer, in which pursuit he was quite successful, and passed away there in 1896. He was a stalwart Democrat in political belief and for a number of years was a commissioner of Johnson county. He was a son of William Edgerton, a North Carolinian by birth and a Quaker who spent his business career as a farmer and cotton manufacturer and was a man of substance for his day. Harriett (Copeland) Edgerton, born in 1844 in North Carolina, was also of English descent. She departed life in 1906. Both parents were devoted members of the Methodist Episcopal church South.

Of their family of nine children, Dr. Edgerton was eighth in order of birth and is one of seven yet living. He received his earlier education in Guilford county, North Carolina and made his professional preparation at Vanderbilt University, Nashville, Tennessee, from the medical department of which he was graduated in 1889. For the first three years thereafter, or until 1892, he practiced in North Carolina; then he came to Lebanon, Tennessee, where twenty years have now been spent in the earnest, attentive and skillful application of his medical knowledge. As a physician he excels, has reaped the reward of a most successful practitioner, and is recognized as of the foremost rank of his profession in this section of Tennessee. Dr. Edgerton has builded his success out of his own energies and ability and the lucrative practice he commands and the very comfortable estate he has accumulated have come to him by no magician's wand but represent the rewards of his own merit. He is a member of the Wilson county and the Tennessee State Medical Societies and of the American Medical Association.

On January 1, 1890, he was married to Miss Willie Pate, daughter of Stephen Pate. Mr. Pate, a native and for years a farmer in Putnam county, Tennessee, now resides with Dr. and Mrs. Edgerton. He is a Confederate veteran of the Civil war and gave four years of loyal service to support the cause of the Southland. The family circle of Dr. and Mrs. Edgerton has been broadened and brightened by the advent of two children, Lucile and Howard, both of whom are now attending school. Mrs. Edgerton is a member of the Christian church, while Dr. Edgerton is a Methodist. Politically he is a Democrat. In a business way he holds a large interest in the woolen mills at Lebanon being president of the Lebanon Woolen Mills, and also has extensive real estate holdings there. He and his family enjoy one of the most beautiful homes of Lebanon.

AMZI W. HOOKER. Conspicuous among the foremost business men of Lebanon, Tennessee, is Amzi W. Hooker, president of the Lebanon National Bank and an influential citizen of this community in other than business relations. He is a college man, a graduate of law, energetic, capable and resourceful, a representative of that type of citizen that not only sustains the prosperity of a commonwealth but pushes its development.

Born at Lexington, Mississippi, December 25, 1865, Mr. Hooker is a son of Judge John J. and Catharine (Beall) Hooker, both natives of Mississippi. The mother, born in 1833, was a daughter of Otho Beall and passed away in 1866, leaving two sons: John J. Hooker, now engaged in the railroad business in Mississippi, and Amzi, who was then but an infant. Judge John J. Hooker, the father, was born in 1823 and died in his native state in 1873. He was educated in Mississippi, was admitted to the bar when about twenty-five years of age and passed a very successful career in law, accumulating a large estate from the remunerations of his professional labors. For a number of years he served as a chancery judge. After the death of his first wife he contracted a second marriage and to that union was born a daughter, Eva B., who is now Mrs. S. S. Hudson, of Vicksburg, Mississippi. Mr. Hudson is one of the prominent men of his state and was formerly state's attorney of Mississippi. Both parents of Mr. Hooker were devout members of the Baptist church and Judge Hooker took a leading part in the work of that denomination in Mississippi. He was of an open-hearted, charitable disposition and substantially supported his religious sentiment by large donations of money for church work. In political belief and adherency he was a Democrat.

Amzi W. Hooker spent his boyhood in Mississippi and in a preparatory school there he laid the foundation for his subsequent collegiate training. After two years of study in Richmond College, Richmond, Virginia, he entered the University of Mississippi and concluded the junior year in the latter institution. He then took a course in a business college at Cleveland, Ohio, and following that he matriculated at Cumberland University, Lebanon, Tennessee, where he completed a course in law and was graduated in June, 1887. Instead of becoming a law practitioner, however, he engaged in the general insurance business and continued in that line ten years. He then embarked in the lumber business and has continued his identification with this line of business to the present time, his lumber sales extending all over this section of the state. As previously mentioned, he is president of the Lebanon National Bank, one of the solid and popular financial institutions of this section of the state, and he is also a part owner of the interests of the Castle Heights Training School at Lebanon and has extensive real estate holdings. With keen business acumen Mr. Hooker has employed his inheritance, both in the way of mental traits and of money, to the best of advantage so that what he has accumulated represents the rewards of his own ability and endeavors.

Mr. Hooker has been twice married. His first marriage occurred in June, 1887, and united him to Miss Gertrude Kirkpatrick, who was born in Lebanon and resided there until her death in 1894, when she

W. P. Burton M.D.

W. P. Bar... ...outh now practically retired from active life, and giving most ... ... P. Barton, of ... ... Teares ... ... the ... ... pract... ... ... so sk... ... ... disease that his s... ... ... in constant de... ... ... culture in his profession. ... ... Dr. Barton is now ... ... to rest, or rather to lead a less strenuous life. His ... rest in publi... ...es remains unabated and his opinions, rip...ed by ... ... knowl... ... of many parts of humanity, are always lis-tened ... ... wisdom of ... to p... ...

W ... ... county, T... ... ... of May 1 ... ... of J. W. a... ... ...ah C. New... ... ... whom were bo... ... ...ess... J. W. Barton was ... ...nd grew up in the ... ...re he was born, receiving his ... ... the country school ... ...for a few ... ... and th... ... ... to farming, in whe... ... ... a f... ... ... and had a ... ... Feb... ... ... county, i ... ... 1872, sa... ... ...es Bennett ... Neal, who ... ...I s... ... their entire lives ... a ...etai... ... born to Mr. and Mrs. B... ... Barton being the ... ... Wilson county, and ... ... B...ton is living with her ... ... of eighty-five. The father d... ... ... of his parents belonged to the Bapt... ... ...re with the Know-Nothing party ...

left a daughter, Katherine. She was a member of the Presbyterian church. In 1901 Mr. Hooker married Alice, daughter of Judge W. H. Williamson, a prominent attorney of Lebanon. Mrs. Hooker's mother, prior to her marriage to Judge Williamson, was the widow of Gen. John Hunt Morgan, the famed raider and Confederate soldier of the Civil war. To the union of Mr. and Mrs. Hooker has been born one son, John J. Hooker, now attending school. Both are members of the Presbyterian church and Mr. Hooker is the elder of his church and is secretary of the board of trustees of Cumberland University. Fraternally he is affiliated with the Knights of Pythias.

W. P. BARTON. Although now practically retired from active life, and giving most of his time to his farm, W. P. Barton, of Mount Juliet, Tennessee, led an active professional life for many years. As one of the most prominent physicians in the various localities in which he practiced he attained a high standing in his profession and became so skilled in diagnosis and the cure of disease that his services were in constant demand and he made a fortune in his professional career. Dr. Barton is now content to rest, or rather to lead a less strenuous life. His interest in public affairs remains unabated and his opinions, ripened by contact and knowledge of many kinds of humanity, are always listened to with the greatest respect, for he has gained wisdom with the passing years.

W. P. Barton was born in Wilson county, Tennessee, on the 12th of May, 1856, the son of J. W. and Sarah C. (Neal) Barton, both of whom were born in Tennessee. J. W. Barton was born in 1819, and grew up in the county where he was born, receiving his education in the country schools. He taught for a few terms and then settled down to farming, in which occupation he spent all of his life. He owned a few slaves and had a good farm, and was accounted one of the successful men of the county. He married Sarah C. Neal on the 11th of March, 1852, she being the daughter of Seth Jordan Neal and Frances (Kimbro) Neal, who were both born in Rutherford county, Tennessee, and spent their entire lives on a farm in their native state. Seven children were born to Mr. and Mrs. Barton, of whom five are now living, W. P. Barton being the third in order of birth. All of the children live in Wilson county, and are all successfully engaged in farming. Mrs. Barton is living with her son, W. P., having reached the venerable age of eighty-five. The father died in 1910, at the age of ninety-one. Both of the parents belonged to the Baptist church, and his political affiliations were with the Know-Nothing party when that party first came into existence, but he afterward became a Democrat. The father of J. W. Barton, was Stephen P. Barton, and his mother was Ellen (Baird) Barton, both of whom were natives of North Carolina. They came into

Tennessee and settled on a farm in Wilson county, about 1800, and here they lived during the remainder of their lives.

W. P. Barton received his first education in the country schools and then was sent to Mount Juliet, Tennessee, for a course in private instruction under T. H. Freeman. He was prepared for college under the tuition of this man, and entering Vanderbilt University was graduated from the institution in 1882. Going thence to the University of Tennessee he completed the course and was graduated from there in 1885. In 1893 he received a degree from the University of Nashville. Most of his studies had been in the scientific or medical field and after leaving college he began the practice of medicine. He first located at Silver Springs, Tennessee, and practiced there for three years. Then he moved to Texas and was located for a time at Fate, later removing to Roy City. He was very successful in his practice here and made a small sized fortune. In 1895 he moved back to Wilson county and gave up his practice. He has not been able to escape entirely from the duties of a physician for a number of his friends simply will not consent to having any one else attend them when they are ill. He owns four hundred and fifty acres of land comprising his home farm, besides two hundred acres nearby, also three thousand eight hundred acres in Rockwall, Collin, Hunt and Deafsmith counties, Texas, and is worth about one hundred thousand dollars.

Mr. Barton and his family are members of the Baptist church, and in politics he is an independent Democrat. He takes much interest in fraternal affairs, belonging to the Masons, in which order he is a Royal Arch Mason.

On the 19th of December, 1889, Mr. Barton married Lou May Mc- Dowell, but she only lived a few months, dying on June 29, 1890. In February, 1895, Mr. Barton married again, his second wife being Gela Curd, a daughter of Dr. J. M. Curd, who lives in Wilson county. She died May 5, 1897, leaving two children; Lou Ellen, who lives at home and W. P. Barton, who is at present attending the Webb School at Bell Buckle, Tennessee.

Mr. Barton began life with little or nothing, but with the determination to succeed, and considering that the first step along the road to success was the acquiring of a good education, he saved rigorously in order to make this possible, teaching school part of the time to pay for his medical education. He feels that the time and money was well spent and certainly no life could be better proof than his that an education means success, provided it is used in the right way.

RUFUS P. McCLAIN. The legal career of Rufus P. McClain, of Lebanon, covers the long period of forty-five years and has been of that character that he has long been recognized as one of the strongest and ablest members of the Wilson county bar and as one of the foremost men of his profession in this section of Tennessee. He holds a no less honorable standing as a citizen, has represented this county in the state legislature, and through different other professional and public services and an upright walk in life has become one of the best known and highly regarded men of Wilson county. It is his native county, the date of his birth being February 28, 1838, and the whole of the nearly three-quarters of a century since then, except while he was serving the Southland as a soldier of the "gray," has been passed in the vicinity where he was born. His parents, John A. and Minerva (Ross) McClain, also were both natives of Wilson county, the former's birth having occurred in 1801 and that of the latter in 1808. John A. McClain passed his career as a farmer and was very successful in that pursuit, being the owner of a fine estate of 400 acres at the time of his death in 1866. His wife survived him two years, joining him in death in 1868. They reared nine of the ten children born to their union and of this family six are yet living, the subject of this sketch being the fourth in the family in order of birth. John A. McClain was a Whig in politics until the breaking up of that party, after which he was a loyal adherent of the Democratic party. Four of his sons, William A., Rufus P., Henry Harrison and John Bell, fought during the Civil war to sustain the Confederacy. He was a member of Cumberland Presbyterian church. William McClain, his father, was a native of North Carolina and passed from the Old North state with the early tide of emigration to Tennessee, settling in Wilson county, where he became an extensive farmer and large slave holder. The family was originally of Irish lineage. Minerva Ross McClain, the mother, was a daughter of Allen Ross, also a North Carolinian, who came to this state in an early day and participated in the warfare against the Indians that then were in this locality and menaced the settlers. He lived to be over ninety ears of age and reared a family of twelve children.

Rufus P. McClain was brought up in Wilson county and was graduated from the literary department of Cumberland University in 1859. In 1861 the Civil war opened and, as previously mentioned, he and three of his brothers entered the Confederate service, Rufus P. becoming a member of Hatton's regiment, which was assigned to Archer's brigade, Hill's divison of the Army of Northern Virginia, and fought under the peerless "Stonewall" Jackson. This was one of the bravest regiments of the Confederate army and saw long, hard and active service. Its opening engagement was at Seven Pines and it participated in the series of battles from Warrenton ford to Shepherdstown, including the capture of Harper's Ferry, and it afterward fought at Sharpsburg, Fredericksburg, Chancellorsville, Gettysburg, the Wilderness campaign and in many other battles of lesser note. Mr. McClain entered the army as a private and was successively promoted to be corporal, quartermaster and finally paymaster for Hill's division, surrendering with his remaining comrades at Appomattox in 1865. On returning to Tennessee he took up the study of law in Cumberland University and was graduated from the law course in 1867. He then commenced the practice of his profession in Lebanon and from that time to the present has been extensively engaged in professional labors, his practice extending to all the courts and establishing for him the reputation of an able, conscientious and successful lawyer. He is and has been for some time attorney for the Nashville, Chattanooga & St. Louis Railway Company. He served as clerk of the county court four years, as clerk and master in equity in the Wilson county court eight years, and sat as special judge of the circuit court twelve months. His public service has also included one term in the state legislature as the representative of Wilson county, his services in that body being of a character alike honorable to himself and satisfactory to his constituents. A first class business man also, he has accumulated a very comfortable estate and is a stockholder and a director in the American National Bank at Lebanon. Another prominent citizen of this name was Josiah S. McClain, an uncle of Rufus P., who served as county court clerk forty years and was one of the best known men of Wilson county.

In 1867 Mr. McClain was united in marriage to Miss Hester Mac-Kenzie, daughter of Alexander MacKenzie, who was a native of Scotland and died in Nashville, Tennessee. Mrs. McClain passed away August 15, 1910. To this union came four children: Jennie M., now Mrs. Joseph Anderson, of Chattanooga, Tennessee; Minnie, who became Mrs. Ewing Graham and resides at West Palm Beach, Florida; Hester, who became the wife of Joseph Brown and resides in Chattanooga, Tennessee; and Alexander M. McClain, who is a traveling salesman. Mr. McClain is a member of the Methodist Episcopal church, South, of which his wife was also a member. Mr. McClain is a Royal Arch Mason and a Knight Templar Mason and has served as worthy master of his lodge. He is also a member of the Knights of Pythias. Politically he is a stalwart supporter of Democratic policies.

DANIEL HILLMAN GOODRICH. A well known citizen of Waverly, Tennessee, is Daniel Hillman Goodrich, a loyal Tennesseean' who wore the ''gray'' in the days of 1861-65 and who is now serving his third term as county clerk of Humphreys county. By paternal descent he comes of New England ancestry, while the Hillmans, his mother's people, were originally a New Jersey family. His birth occurred near Old Dover furnace, Stewart county, Tennessee, October 14, 1837. Justice B. Goodrich, his father, born in Connecticut in 1801, came to Kentucky as a young man and there was married to Jane H. Hillman, who was born in New Jersey in 1811. He had learned the trade of a moulder and furnace man and after his marriage he went into Alabama with his father-in-law, Mr. Hillman, to prospect in iron ores. At Mobile, Alabama,

Justice Goodrich cast the first steamboat shaft cast in the South. While they were in Alabama Mr. Hillman died and Mr. Goodrich then returned to Tennessee. Being of a roving disposition, he followed his occupation first in one locality and then another where there were furnaces, and finally passed away in 1849 in Kentucky, where he died of cholera. During his later years, however, he had taken up the study of medicine, making his professional preparation at the Louisville College of Medicine, Louisville, Kentucky, where he received his degree of M. D., and had practiced medicine in Kentucky and Missouri several years prior to his death. He was a Mason, a Whig in politics, and in religious faith and church membership was identified with the Christian denomination. His wife, who survived him until 1863, also was a member of the Christian church. To these parents were born eight children, of whom four grew to maturity.

Daniel Hillman Goodrich, the fifth of this family in order of birth, was educated in a seminary (Union Academy) near Triune, Williamson county, Tennessee. In 1855, when yet a youth in his teens, he went to St. Louis, Missouri, where he entered the iron and heavy hardware business at No. 15 North Levee. On the 23d day of March, 1861, he joined Company H, Second Missouri State Guard, and was captured at Camp Jackson, on the 10th of May, 1861, by the forces of General Lyon, commanding the Federal forces, and was paroled with the rest of his command, and the members of the First Missouri State Guard, on the night of the 12th of May, 1861. Remaining in St. Louis, Missouri, until July, 1861, he came to Nashville, Tenn. A few days after the battle of Belmont, Missouri, he went to Columbus, Kentucky, and made application for an exchange, through General Polk, commanding the Confederate forces at Columbus, Kentucky. General Polk ordered him back to Nashville, Tennessee, to await an exchange.

Just before the fall of Nashville, Tennessee, 1862, he went to Knoxville, expecting to join Company B, Rock City Guards, First Tennessee (Manny's Regiment) but having nothing to show that he had been exchanged, was not accepted, but was told to follow the regiment until an exchange could be arranged. He continued with the regiment (doing camp service) until after the battle of Shiloh. While in Corinth, he met Maj. H. W. Williams, of General Price's staff, who asked him if he had been exchanged. Answering in the negative, he was ordered to Atlanta, Georgia, to await exchange. Remaining in Atlanta and Marietta, Georgia, about sixty days, hearing nothing from Major Williams, and having no means of getting a living, Mr. Goodrich accepted a position as agent of the Navy Department, to get up iron to make gunboat plates for the vessels under construction, at Mobile, Selma, and Columbus, Alabama, and Savannah, Georgia, Charleston, South Carolina, and Wilmington, North Carolina, occupying this position until the retreat of General Joseph E. Johnston from Dalton, Georgia, when he was placed in charge of the Macon & Western Railroad, as headquarter railroad agent, at Atlanta, Georgia. After the fall of Atlanta, he was sent to Griffin, then to Lovejoy Station, Jonesboro, and then back to Atlanta, Georgia, at which place he was at the close of the war.

Returning to Nashville, Tennessee, he engaged in the hardware and iron business until July, 1866, when he came to Humphreys county, Tennessee, locating at Hurricane Mills, remaining there until September, 1875, when he came to Waverly, Tennessee, where he has remained, being engaged in the dry-goods and other business, until 1893, when he was appointed postmaster, under Cleveland's second administration and served four years, then going into the mercantile business and remained in that until he was elected county court clerk, which office he has occupied ever since.

Mr. Goodrich is a firm Democrat in belief, a member of the Independent Order of Odd Fellows, a member of the Knights and Ladies of Honor, and one of the oldest Masons in the state, having been made a Master Mason in 1858 in St. Louis, Missouri.

On May 19, 1881, he married Miss Sallie C. Hancock, of Wilson county, Tennessee, from which union have been born the following children: Lev. Hancock, now a resident of Pine Bluff, Arkansas; Sophia D., now Mrs. Harry D. Scott, of Memphis, Tennessee; Ellen Louise, Daniel H., and Sarah Hilda (twins) who are at the parental home. The family, except Lev. H., are members of the Methodist Episcopal church, South, of which church Mr. Goodrich has been a steward for thirty years.

REV. SAMUEL A. STEEL, D. D. Dr. Steel, who is now pastor of a large church in Columbia, South Carolina, has long enjoyed the reputation of being a prominent minister of the Methodist Episcopal church, South. He has been in charge of the largest churches of his denomination in the cities of Richmond, Virginia, Columbus, Mississippi, Memphis and Nashville, Tennessee, Louisville, Kentucky, and Kansas City, Missouri, and has filled important positions in the editorial and educational work of his church. His career has been marked by fidelity and earnestness, and he has had his full share of the "heat and burden of the day." Samuel Augustus Steel was born near Grenada, Mississippi, on October 5, 1849. His father was Rev. Ferdinand Lawrence Steel, a native of Fayetteville, North Carolina, and of staunch Irish ancestry; and his mother was Miss Amanda Fitzgerald Steel (nee Hankins), who was born at Paris, Tennessee, a representative of one of the old and honored families of the state. Rev. Ferdinand L. Steel moved from North Carolina to Mississippi in 1845, and soon after entered the ministry of the Methodist church, and was a pioneer preacher all over North Mississippi and West Tennessee. He fell a victim to an epidemic of cholera in Memphis in 1873, in the sixtieth year of his age. His widow survived him a score of years, and died in Nashville, Tennessee, at the home of her son at the advanced age of seventy-six years. When the war for the Union began, Dr. Steel was eleven years old. As the war broke up everything in the South, he was deprived of the advantages of early education, and his childhood and youth were spent amid the turbulent scenes of that terrible struggle, and the chaotic reconstruction period that succeeded it. He vividly describes many of these scenes in his lecture on "Home Life in Dixie During the War," which he has delivered nearly a thousand times throughout the United States. It was a severe school in which he was brought up, but it taught him those lessons of self-reliance, fearlessness and energy that have been characteristic of his career.

He was nearly grown before he had a chance to attend school; but so well had he been taught at home, and so earnestly had he applied himself to study, that within three years after he left the farm in Mississippi, and while still an under-graduate at Emory and Henry College, in Virginia, he was elected chaplain of the University of Virginia; a very high honor, for at that time the chaplain ranked with the professors of the University.

Dr. Steel was too young to enter the Confederate army, and got a well-remembered whipping at home for attempting to do so. General Forrest himself turned him over to his mother for salutary discipline, telling her they had "no cradles at the front," and threatening to thrash him himself if he ran away and came. But he was a fiery little "rebel," and to humor him and keep him at home, his parents allowed him to "run the blockade," and smuggle such things through the Yankee lines at Memphis, as were of use to the Confederates. He became an "artful dodger" of blue-coated pickets, and had many thrilling adventures.

When Dr. Steel left home to go to school on his own hook, he started in as a pupil of Miss Maria Anderson, who had a little school in the country, near Memphis. Here he cut cross-ties for what is now the Illinois Central Railroad, roasted his potatoes in the yard, and slept on a straw pallet; and he feels a deep debt of gratitude to the noble young woman who encouraged him, and assisted him to get a start. From this school he went to Memphis, then to Andrew College, at Trenton, Tennessee, where he spent a year. The pastor of the Methodist church at Hickman, Kentucky, having died, young Steel was appointed to fill his place, and he was in charge of this church for the year 1870. By saving his salary, he was able to go to college, and on the advice of Bishop McTyeire he decided to enter Emory and Henry. College, in the mountains of Southwestern Virginia. Soon after he entered the college, the health of the Methodist pastor at Abingdon, a town not far from Emory, having failed, young Steel was appointed to take charge of the church in Abingdon. While this put a very heavy burden on him it was a very fortunate circumstance. The salary enabled him to continue at college, while his work in Abingdon introduced him to many of the best and most influential people in Virginia. While in Abingdon, too, he met the accomplished lady, Miss Mary Burns, who subsequently became his wife. She was then a teacher in Martha Washington Female College in Abingdon.

It was while he was at Emory and Henry College that Mr. Steel's friends had him elected chaplain of the University of Virginia, where he succeeded the Rev. T. D. Witherspoon, D. D. He spent two years at the university, and while there was happily married to Miss Mary Burns, of Petersburg, Virginia. When he left the university, Mr. Steel was appointed to Broad Street Methodist church in Richmond, Virginia, where he spent three years. Then he was sent to Columbus, Mississippi, where he remained four years; from there he removed to Memphis, Tennessee.

In 1888, Dr. Steel, who was then the pastor of Walnut Street Methodist church, in Louisville, Kentucky, was appointed the Fraternal Delegate from the Methodist Episcopal church, South, to the General Conference of the Methodist Episcopal church, which met in New York City. His address before that body made a profound impression, and has been pronounced one of the finest examples of fraternal oratory. It was while he lived in Louisville that the wife of his youth, to whom he felt that his success was largely due, was called home. Four children had blessed the union, and his mother now took charge of his home.

Four years later, while pastor of McKendree church, Nashville, Tennessee, he was again happily married to Miss Ella Battle Brevard, of Union City, Tennessee. Five children have come to the home as the result of this happy marriage.

In 1894 Dr. Steel, while serving as pastor of West End church in Nashville, was elected by the General Conference, then in session in Memphis, the first general secretary of the Epworth League, and editor of the *Epworth Era*, the new paper published by the church for the young people. Dr. Steel had had some editorial experience, having edited the *Advocate of Missions*, and in company with Dr. Galloway, afterward Bishop Galloway, the *Southern Prohibitionist*, at Columbus, Mississippi. This was the first paper published in the South to advocate the prohibition of the liquor traffic. Dr. Steel's editorial management of *The Epworth Era*, gave that paper a reputation for vivacity, spirit and aggressiveness, such as few religious journals acquire. Indeed, he put so much fire and ginger in it, that it got him into serious trouble with the authorities of his church, and they had him up and tried him. He was entirely too independent to edit a church "organ," and retired from the official tripod at the next General Conference. When his term as Epworth League secretary ended, Dr. Steel spent several years on the lecture platform, where he achieved enviable fame as a popular speaker, especially on themes connected with the war for the Union. In 1898 he accepted the presidency of Logan Female College, at Russellville, Kentucky. From there he went to Lumberton, Mississippi, where he operated for a time the Lamar Manual Labor School. This school failed for lack of funds, but had an important influence in starting the splendid system of industrial schools now conducted by the state. After a brief connection with educational work in Oklahoma, Dr. Steel re-entered the work of the pastorate, and was appointed to Brownwood, Texas. He was called to take charge of the old Memphis Conference Female Institute, located at Jackson, Tennessee. He remained here, however, only a year, for he was needed more in the pastoral work of his church, for which he has always shown a special fitness; and he was appointed to his present position, as pastor of the leading Methodist church in Columbia, South Carolina.

Dr. Steel received the degree of Master of Arts, *pro causa honoris,* from Emory and Henry College in 1881, and that of Doctor of Divinity from Emory College, Oxford, Georgia, in 1884.

Dr. Steel has been greatly blessed in his family, and notwithstanding his extensive travels, he is decidedly a home-loving man. His oldest child is the wife of Mr. John Harvey Creighton, who at present is the efficient secretary of the Y. M. C. A. in Roanoke, Virginia. His second child is the Rev. Edward Marvin Steel, a talented young preacher of the Tennessee Conference, stationed at present at Lewisburg, Tennessee. His third child, beautiful Christine, died in 1898, at the early age of fourteen. The fourth, Miss Miriam, is a teacher in Collegio Isabella Hendrix, in Bello Horozonte, Brazil. The children of the second marriage are: Thomas Brevard, now in college, and the four girls, Gerald, Virginia, Ella Lee, and Chloe Louise, who make up the happy home circle in South Carolina.

WILLIAM HENRY SNEED. The bar of the state, and of east Tennessee in particular, has had no more conspicuous name during the past seventy cr more years than that of Sneed. Ability, personality, character and fine achievement have so long been associated with the name that it has become synonymous with those qualities in the minds of certainly the great majority of members of the profession in Tennessee as well as with thousands of citizens. Beginning in the decade of the '30s and continuing to the end of the '60s one of the very ablest lawyers of east Tennessee, and the associate of many of the eminent men of the time, was William H. Sneed. The mantle of his dignity and ability later fell upon his son, Judge Joseph W. Sneed, who for upwards of forty years has borne a prominent part in public affairs and as a lawyer and judge in Knoxville and vicinity.

At a recent meeting of the bar association of the state, held at the Hermitage Hotel in Nashville, the Hon. William A. Henderson delivered an address entitled: "Some of the Lawyers of East Tennessee Who Are Being Forgotten." Among others he gave his reminiscences of Col. William H. Sneed. These memories form a delightful portrait of a splendid character, whose record is an enduring honor to the history of the Tennessee bar, and for this reason the portion of the address pertaining to Colonel Sneed will be presented here practically as delivered.

"I now draw your attention to Col. William H. Sneed. To revive the memory of him will be interesting to you, and a labor of love for me. I probably knew him better than any man now living.

"For a quarter of a century Colonel Sneed was in the forefront of the distinguished lawyers of east Tennessee. In his time and in that region there was a very able bar. Tennessee lawyers have always taken high rank. From wide experience and observation, I know of none better in the United States. Among his associates were R. J. McKinney, Thomas A. R. Nelson, Landon C. Haynes, Horace Maynard, Thomas C. Lyon, James R. Cocke, Dan Trewhitt, Walter R. Evans, S. B. Boyd, O. P. Temple, Thomas D. Arnold, David M. Key, James T. Shields, John Baxter, and others.

"Colonel Sneed was born in Davidson county about the year 1812. Although an educated man, he was not a college man. In early manhood he read law with Charles Ready, at Murfreesboro, and soon became his partner. In the early forties he was elected to the state senate, and became intimately acquainted with the members from the 'Hill Country of Judea,' as a result of which he located at Greenville, Tennessee. He married at Murfreesboro, and a daughter was born, a beautiful girl who lived many years in Nashville. After moving to Greenville a daughter of Dr. Williams, a prominent man in that locality, became his second wife. He left as children Judge Joseph Sneed, whom you all know as an able lawyer; Thomas Sneed, a business man of Memphis; Mrs. Kate Sneed Jones, of Washington; and Mrs. Fannie Eldridge, of Mississippi. All are living except the eldest daughter.

"I think Colonel Sneed was the handsomest man I ever knew. He was more than good looking. Every excellence of manhood may be compressed into one word, and that word is *strength*; so the opposite may be expressed in the one word *weakness*. The most terse illustration of a mere manikin is in the question so well known to all of you: 'What went you out for to see—a reed shaken by the wind?' Perfect manhood is strength of body, strength of mind, strength of soul. It is a trinity, as most things are on earth and in heaven. Colonel Sneed was of medium height, broad shouldered, deep chested, of heavy build, and with a quick, strong, positive walk. In everything he was intense. Like every strong man, he had many warm friends, and a few bitter enemies. Show me a man without enemies, and I will show you a man of little account. His partners in business in east Tennessee were, first, Judge McKinney, then Judge Temple, then Mr. Cocke, a great-grandson of William Cocke, and still later myself, until I became a soldier. I first knew him when I was a boy. He always called me 'Will,' and continued to do so until the death-bed. As a young man I became more intimate with him.

"He had a heavy suit of hair which rebelled like a lion's mane, and was white as wool. His appearance would indicate that his individuality came largely from his mother. For one term he was a Whig member of Congress, and the ardent supporter of that 'Harry of the West.' He was a conspicuous candidate for the supreme bench against his late partner, Chief Justice McKinney—that grand old judge known to the members of the bar as 'Old Strictissimus.' It is said that Colonel Sneed was defeated by only one vote. It is an interesting fact that many contests of this kind in this country have been decided by a majority of but a single vote in the legislative bodies. Like most Whigs, as the rebellion approached, he was a strong Union man, and took a prominent part in the ensuing campaign. But when Tennessee finally seceded he followed her behests and espoused her cause. When the federal troops approached Knoxville, under Burnside, he refugeed to Liberty (now Bedford City), Virginia, with his family, and remained there until the end of the war. He then returned to Knoxville and, until his death, spent the most of his time in gathering together the fragments of a large estate which had been nearly devoured by the cupidity and animosities of war.

"He never sought to re-enter the general practice. In the various partnerships in which he engaged, certainly the last one, he spent most of his time in equity practice and in the supreme court, although he did much *nisi prius* work. Far beyond the average lawyer, he gave time and labor to the preparation of his cases. He was at his desk early and late. Every document was scrutinized, every witness interviewed, and he went into battle armed cap-a-pie. He took a professional pride in never asking for a continuance of a case, and always resisted such applications from his opponents or from his partners. His manner of argument was loud and intense, with that eloquence that always flows from a settled belief in the justice and truth of one's insistence. He had a habit, in his delivery, of tapping the palm of his left hand with the forefinger of his right, as if nailing attention to his point. The man who believes his own contention is always eloquent. This addiction of his mind was so strong that he would never take the opposite view of any question from that which he had entertained in some other independent case. Many times I have heard him say: 'I am on record against such a view of the law in some stated case.'

"Another peculiarity of Colonel Sneed's life as a lawyer was that he would never prosecute a criminal case. His theory was that when the state alleged a violation of her law by one of her citizens, outsiders should have no place in securing a conviction. For myself, I think this is a good theory, but sometimes faulty practice. I have not always followed his teachings in this regard. But all the law-breakers agreed with him.

As an examiner of witnesses, and in the high art of cross-examination, he was a marked success. His whole manner indicated a desire to unravel and untangle the truth, and, in handling witnesses, he was as kind as a mother talking to her boy. But when he detected fraud, he could be as cruel as a surgeon's scalpel. His manner toward the court showed an honest effort to discover and enforce the law, as an assistant to the judge. As to the jury he was always 'in the box,' as the thirteenth man.

"More than any lawyer I ever knew, he had the art and courage of how to charge a fee. His fees were higher than those of his associates, but I never heard of any dissatisfaction or disagreement on the part of his clients in that behalf. The bar does not seem to appreciate the fundamental principle of humanity to value a thing by the measure of its price. This is the reason why gold is more precious than iron, and the diamond than the garnet. Let me illustrate this by a reminiscence:

"During the prime of Colonel Sneed's life as a lawyer, the county of Campbell, in East Tennessee, was torn asunder by the case of Miller versus Dossett. The litigants were prominent and well-to-do farmers of that country. Each owned a cow, and these cows resembled each other in appearance. Each cow had a calf, and these calves were very much alike also. The animals were being pastured on a small island in Powell's river, when one night a sudden freshet came and one of the calves was washed away. The remaining calf, having some doubt as to his nativity, or possibly from purely selfish motives, then cultivated the habit of sucking both cows. The question involved in the suit was the ownership of the calf. The two old friends became bitter enemies, and went to law. There were actions and cross-actions, of replevin and detinue, indictments for larceny, and several actions for libel and slander, all choking the dockets of the roaring courthouse at Jacksboro. The country took sides like Highland clans. The best lawyers in that end of the state gathered to that feast. On one side were Colonel Sneed, Judge Boyd, Judge Young, Mr. Evans, and other lieutenants; on the other, Horace Maynard, Joseph B. Heiskell, John Netherland, and other lieutenants. After years of hard-fought litigation Colonel Sneed was unsuccessful in his cause, but charged a fee of five thousand dollars, which was cheerfully paid. Horace Maynard and his associates gained the cases, and he received a fee of twenty-five dollars. His explanation was that his actual fee was ten thousand dollars, but all except the twenty-five dollars was paid in glory. * * *

"The testimonial of respect paid Colonel Sneed by the bar of East Tennessee, and the high esteem in which he was held by his brother lawyers, as a man, citizen and lawyer, is evidenced by the memorial presented at the time of his demise, in the supreme court room at the September term, 1869, of that court. These proceedings have been perpetuated by being published at the end of the sixth volume of Caldwell's Reports. It is worthy of note that at this meeting, Thomas D. Arnold,

the senior member of the bar, presided; James W. Deadrick, afterwards chief justice of the supreme court, was chairman of the committee on resolutions; and John Baxter and Thomas A. R. Nelson acted as secretaries. Colonel Sneed has also received honorable mention in Caldwell's 'Bench and Bar of Tennessee,' page 299. At the time of his death, September, 1869, his brother members of the bar took suitable and appropriate action commemorative of his life and avocation, which are published at the end of Vol. VI, Caldwell's Tennessee Reports.

"If you were to select a few of the big lawyers of Tennessee he would be located within the glorious circle of its pride. As a man in political office, he was a patriot of renown; as a citizen he was a born leader of men; the escutcheon of his private life went to the tomb without a stain on its face. As a husband and father he was the soul of love. Colonel Sneed's name has been crystallized in the name of Sneedville, in Hancock county.

"This is a truthful memoir from a friend. What more can tongue or pen say?"

(This article by Mr. Henderson was written May 22, 1911.)

JUDGE JOSEPH WILLIAM SNEED. A few years after the death of Col. W. H. Sneed, his eldest son, Joseph W., gained his first laurels in the law and public affairs, and now for many years has been one of the eminent citizens of Knoxville and East Tennessee, in which time he has held many positions of trust and honor at the hands of the people.

Judge Sneed is a native of Knox county, and received his education at the old East Tennessee University, now known as the University of Tennessee. After the military department was added to the university, he was the first adjutant of the cadets, having been appointed by Captain Mariner, who was the first commandant.

His public career began with a short term as member of the municipal council of Knoxville. In 1886 he was the first city attorney elected under the charter which has just been abandoned for the commission form of government, and was successively elected to this position for four years.

In 1891 Judge Sneed was appointed criminal judge by Governor Buchanan, being at that time thirty-six years of age, his appointment being to fill the unexpired term of Judge S. T. Logan. As criminal judge he stood for election in 1892, and was successful over a Houk Republican, M. F. Caldwell, by 503 majority.

In 1894 he competed for the honors of the circuit judgeship. His opponent was Judge S. T. Logan, and he won the race by a majority of 457. This was a unique political achievement, for he was the only Democrat elected that year to any office, save in some of the minor positions, like constable or justice of the peace, and the election covered practically all the county offices.

In 1902 Judge Sneed was re-elected circuit judge by a majority of

1,261. In the last half century no other Democratic candidate for judicial honors in this part of the state has been so distinctly honored as Judge Sneed. No other Democratic nominee has been elected to a judicial position by entire East Tennessee constituents since before the war, during the decade of the fifties. Yet on all the three occasions of his candidacy he accepted his nomination from the Democratic party and was its unequivocal candidate throughout the campaigns.

In 1901, just prior to his last election, the legislature designated the circuit judge to hold the chancery court for Knox county, which position Judge Sneed filled up to the year 1909. When the courts of the state were redistricted in 1899, Judge Sneed was assigned to hold the circuit court of Sevier county, and he tried both civil and criminal cases for that county. Also by the act of 1899 he was again assigned to the criminal court of Knox county. Thus from 1899 to 1901 he held the circuit and criminal court of Knox county and the circuit court of Sevier county, and continued to hold them until 1902, and from 1901 to 1907 held all the courts of Knox county. After the election of 1902 he was relieved of the court in Sevier county, though this, to only a small degree, lightened the arduous labors of his judicial responsibilities.

During a considerable part of his career as judge the cases that passed under his review numbered in the aggregate more than two thousand each year. It required not only a strong constitution but also legal and executive ability of a high order to dispatch all this business. Despite the demands of this almost unremitting labor, the record of Judge Sneed stands in high light both in the quality and permanence of his decisions. It has been often said of him, and with truth, that only few of his cases were ever reversed by the higher courts, and the tribute is all the greater because he held all the courts of his county.

Judge Sneed cast his first presidential vote in 1876 for Tilden and Hendricks, and has voted for every Democratic candidate for president and vice president ever since. He was recently a delegate to the Baltimore convention which nominated Wilson and Marshall, now president and vice president of the United States. On the nomination of Senator Luke Lea he had the honor to be made chairman of the Tennessee delegation. After the convention he took the leading part in organizing a Wilson and Marshall Club at Knoxville, and gave his enthusiastic support to the candidates throughout the campaign.

Outside of his political and judicial career Judge Sneed has done much important service for his home city. When a member of the city council in 1885 he took the lead in advocacy of the building of a girls' high school, an institution now located at the corner of Union and Walnut streets that has had a splendid usefulness. He was chairman of the building committee until several private citizens were added to the committee membership, when, because of the presence of older men than himself, he voluntarily relinquished the post and Col. W. P. Washburn was appointed chairman.

When the Knox County Reform School was established in 1897, it was provided that the chancellor·and circuit judge of the county should appoint the trustees. Judge Lindsay as chancellor and Judge Sneed as circuit judge together made the first appointments. Through the redistricting act of 1899, Judge Lindsay having gone out of office, Judge Sneed made all subsequent appointments of trustees, except one made by Chancellor McClung, until his own retirement from the bench in 1910. The reform school has been so successfully managed that up to the present time no word of just criticism has been passed, and it is considered one of the best managed institutions of the state, as well as one of the most useful. This record is one that reflects high credit upon its trustees, in the first instance, and is also gratifying to the appointing power, for the destiny of the institution depended upon the wisdom exercised in the selection of its governing authorities. Some time after the organization of the institution, it was provided that a board of trustees, composed of women members, should take the management of the girls' department. The selection of these trustees also devolved upon Judge Sneed, and the record of their work in their special department has been fully as efficient as that made by the board for the entire school.

Since the expiration of his third term of office, on September 1, 1910, Judge Sneed has devoted himself to the practice of his profession. He enjoys a generous share of the legal business in his home city and vicinity, and is regarded as one of the strongest members of the present Knoxville bar.

JOHN WILLIAM SEATON. A man of integrity and honor and one well worthy of the high regard in which he is held throughout the community in which he lives is John William Seaton, of Linden, now clerk of the circuit court in Perry county and for eighteen years prominently identified with educational work in that county. He is a native of Gibson county, Tennessee, where he was born March 1, 1873. Ryan Seaton, his grandfather, was one of the many immigrants to Tennessee from the older commonwealth of North Carolina, his advent here having been made during the forepart of the last century. He was a soldier in the War of 1812 and fought with Gen. Andrew Jackson at the battle of New Orleans. Prior to leaving North Carolina he was married to a Miss Stinson, and on coming to this state located with his family near Pulaski, Giles county, where the remainder of his career was spent as a farmer. He and his wife reared five children, of which family John Green Seaton, the father of John William, was second in birth. John Green Seaton was born in Maury county, Tennessee, May 15, 1840, and there received such educational discipline as the common schools of the period afforded. He was numbered among the gallant sons of Tennessee that fought to sustain the southern cause during the Civil war. In Maury county, in 1872, he was married to Miss Lou Bell, who was born in Lawrence county, this state, June 9, 1848. To this union were born five sons, as follows: John William Seaton of this review; Smith B.; James T.; Benjamin, deceased; and another that died in infancy. The father died September 26, 1878, and later his widow married M. G. Alley. They are now farmer residents near Humboldt, Gibson county, Tennessee.

John William Seaton was educated in the public schools at Trenton, Tennessee, in Scott's Hill Academy, Henderson county, and at the Southern Normal University, Huntington, Tennessee. He then took up the profession of teaching and for eighteen years was employed as an instructor in Perry county and Decatur county. From 1907 to 1909 he was superintendent of public instruction in Perry county and at the same time he continued to be engaged in teaching, as was permissible at that time. In 1910 he was elected clerk of the circuit court in Perry county for a term of four years and is now engaged in that official service. He has also served as a district tax collector in that county.

In 1896 he was united in marriage to Miss Penina Lomax, who is a daughter of John Lomax, a farmer residing near Cedar Creek, Perry county. Six children have been born to this union, namely: Grace, who died in 1898 in her second year; Eugene, who died in 1903 at the age of four; Nettie, O'Dell, John William and Pauline.

In political views Mr. Seaton is a Democrat; in church membership he is identified with the Baptist denomination and is now clerk of the Tennessee Baptist Association.

JAMES WILSON LEWIS. When it is stated that this esteemed citizen of Linden has served as clerk and master of chancery in the Perry county court since 1908, and has been in public service in Perry county in one capacity or another for the last thirty years, further attestation of his worth and standing in that community is unnecessary. Two generations of this family have been native to Tennessee and have sprung from their common ancestor, Aaron Lewis, the grandfather of James Wilson, who was one of the many settlers that came into this state from North Carolina in the opening years of the nineteenth century, and who was one of the first settlers in Perry county. Aaron Lewis located first in the Yellow creek district in Dickson county and there was married to Polly Ann Dickson, who bore him ten children. In 1836 he removed with his family to Perry county, locating on Lick creek, about four miles from the Tennessee river. He was one of the first settlers in Perry county and became one of its most prominent men of that time, serving as the first tax collector of that county. William Kennedy Lewis, his son, who was born in the Yellow creek district in Dickson county in 1827, accompanied the family to Perry county in 1836, and spent the remainder of his life there. He received but a meager education and early took up farming as his vocation, his estate being located along Cypress creek, near the Tennessee river. In the war between the states he espoused the southern cause and as a member of the Forty-second Regiment of Tennessee Infantry fought to sustain it. He enlisted as a member of Captain Hulm's company, which was assigned to the Forty-second Tennessee Regiment under command of Gen. W. A. Quarles and in the army of Gen. Albert Sidney Johnston. This regiment bore a most gallant part at the battle of Fort Donelson, but was captured there, and Mr. Lewis was one of the prisoners taken to Camp Douglass, where he was held seven months before his exchange was effected. He then rejoined the army at Fort Hudson and continued to serve until the closing year of the war. Returning to Perry county he resumed farming and was thereafter engaged in that vocation until his death in 1897. In Perry county, in 1844, he was united in marriage to Miss Susana J. Coleman, who was born in Hickman county in 1829, and died in 1909. They became the parents of six children, the second of whom was James Wilson Lewis of this review. William Walker Lewis, of Hohenwald, Tennessee, is the only other member of the family yet living.

James Wilson Lewis was born in District No. 2 of Perry county, Tennessee, May 12, 1848. Reared in his native county, he there received a common school education and later became a teacher in the country schools of his vicinity. He was also employed for a time as a clerk in a country store. At the age of twenty-seven he entered into the mercantile business with R. J. Howard, under style and firm name of Howard & Lewis, at East Perryville, continuing there until 1880, when he moved to Marsh Creek and was there engaged in the timber business for a short time. His public service began in 1882, when he was elected clerk of the circuit court in Perry county, in which official capacity he served four terms, or sixteen years, and following that he was elected magistrate of the third civil district. On January 1, 1908, he was appointed clerk and master in chancery court in the county of Perry for a term of six years, and is now filling that position. He is a Democrat in his political views.

Mr. Lewis has been twice married. His first wife was Miss Rebecca Josephine Sutton, daughter of James R. Sutton of Perry county, whom he wedded in 1876. At her death on September 23, 1895, at the age of thirty-seven, she left two children: Martha Jane, who is now Mrs. W. J. Bray, of Jackson, Tennessee, and Julia Bertie, who is now the wife of J. C. Ward, of Perry county. In 1897 Mr. Lewis was joined in marriage to Miss Minnie J. Dickson, daughter of J. T. Dickson, of Lick Creek, Perry county. To this union have been born four daughters: Irma Loraine, Dorothy May, Mary Inez and Pearl Vivian. Both Mr. and Mrs. Lewis are members of the Methodist Episcopal church South, and are prominent in church work, the former having served as a steward of his church for a number of years. His fraternal associations are with the Masonic order as a member of the Linden Lodge No. 210, Free and Accepted Masons, and of Linden Chapter No. 156, Royal Arch Masons, and he has served as secretary in both lodges.

GENTRY RICHARD McGEE. A public citizen of Jackson, Tennessee, whose life of educational service should be given more detailed account than we have data to provide, is Gentry Richard McGee, who recently closed his long pedagogic career and is now living retired. Since he was a lad of twelve years of age he has called Tennessee his home, and in more than one way has nobly served his commonwealth. Born in Ebenezer, Mississippi, he was the son of James Gentry McGee, M. D., who spent his entire professional life in that place, and of Mary Ann Ford, who was a native of Pearl River, Mississippi, and a daughter of Rufus Ford. The date of Gentry Richard McGee's birth was September 17, 1840, and he began his life and education as a typical American boy of cultured and well-to-do parents. But in 1850 Dr. McGee's life was cut short by a sudden illness, and within ten days from that time his widow also answered the death summons. Their orphaned son went to the home of a paternal uncle at Trenton, Tennessee, which continued to be his home until he was well launched upon his life's career.

Having received some years of educational training at Ebenezer, Mississippi, young Gentry McGee next entered Gibson Academy at Trenton, under the guidance of his uncle, who was living at that place. After completing the prescribed courses at that school, he matriculated at Andrew College at Trenton, Tennessee, where he passed all courses and examinations, entitling him to the degree of Bachelor of Arts. Before he could return, in order that his degree might be conferred upon him, he was withheld by the call for service which was entailed on all patriotic citizens by the declaration of war between the North and the South.

Mr. McGee enlisted in May, 1861, with the Twelfth Tennessee Infantry, under Col. R. M. Russell. He served in most of the battles of the campaign from Missionary Ridge to Atlanta, concluding with the battle of Nashville. A private when he entered the Confederate army, he was in the course of the war raised to the rank of second lieutenant of Company B.

On the conclusion of the sectional conflict, Mr. McGee returned to Trenton and to his uncle's home. There he proceeded to assist the latter by putting in the crop then due for planting in this locality, and in agricultural activities with his relative, Mr. McGee continued for two years, in the meantime looking to his chosen life work.

In 1867 Mr. McGee took charge of the school at Miller's chapel, where he taught for two and a half years. He then accepted a position as instructor in the academy at Bells. After one year in that institution he organized the schools at Trenton, where he acted both as instructor and as superintendent. For a period of twenty-six and one-half years Superintendent McGee retained this position, steadily building up the school system to one of strength and marked efficiency.

In August of 1899 Superintendent McGee tendered his resignation as head of the Trenton schools in order to accept the principalship of the high school of Jackson. Having officiated in the latter capacity for four years, he was honored by election to the position of superintendent of this city's system of education. His direction of Jackson's schools continued for nine years, at the conclusion of which time, in 1912, he tendered his resignation as superintendent in order to retire to private life, where he is now engaged upon a work that will doubtless establish his name forever in educational circles.

It is Professor McGee's privilege to look back upon a career of the truest type of service the world knows—that in which the faithful, large-hearted educator truly stands *in loco parentis* to unlimited numbers of youths. The lives Professor McGee has touched for good, for stimulated action, for awakened conscience, for inspired purpose—these are legion; nor are their hearts without tribute, both spoken and silent. Printed volumes bear Gentry Richard McGee's name, and the work of his hand and brain, in the shape of a school history of Tennessee, is now in general use in the public schools of the state, and he has for years been gathering material for a complete history of the United States which he expects to bring to completion and publication in the course of the present year (1913), the same being designed for use in the public schools of the country.

Professor McGee's home life was established in 1872. In February of that year he was united in marriage to Miss Sallie Valentine Prentice, of Richmond, Virginia, a cousin of the noted sculptor, Valentine. Mrs. McGee died in 1900. The only child born to them was a daughter, whom they named Ora Belle, and who is now the wife of George H. Brandau, of Jackson.

Through the years he spent here and in Trenton, Professor McGee has made countless friendships in other relations apart from those of his immediate profession. These include those who have come in close touch with him in his connection with the Church of the Disciples, of which he is a member; in his affiliation with the party affairs of the Democracy; and in his membership in various fraternal organizations. Of the latter he belongs to the Masonic order, his mother lodge being at Trenton, where he is a past master, and his later association with Jackson Lodge No. 332, A. F. & A. M., to which he was transferred on the occasion of his removal to this place. He is also a member of the Kenton Chapter of the Knights Templar, and of the Knights of Pythias, No. 16, of which lodge he is past chancellor.

The usefulness of Gentry Richard McGee's life does not by any means cease with the laying aside of his official duties. Still young of heart and mind, still interested in all that promotes the best development of intelligence and character, he is the adviser of many individuals and many organizations. They are not few who both praise and affectionately envy the rich service of this veteran educator.

W. F. WHITE. The tiller of the soil can enjoy to the fullest the bounties of nature, for he earns them well. On the farm there is opportunity for the development of man's physical, mental and moral powers without restraint. From the sweet-scented fields and meadows comes an inspiration which cannot fail in its influence for good—an influence which is satisfying beyond that of the artificialities of city life. In such an atmosphere, in communion with nature, Mr. White has thrived and prospered.

Mr. White's ancestors belonged to a class of wealthy and influential farmers, his maternal grandfather, Benjamin Taylor, who was born in North Carolina and came to Tennessee prior to 1800, owning considerable land; and his great-grandfather, Francis Ketring, being one of the wealthiest men of his time. A German by birth, Francis Ketring came from Pennsylvania to Tennessee accompanied by the soldiers. To each of his large family of children he gave a farm of considerable size.

Coming to Tennessee in 1845 from Virginia, the state of his birth, Willis White, the father of W. F. White, three years later married Barbara Taylor, who was born in Sumner county, Tennessee, and who died in 1879. He was a farmer by occupation, a Democrat in politics, and belonged to the Presbyterian church. His death occurred in 1886. W. F. White has one sister, Katie, who married I. D. Luton and lives in Nashville.

Having finished his education in the common schools of Sumner county, Tennessee, in which county he was born May 30, 1851, W. F. White decided that no occupation presented a better opportunity than did the one in which his ancestors had been so successful, and he accordingly engaged in farming. His choice was a wise one and he is now one of the leading farmers in his section, fraternally affiliated with the Masons, being a Chapter Mason, and in politics a Democrat.

Mr. White married Ella Patterson, daughter of Capt. R. S. Patterson and Tennessee Jefferson of Nashville, Tennessee, and they are members of the Cumberland Presbyterian church. Their home and farm is an object of beauty and utility combined—a model of life in the country, indicative of the prosperity attained by its owner.

GEORGE W. JACKSON. The present judge of the county court of Sumner county received that distinction as a merited honor for his able record in business and citizenship. Judge Jackson, who is a native of this county and represents one of the old families here, began his career as a poor boy, and it has been due to his unremitting industry and fine business ability that he is now recognized as one of the most substantial farmers and public-spirited citizens of the county.

George W. Jackson was born in Sumner county, April 7, 1862, a son of William and Nannie A. (Vanderville) Jackson. The paternal grandfather, Matthew Jackson, a native of North Carolina, brought his family of young children to Tennessee and settled on a farm in Davidson county. He was one of the early settlers here and during the thirties took service under General Jackson during the Seminole Indian war. The old plantation, of which he was the owner, was operated in the early days by slave labor. The Vandervilles, representing the maternal branch of the family, are also among the old citizens of Tennessee, Grandfather John Vanderville having been born and reared in this state, and a son of one of the first settlers.

William Jackson, the father, was born in North Carolina in 1814, and died in 1870. His wife was born in Davidson county, Tennessee, in 1823, and her death occurred in 1887. The father was a boy when his parents moved into Tennessee, settling on a farm in Davidson county. From there he came to Sumner county in 1860, and during the remainder of his life was a successful farmer here. He reared a family of eight children, seven of whom are now living, Judge Jackson being the fifth in order of birth. The parents were both members of the Methodist church. The father was a justice of the peace and for a number of years held the office of coroner in Davidson county. Judge Jackson, during his boyhood days, attended the free schools of Goodlettsville. Starting as a poor boy on a farm, he utilized his energies to the best advantage, and in 1835 bought a farm on credit. The results of the next four or five years' efficient management enabled him to pay for this place, and he has long since been on the highroad of prosperity. At the present time his estate comprises five hundred acres of land, for which he has been offered one hundred dollars per acre. He is also a stockholder in the Bank of Goodlettsville.

In 1885 occurred his marriage to Miss Josie A. Crunk, a daughter of John A. Crunk, one of Sumner county's farmers. Mr. and Mrs. Jackson are members of the Methodist church, in which he has served as steward for fifteen years past. His fraternal affiliations are with the Woodmen of the World. A Democrat in politics, he has never been an active seeker for office, and the honors bestowed upon him by his party have all come unsolicited. The first important public office which he held was that of justice of the peace, to which he was elected in 1892, and in 1912 he became county judge. He is also a member of the board of education.

HIRAM NEAL. It is doubtful if any of the present citizens of Wilson county represents older and better known families in this vicinity than Hiram Neal, president of the Watertown Bank, and for many years a prominent business man and leader in local affairs. The Neals have been settled in this section of Tennessee for much more than a century, and wherever the name is found, it has been associated with substantial character of citizenship, and a solid prosperity in material affairs.

Hiram Neal, himself, is one of the oldest native residents of Wilson county, where he was born on the thirtieth of December, 1841, a son of Ashley and Elizabeth (Waters) Neal. The family came to this vicinity from Kentucky, where the paternal grandfather, Pallas Neal, was born, whence he came to Tennessee when a young man. The first name of his wife was Sallie. By occupation he was a farmer and stock raiser, and he spent most of his active career in Wilson county, where he died. The maternal grandfather, named Shelah Waters, was a native of Maryland, leaving there in 1789 for Virginia, whence he came in 1811 to Wilson county, Tennessee, during the pioneer epoch, and spent the rest of his life in this state.

Ashley Neal, the father, was born in Wilson county in 1803, and died in 1886, at a very advanced age. His wife, also born in this county in 1804, passed away in May, 1865. His lines of business were farming and the raising of stock, and he also was known to a considerable extent as a dealer and trader in stock. His farm consisted of between three hundred and four hundred acres of land, and he owned some slaves, for the cultivation of his crops, during the ante-bellum days. He was also a member of the Grange; in politics during his early life he was a Whig, subsequently a Republican, and although he had been a slave owner, he was a strong Union man in his sympathies. His wife was a member of the Missionary Baptist church. They were the parents of ten children, and five of them are now living, Hiram Neal having been the ninth in order of birth.

Hiram Neal grew up in his home district of Wilson county, and when a boy attended the country schools of that vicinity. His education was completed in Pennsylvania, where he attended school for a time. His practical career commenced on a farm, and he bought sixty acres on credit, which he was able, by his industry and good management, to pay off within the time appointed at the beginning. He is now the owner of one hundred acres of farm land, near Watertown, but has owned much more than this at an earlier period in his career, since he has given his children good farms, and has been prosperous to a very gratifying degree. Mr. Neal is president of the Bank of Watertown, and for the past eighteen years has served his community in the office of justice of the peace.

In 1866 he married Elizabeth Whaley, a daughter of William Whaley, a merchant of De Kalb county, Tennessee. The two children now living are Sallie, who is the wife of C. A. Smith, and resides on a farm in Wilson county; and A. W., who is a resident of Nashville, Tenn. Mr. Neal and wife are members of the Missionary Baptist church, and in politics he has maintained an independent attitude.

J. N. Curd, M. D. One of the most successful farmers and prominent men of Wilson county, Tennessee, is Dr. J. N. Curd, who having spent a number of years of his life as a practitioner of medicine, turned after a time to farming and has made as good a farmer as he did a doctor. He is a man of wide personal popularity, and the respect which his neighbors have for him gives him no small influence on the life of the community. He served in the Civil war and has helped to make the New South out of the ruins of the old, and all through these years he has used his influence and aid in all projects that would be of benefit to the community.

J. N. Curd is a native of Wilson county, but comes of Virginia parentage, his father having been born in the latter state in 1805. His father was W. M. Curd, and his grandfather was John Curd, also a native of Virginia. The Curd family came to America from Ireland, early in the colonial period. John Curd married Elizabeth Lumpkin, also a native of Virginia, in 1801, and early in the eighteenth century they removed to Tennessee where they spent the remainder of their lives. W. M. Curd was only a child when his parents removed to Tennessee, and he received his education in Wilson county, where they settled. On the 22nd of November, 1832, he married Susan Davis, a daughter of N. G. Davis, and his wife, who was a Miss McFarland, both natives of Virginia, who were early settlers in Tennessee and spent all of their lives in the state of their adoption. Mr. and Mrs. Curd became the parents of four children, of whom two are now living; J. N. Curd and his sister, Bettie, who is the widow of W. C. Dodson, and is living in Davidson county. Both the father and mother were members of the Baptist church and Mr. Curd was a member of the Democratic party. He died when a comparatively young man, in 1842.

J. N. Curd grew up in the country and attended the country schools until he had advanced far enough to go away to school. He was then sent to Union University, at Murfreesboro, Tennessee, and later matriculated in the University of Nashville, where he took a course in medicine. He was graduated from this institution in 1867, but before receiving his degree he had been engaged in the practice of his profession, for during the days of the conflict between the states, there was a crying need for anyone who had any pretensions of a knowledge of medicine. He enlisted in the army in 1862 and served throughout the rest of the war as a surgeon in the Confederate army, surrendering with the rest of General Johnston's army to General Sherman, at Goldsboro, North Carolina, in 1865. After the close of the war Dr. Curd became a full-fledged physician and with the experience he had gained on the battlefield it was not long before he had established a fine practice. He was thus engaged for fifteen years and then concluded to retire from the profession and settled as a farmer in Wilson county, Tennessee, near Mount Juliet. He secured, partly by inheritance and partly by purchase, a large farm and has since built a fine home, and is living what is considered by wise people the happiest life of the times, that is, that of a farmer who is well enough educated to enjoy interests outside of his farm, and is prosperous enough to have the comforts and luxuries ordinarily denied to the farmer. His farm contains four hundred and thirty acres and is one of the best kept up farms in the community.

Dr. Curd is a member of the Baptist church, and votes the Democratic ticket as a rule, though he prefers to vote independently when occasion demands. During his professional life he was a member of the county medical association and he also served for eight years as school commissioner.

In 1873 Dr. Curd was married to Ella W. Winter, a daughter of Dr. A. J. Winter, who was a physician in Wilson county for a number of years. Mrs. Curd died in 1887, five children being born of the marriage. Of these, three are living: Elmer, who is a merchant in Wilson county; Edgar, who lives with his father, and May, who married Orvie Hassey, of Davidson county, Tennessee. In 1889 Dr. Curd married Mary Cook, a daughter of Dr. L. M. N. Cook, who was also a physician and had practiced in Wilson county for years. Dr. and Mrs. Curd are the parents of one child, Helen, who is at school in Murfreesboro. Mrs. Curd is a member of the Methodist Episcopal church. The doctor has never had very much time to spend in fraternal affairs, his membership in the Ancient Free and Accepted Masons being his sole allegiance of this kind.

MILTON H. WELLS, M. D. The medical fraternity of Wilson county has one of its ablest members in Dr. Milton H. Wells, of Watertown, where he is city physician, and where during his practice and residence he has taken an active part in public affairs, and has gained the thorough esteem of his professional associates and all classes of citizens.

The Wells family, to which he belongs, was first settled in Overton county, and its name has been associated with local history of that vicinity for upwards of a century. Milton H. Wells was born in Overton county August 11, 1863, a son of Mitchell and Minerva (Matthews) Wells. The paternal grandparents were named Stephen and Nancy (West) Wells. The former was a native of North Carolina, whence he came to Tennessee at an early day. The latter was born in Overton county, and belonged to an early family settled there. The grandfather died in 1875 after a long and successful career.

Both Mr. Wells and wife were natives of Overton county, where the father was born in 1831 and died in 1882, and the mother was born in 1833 and died in 1901. Mr. Wells was an expert machinist. He had studied medicine for a time, but decided not to follow that profession, chiefly on account of ill health. During the war he entered the service of the Confederacy and held the rank of lieutenant for one year, until his honorable discharge. He was for a number of years a justice of the peace, and took considerable interest in Democratic politics, although he never held any other office outside of the one just mentioned. He was a member of the Cumberland Presbyterian church, while his wife was a Baptist.

Milton H. Wells attended for a time the Oak Hill Institute in Overton county, and after his early school days he identified himself with several lines of business in this part of the state. Finally, on determining to enter the medical profession, he became a student in the medical department of the University of Nashville, where he was graduated with the degree of M. D. in 1901. He began practice in Overton county, where he remained until 1911, at which time he came to Wilson county and located near Watertown. For a number of years Dr. Wells taught school, and it was from the savings of this occupation that later he attended medical school and fitted himself for practice. He is city health officer of Watertown, is insurance examiner for two companies, and is the owner of a good farm in Overton county and has other investments. Though he has had to work for all that he has obtained, and has deserved all his good profits, he acquired many evidences of esteem and success, and is one of the best known men in the town.

In 1891 Dr. Wells married Miss Amelia Thomas, of Overton county, a daughter of J. C. Thomas, who was one of the successful farmers of that county. Mrs. Wells is a member of the Christian church, while his church is the Cumberland Presbyterian. Fraternally he is affiliated with the Independent Order of Odd Fellows, and the Modern Woodmen of America, and in the former order has passed all the chairs and has served as district deputy; he is also a member of Comer Lodge, F. & A. M. He has membership in the Wilson County Medical Society, the Upper Cumberland Medical Society, the Tennessee Medical Society, and the Southern Medical Association, while in politics he is a good Democrat.

WILLIS M. LITCHFORD. The cashier of the City and State Bank at Watertown is one of the younger generation of a family which has been identified with Tennessee for the greater part of a century. He is a prospering young business man with growing influence, and his talents, which were first turned to educational work, have found a very attractive field in business and finance. Willis M. Litchford was born in Smith county, Tennessee, August 30, 1889. His parents were Britt T. and Laura (Thomas) Litchford. The family was originally from Virginia, and were located in Tennessee early in the last century. Both the parents were natives of Smith county, the father born in 1862 and the mother in 1858. The father has long been a successful farmer, and his estate in Smith county is estimated to be worth $40,000, and he is also interested in the Citizens' Bank of Watertown, one of its directors, and an influential man in both civic and business affairs. There are five living children in the family, Willis M. being the oldest. The others are as follows: Mary, Frank, Thomas and Julian, all of whom reside at home. The mother is a member of the Methodist church, while the father is a Mason and in politics a Democrat. The paternal grandfather was David Litchford, who was born in Davidson county, Tennessee, where he became a very prosperous citizen, and at the time of his death was said to be worth about $75,000. During the Civil war he had served as a Confederate soldier under General Forrest, and while following that gallant cavalryman was captured and saw many hardships of military life. The maternal grandfather was named Frank Thomas, who was born in Tennessee, in which state he spent most of his life, and he was a soldier, both of the Mexican and the Civil wars, being on the Union side in the latter. While a successful man in business, he was perhaps more prominent in politics. He was one of the leading Republicans of his time, and was chairman of the Republican state committee several times, and also served in the office of the United States marshal for the middle Tennessee district.

Willis M. Litchford received his education at Watertown, and as a schoolboy showed unusual brilliance in his studies, so that he graduated with first honors from the high school in 1910. He then took examinations as a school teacher and was given a life certificate on account of his passing the best examination in this state. He was a member of the County Historical Association, and has always been interested in local affairs. For fifteen months he was engaged in teaching school and then in 1912 assisted in the organization of the Citizens' State Bank at Watertown. This bank has already shown an unusual record of prosperity, and with its capital of $20,000 and its average deposits of $10,000, has afforded an excellent service to the business and financial community and patronage which it represents.

Mr. Litchford is cashier, and also one of the directors of this bank. In 1912, he was married to Miss Prudie Armstrong, a daughter of Lucius Armstrong. Her father is a farmer in Wilson county. Mrs. Litchford is a member of the Presbyterian church, while Mr. Litchford is affiliated with the Modern Woodmen of America and in politics is a Democrat.

ROBERT H. BAKER, M. D. A family which has been resident in Tennessee for more than a century is represented by Dr. Baker of Watertown, in Wilson county. Its members have been farmers, business and professional men and soldiers; have helped create wealth and prosperity, and have always been men of "honest and good report." It is one of the families which preeminently deserve mention in the annals of Tennessee.

Dr. Robert H. Baker was born in Davidson county, Tennessee, June 1, 1847, a son of William D. and Mary (Fuqua) Baker. The paternal grandparents were James and Annie (Saunders) Baker, who came from North Carolina to Tennessee, and were married in Stewart county, this state, in 1811. The paternal grandmother attained the great age of ninety-eight years. The grandfather bought a large quantity of land near Nashville in 1811, and during the remainder of his career was known as one of the large land proprietors and successful men of the vicinity. He was also owner of many slaves.

William D. Baker, the father, was born in 1812, in this state, and died in 1890. His wife, whose maiden name was Mary Fuqua, was born in Davidson county, this state, in 1811, and died in 1893. Her father, Peter Fuqua, came to Tennessee from Virginia, being a minister of the Missionary Baptist church. With his ability as a minister, he also united executive talent in business, and was considered a wealthy man at the time of his death. William D. Baker became a successful farmer, and also entered actively into the political life of his county. For a number of years he was tax collector of Davidson county, and then for twenty-four years served as a magistrate in the same county. His resignation from the latter office was due to ill health. There were eight children in his family, and two of them are living at present, one being the doctor; the other, W. T. Baker, was for eight years judge of the city court of Nashville. The sons, James F., W. T., Frank M. and R. H., were all soldiers in the Civil war; Frank was killed in battle in 1864, while under the command of General John H. Morgan. The father was a Union man, though all four of his sons gave service to the Confederacy. The parents were both members of the Christian church, and the father was a Democrat in politics.

Dr. Robert H. Baker, who has for forty years been one of the leading physicians of Wilson county, received his educational training in the University of Nashville, where he was graduated in the literary department in 1868, and was graduated in medicine in 1873. He began practice in the same year and some years later, during 1880 and 1881, took a post-graduate course in medicine in Cincinnati. He has always been a physician who has endeavored to keep pace with the developments of his time and has striven with marked success to render his services efficient and valuable at all times to his large circle of patients.

In November, 1875, Dr. Baker married Mary Waters, whose father, Hon. Wilson L. Waters of Watertown, at one time member of the Tennessee legislature, was one of the ablest business men of this locality, and both for his wealth and his influence in other ways, was widely known in this part of Tennessee. By reason of his industry and progressive activities and his eagerness to advance the interests of his community and state, he was selected by the officials and a large concourse of people to cast the first shovelful of dirt in the construction of the Tennessee Central Railroad, which work began at Watertown, named in his honor. The six children of Dr. and Mrs. Baker are as follows:

Charles W., of Nashville; Laura, wife of T. L. Hale, a dentist at Watertown; Mary, at home; Ellen Waters, at home; Robert H., Jr., at home; and Mildred, also at home. The family are members of the Christian church.

Dr. Baker was very young at the beginning of the Civil war, but as his sympathies were with the Confederacy, and as his brothers were already in rank, in 1863 he enlisted and saw active service in a number of engagements and hard campaigns. He was escort for General Pettus for some time and was twice captured, but each time made his escape. An Independent Democrat, Dr. Baker was nominated on the Independent Democratic ticket for the state legislature, but was defeated by a small majority. He is a member of the county and state medical societies and of the American Medical Association.

WALTER MALONE, the youngest of a family of twelve children, is a son of Dr. Franklin Jefferson Malone and Mary Louise (Hardin), his wife. He was born February 10, 1866, in De Soto county, Mississippi, about thirteen miles southeast of Memphis, Tennessee.

His father, a surgeon in the Mexican war, and a member of the Mississippi Constitutional Convention in 1868, died January 24, 1873. The death of his father in his son's childhood, deprived him of many early advantages, but he managed to receive those which a country school offered.

From the age of six to sixteen he made his daily trips of three miles, across the state line, into Tennessee to the little schoolhouse. This brought him in close contact with nature. When the school session was over, he worked on the farm, and here found form for the products which were stored in his mind. His first attempt to record them in verse was at the age of twelve; but these youthful effusions his, perhaps, over-critical judgment consigned to destruction.

Between the ages of thirteen and fourteen, he was encouraged by the publication of several of his poems in the *Louisville Courier-Journal.* So, at the age of sixteen, he began writing verse in earnest, and, in 1882, gave out his first volume, "Claribel and Other Poems," to the public. This was a book of three hundred pages, savoring of rural life, and giving promise of poetic genius. This book was greatly admired and highly commended by many; but in later years its author must have regarded it with disapproval, for he sought to destroy every copy he could find.

In 1883 he entered the preparatory department of the University of Mississippi at Oxford. Though he had read much, he had never devoted himself assiduously to elementary text books. His life had been one of freedom in nature's realm, and hence it was with difficulty that he entered upon collegiate work. Mathematics was to him especially distasteful. However, his last years at college were eminently noteworthy.

He won laurels in two oratorical contests, and served three years on the editorial staff of the college magazine—the last year as editor in chief.

In 1885, at the age of nineteen, he published another volume, ''The Outcast and Other Poems,'' a book of three hundred pages. This book elicited favorable comment from such poets as Edmund Clarence Stedman, Oliver Wendell Holmes and others; but this volume, too, the author later sought to suppress. Whittier said of it, ''The book gives promise, but it is not what it would be were the author ten years older. Why, at that age I could not make a respectable rhyme.'' However, despite Mr. Malone's efforts to destroy them, these early volumes are still being read and enjoyed. Some of their poems, altered and recast, are found in his later works. The author's objection to his early works is that they were given out at a time when he did not know the way of the world.

In 1887 he graduated and was admitted to the bar several years later. Making Memphis his home, he formed a co-partnership with his brother, James H. Malone, afterward mayor of Memphis. Realizing that the law is a jealous mistress, he now devoted himself assiduously to it, and his pen was idle until the year 1892, when his best work began. ''Narcissus and Other Poems'' appeared, attracting widespread attention. Two years later came ''Songs of Dusk and Dawn.'' This volume contained many new poems, together with some of the best of his preceding volume. It was generally commended as a work of high art, and Col. M. W. Connolly of Memphis, in one of his inimitable editorials, paid its author a high tribute.

In 1896 followed ''Songs of December and June,'' a little volume of twenty lyrics, and ''The Coming of the King,'' a year later, a collection of eight short stories. This book received high praise from the press, and from writers like Thomas Bailey Aldrich, Charles Dudley Warner, Edgar Fawcett, and others.

In 1897 Mr. Malone retired from the practice of law and went to New York City, where he engaged in literary pursuits, contributing to leading magazines and weeklies. Several years later he returned to Memphis, and resumed the practice of law.

In 1900 he published ''Songs of North and South,'' a volume containing the garnered work of the three preceding years. This excellent volume brought him to the notice of Israel Zangwill, Alfred Austin, and the British and Scotch reviews.

In 1904 his book entitled ''Poems'' came out. This was a complete edition of all his poems, many of them re-written and revised. In 1906 appeared his latest book, ''Songs of East and West,'' a volume of twenty-seven poems containing word pictures of travels in California, Florida, Mexico, Cuba and Europe.

His most widely quoted poem, ''Opportunity,'' first appeared in *Munsey's Magazine* in March, 1905. This poem has received many reprints in all English-speaking countries. It has been framed by lovers of art, and may be seen not only on the walls of the homes, but in many public places. It is generally believed that this poem was written in response to the pessimistic "Opportunity" of Senator John J. Ingalls; but this is not the fact, although the poem is uplifting and presents a phase of the subject diametrically opposed to the view of that author. It is light and cheer to the despondent, comfort to the bereaved and a helping hand to the downtrodden.

In 1905, on petition of practically all the members of the Memphis bar, Mr. Malone was appointed judge of the second division of the circuit court of Shelby county, Tennessee, by Governor John I. Cox, and, by election, has held the office ever since, for he is exceedingly popular in politics and has many friends. As a jurist he has attained marked eminence, for he has a phenomenal knowledge of law and is a man of wonderful versatility.

In his writings there is no tinge of commercialism, for he is an advocate of true art. The utilitarian idea has never entered his mind. He has fought his way to fame against popular fads and capricious fashions. While all of his work has been in a serious vein, Judge Malone is not austere or exclusive. He has his sunny moments, and is genial, cheerful and often generous to a fault. He has taken the language of the flowers, the birds and the trees and made it popular. In him they speak to you their varied language, and you hear their voices and are made glad.

Besides his poems and short stories, he has written three plays: "Poe and Chopin," a mystical and subjective study; "The Valley of the Shadow," a drama based on the yellow fever scourge of 1878 in Memphis. This is a sociological study, advancing a bold plea for the women of the underworld—one of whom is its heroine. "Sam Davis" is a war drama, replete with the spirit of loyalty and patriotism.

With Judge Malone's patient waiting have come appreciation and success. His fame is made, though he is still working on his epic, "De Soto," which he began in January, 1908, and will complete this year. This bold effort is being produced in the measure of "Paradise Lost," and will contain about eighteen thousand lines. It recounts the adventures of that intrepid cavalier in the early days of the Americas, adorning his history with many bright flowers of fiction. Some of its lyric interludes have been published in *Scribner's Magazine, Munsey's Magazine, The Smart Set,* and other leading magazines. Judge Malone has said that this story was a conception of his early youth, the dream of his young manhood, and now, in his maturer years, he will give it out as a finished product of masterful effort and genius.

Many of Judge Malone's best poems have been published in compilations of southern literature. An excellent selection is found in "The Library of Southern Literature," which also contains the best written account of his life from the virile pen of Col. M. W. Connolly, himself a poet and newspaper writer of renown, and the present editor of the *News-Scimitar* of Memphis. There is also a short but choice collection of his poems found in "Southern Writers," by W. P. Trent, published in 1905.

With the completion of "De Soto" Judge Malone has said that he will be ready to die, but he is not yet an old man by any means, and it is to be hoped that his pen will continue active for many years to come.

EDWARD BUSHROD STAHLMAN is one of the men whom American business has rewarded with high position and influence. He began life a poor boy, working not only for his own support but for his family. He went into railroading and learned that complex industry from the ground up, becoming an impersonation of efficiency in the management of both men and practical things. He attained one of the high executive positions on a great railroad, and was one of the big men of the South in transportation circles until his retirement some fifteen years ago. Mr. Stahlman is a Tennesseean by virtue of his many years' residence in Nashville, and is now perhaps best known as publisher of the *Nashville Daily Banner*.

He was born in Mecklenburg, Germany, September 2, 1844, a son of Frederick and Christiane (Lange) Stahlman. His father was an educator and principal of the schools at Leuso, Germany, where the son received his elementary education. The family came to America and located in Virginia in 1855. The father's death soon afterward left the widow with seven young children, and Edward was called into practical service to help support the home.

His career in the railway service began in an humble capacity during the construction of the Parkersburg branch of the Baltimore & Ohio Railroad. He was a hard worker and had the personality of a real leader, so that he was soon placed in charge of responsible duties. In 1863, at the age of nineteen, he came to Tennessee to enter the service of the Louisville & Nashville, and in 1865 located at Nashville, which city has been his home for the greater part of half a century. Here he was cashier of the Southern Express Company for several years. In 1871 he became freight contracting agent at Nashville for the Louisville & Nashville Railroad, and in 1875 was appointed general agent at Nashville. He was made general freight agent in 1878 and traffic manager in 1880. Resigning in 1881, he became vice president of the Louisville, New Albany & Chicago Railroad, a position which he resigned to accept the same office with the Louisville & Nashville, with which road he remained until 1890. After spending about a year in Europe with his family, he became commissioner of the Southern Railway & Steamship Association, with headquarters at Atlanta, Georgia, and continued actively in the transportation service until October, 1895.

At Nashville Mr. Stahlman has been one of the citizens to whom credit is due for the modern era of growth and commercial enterprise. One of the features of the modern business district is the Stahlman office building, and his energy and capital have gone into many other enterprises that have promoted the prosperity of the city. Mr. Stahlman is both the owner and publisher of the *Nashville Daily Banner*.

THOMAS POLK EWING. Not only is Thomas Polk Ewing a young man of eminence in Montgomery county, but he is one who has been known from infancy in this community, which was his birthplace. It has been his privilege to serve his district in a prominent political capacity, doing great credit to the family reputation. The Ewings came out of Kentucky to Missouri. Thompson Ewing, the paternal grandfather of our subject, was a native of Kentucky, whence he removed to Missouri. His name is well known indeed in the Cumberland Presbyterian church, in which he was conspicuous as founder. The major part of his life was spent in Missouri, which was the birthplace of his son, Finis Ewing (1838-1906). The latter was given a good education, and came, at the age of twenty, to the state of Tennessee, where he established himself in Montgomery county. He was twice married, first to Miss Delnia Barker, who bore him one child, but soon afterward passed from earthly life. This child, a daughter named Ella, lived to maturity and is well known as Mrs. T. C. Nimms, of Nashville. Finis Ewing later was united to Miss Frances Douglas Polk, a daughter of Irving and Elizabeth Polk, who were Robertson county farmers. Frances Polk Ewing was born in 1850 and is still living. She and her husband became the parents of seven children, six of whom are yet living. The eldest, Charles Bowman Ewing, lives at Nashville; Finis, the second child and son, is a citizen of Memphis; Bessie is deceased; Maude is Mrs. Leslie Smith and resides at this place; Thomas Polk Ewing, as the special subject of this review, receives detailed account below; Robert Lee Ewing lives at Memphis; and Polly Douglas Ewing became Mrs. B. A. Martin of near Clarksville.

Thomas Polk Ewing was born on April 19, 1883, at the rural property in District No. 1 of Montgomery county which is still his home. He received careful education in the academy at Cumberland City and thereafter entered upon the occupation of farming, conducting and supervising operations on his father's farm; for that gentleman was concerned somewhat in political affairs, in the capacity of district magistrate, which office he filled for no less than twenty-five years, showing in his efforts in the cause of peace no less patriotism than he had exhibited as a soldier of the Civil war.

As an agriculturist of extensive operations, T. P. Ewing has shown no slight executive and managing ability. He manages four hundred acres, chiefly devoted to tobacco raising, and also raises considerable stock. Meanwhile he has achieved a most substantial reputation as one who knows how to serve his Democratic constituency and the local public in general in various civic and political offices. From 1906 to 1912 he filled the office formerly honored so many years by his late father, the magistracy of District No. 1. For two years he was a member of the Montgomery county highway commission and for a similar period of the county board of education. He has been a member of the Tennessee legislature as a representative from Houston and Montgomery counties and is again a candidate for the same office from Montgomery county. While in the legislature he has served on the committee on banking, the committee on agriculture, the committee on county lines, the committee on railroads and the committee on game, fish and forestry; he has also been chairman of the committee on new counties and the committee on investigating state mines. Mr. Ewing has an especial gift for official service and has been prominent as chairman of the Planters' Association.

Mr. Ewing maintains his home at his rural property. His marriage took place on November 8, 1911. Mrs. Ewing was formerly Miss Helen Dodds, of Jackson, Tennessee. She is a daughter of J. S. Dodds, of that place. Mr. and Mrs. Ewing are the parents of an infant son, Thomas Polk Ewing, Jr., born August 7, 1912.

The church affiliations of Mr. and Mrs. Ewing are, respectively, those of the Episcopal and Methodist Episcopal, South. Mr. Ewing is fraternally connected with the Benevolent and Protective Order of Elks, the Loyal Order of Moose, and the Junior Order of United American Mechanics. He is a man whose talents and personality have won him considerable popularity, which promises to increase and to win for him wider opportunities for public usefulness.

NORMAN B. MORRELL. Engaged in the successful practice of his profession in the city of Knoxville for the past twenty years, Senator Morrell is recognized as one of the able and representative members of the bar of eastern Tennessee and is now representing Knox county as a member of the state senate. He has secure vantage place in the confidence and esteem of the people of his home city and county and as a citizen manifests his loyalty to every interest that touches upon the welfare of the community.

Hon. Norman B. Morrell was born in the city of Little Rock, Arkansas, on the tenth of February, 1870, and is a son of Rev. Henry H. Morrell, D. D., and his wife, Mary E. (Badger) Morrell, both of whom were born and reared in Ohio, in which state their respective families were founded in an early day, and with the civic and material history of which the names of both families have been closely identified. Rev. Henry H. Morrell, D. D., was a distinguished member of the clergy of the Protestant Episcopal church, and within the course of his long and consecrated life and service he held important pastorates in various dioceses of the church. From 1881 to 1886 he was rector of St. John's church, in Knoxville, and here, as elsewhere, his memory is revered by all who came within the sphere of his gracious and benign influence. He died in 1889, his devoted wife having preceded him in the year 1876. Five of their children, three sons and two daughters, are now living.

Senator Morrell is indebted to the public schools of Ohio and Tennessee for his early educational discipline, and he had the further advantage of a home of distinctive culture and influence. He attended the University of Tennessee for two years, and in preparation for his chosen profession he entered the law department of the celebrated University of Michigan, and in that institution he was graduated with the class of 1893 with the degree of Bachelor of Laws. Prior to the pursuit of his college career, however, it may be mentioned that Senator Morrell was employed for three years in the offices of the Knoxville Iron Company, and one year with the Mingo Mountain Coal & Coke Company.

Soon after he was graduated from the University of Michigan, the young man was admitted to the Tennessee bar, and since that time he has been engaged in the practice of his profession in the city of Knoxville, where he has built up a large and representative law practice and been concerned in much of the important litigation of the various courts. He is associated in a professional way with Charles Seymour, and is broadly recognized as one of the leading land and title lawyers in Knox county.

Mr. Morrell never aspired to political office until he announced his candidacy for the office of state senator in 1912, being elected by a large majority in November of that year. He has ever given a splendid allegiance to the Republican party, and has rendered effective service to the party on many occasions. His heavy majority at the polls in November was especially pleasing in view of the overwhelming Democratic landslide that attended the election throughout the country. Mr. Morrell presented resolutions in the Republican county executive committee meeting in 1912, which were passed, endorsing William H. Taft, R. W. Austin and the Republican party.

Mr. Morrell was one of the organizers of the Bell House Boys' Association, and was made its first president. He has long shown a most praiseworthy interest in the public school system of his city, and has done good work in that department of civic activity. He was the first secretary of the Knoxville Water Commission, and served most acceptably in that capacity for a number of years. He was also secretary of the charter committee of citizens that drafted the charter for the commission form of government of Knoxville, and has in many another equally telling way manifested his splendid citizenship and his interest in the development and progress of his city.

Mr. Morrell holds membership in the Knox County Bar Association and the Tennessee Bar Association, and is likewise affiliated with the

Royal Arcanum, and both he and his wife are zealous members of St.
John's church, Protestant Episcopal, of which he is junior warden and
On October 10, 1900, Mr. Morrell was united in marriage with Miss
of which his father was formerly rector.
Mary Ogden, daughter of James E. and Elise Porta Ogden. Mr. Ogden
is a native of the Buckeye state and Mrs. Ogden of Brazil, from whence
they. came to Tennessee in their earlier years. The father has for
many years been prominent as a railroad man. Three children have
been born to Senator and Mrs. Morrell: John O., Elise Emma and
James Robinson. The attractive family home, widely known for its
gracious and open-handed hospitality, is located at 1925 Caledonia
street, in this city.

JOHN H. FRANTZ, as one of the senior members of the law firm of
Cornick, Frantz, McConnell & Seymour, of Knoxville, Tennessee, is too
well known both in professional and social circles to need further comment. He has been engaged in the practice of his profession in the city
for a number of years and during this time has built up an enviable
reputation as a lawyer who does not stoop to underhand dealings and
who respects his profession too greatly to drag it down, as have so many
of the fraternity. That such a standard has not prevented him from
attaining success is shown by the large clientele which he has always had.
John H. Frantz is one of a family of nine children, whose parents
were T. P. Frantz and Sarah (Petit) Frantz, both of whom are now dead.
John H. Frantz was born in 1869, on the 15th of February, in the
state of Virginia. He received his elementary education in the public
schools of the state and later attended Central College, Missouri. His
law studies were pursued at the University of Tennessee,. from which he
was graduated with the class of 1894, and he immediately entered upon
the practice of his profession. He has been exclusively engaged in the
general practice of law since that time, for many years as a member of
the firm of Cornick, Frantz & McConnell. In 1912 Charles Milne Seymour was admitted to the firm and the name was changed to its present
reading. The other members of the firm are Howard Cornick and
Thomas G. McConnell. Their beautiful suite of five offices is located on
the fourth floor of the East Tennessee National Bank building.
In politics Mr. Frantz is a stanch Democrat and an active supporter
of his party. He is a member of the Ancient Free and Accepted Masons
and is very popular in the social life of the city, being a member of the
Country Club, the Cherokee Club and the University Club of Knoxville.

MAJ. THOMAS SHAPARD WEBB. Famous among the law firms of the
city of Knoxville, Tennessee, stands that of Webb & Baker. Major
Webb, the senior member of this firm, is perhaps one of the best known
men in Knoxville, and, in fact, in eastern Tennessee. For forty-four

years he has been a practitioner in Knoxville, and the record that he
has made as an upright lawyer and one who is unafraid is only equaled
by the record that he made as a soldier in the Civil war.

Thomas Shapard Webb was born on the 26th of September, 1840, in
Haywood county, Tennessee, the son of James L. Webb and Ariana
(Shapard) Webb. He was one of a family of eleven children and was
reared from infancy in Memphis, Tennessee. After completing his elementary education in the Memphis schools he was sent to Bingham
School, in North Carolina, a famous old school even then. He later attended the University of North Carolina, at Chapel Hill, but in April,
1861, during his junior year, he left the university to enter the Confederate service.

He enlisted at Memphis as a private in Company G of the One Hundred and Fifty-fourth Tennessee Regiment, but was almost immediately
elected first lieutenant, and it was as a lieutenant that he took part in
the occupation of Columbus, Kentucky, and in the battle of Belmont.
Early in 1862 his regiment fell back to Corinth, and then followed the
terrific two-days' battle of Shiloh. When General Beauregard evacuated
Corinth, Lieutenant Webb had the misfortune to be captured, and the
circumstances of his capture were such that he was reported dead, and
consequently lost his rank in the regiment. He was held a prisoner at
Johnson's Island until September, 1862, and as soon as he was released,
after an exchange at Vicksburg, he hastened to report for duty to General
Polk, at Knoxville. It is not hard to imagine the surprise with which this
resurrection of one supposed to be dead was greeted. General Polk
placed the young officer on detached duty, and he remained in Knoxville
until July, 1863, when he received orders to report to General Forrest.
To serve with this dashing cavalry leader was the ambition of many a
boy in gray, and it must have been a joy to Major Webb when he received those orders. General Forrest detailed him with two other men
to raise cavalry and organize the Sixteenth Tennessee Cavalry, of which
company Lieutenant Webb was commissioned major. Under the command of General Forrest, Major Webb now served with his regiment in
the engagement at Collierville, Tennessee, and in the famous battle of
Tishomingo Creek, or Brice's Cross-Roads. In this last battle he fell with
a wound in the ankle that prevented him from seeing any more active
service for about a year. Upon rejoining Forrest he took part in Wilson's raid in the spring of 1865, and shortly after this fought his last
fight at Scottsville, Alabama. He surrendered with his regiment at
Gainesville, Alabama.

, After the war he returned to his neglected studies and completed his
preparation for the bar in Memphis. He passed his examinations and
was admitted to the bar in 1867. He immediately began the practice
of his profession and has continued since that time, being conspicuously
successful. In 1869 he came to Knoxville to live and has been a resident

of that city ever since. As experience came to the aid of legal knowledge, Major Webb's reputation as a brilliant and dependable attorney increased, and he is acknowledged throughout the state as one of the authorities on various legal questions. He has several times had the honor of sitting as a special judge on the bench of the supreme court. The firm of Webb & Baker was formed on October 1, 1908, and their offices are in the Holston National Bank building.

Major Webb was married in February, 1867, to Miss Blanche McClung, of Knoxville. She died on October 15, 1894. On the 11th of August, 1897, Major Webb was again married, his wife being Mary Polk, a daughter of Col. Henry C. Yeatman, of Hamilton place, Ashwood, Tennessee.

JACOB LYTTON THOMAS. Those successful business men who have left the impress of their abilities upon the commercial history of Knoxville have been, almost without exception, men of affairs, with little instruction in science. They have stepped from the counter or office to the management of large interests, demonstrating their fitness to be leaders by soundness of judgment and skill in management. Such a man the generation of business men now passing from the scenes of active business recognized in Jacob Lytton Thomas when he came to Knoxville in 1874, and at once became a leader in business among those who had already reached high rank as merchants. His subsequent career was one of great activity in commercial circles, and in his death, which occurred September 24, 1906, the city lost a man who had done much to add to its prestige and importance.

Jacob Lytton Thomas was born in Nashville, Tennessee, December 3, 1840, one of the seven children of Jesse and Elizabeth (Lytton) Thomas. He received good educational advantages, attending the public schools and the University of Nashville, and after his graduation from the latter institution, in 1861, enlisted in the Confederate army for service during the Civil war. His military career covered a period of three years, and his faithful service gave promise of a characteristic that was to mark his after life—absolute devotion to every duty imposed on him. On his return, Mr. Thomas began his business career with the well-known Nashville firm of Gardner, Buckner & Company, with which he was connected until 1872, when he joined his brother and embarked in the dry goods business, the firm being known as the Morgan-Thomas Company of Nashville. In 1874 he severed his connection with the above firm and came to Knoxville, where he entered the wholesale dry goods business, in connection with Cowan, McClung & Company. During the remainder of his career, Mr. Thomas continued to be identified with this concern, one of the oldest and largest firms in the city, dealing in wholesale dry goods, notions and furnishings. As a member of Knoxville's coterie of leading business men, Mr. Thomas ever showed himself to be the self-contained man of business, whose word was unimpeach-able, whose fidelity was unquestioned, whose judgment of men and affairs was instinctive, one who had attained, by inimitable methods, a competence which he neither hoarded with avarice nor scattered with prodigal ostentation, but enjoyed reasonably, dispensed providently and shared generously. By temperament he was disinclined to public life, but took a good citizen's interest in all matters that affected his com-munity, and in political matters supported Democratic principles and candidates. He was not indifferent to the social amenities, and was well known in Masonry, in which he had attained to the Knights Templar degree.

On June 5, 1873, Mr. Thomas was united in marriage with Miss Lucy McClung, the daughter of Charles J. McClung, and seven children were born to this union, of whom five survive, namely: Jesse, who resides at No. 804 West Main street; Hugh M., whose residence is at No. 1622 Rose avenue; and Charles M., Matt G. and Miss Margaret, who reside with their mother at the beautiful family residence, No. 504 West Main street, Knoxville. The members of the family are affiliated with the Methodist Episcopal church South. The sons are still connected with the firm which their father helped develop.

WILLIAM WALLACE WOODRUFF. Prominent and widely known as a banker and merchant, Mr. Woodruff has been identified with the city of Knoxville for upwards of half a century. In that time he has attained a high position in business affairs, while his judgment and integrity have long been honored by his associates and he has also given much disinterested service that has accrued to the best good of the public, in positions that share greater burdens of responsibility than rewards of honor. He is president of the Woodruff Hardware Company, which operates one of the largest stores of its kind in the city.

William Wallace Woodruff, president of the wholesale hardware firm of W. W. Woodruff & Company, is a native son of Kentucky, born in the town of Bardstown, on the twenty-first day of March, 1840. He is one of the three children born to Ezra and Catherine Woodruff, the father having been a well-known manufacturer at Bardstown. Mr. Woodruff gained his early education in the common schools of Louisville, Kentucky, and on leaving school began his career in business as a clerk in a mercantile establishment. He was just at the outset of his business career and a young man of barely twenty-one years when the war broke out, and in the early days following the firing upon of Fort Sumter in April, 1861, he was appointed adjutant of the Thirteenth Kentucky Volunteer Infantry. His service continued to the end of the war, and he was discharged in January, 1865. Enlisting as a private, he was made adjutant, and during his service promoted to the rank of captain of Company D, and he left the service with that rank.

Upon his return from the front Captain Woodruff located at Knoxville, where he established soon after the wholesale hardware firm of which he is now senior member. His business career has had its setbacks and its hard times, like that of every successful record of enterprise, but on the whole he has maintained a front rank among the local merchants, and is now one of the leading men in the business and fiancial affairs of the city of Knoxville. Besides his presidency of the concern which bears his name, he is vice president and director of the East Tennessee National Bank and the Knoxville Real Estate Company and the Knoxville Ice Company. Since 1906 he has led a practically retired life, having retired in that year from the close supervision of his business, and now turns over the details of management to his junior associates. His son, W. W. Woodruff, Jr., is vice president of the company, and an able representative of his honored father in the business.

Mr. Woodruff is president of the board of trustees of the Tennessee Deaf and Dumb Institution, as well as president of the Carlson & Newman College at Jefferson City, Tennessee, and he and his family are communicants of the Baptist church in Knoxville.

The Baptist church of this city has for a number of years had no more liberal member than Captain Woodruff. He is a member of the Masonic order and of the Cherokee Country Club, as well as the local chapter of the Sons of the American Revolution.

In 1865 Captain Woodruff was united in marriage with Miss Ella T. Connelly, a native of Frankfort, Kentucky, and to them eight children were born, of which number five are yet living. The handsome home of the family is located at No. 1401 West Cumberland avenue.

COLONEL ROBERT LEE BEARE. In the personality of Robert Lee Beare are combined military talent and mercantile efficiency. Tennessee has been his chosen state since 1890 and Jackson his adopted home since 1906. His native state is Mississippi, and Virginia the nativity of his parents. His father, David Sieg Beare, was a jeweler by vocation and when he removed from Virginia settled his family and business in Aberdeen, Mississippi. His wife was Sarah Taylor, born in Staunton, in the Old Dominion state. It was in the early sixties—just before the war—that David Beare became a resident of Aberdeen, and there it was that to him and his wife Sarah the son was born whom they christened Robert Lee. His date of birth was December 2, 1864.

In the public schools of that Mississippi town Robert Lee Beare received his intellectual training. In 1885 he entered the United States Signal Corps, to which he gave service for one year. At the end of that time he accepted the official position of manager for the Western Union Telegraph Company at Aberdeen, Mississippi, his native home. He continued in this capacity until 1895.

In the meantime Mr. Beare, who is of an enterprising bent, had been establishing an ice business at Humboldt, Tennessee. Begun in 1890, it had by 1895 reached such proportions that it required the whole attention of its originator and owner. In the latter year he resigned his position with the Western Union Company and proceeded to further enlarge his ice manufactory. In 1906 he sold the plant. Removing to Jackson, he built a large establishment for the manufacturing of ice. This he has since continued to operate, combining with those activities the management of a coal and wood business.

It is of special interest to note the steadily increasing military prominence of Mr. Beare. In 1903 he was elected captain of Company G in the National Guard of the state of Tennessee. In 1906 he was made lieutenant-colonel of the Second Regiment in this same body. When, in 1907, the colonel of that regiment resigned, Robert Lee Beare was actively in command. In 1908 the First and Second Regiments were consolidated and Colonel Beare was honored by being retained in command of the reorganization.

City affairs have sought his incumbency of office. In 1910 he was elected alderman from the Fourth ward, in Jackson. He served for the stated term, but declined to consider re-election, because the multiplicity of his other duties was such as to prevent his giving as much time to city business as he felt the alderman's office should require. At reorganization of the state he accepted appointment as one of the three election commissioners, which office he still holds.

Col. Beare's prominence in the business capacity mentioned above, added to his membership in the directorate of the Union Bank and Trust Company of Jackson and his presidency of the O'Malley-Beare Valve Company of Chicago, have made him an especially intelligent president of the Merchants' and Manufacturers' Association. In that capacity he served for the term of 1911. As this association is one ruling only one-term presidencies, Colonel Beare has retired to general membership in it. He is, however, one of the most competent and energetic members in this body and in divers other ways lends willing assistance to any movement or measure that tends to the further development of the city's resources.

The political stand which Colonel Beare takes is that of an Independent Democrat. He is a member of various fraternal orders and the church connection of himself and his family is with the Methodist branch of the church.

Mrs. Beare—nee Mary Reiney—is a daughter of the late Col. G. K. Reiney, of Humboldt, Tennessee, and a niece of the late Col. F. B. Fisher. The marriage of Miss Reiney and Colonel Beare took place in 1906. They are the parents of two children, a daughter named Mary Hortense and a son called Robert Lee Beare.

JOHN MINNIS THORNBURGH. One of the strongest combinations of legal talent in Knoxville is the firm of Powers & Thornburgh, composed of J. Pike Powers, Jr., and John M. Thornburgh, whose offices are in the Empire building. The firm, since its organization in 1905, has had a generous share of the practice of office and courts, and its services have been employed in many of the important cases during this period.

Mr. Thornburgh, who represents the third generation of the family name in connection with the bar and public life in Tennessee, has been winning success in the law for the past ten years, and has also gained distinction in politics and enjoys many high social connections.

One of the four children of former Congressman Jacob M. Thornburgh and his wife, Laura Emma (Pettibone) Thornburgh, John M. Thornburgh, of this review, was born in the city of Knoxville, November 10, 1881. His father was a son of Montgomery Thornburgh, a prominent lawyer of Jefferson county, Tennessee, and was born in that county on July 3, 1837. He died at Knoxville on the 19th day of September, 1890. Jacob Montgomery Thornburgh had just been licensed to practice law when the Civil war broke out, and he crossed the mountains into Kentucky in 1861 and joined the Union army. He was afterwards commissioned lieutenant colonel of the Fourth Tennessee Cavalry. He made an enviable reputation as a soldier and officer, and was for some time the commander of a brigade. He was mustered out in July, 1865, and in the following year President Johnson tendered him a major's commission in the regular army, which he declined. He was district attorney from the third judicial district from 1866 to 1871, and in 1872 he was elected to congress, succeeding himself in the office in 1874 and in 1876. After retiring from congress he formed a partnership with Judge George Andrews, which continued until the death of Judge Andrews in 1889, and his own death followed within a year from that time. He was an industrious, popular and successful lawyer, especially noted for his ability as an advocate, and his position in political and professional life in his time was one of the most secure. His honored father, Montgomery Thornburgh, was in his day one of the leading citizens of Knox county, where he practiced law and also followed farming, was a member of the legislature and served in the office of attorney general of the county.

John Minnis Thornburgh was educated at Columbia University, New York, and at the University of Tennessee, where he was graduated A. B. in 1901 and LL. B. in 1902, being valedictorian of his class in the latter year. Admitted to the bar to practice in all courts of Tennessee in 1902, he was subsequently, on March 8, 1909, admitted to the bar of the United States supreme court. From 1903 to 1905 he was connected with the firm of Cornick, Wright & Frantz, and in 1905 formed the association with Mr. Powers which has proved so successful for both of them. Since July, 1911, Mr. Thornburgh has been serving as United States commissioner. He has been a member of the Knox county Republican executive committee since 1906, was a delegate to the state gubernatorial convention of 1910, and in the same year was a candidate for the Republican nomination to the office of attorney general of Knox county.

Mr. Thornburgh is a member of the Phi Gamma Delta fraternity and the Phi Kappa Phi honor fraternity, and affiliates with the Knoxville Lodge No. 160, B. P. O. E.; Council No. 645 of the Knights of Columbus, and is a member of the Cotillion Club and the Cherokee Country Club. He is a communicant of the Church of the Immaculate Conception.

Mr. Thornburgh was married on October 11, 1910, to Miss Sara Matlock, daughter of Mr. and Mrs. H. H. Matlock, of Riceville, Tennessee. They have one son, Henry Matlock Thornburgh, born April 30, 1912.

JOHN E. ROBERTSON. Highly respected both as a citizen and as a public official is John E. Robertson, revenue officer and postmaster of Springfield, Tennessee. He is a son of Logan T. and Elizabeth (Wells) Robertson and a grandson of George W. Wells, a man of unusual distinction in Crockett county. That community was the native home of George Wells, and there he had always lived until the period of the Civil war. He was one of the rare southerners who disapproved of secession and believed in the right of the national government to enforce unity in the great family of states whose very name is indicative of union. As Mr. Wells had the courage of his convictions and deceived no one in regard to his opinions, it became necessary for him to go, as an exile from his southern home, to Illinois, where he temporarily settled in Duquoin. After the close of the war, he returned to Crockett county, the beloved home of his childhood, and there he remained throughout the residue of his life, with the friends of a lifetime. He had not gone so far as to demonstrate his loyalty to the government by taking up arms against his neighbors, but he had two sons who felt it their duty to serve the Union as soldiers in the Federal army. These two young men, John W. and Everett Wells, were both killed in the engagement at Fort Pillow. After the period of renewed peace was begun, Mr. Wells was again accorded his old place in the hearts of his friends of opposite opinions. He was, indeed, a very prominent citizen, serving for twenty years as justice of the peace and receiving every tribute of genuine respect. The man whom his daughter married—Logan Robertson—was a carpenter for many years, only laying aside that occupation in 1880, to retire to his farm in Crockett county, where he now lives, at the age of eighty-one years. Elizabeth Wells Robertson died in 1884 at the age of forty-eight. She and her husband were both connected with the Missionary Baptist church. Logan Robertson is a Republican in politics and is a member of the Independent Order of Odd Fellows. Of the four sons yet living, who were born to Logan and Elizabeth Robertson, the second was John E., the date of whose birth was November 6, 1863, and whose birthplace was Chestnut Bluff, Tennessee.

At his own home John E. Robertson was given the opportunities for education which the public schools offered and later spent one year in advanced study at the South-Western University, located at Jackson, Tennessee. He then engaged in the profession of teaching, which he continued for two years. At the end of that time he entered the revenue service as assistant store-keeper and gauger. In 1892 he located in Springfield, which has ever since been his home.

In 1894 Mr. Robertson was united in marriage with Miss Fannie Dylus, a daughter of Finis Dylus, a native and lifelong resident of Robertson county. One child has been born to Mr. and Mrs. Robertson and was christened Lula D. Robertson. She is at home with her parents. Mrs. Robertson is a member of the Methodist church, her husband being connected with the Baptist denomination. He is affiliated with the secret societies of the Independent Order of Odd Fellows and the Free and Accepted Masons.

In 1906 Mrs. Robertson received the appointment to the postoffice of Springfield and is nominal postmistress, having retained the office since that time. Mr. Robertson undertakes many of the responsibilities and duties of the office, ably discharging the same.

ROBERT ALEXANDER KIMBEL, of Linden, has been registrar of Perry county thirty-one years, or since 1882, and has the distinction of having given the longest continuous service in one position of any present office holder of Tennessee. This long continuation in public service speaks more eloquently than words can do as to the position Mr. Kimbel holds in the confidence and esteem of the people among whom he has lived since his birth. The name he bears is one that has been prominent in the public life of this county for full three-quarters of a century and has throughout that long period remained locally significant of the most worthy order of citizenship.

The Kimbels are Scotch and the family was founded in this country by William Kimbel, the grandfather of Robert A., who emigrated here from Scotland along in the latter part of the eighteenth century and settled in Alabama, where he followed his trade as a brick mason. Dr. Franklin H. Kimbel, his son, born in Alabama in 1799, grew to manhood in his native state and there was prepared for the profession of medicine. He came to Tennessee when a young man, locating first in Waynesboro, but removing later from thence to Perry county, where he spent the remainder of his career in active service as a physician, passing away in 1864. He became a very prominent citizen of this county and twice represented it in the Tennessee state legislature, first in 1851 and 1852 and again in 1855-56. He was also clerk of the circuit court in Perry county during the '40s, and in 1860 was county court clerk. In political allegiance he was a staunch Democrat. In 1840, in Perry county, Tennessee, he wedded Eliza King, who was born in Cheatham county, Tennessee, in 1813 and who departed life in Perry county in 1883. Six children came to this union, viz.: Robert Alexander Kimbel, the immediate subject of this review; Benjamin F., who served under Captain Whitwell, in Colonel Cox's regiment, in General Forrest's army during the Civil war and died in a Federal prison; Elizabeth, deceased in infancy; James Wiley and John Nathaniel, twins, the former of whom is deceased and the latter of whom resides in Perry county; and Sims Allen, also a resident of Perry county.

Robert Alexander Kimbel, the eldest of this family, was born at Buffalo River, Perry county, Tennessee, September 26, 1841, and received his educational discipline in the early public schools of this county. His public service began in 1882, when he was elected to the office which he has held continuously since, that of registrar of Perry county, in which position his service has been of the most worthy and efficient order. He is a Democrat.

Mr. Kimbel has been twice married. In 1890 he wedded Miss Martha Broyles, of Savannah, Tennessee, and to their union were born two children: Herbert Franklin, now deceased, and Hundley Broyles, who married Miss Bertha Willer of Savannah and is manager of the Cumberland Telephone Company at Waynesboro, at the age of nineteen. Mrs. Kimbel passed to rest in 1896, a consistent member of the Methodist Episcopal church South. In 1902 Mr. Kimbel took as his second wife Miss Fannie Ellis, of Franklin, Tennessee. Both are members of the Methodist Episcopal church South; Mr. Kimbel has been trustee of his church for many years.

KINNARD TAYLOR McCONNICO. One of the strongest firms of the Nashville bar is that of Pitts & McConnico, composed of John A. Pitts and Kinnard T. McConnico. The junior member has been identified with the profession in this city for fifteen years, and has a record of achievement and success in both the law and in public affairs.

Mr. McConnico, who represents an old Tennessee family, was born at Cornersville, Marshall county, this state, on February 13, 1875. His parents, both natives of Tennessee and of Scotch-Irish lineage, were George H. K. and Sarah Josephine (Taylor) McConnico. The McConnicos originally settled in Virginia, from there came to Williamson county, Tennessee, where a number of families of the name have since resided, and many of the members have been prominent. The Rev. Garner McConnico, great-grandfather of the Nashville lawyer, was a pioneer minister of the Primitive Baptist church in Tennessee. George H. K. McConnico, the father, now deceased, was a Confederate soldier throughout the war, being a private of Company A of the Forty-fifth Tennessee Infantry.

The family residence was established in Nashville when the son Kinnard T. was seven years old, and here he was reared and educated.

From the public schools he entered Vanderbilt University, where he took the literary course and later studied law, being graduated in 1896 with the degree LL. B. Since that time he has practiced in this city with growing distinction and success. In 1902 he was elected city attorney for four years, but resigned after three years and in April, 1905, joined Mr. Pitts in their present partnership. Mr. McConnico is a Democrat and a member of the Knights of Pythias. He was married in 1906 to Miss Nina Ferris, daughter of the late Judge John C. Ferris, of Nashville.

HENRY J. HARLEY. As a representative of the manufacturing interests of Davidson county, and an honored and respected citizen of Nashville, Henry J. Harley, vice-president of the Smith, Herring & Baird Manufacturing Company, and likewise of the Harley Pottery Company, is the subject of this brief history, wherein are recorded some of the more important and interesting events in his life. He was born on a farm in Jackson county, Tennessee, June 27, 1838, a son of George Washington Harley, coming from pioneer stock.

His grandfather Hiram Harley, a native, as far as known, of North Carolina, came from there to Tennessee in the very early part of the nineteenth century, making the removal with teams. Locating in Jackson county, he bought land on the Blackburn fork of Roaring river. Tennessee was then but sparsely settled, wild game of all kinds being abundant, while the streams were well filled with fish. There were no railways in the state, and no convenient markets in the county. Owing to an entire absence of mills of any kind, he, in common with the other pioneers, used to manufacture his own meal, pounding the corn with a pestle in an iron mortar. In 1850, then a man well advanced in years, he again started westward, going to Missouri, settling as a pioneer in the vicinity of Springfield, buying a tract of land about twenty-five miles southeast of that city, and there residing until his death. He was killed during the Civil war by bushwhackers, being then ninety years of age. His wife, whose maiden name was Elizabeth Stafford, survived him several years, rounding out nearly a century of life. They reared a family of five children, as follows: Harriet, Elizabeth, Matilda, George W., and Andrew.

Born in North Carolina, George W. Harley was but a babe when brought by his parents to Tennessee, where he grew to manhood. Subsequently buying land near the parental homestead, he cleared and improved a good farm, on which he was engaged in agricultural pursuits until his death, at the comparatively early age of fifty-nine years. He married Margaret Lawson, who was born in Jackson county, Tennessee; her father, Robert Tilford, it is said, was a native of Scotland, and her mother was a member of the well-known Sevier family. She died at the age of sixty-six years, having reared eight children, namely:

. Henry J., Samantha, James A., Hiram E., Lewis, Elizabeth, Absalom, and Eliza.

Brought up in his native county, Henry J. Harley obtained his early education in the typical pioneer log cabin, attending a free school two or three months each year. The rude cabin was made of rough logs, with an earth chimney and a puncheon floor, and its pupils came there from anywhere within a radius of five miles. In 1853, when he was fifteen years old, his Grandfather Harley visited relatives and old-time friends in Tennessee, and when the grandfather returned to his home in Missouri he accompanied him, they being four weeks in making the trip, taking turns in riding the one horse which they had between them. He found wild game of all kinds plentiful in Missouri, and from the deer which he shot during the following winter he realized a little money.

Going to Springfield in the spring of 1854, Mr. Harley found it to be a small but flourishing inland town, with stage connections for St. Louis and other points. The greater part of Missouri was then owned by the government, and people wishing to enter land were obliged to register at the land office in Springfield, and then patiently wait in the large crowd that was always in evidence until his name was called, sometimes waiting two weeks or more. He sought and obtained work on a farm, and at the end of four months of steady labor was paid the sum of sixty dollars in gold. With his earnings in his pocket he started homeward, walking to St. Genevieve, on the Mississippi river, and on the way passing Iron Mountain. There were then no railways in Missouri; on the plank road which had been laid to St. Genevieve, a distance of forty miles, all the ore was drawn with teams. From that place Mr. Harley came via the Mississippi, Ohio, and Cumberland rivers to Nashville, Tennessee, where he purchased a fine suit of clothes. The vest, which was a fancy one, and decidedly dressy, was ornamented with hand-painted decorations.

From that time until the outbreak of the Civil war, Mr. Harley was busily employed in tilling the soil. In July, 1861, he enlisted, from his old home in Jackson county, in Company G, Twenty-fifth Tennessee Volunteer Infantry, of which he was commissioned first lieutenant. After the engagement at Chickamauga, he was detailed as supernumary officer, and ordered to report to General Gideon J. Pillow, at Marietta, Georgia. He subsequently had to report first to Colonel Lockhart, at Montgomery, Alabama, and later to Major Tazewell Newman, at Guntersville, Alabama, continuing in active service until the cessation of hostilities.

Returning home barefooted and ragged, Mr. Harley commenced farming on rented land, with his wife, occupying a log cabin. Successful in his operations, he continued as a tiller of the soil until 1871, when he accepted a position with the Phillips & Buttorff Manufacturing Company, of Nashville, for which he was traveling salesman for three years.

In 1874 he was elected clerk of the county court of Jackson county, and at the expiration of his term, in 1878, was re-elected to the same office. Resigning in 1880, Mr. Harley resumed his former position as commercial salesman for his former employers, and continued with the firm until 1890. From that time until 1908, a period of eighteen years, he was general manager of the Broad Street Stove and Tinware Company's establishment. During the past four years, since 1908, Mr. Harley has been associated with the Smith, Herring & Baird Company, of which he is vice-president, being also vice-president of the Harley Pottery Company. He is likewise much interested in the Cumberland Steamboat Company, and in other enterprises of importance.

Mr. Harley married, January 17, 1860, Mary E. McKoy, who was born in Coffee county, Tennessee, a daughter of Hiram and Margaret (McDonald) McKoy. Five children have been born of the union of Mr. and Mrs. Harley, namely: Maggie, James M., Hiram, William H., and David R. Maggie, wife of W. Y. Hart, has three children, Chester K., Mary, and Eugenia. James M. Harley married Willie Ann Vaughan, and they are the parents of two children, Elmore and Mattie Lee. Hiram, whose death occurred August 13, 1892, married Jessie Phillips, by whom he had one child, Mary Kate. William H. married Florence Roach, and they have three children, Ruth, Rachel, and Rebecca. David R. married Jennie Vaughan. Elmore Harley, Mr. Harley's grandson, married Alta Jarrett, and they have three children, Johnson, Jarrett, William Leslie and Anna Elizabeth. Mary Kate Harley, a granddaughter of Mr. and Mrs. Harley, married Hugh Martin, and has one child, Mary Elizabeth Martin.

Mr. and Mrs. Harley are members of the Christian church, and for full forty years Mr. Harley has belonged to the Ancient Free and Accepted Order of Masons.

WILLIAM THOMAS HARDISON. For many years prominently identified with the business life of the city of Nashville, William Thomas Hardison has contributed largely towards the development and advancement of the city's mercantile prosperity, and is now living retired from active pursuits, enjoying a well-earned leisure. A son of Humphrey Hardison, he was born, March 20, 1839, in Maury county, Tennessee, of substantial pioneer stock.

His paternal grandfather, James Hardison, who was of Scotch ancestry, was born and reared in North Carolina, and was there married. In 1808, accompanied by his family, he migrated to Tennessee, making the journey overland with teams, one wagon and a cart holding all of their household possessions and their farming implements. He located as a pioneer in Maury county, settling there while the country roundabout was still in its primitive condition, the dense forests being inhabited by the wily Indian and the wild beasts native to the country, neither, however, proving very troublesome. For many years after he established his home in Tennessee there were no railroads near him, Nashville, forty-five miles away, being the nearest depot for supplies. He purchased land, and on the homestead which he improved spent the remainder of his life, both he and his faithful wife living to a good old age.

Born in North Carolina, Humphrey Hardison was a small boy of four years when he was brought by his parents to Tennessee.˙ Growing to manhood in pioneer days, he received a limited education in the district schools, but while assisting his father became familiar with the various branches of agriculture. Beginning life for himself, he purchased sixty acres of land on Duck river, twelve miles east of Columbia, and at once began to clear the tract of its heavy growth of timber. Having but one hired man to assist him in his arduous task, the work was necessarily slow. He embarked in the livestock business, making a specialty of raising mules and saddle horses. He was very successful in that industry, and as his means increased he added to his landed possessions until he had seven hundred acres in one body besides outlying tracts in that vicinity, and six hundred and forty acres of land in Texas. He operated with slave labor, and was easily the leading stock raiser and dealer of Maury county for several years, and a man of prominence in agricultural circles until his death, October 11, 1874.

Humphrey Hardison married Harriet Woolard, who was born in Tennessee, a daughter, and only child, of Silas and Lucretia (Robinson) Woolard, natives of North Carolina, and early settlers of Maury county. She died at a comparatively early age, being but forty-five years old when she passed to the life beyond. Ten children were born of their union, as follows: Marshall, who served in the Confederate army, and was captured at Fort Donelson, died while in prison; James, who likewise enlisted in the Confederate service, died soon after entering the army; Jane became the wife of George W. Patterson; Sarah married J. C. Ligett; Margaret Sophronia married J. M. Patterson; William Thomas, with whom this brief sketch is chiefly concerned; Richard Calvin, who, early in 1861, enlisted in the Confederate army, and was commissioned lieutenant of his company, was honorably discharged in 1862, on account of physical disability; Victoria became the wife of William Wilcox; Humphrey enlisted as a soldier in 1864,, and served until the close of the war; and Sherod T.

On attaining his majority William Thomas Hardison took up his residence in Texas, which was then a typical frontier state, with but forty miles of railroad within its borders. He found employment as clerk in a store at Paris, but when, a few months later, war between the states was declared, he returned home, and at once enlisted in Company F, First Tennessee Cavalry, under command of General Armstrong and later of General Forrest, the famous Confederate cavalry leader. Mr.

Hardison continued with his command in all of its many campaigns, marches and battles until the close of the conflict, being in Greensboro, North Carolina, at the surrender. He was allowed to retain his horse until he reached Strawberry Plains, Tennessee, where, with others, he took passage for Nashville in a box car.

On arriving home, Mr. Hardison assisted his father in the harvest field for awhile, and later taught school two terms. Changing his occupation, he then dealt in horses for a time, buying in Indianapolis, Indiana, and selling in his home state. He subsequently managed his father's farm for a year, and then embarked in agricultural pursuits on his own account, assuming possession of a small farm which his father had given him, it being located in Marshall county. Disposing of that at the end of a year, Mr. Hardison moved to Obion county, Tennessee, where he bought a tract of timbered land, and, at a crossing of the roads, established a general store, which he conducted successfully for two years. Coming then to Nashville, a city of but thirty-five thousand inhabitants, Mr. Hardison bought a third interest in a retail grocery store on Broad street. Selling out his interest four years later, he, with two others, purchased a wholesale grocery house and stock, and conducted a substantial mercantile business, as a member of the firm of Harsh, McLean & Hardison, until 1890. Selling out in that year, Mr. Hardison purchased a half interest in the business of Mr. E. A. Ireland, with whom he was associated for five years. He then bought out his partner, and remained as sole proprietor of the establishment until succeeded by his son, Humphrey Hardison, who still continues the business with characteristic success.

A man of great executive and financial ability, Mr. Hardison has been prominently identified with various enterprises of note. For five years he was president of the Broadway National Bank, and on resigning that position served for two years as director, being then succeeded by his son Humphrey. He has also served as director and vice-president of the Wilkinson County Undertakers' Association.

Mr. Hardison married, October 29, 1867, Martha G. McLean, who was born in Marshall county, Tennessee, a daughter of Andrew and Elizabeth (Denney) McLean. Mr. and Mrs. Hardison have two children living, namely: Elizabeth McLean, widow of M. A. Montgomery; and Humphrey, who succeeded his father in business. Blanche, their eldest child, lived but one year, and William T., their youngest son, died at the age of twenty-one years. Humphrey Hardison married Elizabeth E. Escott, and they have two children, William Thomas Hardison, the second; and Frances Scott Hardison. Mr. and Mrs. William Thomas Hardison united with the Presbyterian church when young, and have reared their children in that faith.

E. B. Chappell, D. D.   As Sunday school editor for the Methodist
Episcopal church South, Dr. Chappell has the distinction of writing for
more people than any other editor or writer in the entire South. He is
one of the senior men in southern Methodism, has been connected with
the ministry and official work of the church for more than thirty years
and now occupies one of the most responsible places in the church service.

Dr. E. B. Chappell was born in Perry county, Tennessee, December
27, 1853, a son of W. B. and Elizabeth (Whitaker) Chappell. The Chappell family came from England and settled in Virginia in the year 1635,
and has been represented in southern civic and professional life for many
generations. The paternal grandparents were William and Sallie
(Palmer) Chappell, both of whom were born in Virginia, moved out to
Tennessee in 1827, locating on a farm in Maury county near Columbia.
The grandfather was a man of ability, both in business and public affairs,
owned a number of slaves and conducted a large plantation. Nearly all
his active life he was a class leader in the Methodist church.

Mrs. W. B. Chappell, the mother, was born in North Carolina, in 1831,
and is now deceased. Her husband was born in Tennessee in 1828 and
died in 1900. He was educated in this state and spent all his life here.
By occupation he was a farmer, and was a man of more than usual education for his day. He filled the office of county surveyor and was very
influential in his community. For many years he was officially connected with the Methodist church and took much part in Sunday school
work. In politics he was a Whig and later a Democrat. He was twice
married, and by the first marriage there were four children. After the
death of his first wife he married a Miss Gillham, and there were five
children by that union. E. B. Chappell was the oldest child. The
others are as follows: W. W. Chappell, who resides on a farm near
Nashville; Sallie, wife of E. S. Gillham, a resident in west Tennessee;
Anna, wife of H. A. Grimes, of Oklahoma. The children of the second
marriage were: Charles P., a merchant of Tupelo, Mississippi; Summers.
a farmer in Wayne county, Tennessee; Mrs. Grady Jones, of Waverly,
Tennessee; Rev. A. C. Chappell, in the ministry of the Methodist church
South at Waco, Texas; Rev. C. G. Chappell, also a minister of that denomination and stationed at Gatesville, Texas. Both the latter are prominent
in the ministry and have excellent charges. The maternal grandparents
of E. B. Chappell were James Whitaker and wife, the latter being a
Lyon. They were born in North Carolina, came to Tennessee in 1846,
settling in Wayne county, where the grandfather was a farmer and prosperous planter.

E. B. Chappell received his education at the Webb School, at that time
at Culleoka, Tenn., and was graduated from Vanderbilt University in
1879. The first two years after his graduation he spent as principal of
a conference school and in 1882 took up the active work of the ministry
in the Texas conference. He preached in Texas for nine years, being

stationed at LaGrange, San Antonio and Austin, having the best appointments in the state. Then removing to St. Louis he served two of the leading churches of that city, and in 1898 came to Nashville, where he was pastor of the West End church for four years and of McKendree church for four years. In May, 1906, he was elected to his present office as Sunday school editor of the Methodist church South. He is also chairman of the Sunday school board of the church.

Mr. Chappell married Miss Jennie Headlee, daughter of Rev. J. H. Headless, of the St. Louis conference. The marriage was celebrated in 1880 and four children have been born, namely: F. W. Chappell, a civil engineer, who makes his home at Dallas, Texas; Ethel, who married W. A. Smart, and lives at Portsmouth, Virginia, her husband being a pastor of the Methodist church there, and his father one of the distinguished ministers of the denomination; Helen, at home; and E. B. Chappell, Jr., in business at Houston, Texas. Mr. Chappell is prominent in the Masonic Order, having attained thirty-two degrees of the Scottish Rite.

JOSEPH D. HAMILTON. Treasurer of the Board of Missions for the Methodist Episcopal church South, Mr. Hamilton has held this responsible position for the past fifteen years, and is one of the ablest men connected with the business organization of the church. He is a native of Nashville, and for many years was in business in this city, previous to his election as treasurer of the Board of Missions.

Joseph D. Hamilton was born at Nashville, December 15, 1845, and the family had been identified with the country west of the Alleghenies for more than a century. His parents were Mortimer and Emeline (Hill) Hamilton. His paternal grandparents were Joseph D. and Sallie (Morgan) Hamilton, the former a native of Rockbridge county, Virginia, whence he moved into Kentucky as an early settler, and for many years was cashier of the bank of Russellville. Joseph D. Hamilton was a man who enjoyed unusual success, although his life came to a premature end. The maternal grandparents were Thomas and Sallie (Woods) Hill. The former was a native of Kentucky, and was a first cousin of General A. P. Hill, of Confederate fame. He followed business as a merchant and was owner of a line of steamboats and previous to the war owned many slaves.

Mortimer Hamilton, the father, was born in Russellville, Kentucky, in 1816, and died in 1879. His wife was born at Nashville in 1816, and her death occurred in 1907. The father was educated in Kentucky, but when a young man moved to Nashville where he was in the drug business during the remainder of his life. He and his wife had eight children, only three of whom are now living, the two daughters being Mary and Emeline, both unmarried. The father was very prominent in the affairs of the Methodist church South, serving as an official in his church until death. He was a Democrat in politics, and a Mason who took all the degrees of the York Rite, including the Knights Templar, and held the various chairs in his lodge.

Joseph D. Hamilton received his education in the public schools, and just before the close of the war enlisted and saw brief service with the Twentieth Tennessee Regiment of Infantry. Returning from this experience he engaged in the hardware business with his uncle, J. M. Hamilton, at Nashville, the firm being known as J. M. Hamilton & Company. Some time later he became identified with the manufacturing of paper and bags, under the name of Morgan & Hamilton Company. This was his active business line until 1898, when he was elected treasurer of the Board of Missions of the Methodist Episcopal church South. Mr. Hamilton has the important responsibility of handling a million and a half dollars every year, and has charge of the funds collected in all the churches of the Southern Methodist denomination for missions. He gives his whole time to this business and has no other commercial interests.

In 1891 he married Miss Mary G. McTyeire, oldest daughter of Bishop H. N. McTyeire, whose name was for years a household word in Methodism and who was the founder of Vanderbilt University at Nashville.

Mr. Hamilton is a Democrat in politics, and is a steward in the McKendree church at Nashville, being also a member of the official board.

DAVID R. PICKENS, M. D. Representing one of the oldest families of Marshall county, Dr. Pickens has been extending the recognition of the name in the field of medicine and surgery, and is accounted one of the ablest young surgeons of Nashville, where he has had prominent connections and a large practice.

David R. Pickens was born in Mooresville, in Marshall county, Tennessee, August 9, 1882, a son of Z. R. and Nannie L. (McKibbon) Pickens. The founder of the Pickens family in Tennessee was Hamilton Pickens, great-grandfather of the doctor, who came from South Carolina to this state and was one of the early settlers in Marshall county. His brother served as one of the early governors of South Carolina, where the name is particularly well known. Grandfather David B. Pickens was born in Marshall county, Tennessee, in 1812, more than a century ago, and lived to be eighty-five years of age. He was a successful farmer and trader. Z. R. Pickens, the father, was born in Marshall county, in 1860, had a high school education at Mooresville, became a farmer and stock dealer, and for the past fourteen years has resided at Belle Buckle, where he has built up a large business in buying and selling mules, being probably the best known dealer in these animals in the state. He is a member of the Presbyterian church in which he has taken considerable interest, and in politics is a Democrat. His wife was born in Maury county, in 1863, a daughter of J. Van McKibbon, who was a native of Maury county, and a substantial farmer there. Z. R. Pickens and wife had five children, namely: David R.; Xennie, wife of William Bonner, a

merchant at Belle Buckle; William F., a farmer at Mooresville; Mackie, wife of Lesley Davis, of Belle Buckle, and Z. R., Jr., who is in the same business as his father, and the two are associated.

Dr. Pickens when a boy attended Webb school, and later took two years in the literary department of the Vanderbilt University. From that he began the study of medicine, and was graduated M. D. in 1907. His first experience was in the city hospital at Nashville, and he also spent two years with Dr. R. E. Fort, in the latter's private hospital. In 1910 he established himself in independent practice, and has since enjoyed unusual success. He has made a specialty of surgery, and is at the present time instructor in surgery in the Vanderbilt University. Dr. Pickens is a member of the Delta Kappa Epsilon fraternity, and the Alpha Kappa Kappa medical fraterity. He belongs to the Elks Lodge No. 72, and is a member of all the medical societies and associations. In politics he is a Democrat. He gives all his time to his profession, in which he has already won a high place.

HON. CHARLES C. GILBERT. One of the most progressive members of the present legislature is Charles C. Gilbert of Nashville, in which city he has been well known for his success in the automobile business, and as the enterprising assistant secretary of the board of trade. Mr. Gilbert is young, came up through the ranks, has a keen conception of modern tendencies, and requirements of business and civic life, and his influence and creative activity in the legislature have been directed to measures of the most practical character and affecting broad and vital interests in the state.

In Bethel, Giles county, Tennessee, Charles C. Gilbert was born March 12, 1877, a son of John C. and Tranquilla (Gracy) Gilbert. His grandfather, Calvin G. Gilbert, came from North Carolina, settling in Giles county, and was the founder of the Gilbert family in this state. The maternal grandfather was J. A. Gracy, for many years a Presbyterian minister, and one of the organizers of the Cumberland Presbyterian church, his home during most of his life being in Lincoln county, where his daughter, the mother of Mr. Gilbert, was born. The mother now lives in Texas. The father, who was born in Giles county, was educated there, was a farmer, and provided well for his family. When the war broke out, he organized a company, and as captain in the Twenty-Third Tennessee Regiment went through the struggle from beginning to end. He was wounded in three different battles, was captured and spent several months in Federal prisons. After the war he returned to Giles county. He was an active member of the Cumberland Presbyterian church, and prominent in Masonry, having taken thirty-two degrees of the Scottish Rite in that order. In politics he was a Democrat. He and his wife were the parents of thirteen children, six of whom are now living, and the Nashville legislator was ninth in order of birth.

In the schools at Lawrenceburg, Tennessee, Charles C. Gilbert received his first training, and continued in the public schools of Nashville. To earn his way during the early stages of his career, Mr. Gilbert learned and practiced stenography, an avenue through which so many young men have reached a useful place in commercial affairs. He kept up that work for twelve years, and eventually engaged in the automobile business, organizing the Southern Automobile Company, a concern which his vitalizing energy made very successful. He also has the distinction of having organized the Nashville Automobile Club, and was its first secretary. On returning from that place he became assistant secretary of the Nashville Board of Trade, with which important organization he has since been connected.

Mr. Gilbert is one of the most vigorous exponents in Tennessee of the good roads movement. He has attended conventions all over the United States, and on many different occasions, has spoken and argued the material benefits to be derived from well made and serviceable highways. In politics he is Democratic, and served two years in the city council. Later he was nominated to the assembly, but refused the nomination. In 1912 he accepted this honor when again proffered him, and was elected. During his legislative career he has introduced the banking law for state banks; has brought in the measure providing for a highway department in the state; has been one of the chief movers in a general law, providing for commission government in the cities of the state; another bill of which he is the author allows counties to issue their own bonds without previous legislative permission. Mr. Gilbert fought hard against capital punishment, but lost the bill abolishing that institution.

In June, 1900, Mr. Gilbert married Miss Alma Badford, of McMinnville. To their marriage have been born three children: Mary L. who is in school; Charles C., Jr., and Elizabeth, the latter being one year of age. The family worship in the Presbyterian church of which Mr. Gilbert is an elder, and for thirteen years has been superintendent of the Sunday school. He is a member of the Masonic Order and of the Knights of Pythias. He has done much work as a speaker for the Boys Corn Club and for the promotion of agricultural improvement.

REV. WARNER T. BOLLING, D. D. Dr. Bolling was one of the distinguished members of the clergy of the Methodist Episcopal church, South, and in his high calling has labored with all of consecrated zeal and devotion. It is needless to say that he was a man of fine intellectual attainments, and further than this, he was a most effective pulpit orator and possessed of an executive ability that has enabled him to further the temporal, as well as the spiritual prosperity of the various churches which he served. He was at time of his death, April 16, 1913, pastor of the church of his denomination at Clinton, the judicial center of

Hickman county, Kentucky, this attractive little city being situated about fourteen miles distant from the boundary line between that state and Tennessee. There is all of consistency in according to him specific consideration in this publication, for though he was not a resident of Tennessee, he was a member of one of its gallant regiments in the Confederate service in the Civil war, and had otherwise been concerned in various ways with Tennessee affairs.

Dr. Bolling was a scion of staunch and patrician old southern stock and a representative of families that were founded in Virginia, that cradle of much of our national history, in the colonial epoch. He was born in Greene county, Alabama, on the 25th of May, 1847, and was a son of Warner T., and Harriet E. (Smith) Bolling, both of whom were born and reared in Virginia. Warner T. Bolling removed from the Old Dominion state to Alabama when a young man and in the latter state he became a successful planter, his operations having been carried forward on a somewhat extensive scale. He suffered great losses through the ravages of the Civil war, as did most of the planters of the southern states, and both he and his wife continued to reside in Alabama until their death. They were devout and zealous members of the Episcopal church; they lived "godly, righteous and sober lives;" and they ever commanded the high esteem of all who knew them. Of their children, three sons and one daughter attained to years of maturity none of whom are now living. Dr. Bolling, of this review, was the youngest in the family and the only one of the number to enter the ministry. One brother, Robert P. Bolling, was engaged in mercantile business, and another brother, George S., served in the quarter-master's department of the Confederate army of the Civil war.

On the old homestead plantation Dr. Bolling passed the days of his childhood, under the conditions and influences of the fine old southern regime,—a patriarchial system that gave to American history its only touch of generic romance. He was a lad of about fifteen years at the inception of the war between the states, and his youthful loyalty to the south was shown forthwith and in an insistent way. He tendered his service in defense of the cause of the Confederacy, by enlisting in May, 1861, and was attached first to the Harris Zouave Cadets, in Memphis, Tennessee, as Company D of the 154th Sr. Tennessee Regiment. Then he re-enlisted as a private in Company C, Second Tennessee Infantry, and with this gallant command he served from May, 1861, to May, 1865, the entire period of the great conflict between the north and the south. It was his to participate in many important engagements, besides innumerable skirmishes and other minor conflicts, and he proved a valiant and faithful young soldier in battling for a cause which he believed to be right and just and the story of which is written in words pregnant with the evidences of devotion, suffering and sacrifice. The Doctor took part in the battles of Shiloh, Perrysville, Murfreesboro, and Chickamauga,

Ringgold Gap—the entire Atlanta campaign from Dalton to Jonesboro—Franklin and also Lost Mountain and Nashville, and in the last mentioned engagement he received a severe wound in the right arm. At the battle of Nashville, he was captured by the enemy, in December, 1864, and he was held a prisoner at Camp Chase, Ohio, until the close of the war, his parole having been granted in May, 1865. Dr. Bolling ever retained the deepest interest in his old comrades in arms and signified the same by his affiliation with the United Confederate Veterans' Association.

In the schools of his native state Dr. Bolling gained his preliminary education, which was supplemented by a classical course in historic old Emory and Henry College, at Emory, Virginia, an institution maintained under the auspices of the Methodist Episcopal church, South. His theological education was acquired in the conference course of studies, and in 1868 he was ordained in the ministry, at Paris, Tennessee. In 1886 he received the degree of Doctor of Divinity from St. Charles College, Missouri, in recognition of his high attainments and exalted service in the church, and in 1909, the same degree was conferred upon him by Peabody Institute, at Nashville, Tennessee.

Dr. Bolling labored in his high vocation for more than two score years, within which he garnered a generous harvest in the aiding and uplifting of his fellow men and in making his angle of influence constantly expand in beneficence and zeal, as an earnest worker in the vineyard of the divine Master. He joined the Memphis conference in 1868 and for nearly twenty years was one of the distinguished and influential representatives thereof, the while he had the affectionate regard and high esteem of the various communities in which he held pastoral charges, including those at Lexington and Covington, Kentucky; Hannibal, Missouri; Centenary Church, Fayette, Missouri; St. Paul's, Denver, Colorado; Columbus, Mississippi; Shreveport, Louisiana; Jackson, Mississippi; the Central Methodist church in Memphis, Tennessee; the Broadway church in Paducah, Kentucky; and the church at Fulton, that state. He was transferred to the West Virginia conference in 1880 and remained in other conferences to do special work directed by different Bishops of the Methodist Episcopal church, South, returning to the Memphis conference in 1904, where he remained until his death. The Kentucky towns he lived in, are included in the bounds of the Memphis conference. He held the pastorate of the church of his denomination in Clinton, Kentucky, from November, 1912, to April 16, 1913, on which date he died. He was buried in Forest Hill cemetery, Memphis, Tennessee, his former home, on April 17, 1913.

Dr. Bolling was first married to Miss Mary Coley, of Milan, Tennessee, in 1870. Robert E., Margaret E., and Cora were children of this marriage, Cora dying in infancy, in 1873.

Dr R.H.Baylor

At Huntington, West Virginia, on the 5th of September, 1883, was solemnized the marriage of Dr. Bolling to Miss Willie R. Jeter, who was born and reared in Virginia and who is a daughter of the late William Ryland Jeter, an honored and representative citizen of that state. Mrs. Bolling is a woman of most gracious personality and in her gentle influence she has effectively supplemented the endeavors of her husband in his pastoral work. Of the nine children of Dr. and Mrs. Bolling, two are deceased: Warner Tapscott, who passed away at the age of five years, and Arthur Davis, who was three years of age at the time of his death. The surviving children are: Margaret E., Robert E., Louise, Mary, Helen Meade, Gladys and Randolph P. Robert E. is a bachelor living in Detroit, Michigan; Margaret E., married E. H. Mullen of Columbus, Mississippi, and is now living in Los Angeles, California; Louise L., married John W. Fitzhugh of Jackson, Mississippi, and now lives in Memphis, Tennessee; Mary Randolph married Dudley Porter of Paris, Tennessee, where they live; Gladys Garland married George L. Alley of Fulton, Kentucky, where they now reside; Helen Meade resides at home; Randolph Peyton, thirteen years, also resides at home.

The late Rev. Dr. Bolling during nearly the last eight years of his life was a regular correspondent for the *Sunday Commercial Appeal,* writing for a number of years under "Reflections."

DR. ROBERT H. BAYLOR. A veritable dean of physicians is Dr. Robert H. Baylor, of Erin, Tennessee. The incidents of his life have covered numerous states, and some of its experiences have been scarcely less than romantic. His native state was Virginia, where his father, John Baylor, born just on the threshold of the nineteenth century, had come as a pioneer from North Carolina. In the Old Dominion state John Baylor had followed the combined vocations of wagon-maker and farmer, and had become quite successful. He was a member of the historic Whig party and of the Methodist church. To the same religious fold belonged his wife, Elizabeth Young Baylor, also a native of Virginia. They were the parents of eleven children, the fifth of whom was christened Robert H. He was born on September 24, 1836, and was destined to carve for himself the varying fortunes that have made his life a successful one.

In one of the little log school houses that were once numerous in Virginia, Robert H. Baylor received his elementary education. He was a studious youth, whose love of learning caused him to carry "his book" with him when he followed the plow in the fields of his father's farm. Thus growing into habits of agricultural life, he continued in such occupation until he was a young man of twenty-four years of age. At that time he left his home, going to Mobile, Alabama, where he entered the Confederate navy. He continued in the service about two years, on the steamer Selma, being that ship's hospital steward. He was made a prisoner of war on August 5, 1864, at Mobile, during the battle of Mobile Bay. He was transferred to New Orleans and later to Ship Island, remaining there until the close of the war, after which he went to Vicksburg, Mississippi, and thence to Galveston, where he engaged in selling drugs. While thus engaged in the southern city he took advantage of lectures given at the medical college there, although he did not matriculate in said institution. Later plans led him to go to Louisville, where he pursued a regular course of study in the Louisville Medical College. He had left a reserve supply of money in the hands of a Galveston acquaintance who was to hold the sum in trust, but who failed in business and lost the funds entrusted to his care. There was nothing for the newly fledged physician to do but to attempt to return to Galveston without resources. He therefore undertook to make the journey on foot.

When he reached Danville, Tennessee, he made a sojourn at that place, where he taught school for a few terms. Incidentally he met a student physician from Nashville, with whom he arranged to buy the latter's outfit of medical supplies. Thus equipped, Dr. Baylor began his practice as a young doctor of medicine. Danville was the field of his initial practice.

Dr. Baylor married Miss Martha Edmonia Edwards, of near Elkton, Todd county, Kentucky. Their home had been blessed with four children and the medical career of the doctor was well under way after six years of residence in Danville. He then in 1884, removed to Stewart, Tennessee, where for eighteen years he was in active general practice, largely among the rural residents. At the end of that period he purchased a property near Tennessee Ridge, on which he lived for one year. In 1900 he removed to Erin, Tennessee, where he is still actively at work in professional duties. He is the owner of a small farm, in which he is recreatively as well as financially interested. He holds the responsible position of health officer of Houston county. The doctor's sympathies are Democratic, but his more mature theories are conservatively and sanely socialistic.

Dr. Baylor's life is enriched by its present useful activity; by its wealth of significant memories; and by the mutual interest of his four sons, all of whom are living worthy lives. Robert A. Baylor is at Winnipeg, Canada; Willard Hudson Baylor is a painter in Erin, Tennessee; Everett Ralston Baylor is a bookkeeper in a wholesale grocery at Nashville; and Lloyd Ellingwood is at home with his parents.

SCOTT PRESTON FITZHUGH. The list of Dover's promising barristers would be far from complete without the name of Scott Preston Fitzhugh, one of the youngest but also one of the most talented members of the bar in this community of Tennessee. The Volunteer State has known well and estimably four generations of the Fitzhugh family. The founder in this commonwealth of the Tennessee line of this originally Scotch family was James Fitzhugh (the great-grandfather of S. P. Fitzhugh), who was a native of Virginia. With his wife he settled in Stewart county, on a rural property near Dover. Here he followed farming and reared his children. His son, James Y. Fitzhugh (the grandfather of our subject) became a planter to some extent and combined with his agricultural industry considerable ministerial service in the Free-Will Baptist church. He married and of the eleven children who were born to him the eighth was Pinckney Preston Fitzhugh (the father of Attorney Fitzhugh). Successful, like his father, in the acquisition of much real estate, P. P. Fitzhugh became a planter and a dealer in both lumber and real estate. His business is very extensive and he is also from time to time the incumbent of important political office; in the last two sessions of the state legislature in Tennessee he was honored by representing Stewart county in that body of lawmakers. He is active in the religious interests of the Southern Methodist church, as is also Mrs. P. P. Fitzhugh. He is also prominent in the Dover lodge of the Knights of Pythias and in the Dover lodge of the Ancient Free and Accepted Masons. Both he and his wife (who was formerly Miss Missouri Whitford, and a daughter of Willis Whitford of Stewart county), are natives of this county, the husband's date of birth having been September 22, 1853, and the wife's February 14, 1856. It was in the same community that they were married in 1874. Their eight children are now located as follows: Effie, Mrs. R. L. Lancaster, in Stewart county; Ellie, Mrs. W. A. Taylor, in Houston county; Ettie, Mrs. George Sikes, in Stewart county; Martha, Mrs. Joel Carney, in Stewart county; Maggie, Mrs. Nelson Sikes, in Stewart county; Scott P., the subject of this genealogical and biographical review, in Dover, Tennessee; Genie Fitzhugh, in this county; and Comer Fitzhugh, in the state of Colorado.

The seventh in order of birth and the eldest son of his parents was Scott Preston Fitzhugh, who was born on the paternal property near Dover, in Stewart county, on December 15, 1888. His education was pursued in successive public and private schools at Dover, Big Rock, Cumberland City and Dickson. This general equipment of an intellectual sort he made the background for the definitely purposive research in various branches of legal lore, which he studied at Cumberland University, located at Lebanon, Tennessee. Mr. Fitzhugh's law course was completed in 1910 and he was in that same year admitted to the bar of Tennessee.

Such was Mr. Fitzhugh's standing in his native community that he found Stewart an advantageous location in which to begin his practice. In 1910 he formed a partnership with Porter Dunlap, with whom he still continues sharing offices and possessional interests. Aside from his legal business, Mr. Fitzhugh is a stockholder in the People's Bank and Trust Company of Dover. His political allegiance is of course given to the party which his father and grandfather have so loyally represented—that of the Democrats.

Social and fraternal connections appeal to the genial nature of Scott Preston Fitzhugh, who is a member of the Modern Woodmen of America, at Dover Camp; of the Ancient Free and Accepted Masons, at Dover lodge; of the Order of the Eastern Star, at Dover; and to the Kappa Sigma collegiate fraternity, in the Theta chapter at Lebanon University.

In the same year in which his professional career began, Mr. Fitzhugh won as his bride Miss Gertie Riggin, of Lesbin, Stewart county. Mrs. Fitzhugh is a daughter of A. W. Riggin, of that place. Both she and her husband are exemplary members of the Methodist church South, in Dover. Their home is an attractive one and both are social favorites in the community.

HERBERT EWING LARKINS, M. D. One of the old and honored families of Dickson county, Tennessee, members of which have been prominent in military and civic life, in business, agriculture and the professions, is that bearing the name of Larkins, which was founded here prior to the year 1800. A worthy representative is found in Herbert Ewing Larkins, M. D., of Charlotte, whose rapid advance in the fields of medicine and surgery is gaining him a recognized place among the leaders of his profession in this part of the state. Dr. Larkins is a native of Charlotte, born July 25, 1878, a son of Joseph Henry and Elizabeth (Corlen) Larkins.

Hugh Larkins, the founder of the family in this country, emigrated from Ireland during Colonial times, enlisted in General Washington's army, and fought valiantly during the War of the Revolution, and some time after the close of that struggle made his way to Tennessee, here founding the family in Dickson county. Among his children was Joseph Larkins, who became the father of Clark Larkins, the latter being the grandfather of Dr. Larkins. Joseph Henry Larkins was born in 1843, in Dickson county, and grew to manhood on the large plantation of his father, who was an extensive slave-holder. At the outbreak of the Civil war, although but a lad, he enlisted in the Forty-ninth Regiment, Tennessee Infantry, in a company organized by Captain Green. Subsequently he served in General Johnson's army, seeing much hard service, and at Bentonville, North Carolina, was severely wounded. On completing a valiant service, he returned to his farm in Dickson county, where he continued to follow the occupation of agriculturist until his death, in November, 1905. In his early life Mr. Larkins studied to enter the ministry of the Cumberland Presbyterian church, but after a short time gave his attention to other pursuits, and in the latter years of his life was affiliated with the Methodist Episcopal church South. In political matters he was a Democrat, but was never desirous of holding public office. Mr. Larkins married Elizabeth Corlen, who was born in Dickson county in 1843, and they had a family of nine children, as follows: Susan Blake, who married John Loggins; Fostina, who became the wife of Van E. Elazer; Zanie; Eula Frances, who married T. M. Overton; Melbia, who married Miner Elazer; S. F., living in Dickson; Dr. Herbert Ewing; and Wellington and Virgie, living at home.

Herbert Ewing Larkins received his early education in the public schools of Charlotte, following which he became a student in Durkin College, there receiving the degree of Bachelor of Laws. In 1909 he was graduated from the University of Nashville with the degree of Doctor of Medicine, and since that time has been engaged in practice at Charlotte. His abilities here were soon recognized and as the generous and sympathetic nature behind the skill of hand and professional judgment became appreciated his practice continued to rapidly increase. At this time he is known as one of the leading practitioners of the younger generation, and as such holds a deservedly high place in the respect of his professional colleagues and of the public at large. Dr. Larkins is inclined to favor the Democratic party, but reserves the right to vote independently, regardless of party lines, and the duties of his large practice have precluded any thought of entering the public arena in search of preferment.

On June 29, 1910, Mr. Larkins was married to Miss Eva Corlen, daughter of J. K. and Betty Corlen, of Charlotte, and this union has been blessed by the birth of one son: Wilmer Holland, born February 13, 1912.

RICHARD H. PHILLIPS. Especially fortunate in the quality of her journalism, Waverly is the home of the *Humphreys County Democrat*, organized and conducted by Richard H. Phillips. He is a native of Humphreys county, where he has hosts of friends.

In family origin, Mr. Phillips is of combined Missouri and Tennessee parentage. His father, James Phillips (1837-1881) was born in Missouri, where he lived until 1861. Coming at that time to Tennessee, he discontinued his occupation of blacksmith and wagon-maker while serving in the Confederate army. Enlisting in Forrest's Cavalry under Captain Randall, in Hickman county, he served through the war. Given a furlough in 1863 he was apprehended on his way back to his regiment and was taken prisoner near the Hickman county line. He made a desperate fight for his liberty, receiving no less than seven wounds in the encounter, and was taken to Camp Chase, where for nearly two years he lay in prison, before his exchange was accomplished. Those long, horrible months were not without seriously detrimental effect upon his physical constitution. Much broken in health, he returned to Tennessee, where he resumed his place among his family and friends. He had been married in Humphreys county in 1863 to Miss Sarah Plant (born in Stewart county in 1840), and as years passed they became the parents of six children. With this family he presently removed, in 1875, to Hickman county, Kentucky, where he continued to work at his trade during the remainder of his life. He is remembered as a Democrat of decided opinions. He was a member of the Ancient Free and Accepted Masons at Clinton, Kentucky, and of the Methodist Episcopal church. Of the latter his wife, Sarah Plant Phillips was also a member. She survived him for a number of years and in the course of that time remarried, becoming Mrs. Thomas A. Wiggin. Her earthly life closed in 1909, but Mr. Wiggin is still living, a resident of Humphreys county.

Fifth of the children born to James and Sarah Phillips was the son whom they named Richard H., and whose career forms the chief subject-matter of this biographical review. His birth occurred on June 16, 1870, in Humphreys county, Tennessee. His education was pursued at Clinton College, Kentucky, and was supplemented by his very familiar acquaintance with the type-case, which early attracted his interest. He was, indeed, but thirteen years of age when his apprenticeship as a printer began. He learned this work with one W. A. Jones, a French-Canadian printer who was at that time engaged on the *Times-Journal* of Waring, Tennessee—a news sheet that is now no longer published.

After this early apprenticeship, Mr. Phillips next followed the interesting and developing fortunes of a journeyman printer. For fifteen years he was thus engaged at various places. In June, 1910, he came to Waverly, purchased a new printing-plant and organized a weekly paper which he named the *Humphreys County Democrat*. This sheet, which is of course an organ of the good old Southern party, has proved to be very successful, having both a wide circulation and a good advertising patronage. Mr. Phillips is to be congratulated on the good results of the venture.

In all political affairs of the city, county and state, as well as in great national affairs, Editor Phillips is actively interested. Social fraternities also claim a due share of his attention, including him as a member in the Independent Order of Odd Fellows, Waverly lodge No. 104; and in the Knights of Pythias of Huntington (Tennessee) lodge No. 63. He is connected with the Presbyterian church of Waverly, that congregation also being the church home of Mrs. Phillips.

As Miss Della Blair Plant, of Humphreys county, Mrs. Phillips was very well and popularly known before her marriage. Her parents, J. H. and Mary E. Plant, represent one of the oldest of the families in this locality. Mr. Plant is a Confederate veteran and a man of prominence in the community. The year 1900 was the date at which Miss Plant became Mrs. R. H. Phillips. She and Mr. Phillips have welcomed four little daughters into their home. The eldest, Mary Lou, met a death all too tragic at the age of seven, when on January 26, 1908, her baby life was forever stilled by an explosion of blasting powder. Her sisters,

Ella Mae, Mattie Gould and Virginia, live to fill their parents' home with flower-like charm and with budding promises of the future. The editor and his family form a valued acquisition to the business, political and social interests of Waverly.

JOSEPH LARRY BYRN, M. D.   The patronymic ''Byrn'' indicates with singular clearness the origin of the family of that name, and the house of Byrn was first established in America by Larry Byrn, the great-grandfather of the subject of this brief review, who came from Ireland and settled in Tennessee, homesteading a piece of land at the head waters of Yellow Creek. Here the pioneer, then in his young manhood, established a little grist mill, and one day he started to the mill with a load of corn. He was never seen again. The most thorough search was made throughout the country, but the miller was gone, his disappearance being as complete as if the ''earth had opened and swallowed him,'' to quote the proverbial statement. Indians frequented that section of the country in those days, and it was always supposed that he had been attacked by a hostile band and made away with, but beyond conjecturing as to his possible fate, nothing was ever known. He left a young son, Larry, who grew to manhood in Dickson county, and there passed his early life as a farmer and saddler. He served in the Mexican war, and after returning home, retired and led a quiet, peaceful life until death claimed him.

S. M. Byrn, the son of Larry Byrn II., was born, reared, educated and married in Dickson county, and there passed the greater part of his life. He was a farmer, merchant and stock trader, and led a busy life, his home and the center of his business activities being at Fowler Landing, in Humphreys county, to which county he moved in about 1857. He was a prominent and well-to-do man, and at the outbreak of the Civil war he formed a company of light artillery, but not having an acquaintance with military tactics, Captain Lannie was placed in charge of the company, Mr. Byrn being first lieutenant. He served with valor until the battle of Fort Donelson, when he fell before the enemy's fire, his military career ending there. He was a Democrat, and a member of the Methodist Episcopal church. He was ordained to preach in about 1860, but never occupied the pulpit regularly, although he had in previous years supplied whenever his services were in demand. He was a member of the Masonic fraternity. He was born in 1830, and was still a young man when he died in battle. He married Sarah Rogers, born in Dickson county in 1831, their marriage taking place there in 1848. Four children were born to them, Dr. Joseph Larry Byrn being the eldest of that number, and but one other besides himself being alive today— Mollie, the widow of P. J. Davis.

Dr. Byrn was educated in the public schools of his native community and under the instruction of Dr. E. E. Larkins, at Charlotte. Following that he engaged in the timber business for some two years, after which he opened a store at Beggarville, which he conducted for six years. He then entered a medical school at Cincinnati, the Eclectic Medical College, and in 1886 took his degree of Doctor of Medicine. He began the practice of his profession at Beggarsville, Humphrey county, in the same year, and here he continued until 1895, when he went to Union City, there continuing in practice until 1897. He then came back to Humphrey county and settled on a farm near Plant, and here he is engaged in farming and in practicing his profession, dividing his attention between the two occupations. He has a fine place of one hundred and sixty acres which he keeps up in a most admirable manner, and is as prominent as a successful farmer as he is in his medical capacity.

In 1872 Dr. Byrn was united in marriage with Miss Annie Bone, the daughter of John Bone, of Beggarsville, and they have seven children: Eddye Lee, of Hickman, Kentucky; Nancy Cornelia, married John Warren, of Humphrey county; Carrie Willie, of Camden, Tennessee; William Joseph, of Hickman, Kentucky; Fannie, the wife of Roscoe White; Stella, married John Fowler and lives in Camden, Tennessee; and Thomas A., who is at home.

Dr. Byrn is an Independent Democrat, and fraternally he is a member of the Independent Order of Odd Fellows, affiliating with Denver Lodge No. 606, and the Encampment at Waverly. He is a good citizen; a devoted family man, and enjoys the esteem and confidence of all who share in his acquaintance in the county which he has been identified with for so many years.

JOHN J. JONES. A stranger invariably forms his estimate of the enterprise and prosperity of a community from its buildings. If substantial and of tasteful and appropriate design it betokens a thrifty and progressive order of citizenship. The contractor, builder and architect is therefore a very important factor in influencing and shaping the material advancement of a community, for his tastes, knowledge and judgment are largely relied upon by those who have need of his services. It is this line of endeavor to which John J. Jones, of Union City, Tennessee, has directed his attention throughout his business career. By nearly twenty years of experience as a carpenter and twelve years of successful activity as a contractor he became well qualified to take a place among the leading contractors of Union City upon his location there in 1910, and this he has done. In the two intervening years since then he has been more than kept busy, for in 1911 sixteen houses were erected under his direction and thus far in 1912 the number has reached eleven, two of them being large store buildings. His work extends to Hickman, Mayville and Fulton, Kentucky, and he averages ten workmen in his employ. Mr. Jones is not only a skilled mechanic but he also understands the work of the architect and usually draws up his own plans. The whole period of his independent activity has been given to this line of work.

John J. Jones was born in 1875 at Mayfield, Kentucky, where he grew up, received his education and learned his trade. He is the youngest of six children that came to his parents, H. R. Jones and Sarah Adcock Jones, both of whom were natives of Kentucky. In 1886 was solemnized the marriage of Mr. Jones and Miss Lulu M. Ryckman and to their union have been born three children, viz.: John R., James E. and Mary Agnes. In church membership both Mr. and Mrs. Jones are identified with the Baptist denomination, and fraternally Mr. Jones is a member of the Woodmen of the World. They are most estimable young people and well worthy of the high respect and esteem accorded them by their associates. Fair dealing and integrity of purpose are evidently the principles adopted by Mr. Jones in his business transactions and by his character and the success he has attained he well merits recognition among the representative men of Union City.   ·

HERMAN DEITZEL, JR. Scientific agriculture is no longer a high-sounding phrase, and farming, formerly an occupation in which the surplus sons of the old-time large families engaged as their natural and only means of livelihood, has been brought to the front as one of the professions and one that demands careful preparation and that returns sure and generous compensation. Each year witnesses remarkable progress along this line and to understand this aroused and continued interest, the work carried on by the progressive and enterprising agriculturists must be considered. Among the farmers of this class found in Obion county, none have achieved better results than Herman Deitzel, Jr., whose valuable property of 380 acres of land, situated near Union City, has been brought up to the highest state of cultivation. Mr. Deitzel, although still a young man, has risen to a high place in his chosen calling, and his career has been marked by steady advancement and constant industry since early youth. He was born in Union City, Tennessee, in 1883, and is a son of Herman and Josephine (Cloys) Deitzel. His father, a native of Germany, emigrated to the United States in 1869, and in the following year came to Tennessee, where he spent the rest of his life in various pursuits, principally the hardware business, and became a successful man. He and his wife were the parents of ten children, of whom seven are still living, and Herman is the second in order of birth.

Herman Deitzel, Jr., was reared and educated in his native city, and what time he could spare from his studies he spent in working in his father's store, thus demonstrating an industrious spirit at the age of ten years. Ambitious and thrifty, he carefully saved his earnings, having decided to become a farmer, and on reaching his majority he invested his capital in a tract of land near Union City. He at once engaged in agricultural pursuits, and as the years have passed he has added to his land from time to time, now having 380 acres in the highest productive state. Mr. Deitzel has not devoted his entire time to general farming, as stock raising and dairying have also held a part of his attention. His crops consist of corn, wheat, oats, clover, timothy and alfalfa, and in 1912 he devoted twenty acres to tomatoes. In his fine herd of Jerseys are to be found some of the best cattle in the state, and these animals always bring top-notch prices in the markets. His dairy herd consists of thirteen animals, and he also carries about twenty-five head of young stock, from which to draw and also to supply the home market. His breed of hogs are of a strain of superior quality, and well adapted for speedy growth and quick returns. Models of neatness, Mr. Deitzel's farm buildings are in a first-class sanitary condition, are well ventilated and lighted with electricity, while his residence is modern in architecture and equipped with up-to-date conveniences. Modern machinery is used throughout the premises, and the entire property gives eloquent evidence of the presence of ability, thrift and good management. Some there are who regard the tiller of the soil as one whose vocation is deserving of but little consideration. There can be no more erroneous idea. To the farms must the nation look for its sustenance, and to those agriculturists of Mr. Deitzel's class it owes a debt of gratitude. Also from the farm have come some of the most public-spirited of any community's citizens, ready to support movements calculated to advance their localities and giving their time and means in the cause of education and morality. Mr. Deitzel belongs to this class, and has so conducted himself that he has the entire respect of his neighbors and fellow-citizens.

On October 12, 1909, Mr. Deitzel was married to Miss Ella Harris. daughter of Anselmo Harris, of Obion county.

BASCOM C. BATTS. Among the successful and prominent devotees of the great basic industry of agriculture Bascom C. Batts holds prestige as an agriculturist who is self made. He has ever been on the alert to forward all measures and enterprises projected for the good of the general welfare and he has served his community in various official positions of important trust and responsibility. He has served as magistrate of Guthrie, Kentucky, for the past fourteen years, and for one term was judge of Todd county, Kentucky. He is the owner of a finely improved farm of two hundred and seventy-five acres, the same being located some miles distant from Guthrie.

August 25, 1854, in Robertson county, Tennessee, occurred the birth of Bascom C. Batts, who is a son of Jeremiah and Mary Ann (Byrnes) Batts, the former of whom was born in North Carolina, August 16, 1804. and the latter of whom was a native of Robertson county, Tennessee, where she was born May 8, 1810. Jeremiah Batts came to Tennessee with his parents when he was a child of but six weeks old. The family located in Sumner county and remained there for one year, at the end of which removal was made to Robertson county. In the latter place the young Jeremiah was reared to maturity and educated and his entire active career was devoted to agricultural pursuits. He died in Robertson county December 27, 1886, and his cherished and devoted wife passed away February 8, 1867. They were the parents of thirteen children, of whom Bascom C. was the youngest in order of birth. Jeremiah Batts was a son of Jeremiah Batts, Sr., who, after locating in Robertson county, here purchased a section of land for fifty cents per acre. He was a well-to-do farmer and a slave owner. The maternal grandfather of the subject of this review was James Byrnes, who was born and reared in Virginia and who was an early settler in Robertson county, Tennessee, where he was a saw-mill man and a farmer. Jeremiah Batts, Jr., was a Democrat in politics and he served as a magistrate for a period of thirty years prior to his demise. In religious matters he and his wife were devout members of the Methodist Episcopal church.

To the public schools of Cedar Hill, Tennessee, Bascom C. Batts is indebted for his preliminary educational training, which was later supplemented with a course of study in Vanderbilt University at Memphis. He early began to assist his father in the work and management of the old home farm, a part of which he later owned. He bought his present finely improved estate of two hundred and seventy-five acres in Todd county, Kentucky, and here has since maintained his home. His political allegiance is given to the Democratic party, in the local councils of which he has long been an active factor. For the past fourteen years he has served as a magistrate and for one year was county judge. He is a man of fine mentality and broad human sympathy. He thoroughly enjoys home life and takes great pleasure in the society of his family and friends. He is always courteous, kindly and affable and those who know him personally accord him the highest esteem. His life has been exemplary in all respects and he has ever supported those interests which are calculated to uplift and benefit humanity, while his own high moral worth is deserving of the highest commendation. He is a Mason and a member of the Knights of Honor.

May 12, 1880, was solemnized the marriage of Mr. Batts to Miss Lizzie Wood, a daughter of Jonathan Wood, who was a hardware merchant at Clarksville for a number of years. Mr. and Mrs. Batts have one son, B. F., who is studying law in Jonesboro, Arkansas. The Batts family are devout members of the Methodist Episcopal church.

WILLIAM M. GREEN, D. D. In 1907, after half a century of continuous service in behalf of his church, Dr. W. M. Green retired from the duties which had absorbed his energies for so long, and is now quietly spending his declining years at the home of his son-in-law, James H. Parkes, in Nashville vicinity. Dr. Green's career has had an important influence for the promotion of religion and benevolence in Tennessee and the South, and he has been one of the most eminent figures in the Methodist church South. Besides the accomplishments of his own life time, he also represents some of the oldest and most prominent families in Tennessee, and his relationship has been with men who were pioneers of the church and in public affairs in Tennessee.

William M. Green is a native of the city of Nashville, born October 17, 1838, a son of Alexander L. P. and Mary Ann (Elliston) Green. The founder of the family in Tennessee was the paternal grandfather, George Green, who married Judith Stillman. Grandfather Green was a native of Maryland, and was married in Albemarle county, Virginia, in 1776. He then entered the Revolutionary war, and served as a patriot soldier until its close. He was with the central division under Campbell in the battle of King's Mountain. When the war was over he went back to his home in Virginia, gathered his family and possessions together, and then crossed the mountains into east Tennessee. He later moved to Alabama, where his death occurred. By occupation he was a farmer, and one of the pioneers who cleared out his share of the wilderness, and did much to plant civilization on a solid foundation. The maternal grandparents of Dr. Green were John and Ann T. (Ridley) Elliston. John Elliston, a native of Kentucky, came to Tennessee when a young man and with his uncle opened the first silversmith store in Nashville. The Ellistons were noted as business men in early Tennessee. Grandfather Elliston manufactured probably the greater part of the jewelry which was sold from his store, and much of the tableware which was used by early families in Nashville and vicinity came from his establishment, and he also made many of the old tall clocks which stood in the corners of some of the old homes.

The history of Southern Methodism gives a prominent place to the late Alexander L. P. Green. He was born in Sevier county, Tennessee, June 26, 1806, and died July 15, 1874. Educated in the common schools of Sevier county and in northern Alabama, he began preaching when a very young man, and in his time was one of the leaders of the church. He continued active work in the ministry until 1871, at which time he was chosen treasurer of Vanderbilt University. He was likewise successful in a financial way, and at the time of his death was owner of considerable property in Nashville. He and his wife were the parents of five children, only two of whom are now living, one being Dr. Green, and the other Anna, who married Rev. R. A. Young, whose name is familiar in Tennessee Methodism. The elder Dr. Green was in politics a Whig until war time. He held the pastorate of McKendree church at Nashville, was pastor at Franklin and was one of the old-time circuit riders during his younger years. The greater part of his career was spent as a presiding elder. When a young man he was assistant to an older brother as commissioner of the Cherokee Indians in northern Alabama for three years, and it is related that during that time he never had a hat on his head. Later he was one of the commissioners who founded Vanderbilt University at Nashville. When the Methodist church of America was divided in 1844, the late Mr. Green had a more than passive part in that division, and was one of the leaders in the organization of the M. E. church South in 1845.

Dr. William M. Green, when a boy, attended the private school maintained by Alfred Hume, who in his time was one of the leading educators of Tennessee. He later was a student in the University of Nashville, and entered the ministry and began his first pastorate in June, 1858, continuing until 1907. He later served a time as agent for the Sunday school board in the Church Publishing House, and for four years was associate editor of the *Midland Methodist*. In the Tennessee conference, Dr. Green is familiarly known as "Four Year Billy Green," owing to the many pastorates and other positions of church service which he filled for the exact periods of four years. He was pastor at Columbia for four years, Franklin four years, Gallatin four years, West End four years, and divided a period of eight years between the Nashville City Mission and the North Nashville Mission. He wound up his period as a minister with four years at the South End church. His work in the pulpit and as a pastor has also been interspersed with much literary and administrative accomplishments. From his pen were contributed seventy-five short sermons that were published in the *Nashville American*. He also wrote the life of his father. Also should be noted his assistance rendered to the city in opening the street car transfer station, and his co-operation with the board of trade a number of years ago when he suggested changing many of the names used to numerals in the revised nomenclature of the streets of Nashville.

Dr. Green was married September 25, 1866, to Josephine Searcy, daughter of Dr. William W. and Emeline (Johnson) Searcy. The Searcy family is one of the oldest and most prominent in Tennessee. Dr. Searcy was born in Nashville, was a physician who practiced in this city and vicinity for half a century, and was a man of splendid education and many high attainments, which he devoted unselfishly to the work of his profession and to the welfare of society. He was a graduate of the University of Nashville and, later, of the University of Pennsylvania. Frequent articles came from his pen and were published in medical journals and newspapers. Dr. Searcy was born in March, 1810, and died in March, 1874. His father was Col. Robert Searcy, a prominent lawyer and judge of Tennessee, who fought with General Jackson in the early years of the century. Judge Searcy was an influential Mason, and it is noteworthy here that he made the long journey by horseback to North Carolina, and obtained the charter for the first

Masonic lodge in Nashville. Dr. Green and wife were the parents of two children, namely: Mrs. James H. Parkes, whose husband is one of the leading business men of Nashville; and Frank Searcy Green, who is in business with J. H. Fall & Company of Nashville. The son has inherited his father's love for literature and has collected quite a choice library. Mrs. Parkes is a graduate of Columbia School, and has much literary ability, and is the author of a book of travels. Dr. Green has been for years a member of the Masonic order and is independent in politics. He is the owner of considerable property in Nashville, but his best possessions consist in his disinterested services to his church and to society.

ROBERT J. STONE. One of the public-spirited and progressive agriculturists of Cheatham county, Tennessee, is Robert J. Stone, residing near Neptune, a young man of sterling personal qualities and of good education who through sagacious and sapient business ability has achieved no uncertain success in a financial way and as a citizen of the progressive stamp has become one of the foremost men of his community. He has twice represented Cheatham county in the Tennessee state legislature, each time with credit to himself and to his constituents, and has always taken a loyal interest in all affairs relating to the civic progress of his community and state.

Robert J. Stone was born in Dickson county, Tennessee, March 15, 1878, a son of Robert B. Stone and a grandson of Hardaman Stone, both of whom were at one time prominently identified with iron manufacture in this section of Tennessee. Robert B. Stone, the father, was born in Dickson county, Tennessee, in 1847, and is yet living, being now a resident of Cumberland Furnace, Dickson county. He first entered the iron business with A. W. Vauley, subsequently serving for many years as general manager for the Droullard Iron Company at Cumberland Furnace, of which he was also one of the stockholders. When the company disposed of its interests there Mr. Stone, with H. C. Merritt, H. N. Leach, E. H. Stine and W. H. Neblett as partners, bought all of the stock and lands of the concern, the latter comprising some 20,000 acres, and divided the land into small tracts ranging from fifty to five hundred acres. They have now disposed of practically all of this. Mr. Stone now deals in cattle and stock and among his extensive personal realty holdings is eight hundred acres of farm land in Cheatham county. He has been very successful in business affairs and his accomplishments in a financial way represent the application of shrewd business acumen and years of industrious and energetic endeavor, for he began his career with very limited advantages in the way of capital. The old Droullard home at Cumberland Furnace also passed into his possession and is his present residence. During the Civil war he served in the Confederate army under General Forrest one year, or until the surrender of Fort Donelson. He has always been a Democrat in political adherency, and fraternally is affiliated with the Masonic order as a member of the blue lodge, chapter and commandery. He is a communicant of the Episcopal church. Hardaman Stone, his father, was born in North Carolina and came to Tennessee as a young man, subsequently becoming an iron manufacturer and a wealthy man for his day. He helped to build the Nashville & Memphis Railroad. Robert B. Stone has been twice married. His first wife was Miss Sarah Jackson, who was born in Dickson county, Tennessee, in 1842, and passed away in 1882, a consistent member of the Methodist Episcopal church. She was a daughter of Epps Jackson, an early settler in Tennessee and a prominent iron manufacturer who operated the old Carroll furnace in Dickson county for many years. To this union were born six children. Robert J., our subject, being one of four now living. In 1886 he took as his second companion Miss Kate Richardson, who is yet living.

Robert J. Stone, our immediate subject, grew up in Dickson county and was educated in the Edgewood Normal School and at Cumberland University, from which latter institution he was graduated in 1900. He entered into independent business activity as a farmer and stockman in Cheatham county and has continued thus identified to the present time. He owns 1,000 acres in this county, raises tobacco, corn and hay and feeds many cattle and hogs. He is especially interested in Hereford cattle and owns a fine herd of that strain, and in every respect is keenly awake to the advanced agricultural spirit of the day.

In December, 1900, Mr. Stone was united in marriage to Miss Lola Russell, of Franklin, Kentucky, and to their union have been born three daughters, Lucile, Emily Katherine and Lola. Mrs. Stone is a member of the Presbyterian church. Mr. Stone affiliates with the Knights of Pythias and the Sigma Alpha Epsilon college fraternity. Politically he is a Democrat and during his two terms as a member of the Tennessee state legislature he was chairman of the waterways and drainage committee and was a member of the judiciary, agricultural and other committees, his whole service being that of the ablest order. As a young man of ambition, character and ability he has put intelligence and energy into all of his undertakings and ranks among the most forceful men and the most respected citizens of Cheatham county.

CHARLES EBEN NORTHRUP. One of the most successful business men of Gallatin, a lumberman who has been a resident of this city since 1894. Mr. Northrup began life a poor boy, but at the end of eight years had accumulated a considerable fortune of thirty thousand dollars. Then owing to business reverses, the result of the panic of the early nineties, he lost most of this, although he did not become bankrupt. It was at the conclusion of this unfortunate epoch in his life that he came to Tennessee, and since the first years has been steadily prospering and is now reckoned one of the substantial men and influential citizens of Gallatin.

Mr. Northrup was born in Steuben county, New York, February 10, 1854, a son of William H. and Sarah (Tompkins) Northrup. Both of them were natives of that state. The paternal grandfather was named Ebenezer Northrup, who was born in New Jersey, later moving into New York state, where he followed farming, and where his death occurred. The maternal grandfather was John Tompkins, who married Julia Jordan. Both were natives of New York, and at an early date moved into the state of Ohio. The wife of John Tompkins made one return trip to New York on horseback.

William H. Northrup, the father, was born February 8, 1828, and died in June, 1907. His wife was born in August, 1827, and died March 1889. William H. Northrup in his early career moved to Ohio, where he became a soldier of the Union, with the Fifty-fifth Ohio Infantry, and served three years. Most of his service was in the army hospitals. Following the war he settled on a farm in Michigan, where he died. He and his wife had five children, C. E. being the second in number. The parents were both members of the Baptist church and the father was a Republican in politics.

Mr. Northrup in his early life attended the Michigan country schools and made his start in the world as a farmer. As already mentioned, he became quite successful, accumulating property which was valued at about thirty thousand dollars, and was considered one of the most prosperous and substantial men of his community up to the panic of '93, which involved him as it did thousands of other honorable and seemingly substantial citizens of this country. While he got out of the situation with honor and was not a bankrupt, paying a hundred cents on the dollar, yet the misfortune was sufficient to cripple him for the time. In 1894 he moved to Gallatin, since which time his prosperity has continued to go forward. He has a large lumber business and planing mills and ships his products throughout this vicinity. He is also owner of a large amount of timber lands and farm property.

He was married in 1882 to Miss Della Heath, who was born in Michigan, and whose death occurred March 28, 1904. Mr. and Mrs. Northrup were the parents of two children. Eva married Arthur Workins and now lives in Gallatin; Frank H. is associated with his father in business. In September, 1906, Mr. Northrup married Anna Branson, whose maiden name was McLaughlin. She was born in the state of Pennsylvania. They are members of the Presbyterian church, and he is affiliated with the Masonic order. In politics he is a Progressive Republican.

JOHN H. G. SLAUGHTER. At St. Bethlehem in Montgomery county the leading business man and citizen for many years has been John H.

R.E.L. Mountcastle

G. Slaughter. He was for twenty years the postmaster of that town and is now the magistrate of his home district. The agricultural implement and hardware business now conducted under his name, and one of the most prosperous mercantile enterprises in this part of the county, was founded by him in 1887.

Mr. Slaughter was born in Christian county, Kentucky, April 2, 1862, a son of G. H. and Amelia (Bowman) Slaughter. The paternal grandfather, Henry Slaughter, was a native of North Carolina, whence he moved to Tennessee, and became a large planter and slave owner before the war. The maternal grandfather, John Bowman, a native of Virginia, was a farmer and miller, and also owned many slaves.

The father, G. H. Slaughter, was born in North Carolina in 1828, and was a child when his family came west to Tennessee. For a number of years his home was in Nashville, where as agent for the Nashville, Chattanooga & St. Louis Railroad he had the distinction of selling the first railroad ticket in Nashville. He acted as teller in one of the Nashville banks for a long time, and was very influential as a citizen. It was due to his efforts that the streets of that city were first given number and names. A Democrat in politics, he was for thirty years a justice of the peace, and was a member of the lower house of the legislature two terms and for two terms was in the state senate. He belonged to the Missionary Baptist church, while his wife was a member of the Christian denomination. His death occurred in 1897, while his wife, who was born in Kentucky in April, 1837, died on December 25, 1909. They were the parents of four children, namely: Mollie, the wife of W. B. Whitfield, of St. Bethlehem; John H. G.; Sallie, the widow of E. F. Liggin, and May, the wife of B. W. Meriwether.

During the youth of John H. G. Slaughter the family lived in Montgomery county, and in this county he received his education partly in the country schools and at Clarksville. Farming was the occupation to which he was reared and to which he gave a number of years, until 1887, when he established the business at St. Bethlehem which he has since built up to such successful proportions. He also owns a farm in this county. What he has acquired in business has been the result of his own efforts, for he has always been industrious and has never departed from the conservative, substantial roads which lead to material success. In politics he is a Democrat, is affiliated with the Woodmen of the World, and he and his wife are members of the Christian church.

He was married in February, 1884, to Miss Ettie Watts. Her father, Dr. D. A. Watts, was a prominent physician and druggist of Paducah, Kentucky, which was her early home. Mr. and Mrs. Slaughter are the parents of two children, Julia and Harry, both at home.

ROBERT EDWARD LEE MOUNTCASTLE. A notable success in the law, together with prominence in affairs of citizenship, has combined to promote Mr. Mountcastle to a front rank among Knoxville lawyers. He has been a member of the bar of this state for more than a quarter of a century and at the present time is a member of the well-known law firm of Shields, Cates & Mountcastle, whose offices are in the Empire building at Knoxville.

Robert E. Lee Mountcastle was born at Jefferson City, Tennessee, February 21, 1865. The family is one of Scotch-Irish ancestry and descent, and long since settled in Tennessee, its earlier ancestors having belonged to that vigorous race of Scots who first settled in the mountain districts of western Pennsylvania, Virginia and the Carolinas, and subsequently moved down the slopes of the Allegheny into the Ohio valley. A. J. and Cornelia Frances (Williams) Mountcastle were the parents of seven children, including the Knoxville lawyer. As a boy Mr. Mountcastle attended the common schools and in June, 1880, was graduated from Carson and Newman College at Jefferson City, with the degree of Bachelor of Arts. He also took B. A. degree at the Washington and Lee University at Lexington, Virginia, in 1882, and after his admission to the bar practiced law at Lynchburg for seven years, then removed to Morristown and became a partner with Senator-elect John K. Shields and his father, Jas. T. Shields. He removed to Knoxville in 1902 and entered the firm of Shields, Cates & Mountcastle, of which he is now a member.

Mr. Mountcastle, it will not be denied, is one of the strongest Democratic leaders in Tennessee. In 1904, at St. Louis, he was elected a member of the national Democratic executive committee, and he has continued to retain that position. His seat upon the committee was contested in 1912 by Col. John J. Vertrees, but he was retained by the committee, only one vote being cast for the contesting candidate. Mr. Mountcastle has never aspired to political office. In the free and untrammeled judiciary campaign of 1910, as it was known, he was one of the most active leaders in the interest of the candidates on the free and untrammeled ticket. It was because of his support of the judiciary that the so-called regular Democratic state convention, which nominated a candidate for governor, declared the place of Mountcastle upon the national committee to be vacant, and Colonel Vertrees elected to the office, but as has already been mentioned, Mr. Mountcastle was retained on the committee. He was re-elected to the committee by the national Democratic convention at Baltimore, over Senator Nat Baxter, Jr.

In 1902-03 Mr. Mountcastle was president of the State Bar Asso-United States senate, Mr. Mountcastle was the manager of Judge Shields, a place in which he performed most excellent work in the interests of his colleague. He is admitted to be one of the ablest floor leaders in Tennessee in a political convention, as well as one of the ablest pleaders at the bar.

In the recent campaign of Judge Shields for the election to the ciation, of which he has long been a member. He is affiliated fraternally with the Masonic order and he and his family are members of the Presbyterian church.

Mrs. Mountcastle, prior to her marriage, which took place in 1890, was Miss Eliza Bird Solomon, a daughter of E. Y. Solomon. The children of Mr. and Mrs. Mountcastle are Louise, Paul, Fred and Marguerite. The family residence is at 1405 Laurel avenue.

STEWARD D. TINSLEY. A representative agriculturist of Montgomery county, Steward D. Tinsley is a well-known resident of Southside, where his large and well-appointed farm gives substantial evidence of the excellent care and skill with which it is managed. He was born January 5, 1851, in Montgomery county, a son of Oliver Tinsley. His grandfather, Lindsey Tinsley, came from Virginia, his native state, to Tennessee at an early day, and for a number of years thereafter ran the ferry at Nashville.

Born in Amherst county, Virginia, in 1815, Oliver Tinsley was but a boy when he came with his parents to Tennessee. Acquiring his early education in Nashville, he remained in that city until 1838, when he accepted a position with Robert Baxter, of Montgomery county, for whom he managed a furnace for ten years. He subsequently managed another furnace for twenty years, when he purchased from its owner the entire plant, including the furnace, land and other property. Turning his attention then to agricultural pursuits, he carried on general farming until his death, in 1884. An able business man, he acquired a handsome property, at the breaking out of the war between the states being worth about $60,000. During the conflict he lost all of his personal property, but retained about two thousand acres of land. He was a stanch member of the Democratic party, and belonged to the Ancient Free and Accepted Order of Masons. He married Eliza Harper, who was born in 1815 in Tennessee, her father, David Harper, having come to this state from North Carolina in early life. She lived to a ripe old age, passing away September 13, 1906. She was a most estimable woman, and a faithful member of the Methodist Episcopal church. Nine children were born of their union, one of whom, B. W. Tinsley, served in the Civil war as a member of the Fourteenth Tennessee Volunteer Infantry.

The youngest member of the parental household, Stewart D. Tinsley, received a limited education in the district schools, which he attended as opportunity offered, at other times assisting in the care of the home farm. Being industrious and economical, he began in early life to accumulate money, and invest it in land and other property. Successful in his undertakings, Mr. Tinsley has now a fine farm of upwards of five hundred acres of land, and in addition owns a grist mill, a saw mill, and a store. He makes a specialty of raising fine mules, and deals to a considerable extent in Hereford cattle and Berkshire hogs.

On June 25, 1872, Mr. Tinsley was united in marriage with Ella Hunter, a daughter of Drew and Nancy A. (Dean) Hunter, who were born, reared and married in Dickson county, Tennessee. Mrs. Tinsley is a consistent member of the Methodist Episcopal church South, with which she united when young. Politically Mr. Tinsley is a Democrat, and has served in various public positions, having been constable two years, and sheriff six years, while for twelve years he was postmaster at Big Four.

FIELDING L. PITTMAN, general manager of the Union City Cotton Gin, Union City, Tennessee, is one of the enterprising, up-to-date young men of the town. He was born in Gibson county, Tennessee, in 1884, only child of L. G. H. and Lottie (Goodman) Pittman, both natives of the "Volunteer" state. His maternal grandfather, Fielding Goodman, was a man of prominence and influence, a farmer with large land holdings in Central Tennessee, where he filled many local offices. For a number of terms he served as sheriff of Gibson county. He and his wife, Nancy (Robinson) Goodman, had four children, who became representative citizens, engaged chiefly in agricultural pursuits.

Fielding L. Pittman was reared on his father's farm and received his education in the common schools. His early life was spent in the study and practice of mechanical engineering. After three years devoted to this line of work, he turned his attention to the cotton business, and for the past two years has been identified as manager with the Union City Cotton Gin. This prosperous concern was incorporated in 1910 by a company of Union City men, and Mr. Pittman, who up to that time had had ten years' experience in the business, was placed in charge, and to his efficiency as general manager is due the success of the company. The plant covers an area of two acres, and the output of the gin in 1911 was 1,600 bales of cotton.

Mr. Pittman has numerous fraternal affiliations. He belongs to the F. and A. M., the O. E. S., the I. O. O. F., the W. O. W. and the B. P. O. E., in some of which he has served officially. He is a past noble grand of the I. O. O. F. and a past commander of the W. O. W. The only public office he has filled is that of revenue commissioner of Gibson county.

BURTON SANDERSON. One of the enterprising general merchandise concerns at Oakwood in Montgomery county is that conducted by Burton Sanderson, who has employed a fine energy and ability to building up a trade which might be envied by many of the merchants of larger cities.

Mr. Sanderson was born in Stewart county, Tennessee, April 9, 1885.

a son of Frank and Minnie (Harrison) Sanderson. Both parents were natives of Stewart county, where their respective families had early become established. The father was born in 1850 and the mother in 1852. After a common school education in such schools as then existed, Frank Sanderson began his career without capital and with reliance solely on his industry and honesty of purpose. Working by the day or month, he in time acquired the means to purchase a farm in Stewart county, where he gained a position among the substantial citizens. In 1899 he sold his farm and moved to Montgomery county, where he owns a good homestead and is still an active producer of the agricultural crops. In politics he is a Democrat and he and his wife are members of the Christian church. Their seven children are named as follows: James E., a resident of Stewart county; Callie, a resident of Oakwood; Viola, the wife of Hiram Foster, of Montgomery county; Leonard, who lives with his parents; Burton; Ada, at home; and Mannie, a resident of Jordan Springs, Tennessee.

The family having moved to Montgomery county when he was fourteen, Burton Sanderson finished his education in the district schools of this county, and while still a boy began working for his living and the means for a larger career. After some years of industry he was able to start his general store in Oakwood in 1910, and since then he has been rapidly advancing to prosperity. He also owns a farm and gives it such attention as he can spare from his store.

On July 5, 1911, Mr. Sanderson married Miss Gracie Ferrell. Her father is Drew Ferrell, for many years a Montgomery county farmer, and now proprietor of a store at Needmore in district No. 9. Mr. Sanderson is a member of the Christian church and politically is a Democrat.

C. C. CONN. Among the valued citizens of any community. are constructive men, men who have genius and the ability to apply it in material development; but when moral stamina and high ideals of what constitutes good citizenship are added to their assets for usefulness in society, they become true factors of development and progress, not only in a material way but along all lines. C. C. Conn, of Union City, Tennessee, is such a gentleman, a prominent contractor and builder who in this capacity has erected such structures there as the Nailing building, the D. J. Caldwell home, the Neblett home and the residences of Herman Deitzel, C. T. Moss, G. B. and W. L. White, G. L. Porter, J. M. Brice, as well as numerous other less important, all mute testimony of the quality of his workmanship and his skill and taste as a builder. For the most part he is his own architect and works from his own plans. He has spent twenty-one years as a carpenter and the last ten years of that time he has also operated as a contractor. He has long been a resident of this vicinity, but first made his home in Union City about three and a half years ago.

Born in Obion county, Tennessee, in 1866, he was reared and educated in his native county and began his chosen occupation as soon as he left school, following it successfully to the present time. He is a son of Jesse Conn and Louise (Waddle) Conn, the former of whom was born in York, Pennsylvania, while the latter was a native of Maury county, Tennessee. Jesse Conn migrated to Tennessee in 1861 and engaged in the milling and lumber business in Obion county, acquiring extensive business interests in this connection. By trade he was a carpenter and it was under his careful direction that his son learned carpentry and became a skilled workman. There were ten children in the elder Conn family, five of whom are living at this time. Of those surviving, two have followed agricultural pursuits and two are carpenters. They all have assumed worthy stations in society and have so ordered their lives as to command the respect of all who know them. Mr. Conn of this review is affiliated fraternally with the Masonic order, the Loyal Order of Moose and the Woodmen of the World.

JOSEPH E. REEDER. In a day when truly successful editorship requires not only executive ability, but also originality, it is gratifying to happen upon such an able opponent of journalism as we find Joseph E. Reeder, editor of the *New Idea,* a leading Tennessee newspaper published at Burns, Tennessee.

Genealogically Mr. Reeder is a product of Tennessee and other southern states, with a mingling of Pennsylvania blood. In the Keystone state lived his maternal grandfather, Joseph Walp, and there was born the daughter of the latter, Miss Almira Anna Walp. Her birth occurred in 1862 and it was in her girlhood that she and the other members of her father's family came to Dickson, Tennessee, where ties of wifehood and motherhood awaited her. North Carolina had been the earlier home of the Reeder line. That state was the birthplace of John Reeder, paternal grandfather of him who is the special subject of this review. Tennessee was for a brief early period a chosen location of John Reeder, who there married a Miss Hall, a native of Dickson county. They removed thence to Mississippi, where they lived for some time, during which their son, J. H. L. Reeder, was born. The family later returned to Tennessee, which from the age of seven continued to be the home of J. H. L. Reeder. When the Civil war thrilled all hearts to anxiety and with fear or courage, according to their temperaments, he enlisted in Company K, Eleventh Tennessee, under General Forrest, and with him served in all important engagements. He held the rank of sergeant and the quality of his service may be well guessed from the fact that he was three times wounded. Of his scars, however, he has made little account, speaking of each as a slight affair. He participated

in thirty-one skirmishes and twenty-one battles during the four years of
his service. He subsequently took up the study of medicine, which he
practiced in Dickson county, where his rank was second to none and his
practice during his life was one of the largest in the county. In 1876 he
married Miss Almira Anna Walp, above referred to. They became the
parents of eight children, of whom seven are yet living. Kate Reeder,
the eldest daughter, became Mrs. Charles A. Robinson, now of White-
ville; Elzina is Mrs. George Harris, of Nashville; Joseph E., the eldest
son, is the special subject of this review and of detailed account below;
Edward Reeder is one of the citizens of Burns; Elmer C. Reeder is a resident of Kingston Springs, in Cheatham county. Miss Roma Reeder and
her sister, Miss Alma, are members of the parental household.

In District 4 of Dickson county, Joseph Eugene Reeder was born on
December 21, 1877. His education was, as he puts it, that of the country
schools and of the type-case, for at the age of twenty he began his active
career in a printing office. In combined capacities of printer and editor
he served for some time the *Home Enterprise*, a well-known publication.
Resigning this position, he was connected for five years with the *Daily
American* For one year he was a member of the staff of reporters for
the *Nashville Banner*.

It was in 1905 that the *New Idea* was established at Burns by Mr.
Reeder. In the meantime he held for five years his road position, but
his present duties as editor and manager require his full attention for
the two publications of which he has charge. The *New Idea* is issued
weekly and is independently Democratic. Its inherent principles are
those of the good old Southern party, but the paper is permeated with
the spirit of progress which marks all genuinely wideawake enterprises
and its strongest influence is the desire for the greatest good of the community. This publishing plant also issues a monthly periodical of the
magazine class, called *The Home Defender*.

Mr. Reeder is personally a Democrat. His fraternal connections
are with the Independent Order of Odd Fellows, with the Knights of
Pythias and with the Modern Woodmen of America. His church interests are broad in sympathy, but he is not formally connected with any
church organization. Mrs. Reeder is a member of the Church of the
Disciples.

Editor Reeder's home was established in 1908, at which time he was
united in marriage to Miss Jessie McWilliams, daughter of W. McWilliams, of Dickson, Tennessee. Mr. McWilliams is a native of Pennsylvania and Ohio was the birthplace of his daughter, Mrs. Reeder. In the
social life of this locality, the Reeders occupy an important place. Editor
Reeder's human interests are as practical as they are wide, and his publications attract extensive and favorable attention. His favorite avocation is related to agricultural affairs, as he owns a fine farm near the
city. In whatever line his interests lie, however, all contribute to his

greater ability in acting as interpreter, through the press, of the chief needs and the highest principles of the people of this town and vicinity.

WALTER HARDING DRANE. Was born in Montgomery county and has passed his life thus far within its confines. His natal day was February 8, 1870, and he is the son of William McClure and Amelia Washington (Haddox) Drane.

William McClure Drane was born in Clarksville in 1826, and died there on the 23d day of December, 1909. He was the son of W. H. Drane, a native of Montgomery county, Maryland, born there in 1797, and he came as a boy with his father's family to the old settlement at Clarksville early in the nineteenth century. He was a physician, but eventually gave up his practice to engage in the tobacco business, in which he made an independent fortune, and he was ranked among the most eminent citizens of Clarksville of his time. His wife was Eliza J. McClure, a daughter of one of the oldest families in Montgomery county. His son, William McClure Drane, followed him in the tobacco business and like him was one of the most successful men of his community and time. He was active and prominent in the life of the county until his last years. His wife was born in Todd county, Kentucky, in 1836, and was a daughter of Joseph Haddox, a farmer and old resident of Todd county. She died in 1907. Eight children were born to these parents.

Walter Harding Drane received his early education in his home, under the supervision of a governess, but he later attended the public schools of Clarksville, finishing his education in the Southern Presbyterian University and the Broadhurst Institute of Clarksville. Being the youngest of the family, he remained in the home longer than any of the others and when he reached man's estate, busied himself in the care of the home place, a fine farm of two hundred and twelve acres. In addition to this he rents some three hundred acres, his being one of the best improved properties in the country. He raises considerable tobacco, hay and corn, and has a fine herd of registered Jerseys, of which he makes a specialty. He also is interested in Berkshire hogs and has a goodly representation of registered hogs on the place, as well as a number of thoroughbred saddle horses, Montgomery Chief being sire of some of his finest horses. One of his favorite horses is Avelyn, now in the show ring, and she has already taken a number of prizes.

Mr. Drane is a Democrat and is magistrate for district No. 7 of Montgomery county, being the first of the name to hold office of any kind. He is identified with a number of prosperous concerns, among which are the First National Bank and the Clarksville Ice & Coal Company. Mr. Drane is unmarried.

MATTHEW SANDERS. An enterprising and practical agriculturist, Matthew Sanders, of Montgomery county, is prosperously engaged in his chosen calling in district 18, where he owns and occupies the farm on which his birth occurred, December 10, 1875.

His father, the late Wiley Green Sanders, was born in Dickson county, Tennessee, near Charlotte, in 1824, and was there reared. Soon after his marriage he began farming for himself in his native county, living there until 1867. Coming then to Montgomery county, he purchased two hundred acres of land in District 18, and by well-directed toil soon placed his estate in a fine condition. Here he lived until his death, which occurred in 1905, at an advanced age. He was a worthy and highly esteemed citizen, a Democrat in politics, and a consistent member of the Methodist Episcopal church, South. The maiden name of his wife was Tillie Ava. She was born in 1830 in South Carolina, and died on the home farm, in Montgomery county, Tennessee, in 1903. Of the eight children born of their union four are now living, as follows: Thomas, of Clarksville, Tennessee; Finney, a resident of Kentucky; Betty, wife of Daniel Proctor; and Matthew, the special subject of this brief personal narrative.

As a boy and youth Matthew Sanders took advantage of his limited opportunities for advancing his education, and when out of school assisted his father on the home place, thus obtaining a practical knowledge of agriculture in various branches. Succeeding to the ownership of the home farm, Mr. Sanders has carried on the improvements previously inaugurated, and has now a fine farm of one hundred and sixty-seven acres, on which he raises the staple products of the region, his principal crops being tobacco and corn.

Mr. Sanders married, December 5, 1902, Miss Hettie Eads, a daughter of J. S. Eads, and to them three children have been born, namely: Annie Mae; Roy, and Ava. Politically Mr. Sanders is a straightforward Democrat, and for the past six years has served as magistrate, an office for which he is well qualified, and to which he was re-elected in 1912. He is also notary public, and a member of the Montgomery County High School Board, and for four years was a school director. Fraternally Mr. Sanders is a member of Palmyra Lodge, Ancient Free and Accepted Order of Masons; of the Independent Order of Odd Fellows; and of the Junior Order of United American Mechanics. Religiously he belongs to the Cumberland Presbyterian church, of which Mrs. Sanders is also a member.

ROBERT F. FERGUSON, M. D. Any biographical work of the representative men of Tennessee would be decidedly incomplete did it not record the incidents in the career of one whose labors here have covered a period of more than thirty-five years, and whose long experience and acknowledged abilities place him in a foremost position among the professional men of Montgomery county, Robert F. Ferguson, M. D., of Clarksville. Dr. Ferguson belongs to one of the old and honored families of the state, members of which have been prominent in various walks of life, and was born September 17, 1855, a son of Robert F. and Nancy M. (Barker) Ferguson.

Robert French Ferguson, the paternal grandfather of Dr. Ferguson, was born in Pennsylvania, whence the family had come from Scotland at an early day. He was a preacher of the Christian church, and married Hannah Champlain Babcock, who was born in Stonington, Rhode Island. Among their children was Robert French Ferguson, Jr., who was born at Springfield, Massachusetts, February 10, 1815, and received his education at William and Mary College, Williamsburg, Virginia. With his brother, Jesse Babcock Ferguson, who subsequently became one of the greatest preachers Tennessee has ever known, Mr. Ferguson removed as a young man to Howardsburg, Kentucky, and became engaged in publishing a newspaper. In 1844 he took up farming, and settled on the old Babcock farm in Montgomery county, Tennessee, having married Nancy M. Barker, who was born November 17, 1820, at ''Cloverlands,'' a farm in Montgomery county. She was a daughter of John Barker. who was considered the richest man in the county. Mr. Ferguson became one of the leading agriculturists of his locality, and at the time of his death, May 12, 1882, owned 1,500 acres of land. He reared a family of nine children, of whom six still survive, and Robert F. was the sixth in order of birth. Mr. Ferguson was a Democrat, and was well known in political circles during his day, being sent to the state legislature, helping to reconstruct the state after the close of the Civil war, and lending his aid and influence to United States Senator James Bailey. He was prominent in journalistic work, frequently contributing to 'the *New York Tribune* and the *Cincinnati Enquirer,* and was also active in the work of the Congregational church, erecting a church on his own farm, which he attended at the time of his death. His wife passed away in 1884.

John Barker Ferguson, son of Robert French Ferguson, Jr., was born March 7, 1858, at the farm known as ''Summertrees,'' which was named after an estate mentioned in one of Scott's works. The youngest of his parents' nine children, he received his education in the neighborhood schools, and subsequently received the degree of Bachelor of Arts in the Southwestern Presbyterian University at Clarksville in 1877, following which he taught school for one year with Lyon Gardner Tyler, now president of William and Mary College, in a preparatory school at Memphis. He then taught two years in the neighborhood schools, but on the death of his father returned home and took charge of the homestead place, of which he had charge until 1896. At that time he opened a preparatory school, and for eight years was engaged in conducting it. but since 1904 has devoted all of his attention to cultivating the soil. Like his father, Mr, Ferguson has taken a great deal of interest in church work, and has been lay reader for the Clarksville District of the Metho dist church, and was conference leader for one year. He is now District Hospital Commissioner for the Clarksville District, and president of the Methodist Sunday School Association. In politics a Democrat, he reserves the right to vote for the candidate he deems best fitted for the office, while his fraternal connection is with the Masons, he being master of his lodge. Mr. Ferguson's 530 acres are in a high state of cultivation and, devoted to diversified farming, they yield large crops. On November 7, 1883, Mr. Ferguson was married to Miss Carrie J. Morris, of Louisa county, Virginia, daughter of James Morris, and they have two children: Susanne and John B

Robert F. Ferguson received his early education in the common schools, following which he went to the University of New York and the College of Physicians and Surgeons, and graduated in medicine at Nashville in 1876. On receiving his degree, he returned to his home and began practice, entering with zeal upon the work for which he had been trained. Success met his efforts to such a degree that his practice now extends over three counties, and no man in his profession is held in higher respect or esteem. The constant opportunities for real estate investment and his inherent business abilities have enabled the Doctor to accumulate 350 acres of valuable land, on which is situated his modern residence, and he has various other holdings and interests. He takes an active part in the work of the Montgomery County Medical Society, the Tennessee State Medical Society and the American Medical Association, and holds membership in John Hart Lodge No. 103, and the local chapter of Masonry. In political matters Dr. Ferguson is a Democrat.

In 1890 the Doctor was married to Miss Jennie F. Lester, daughter of Robert F. Lester, a native of Virginia. Mr. Lester was for some years a prominent merchant, and later entered the tobacco business, but the Civil war caused financial reverses and his last years were spent at the home of his son-in-law. Dr. and Mrs. Ferguson have three children: Jennie L., Mary Merriwether and Robert F., all at home. The family is connected with the Methodist church South, and both Dr. and Mrs. Ferguson have been identified with various movements of a religious and charitable character.

CHARLES NICHOLAS MERRIWETHER. Among the successful agriculturists and large landowners of Montgomery county, the name of Charles Nicholas Merriwether holds prominent place. Given excellent educational advantages and trained for a scientific career, he preferred to become a tiller of the soil, and such has been his success that he has never regretted his choice. Today he is the owner of 600 acres of highly cultivated land, in district No. 6, on which he is annually raising large crops, and his many years of experience make him known as one of his section's acknowledged judges of agricultural conditions. Mr. Merriwether was born February 14, 1849, in Arkansas, and is a son of Dr. James H. and Lucy (McClure) Merriwether.

Dr. Charles Merriwether, the paternal grandfather, was born in Virginia, and as a young man entered upon a medical career, the rest of his life being spent in practice in Kentucky and Tennessee. He was the first of the family to come to this state, where he secured the present farm of Charles N. Merriwether on a government grant, and here his death occurred, as did that of his wife, Mary (Walton) Merriwether. Among their children was James H. Merriwether, who was born in 1814, in Montgomery county, Tennessee, and who inherited the inclination of his father and followed in his footsteps as a physician. He was educated in the University of Virginia and the University of Pennsylvania, receiving the degree of Doctor of Medicine from both institutions, following which he practiced for the greater part of his life in Tennessee and Arkansas, but on his retirement went to Todd county, Kentucky. He was married in Montgomery county, Tennessee, to Lucy McClure, who was born at Clarksville, Tennessee, in 1822, daughter of James McClure, a native of the Keystone state, who emigrated to Tennessee at an early date. Dr. and Mrs. Merriwether had a family of eight children, of whom six are living: Lizzie, who married A. M. Barker; Charles N.; John H. and William D., of Todd county, Kentucky; Hunter McClure, of Clarksville, Tennessee; and Gilmer, who lives in Kansas City, Missouri.

Charles Nicholas Merriwether received his early education in the public schools, following which he attended Washington and Lee University, and at one time was a student under Gen. Robert E. Lee. On receiving his degree of Bachelor of Sciences, Mr. Merriwether took up civil engineering and mining engineering at Birmingham, Alabama, in the manufacture of iron, but two years later made removal to Montgomery county, Tennessee. At this time he is the owner of the old family homestead of 600 acres, located in District No. 6, near Trenton, Kentucky. Mr. Merriwether raises diversified crops, and has been uniformly successful in his operations, owing to industry, intelligence and well-directed efforts. He believes in the use of modern machinery and up-to-date methods and takes pride in getting the best possible results from his land. Politically, Mr. Merriwether is a Democrat, but public life has not appealed to him, his achievements along agricultural lines satisfying his ambitions. With Mrs. Merriwether, he attends the Christian church, and all movements tending to advance religion, education and morality receive their co-operation and support.

In 1873 Mr. Merriwether was married to Miss Kittie Tutweiler, daughter of Prof. Henry Tutweiler, of the University of Alabama, and six children have been born to this union, namely: Lucy, who married H. L. Patterson, of Montgomery county, Tennessee; Robert Tutweiler, living in Kansas City, Missouri; Henry Tutweiler, of Mobile, Alabama;

Lennie, of Montgomery county; and Nicholas Hunter and Peola Ash, who live at home with their parents.

JAMES CLAIBOURNE HOBBS. For three generations the charm of the fields has held this nature loving family, into which was born in Humphreys county, near the mouth of the Buffalo river, James Claibourne Hobbs, on the 8th day of February, 1866. He was the third child of his parents, Jesse P. and Mary Louise (Darden) Hobbs, and is the only one of the three now living. Sorrow touched these parents heavily in the early death of three of their four children, and both died young in years,—the father when James C. was three years of age and the widowed mother about three years later.

Jesse Hobbs was born in Hickman county in 1836 and was the son of Claibourne Hobbs, himself the son of John Hobbs, the great-grandfather of the subject. John Hobbs came to Tennessee from his native state, Virginia, in an early day, and located in Hickman county, where he devoted himself to farming life. There his son Claibourne grew to young manhood and married Rose White, rearing a large family. This son came to Humphreys county in young manhood and settled on Duck river, and there, like his father, devoted himself to farm life. He owned a pleasant farm and was the owner of a quantity of slaves. His son, Jesse P. Hobbs, came to Humphreys county as a young man and here married and settled down. He continued to be associated with his father in the farm work until he reached his majority, when he bought land of his own and began in an independent way. With the outbreak of the war he joined the Confederate forces, and served through the war with the rank of lieutenant. He was severely wounded in action at Fort Donelson, and was not sufficiently recovered to return to the service before the close of the war. He went to his home in Humphreys county when quiet was once more restored, but the young man never regained his strength and died in 1869. His widow survived him for ten years. She was a member of the Baptist church.

James Claibourne Hobbs was educated at Dickson College and Cumberland University at Lebanon, taking his A. B. and A. M. degrees from Dickson and his LL. B. from Cumberland in 1897. In the same year he was admitted to the bar in Erin. He began practice with Herman Dunbar, who opened a branch office in Nashville, and it was the expectation of Mr. Hobbs to join his partner in that city, but the death of Mr. Dunbar after an association of about two years changed his plan in that respect, and he has since continued in practice in Erin alone, with the exception of a period of five years when he was the business associate of Mr. J. E. Kennard.

Mr. Hobbs has been active in politics and has deported himself in a manner highly creditable to him in his community with regard to his political service. He was chairman of the congressional committee for six years, and was elected to the state senate in 1899 on the Democratic ticket, serving in that body on the rural bills committee and on the committee on ways and means. He has shown in a convincing manner that he knows good laws from poor ones, and that he knows something of what laws are wanting and how best to frame them for the ultimate good of the people.

Mr. Hobbs is associated with a number of fraternal organizations, among them the Knights of Pythias, in which he has membership in Emerald Lodge No. 58, and the Order of Ben Hur, in which he is a member of Erin Lodge.

In 1890 Mr. Hobbs married Miss Nettie Helen McCauley, the daughter of G. H. McCauley, of Erin. Eight children have been born to these parents: Helen; J. Moody; Alice; Flora Louise; Mary Gustava; Sarah Gertrude; Doris and Floy.

Mr. and Mrs. Hobbs are members of the Presbyterian church of Erin, and have reared their family in that faith. They are among the most highly esteemed citizens of Erin, where they are popular in the best social activities of the town, and where their circle of friends is not smaller than that of their acquaintances.

DOUGLAS K. COPPEDGE. Vocations of a scholarly sort have been those chosen by the successive representatives of the family line to which Douglas K. Coppedge belongs. The clerk of the Stewart county court has been known throughout his lifetime in this region, as were also both his parents. His paternal grandfather, Alexander Humphreys Coppedge, came in an early period from the adjacent commonwealth of North Carolina to the Volunteer state, where he promptly determined upon a location in the promising section of Stewart county. He married Miss Emmeline Elliot, who was also a North Carolinian by birth and youthful residence. Alexander Humphreys followed a profession which in those days was one of far greater difficulty and far less remuneration than now, —that of school-teaching. This work he pursued in Stewart county, where he spent the greater part of his life. There his children were born and educated. They were eleven in number, the youngest being Charles Coppedge, now well known in Stewart county, both in his own person and as the father of the subject of this sketch. Charles Coppedge's birthplace was in District No. 6 of this county and the date of his birth was March 16, 1845. He was but an infant when his father died, and he early developed manly traits and an interest in those pursuits involving a considerable degree of brain work. His first self-supporting endeavors were carried on in the capacity of a bookkeeper for the Woods Tatemen Iron Company. With this establishment he continued until the interruptions of the Civil war interfered with their activities. When the war closed and the company was re-established, he resumed work in the furnaces. In 1878 he accepted the office of trustee of Stewart county and continued

therein until 1884. In 1882 he became connected with Walter Brothers, a Dover mercantile house, and remained thus associated until 1890. Since 1896 he has been devoting his time and attention to the affairs of his farm property near Dover. Mrs. Charles Coppedge, who in girlhood was Miss Frances Josephine King, was also a native of Stewart county, her birthplace being in District No. 5 and the date of her birth March 9, 1852. Her marriage to Charles Coppedge took place on November 17, 1870. Their children were six in number: Ruby, Terese (now deceased), Douglas, Erle, Grace and Harold.

Douglas K. Coppedge, third in order of birth and the eldest son of his parents, was born near Dover, in Stewart county, on March 29, 1882. He gathered his knowledge of books from the public schools of his native community and at a comparatively early age sought a field for independent efforts. His first vocational venture was in the mercantile line, in the capacity of salesman in a general merchandise store at Bear Springs.

The satisfactions of agricultural existence for a time appealed to Mr. Coppedge, who in 1901 entered upon the farming occupation, continuing it for nine years. In 1910 he was honored by election to the office of clerk of the court of Stewart county, a position for which he is well qualified. This office he still holds, performing its duties successfully and ably. He is still interested in farming to a considerable degree.

Mr. Coppedge's domestic life was established on June 28, 1911, at which time he won as his life's companion Miss Rose Thomason, a daughter of the late Edwin Thomason of Davidson county. They are cosily situated at their home in Dover and are active in church and social interests of the place. Mr. Coppedge, like his parents, has always been connected with the Methodist church South. Mrs. Coppedge is a member of the Presbyterian church.

Douglas Coppedge and his father are both members of the fraternal order of Ancient Free and Accepted Masons, in Phoenix Lodge No. 270, of Dover. The Modern Woodmen of America, Big Rock Camp, also claim the membership of D. K. Coppedge. Both he and Charles Coppedge are loyal Democrats of the characteristically southern type.

COL. CARY F. SPENCE. A representative citizen of the city of Knoxville and one who has had distinctive influence in connection with business and civic activities in this beautiful and thriving industrial center, Colonel Spence is now serving in the office of postmaster and is known as one of the most loyal and progressive citizens of this section of the state, where he is widely known and commands secure place in popular confidence and esteem.

Cary F. Spence was born at Knoxville, Tennessee. on the 21st of January, 1869, in the house wherein he now resides, and is one of the five children of his parents, who were Dr. John Fletcher and Elizabeth

(Cary) Spence. His father was chancellor of the American University of Harriman, Tennessee, and chancellor of Grant University of Athens, Tennessee. He was one of the best known and most highly esteemed men in the state. He was long identified with educational work, and was manifestly deserving of the high place that he held.

At the inception of the Civil war he tendered his services in defense of the Union, and he became captain of a company in the Forty-second Ohio Artillery, with which command he participated in many of the important conflicts between the North and the South. With the close of the war he established his home in Tennessee, where he continued to reside until his death.

Col. Cary Fletcher Spence is indebted to the public schools of Knoxville for his early educational discipline, the same having been supplemented by an effective course in Grant University, in which he was graduated in the year 1890. In the same year he received the degree of Bachelor of Arts. During his college career the young man attained a national prominence in athletics as a track runner, winning the one hundred yard and the two hundred and twenty yard dashes at the meet of the Amateur Athletic Union in Philadelphia in 1892. He later became a member of the Columbia Athletic Association of Washington, and in 1893, while representing that association at the World's Fair in Chicago, won the distinction of finishing second in the two hundred and twenty yard dash.

In 1891, just following his graduation from Grant University, better known today as the University of Chattanooga, of which his father was then president, Colonel Spence entered business for the first time as a clerk for the Knoxville Building & Loan Company, leaving them a little later to associate himself with the Greer Machinery Company, with which he was prominently connected in the capacity of vice-president. He remained there for four years, withdrawing in 1898 to volunteer his services as a soldier in the Spanish-American war, and was appointed first lieutenant and regimental adjutant in the Sixth United States Volunteer Infantry, receiving his appointment from President McKinley, and in the following year, 1899, was promoted to the rank of captain in Porto Rico. He has been a continuous member of the national guard of the state for thirteen years, and is the highest ranking officer in that body today, bearing the rank of colonel. Following his return to Knoxville in 1899, Colonel Spence became president of the Spence Trunk & Leather Company, a firm that has since become one of the substantial and prosperous concerns of the city, with a growing business of both a wholesale and retail order, and is president of the Island Home Park Company, which owns and has improved the beautiful resort park that gives title to the corporation and which in itself constitutes one of the noteworthy attractions of the Knoxville district.

In his political activities Colonel Spence has been an enthusiastic

supporter of the cause of the Republican party, and has been an active
and effective worker in its ranks. On February 1, 1911, he was appointed
postmaster of Knoxville, and in this important position he has given an
excellent and popular administration, in which he has affected many
improvements in the service and brought the same up to a standard
especially high, as compared with that of other cities of the same com-
parative population and commercial importance. Colonel Spence is dis-
tinctively progressive and public spirited in hs civic attitude and takes a
lively interest in all that touches the welfare and advancement of his
native city, where his circle of friends is coincident with that of his
acquaintances. He is one of the more active members of the Knoxville
Board of Trade and in 1909 and 1910 served as its president, and is
now first vice-president of the Board of Commerce of Knoxville,
Tennessee.

His military record has already been touched upon briefly, and it is
unnecessary to enter into further detail concerning the same, but it may
be mentioned that he is president of the Tennessee Sons of the American Revolution; is a member of the military order of the Loyal Legion,
as he is also of the Military Order of Foreign Wars and the Spanish-
American War Veterans' Association. Fraternally Colonel Spence is
affiliated with the Knoxville lodge of the Benevolent Protective Order of
Elks, and is a member of the Cumberland, Cherokee, Country and Ap-
palachian Clubs. All these are representative clubs of Knoxville, and
in addition to his membership in them Colonel Spence is a member of
the Army and Navy Club of New York City.

Colonel Spence was married to Miss Nan Crook of Baltimore, in
which city she was born and reared. She is the daughter of George W.
Crook, a representative citizen of that city. Two children have come
to the Spence family: Eleanor E. and Shirley C.

DR. F. A. MARTIN. The five years of Dr. Martin's medical practice
in Cumberland City have been such as to demonstrate his thorough
knowledge of his science and the high quality of his professional judgment. His family is one of those that are best known in Stewart county,
although Dickson county was the location in which the Martins first
settled. The first of these to locate in Tennessee was Jerry Martin
(grandfather of the subject of this review), who came to this state
from North Carolina. He was prominent for a number of years as a
county official in Dickson county. His son, E. P. Martin, was born in that
locality, and there he received his somewhat limited education. He gave
willing service to the cause of the South during the Civil war, in which
he served with the rank of lieutenant, under General Forrest. When
peace had returned to the land, E. P. Martin removed to Big Rock, where
he engaged in mercantile and milling business, an occupation which he
still continues, with an excellent degree of success. He is a Democrat in

politics and a Baptist in church affiliation. Mrs. E. P. Martin is a native
of Montgomery county, where in her girlhood she was known as Miss
Irene Reynolds. Of the eight children who have been born to them
the seventh in line was F. A. Martin. The place of his nativity was Big
Rock, in Stewart county, and the date of his birth was February 9, 1880.

The general education of F. A. Martin was completed in Cumberland
City Academy. He had chosen the University of Tennessee as his professional alma mater and went to Nashville in order to enter that institution. He completed his medical course in 1907 and after taking his
degree, he settled in that same year in Cumberland City, where he at
once began practice. Success has attended his efforts and his patronage
is steadily increasing. He is interested in all events and in all periodicals that further the science of medicine. He is a member of the Montgomery County Medical Society and of the Tennessee State Medical
Society.

Dr. Martin is a man of sturdy Democratic views. His fraternal
interests are with the organizations of the Masonic order, his membership in that society being in Charity Lodge No. 307.

On July 11, 1911, Dr. Martin and Miss Blanche Robinson were
united in marriage. Mrs. Martin is a daughter of the late Robert Robinson, the L. & N. conductor whose life was sacrificed in the railroad
wreck on that line. Dr. and Mrs. Martin are among Cumberland City's
most highly regarded and popular citizens.

A. S. PROSSER. One of the ablest lawyers of the Knoxville bar was the
late A. S. Prosser, a soldier of the Union army during the Civil war,
mustered out in Tennessee, and taking up his residence at Knoxville soon
afterwards. For many years, until his death, he was one of the leading
attorneys, enjoyed a large private practice, was esteemed for his unfaltering observance of the best ethics of the profession and for his solid integrity in all the relations of life.

A. S. Prosser was a Pennsylvanian by birth, born in that state December 4, 1838. He was the third in a family of four sons, whose parents
were David and Rachael (Williams) Prosser, both of whom were born in
Wales, were married there, and came to America in 1832, locating first
near Harrisburg, and subsequently at Johnstown, Pennsylvania. The
mother died in 1842, and the father subsequently married Mariah Kenton, a native of Bedford county, Pennsylvania, and she became the
mother of eight children. David Prosser, the father, had the distinction of being the first man to open a coal bed in western Pennsylvania.
He lived a long and useful life, and his death occurred in 1884.

The late Mr. Prosser spent the first fifteen years of his life on a farm,
and most of his early education was obtained in the public schools of
Johnstown, Pennsylvania. He subsequently moved out to the state of
Illinois, where he was occupied up to the breaking out of the Civil war.

Then on April 19, 1861, only a few days after the firing on Fort Sumter, he enlisted in the Tenth Illinois Infantry, and was in service with the commissary department until 1864. At that date he was transferred to the Second Tennessee Cavalry of the Union army as first lieutenant. Lieutenant Prosser was mustered out on July 9, 1865, at Nashville, and remained in that city until February, 1866. At that date he located in Knoxville and entered the law firm of Maynard & Washburn, one of the old and distinguished law firms of the city. He was subsequently admitted a member of the firm and the title changed to Washburn & Prosser, a combination which continued until January, 1870, after which date Mr. Prosser was engaged in practice alone until the time of his death, which occurred June 16, 1894. Mr. Prosser in 1869 served as attorney general pro tempore for the state of Tennessee.

In 1875 Mr. Prosser married Lizzie Brown, daughter of Judge George Brown, a native of Monroe county, Tennessee. One child was born to their marriage, Brown Prosser, who is now well known in the business circles of Knoxville as a merchandise broker, with his offices in the Henson building. Mrs. Prosser and son reside on Rutledge Pike.

JOHN W. ANDES. Many years have passed over the head of the Hon. John W. Andes, of Knoxville, Tennessee, but he is still the same sturdy, clear headed man that he was in the days when he was helping to defend the Stars and Stripes against the onrush of the Confederate forces. He is now a notary public and a claim and pension attorney of Knoxville, and is widely known in the city. The experience of many years of wise living have shown him the way into the hearts of men and the respect and affection which is accorded him comes from the personal friendship and warm admiration of those with whom he comes in contact. A southerner by birth, when the war broke out he had the necessary courage to stand by his convictions and fight against the breaking up of the Union, and this has been typical of his whole life.

The Hon. John W. Andes was born in Tennessee, on the 28th of May, 1838, one of the three children of his parents, who were John and Lettie (Murphy) Andes. His father was a Virginian by birth and followed the occupation of a farmer throughout his life. John W. Andes received from the public schools of the state what in those days was considered an education but which in reality consisted principally of learning to read and write. Turning to the only occupation which was open to a young southerner in those days unless he chose to become a professional man, John Andes became a farmer. He continued this until the Civil war broke out and then enlisted in Company K of the Second Tennessee Cavalry as lieutenant in his company and served throughout the war, being discharged from the service on the 6th of July, 1865.

He left the army to take up his old life again and turned to the only occupation which he had followed. He was successful as a farmer and for many years continued in this occupation. In 1901, however, he gave up the farm and came to Knoxville to live. Previous to this, in 1890, he had been appointed pension agent by the commissioner of pensions and has served in this capacity since that time. His office is located in the Sedgwick block and in addition to being notary public and claim and pension attorney, he also is engaged in taking acknowledgments and in handling deeds and similar interests.

Mr. Andes is a member of the Republican party and has served his party faithfully and well. He was elected a member of the state legislature in 1889 and served through 1889 and 1890. In his fraternal relations he is identified with Masonic Lodge No. 144 of Knoxville, Tennessee. He also belongs to the Grand Army of the Republic and to Ed Maynard Post No. 14. He and his family are all attendants of the Methodist Episcopal church.

On the 27th of June, 1867, Mr. Andes was married to Miss Sarah C. French of Knox county, Tennessee, a daughter of Michael French. Eight children have been born to Mr.. and Mrs. Andes, namely: James A.; Addie E., wife of W. L. Murphy; Ulysses S., now in Philippine Islands, at Manila, at the head of normal school at that place; and Belle, Frank A., Ethel, Ernest W., and John W., all of Knoxville, Tennessee.

W. T. KENNERLY. Beginning his career as a stenographer, one of the best avenues of approach to many commercial and professional activities, then winning his degree in law, and applying a fine industry with his natural ability to his early practice, Mr. W. T. Kennerly has for ten years been one of the rising members of the Knoxville bar, and has attained a place with the best of his contemporaries. Mr. Kennerly is the present city attorney of Knoxville.

Born in Henry county, Tennessee, August 29, 1877, he was one of a family of five children whose parents were C. M. and Sarah A. (Travis) Kennerly. The family is of Irish lineage, and the father followed the occupation of farmer. The names of the paternal grandparents were John W. and Martha (Ross) Kennerly, and of the maternal grandparents, Dr. Joseph H. and Eliza (Crump) Travis.

Beginning his education in the common schools of Henry county, Mr. Kennerly learned stenography, and for several years used that accomplishment as a source of self-support and a means to a broader field of work. In 1901 he had completed his studies in the University of Tennessee and won the degree of LL. B., and has since been engaged in active practice. He is a member of the strong legal firm of Pickle, Turner & Kennerly. His election to the office of city attorney occurred January 27, 1912.

During the Spanish-American war Mr. Kennerly was first sergeant in Company L of the First Tennessee Infantry, and is now a member of the Spanish War Veterans. He was for four years chairman of the Knox county Democratic executive committee, and four years a member of the state Democratic executive committee. He is affiliated with the Phi Kappa fraternity, the Masonic lodge, and the Knights of Pythias, and his church is the Methodist South. His marriage occurred March 15, 1906, when Miss Ola D. Robertson, daughter of G. C. and Emily C. Robertson, became his wife. They have two children, Robert T. and Warren W.

MATTHEW S. McCLELLAN. Of the old and well remembered merchants of Knoxville, one of the most prominent was the late Matthew S. McClellan, who for forty-five years was in business in the city and at the time of his death was at the head of the credit department of the well-known shoe firm of McMillan-Hazen Shoe Company. A successful business man, he displayed much public spirit in the civic affairs, and was a kindly and highly esteemed associate and friend. His death, which occurred February 2, 1912, closed a career of substantial achievement and good citizenship.

One of a family of eight children born to William and Margaret McClellan, the late Matthew S. McClellan was born at Powells Station, Tennessee, January 26, 1849. He attended the public schools of his native county, and subsequently was a student in the University of Tennessee. The beginning of his practical career was coincident with the uplift movement in business which followed a few years after the close of the war, and his energy and ambition found its first important outlet in the mercantile line in partnership with Col. J. M. Toole. After this co-partnership had continued for some time he became identified with the Gaines Brothers in the shoe business at Knoxville, and subsequently became associated in the shoe business with R. S. Payne. This enterprise subsequently went under the firm title of McNulty, Payne & Company, Mr. McClellan being a partner in the enterprise, and a later reorganization resulted in the firm name of McMillan, Hazen & Company, probably the largest and most prosperous wholesale shoe company in Knoxville. Mr. McClellan was identified with this firm as one of its guiding spirits until his death. He was at that time secretary and treasurer of the company and had given the best years of his life to the extension of its business throughout this part of the South.

The late Mr. McClellan was for one term an alderman representing the Seventh ward in the city council, and his name was frequently associated with the voluntary organizations of business men or citizens in effecting some important improvement in this section of the city.

Mr. McClellan was married on October 26, 1871, to Miss Hannah E. Wallace, a daughter of Robert Wallace. Their children, six in number, are named as follows: Hugh, who is one of the well-known and prosperous business men of Atlanta, Georgia; Samuel B., in the manufacturing business; Robert W., V. P. with the S. C. Dismukes Hat Co., at Knoxville; Lula, wife of Edward C. Briscoe, one of Knoxville's business men and a resident of 1510 Laurel avenue; Harriet, the wife of James W. Young, who died September 20, 1908, and Miss Elizabeth, who resides at home with her mother in the old residence at 1221 Laurel avenue. The late Mr. McClellan and his family were all communicants of the Southern Methodist church. In his home Mr. McClellan was loved as a kind and generous father and husband, and among all his business associates he had a reputation for solid integrity which was never impeached. His remains now rest in the Old Gray cemetery at Knoxville.

CAPT. JOHN M. BROOKS. One of the most highly esteemed citizens of Knoxville is Capt. John M. Brooks, who for some years has been in the insurance business in this city and has spent most of his life in Tennessee. Captain Brooks is a veteran of the Confederate army and won his rank as a soldier of the South. He has long been one of the influential men in the Democratic party and following the end of the war had a very important part in the reorganizing of the Democracy in eastern Tennessee. He is a former mayor of the city of Knoxville and has given public service in many important capacities during his long and active career.

John M. Brooks was one of a family of nine children, whose parents were Joseph A. and Margaret (McMillan) Brooks. He was born October 28, 1840, and during his youth received an excellent education, first in the common schools and then in the University of Tennessee, or the University of East Tennessee, as it was then known. With the outbreak of the war in 1861 he was among the first to answer to the call of duty to the Southland, and went into service in Company I of the Second Tennessee Cavalry. His service continued for more than four years until the surrender of General Johnston in North Carolina.

The first important public service of Captain Brooks on returning from the war was, as has been mentioned, in the reorganization of the Democratic party in this state. He was then identified for many years with business in Knoxville, after which he went to Middlesboro, Kentucky, where he was connected with a land company of that place and during his residence there served in the office of mayor. On returning to Knoxville in 1906 he engaged in his present business, the handling of insurance, and his success has been far beyond his expectations. The captain has many friends and his character and personality have kept him continually in high esteem.

Politically he is an independent Democrat. He supported Governor Hooper during his candidacy and has always been an active worker for party success.

Captain Brooks was elected mayor of Knoxville in 1908 and gave two years of excellent service to the city. Since leaving the office of mayor he has been a member of the board of education. He is one of the most honored members of the Confederate Veterans of the state and that body has promoted him to the office of brigadier general of the veterans' organization. Fraternally he is a thirty-second degree Mason, and has membership in the Sons of the American Revolution. He and his family are communicants of the Presbyterian church.

ALFRED Y. BURROWS. One of the leading lawyers of Knoxville, Tennessee is Alfred Y. Burrows, a native Tennesseean who has honored his profession and his state by the able order of his services.

He was born in Fayette county, Tennessee, November 30, 1869, and is one of the five children that came to his parents, Benjamin F. Burrows and Matilda A. (Young) Burrows. The father was a very prominent contractor of Fayette county, Tennessee, where he resided until his death in 1892.

Alfred Y. first received a common school education in his native county and then later attended the University of Tennessee. Following that he completed the law course in the same institution and was graduated in law as a member of the class of 1899, of which he was president. He was admitted to the bar in 1899 and immediately thereafter commenced his practice in Knoxville, where he has continued to the present. He excels as a lawyer and has long held a foremost place at the Knoxville bar. Mr. Burrows has offices in the Empire building. In political affairs he is affiliated with the Democratic party and he is now city attorney of Park City as well as being counsel for a number of other large corporations. He is prominently identified with the Masonic fraternity, being a thirty-second degree Scottish Rite Mason, a past high priest of the Royal Arch Masons and a past master of the Free and Accepted Masons and past eminent commander of Knights Templar.

On June 2, 1891, was solemnized the marriage of Mr. Burrows and Miss Mary E. Atkin, a daughter of Capt. J. J. Atkin, who formerly served the city of Knoxville as chief of police. Mr. and Mrs. Burrows have two children, Bessie and Frank J. The family are communicants of the Methodist Episcopal church South. Their residence is at 1720 Washington avenue, Park City.

LEONIDAS D. SMITH. Division counsel at Knoxville for the Southern Railway Company, Mr. Smith has attained one of the most important honors and positions of service open to the legal profession of east Tennessee. He has been connected with corporate practice of a more important character for many years, and has been a successful member of the Tennessee bar for fully a quarter of a century.

Leonidas D. Smith was born in Sparta, Tennessee, November 25, 1866. His parents were William G. and Amanda (Templeton) Smith, who had a family of seven children. The late William G. Smith had a prominent place as a member of the Tennessee bar, and was actively engaged in practice until his death which occurred at Sparta in 1909. His wife died a year later in 1910.

The career of Mr. Smith was started with a public school education, and he was subsequently a student in the University of Tennessee, where he completed his literary studies. As a preceptor for his legal studies he was fortunate in having Col. H. C. Snodgrass, one of the most eminent lawyers of Tennessee, who had served the state in the office of attorney general and was also a member of congress. Under his direction Mr. Smith continued his studies until his admission to the bar in December, 1887. He at once began practice and became a member of the firm of Jourolman, Welcker & Smith, a partnership which enjoyed many distinctions and successes in the profession and existed for many years until dissolved on March 1, 1913. As division counsel for the Southern Railway Company, Mr. Smith has full occupation for all his professional energy, but in previous years was associated with many important cases in the higher courts of the state.

Mr. Smith in 1911 and 1912 served as president of the Tennessee State Bar Association. Fraternally he is affiliated with the Independent Order of Odd Fellows, the Masons and the Knights of Pythias, and is a Democrat in politics. His office is in the Holston National Bank building at Knoxville. Mr. Smith married Miss Ella Wallace, daughter of Simon D. Wallace, one of the prominent citizens of White county, Tennessee. The one child born to their union is Keilah C. Mr. Smith and family worship in the Christian church, and their residence is at 615 West Church street in Knoxville.

HORACE VAN DEVENTER. Now clerk of the United States District Court for eastern Tennessee, Mr. Van Deventer has been identified with the bar of this state for about twenty years, a period which has been one of influential achievement and varied service in public life. He is a veteran of the Spanish-American war, has been a member of the state legislature, and has associated himself with many of the movements in social and civic affairs which give distinction to the city of Knoxville.

Horace Van Deventer is a native of Clinton, Iowa, where his birth occurred July 22, 1867, one in a family of six children, his parents were James Thayer and Letitia (Flournoy) Van Deventer. Few of the younger generation of the Tennessee bar have been more liberally educated than Mr. Van Deventer. He attended the public schools at Clinton and from there entered the Michigan Military Academy at Orchard Lake, a preparatory and military school, from which he was graduated in 1886. He then became a student in the University of Michigan, where he was graduated with the degree of Ph. B. in 1890. From that university he took up his law studies, which were pursued in probably the foremost school of the time in the country, the Harvard Law School, and he was graduated in 1893 and received the degree of LL. B.

Since his admission to the bar Mr. Van Deventer has been an active member of the Knoxville bar. His record of public service began as city attorney for West Knoxville, a position he held during 1895-97. In the fifty-second general assembly of Tennessee he was a senator from Knox county. In 1905 he began his services as clerk of the United States District Court, for the eastern district of Tennessee, and his official term has continued now for nearly ten years. During the Spanish-American war in 1898-9 he was a captain in the Sixth United States Volunteer Infantry under Colonel Tyson, and also held the ranks of first lieutenant and regimental quartermaster in the same regiment. He was with the regiment during the Porto Rico campaign and after his muster out resumed his practice in Knoxville. His law offices are located at 202 Van Deventer building.

Mr. Van Deventer was married April 9, 1902, to Mary Lurton Finley. Mrs. Van Deventer is a daughter of the Hon. Horace H. Lurton, whose career as a jurist is familiar to all Tennesseeans, and who is now a member of the supreme court of the United States. Mrs. Van Deventer who has been prominent in the social circles of both the Tennessee and national capitals as well as in Knoxville was recently appointed by Hon T. Asbury Wright as president of the Woman's Board of the First National Conservation Exposition to be held in Knoxville in the fall of 1913. Mr. Van Deventer and his wife are members of the Episcopal church. He has membership in the Military Order of Foreign Wars, the Tennessee Society of the Sons of the American Revolution, the Holland Society of New York, and his fraternities are the Masons, the Alpha Delta Phi, Peninsular Chapter, and he is a member of the Cherokee Country Club and the University Club of Knoxville. His residence is at 945 Temple avenue, Knoxville.

HARRY SAMUEL HALL. One of the young and progressive lawyers of Knoxville, with offices in the McNutt building, Mr. Hall has rapidly attained success and prestige since opening his practice in 1906. He has also important interests in local business affairs, and in the city which has been his lifetime home he has always occupied a high social position.

Harry Samuel Hall was born at Knoxville, July 4, 1884. There were four children in the family, and his parents were Isaac and Mary Ella (Alexander) Hall. The family is of Scotch-Irish ancestry.

Reared in his native city and attending the local schools, Mr. Hall graduated from the University of Tennessee with his degree in law in 1906, and in October of the same year was admitted to practice in all state and federal courts. He then became associated in practice with the late Judge D. D. Anderson, former judge of the circuit and criminal court, with offices in the McNutt building. Since the death of Judge Anderson he has continued to practice alone. Mr. Hall is also president of the Hall Lumber Company of Knoxville.

He has membership in the County and State Bar Associations, is affiliated with Lodge No. 234, Knights of Pythias, at Knoxville, his Greek letter fraternity is the Theta Lambda Phi, and he and his family are members of the Methodist church. Mr. Hall belonged to Company B of the Tennessee State Guards, in which he held the offices of second and first lieutenant. His other fraternal orders are the Eagles and the Red Men. Mr. Hall in 1910 was the Democratic nominee for the office of representative from Knox county and he made a strong though unsuccessful campaign.

April 2, 1908, Mr. Hall married Miss Bessie G. Johnson, daughter of John W. and Fannie L. Johnson. They are the parents of two children, Mary Frances and Irma Eugene. The Hall residence is on Washington pike.

CORNELIUS E. LUCKY. The subject of this sketch, Cornelius E. Lucky, was born February 25, 1841, in the village of Jonesboro, the oldest town in the state, and the capitol of the short-lived state of Franklin. He was the sixth child in the order of birth in a family of nine children, he and three sisters are now living.

Mr. Lucky was the son of Seth J. W. Lucky and Sarah Rhea Lucky, both of Scotch-Irish descent, Presbyterians, and connected with old families, that were founders of the state of Tennessee.

Seth J. W. Lucky was born in Greene county, in 1799, educated in that county, graduated at Greeneville College, and began the practice of law in Jonesboro, became circuit judge in 1841, then chancellor, continued his judicial career until his death in 1869, being at that time chancellor of the first chancery division of the state. Judge Lucky was always a Whig although never taking any part in party politics, was identified with every temperance movement of his time, and was an unwavering Union man during the Civil war.

His son, the subject of this review, gained his early education in the schools of Jonesboro and Blountville, entered Emory & Henry College, Virginia, in the fall of 1860, and left there in April, 1861, the college closing at that time on account of the impending Civil war.

Mr. Lucky being strong in his conviction touching the issues to be settled by war deemed it his duty to go with his state and so in 1862 enlisted as a private, assisted Col. Nathan Gregg in raising a company in Washington county, which upon the organization of a regiment became Company K, in the 60th Tennessee Infantry, C. S. A. Lucky having been chosen orderly sergeant of Company K. This regiment, soon after its organization, was sent South and participated in the battles around and near Vicksburg, Mississippi, losing a portion of same by capture at the battle of Big Black river, Mississippi.

The major part of the regiment entered Vicksburg with Pemberton's command and passed through that noted siege. General Pemberton, by surrendering on July 4th, obtained very favorable terms, as the entire command was paroled, allowed to return to their homes and remain there until duly exchanged. Mr. Lucky was with his regiment during this entire period, and was paroled on July 4, 1863, and returned to his home.

The 60th Tennessee was not exchanged until July 1, 1864, its members remaining at their homes on their paroles. When said regiment was exchanged, Mr. Lucky re-entered the army with his command, which was then mounted, and served with it until the end of the war, campaigning in east Tennessee and south West Virginia.

The regiment, or that part of it not captured at the battle of Big Black river, was with General Early in south West Virginia, when General Lee surrendered, and thereupon it started to join General Johnson, in North Carolina, but when within a few miles of Greensboro, North Carolina, learned of General Johnson's surrender, and then the men and officers of that regiment returned to their homes, where possible, Mr. Lucky surrendering to the Federal forces at Jonesboro, his home. He was sent from that place to Nashville, Tennessee, where he took the oath of allegiance to the United States government. Mr. Lucky was a non-commissioned officer during his entire military service, although he acted as quartermaster of his regiment during the last six months of the war. On his return from Nashville, Mr. Lucky learned of his indictment for treason, he at once surrendered to the civil authorities, gave bond for his appearance, and applied for and obtained a pardon from President Andrew Johnson.

After the close of the war, Mr. Lucky spent a year as a clerk in a business house and in a law office, the latter service being in Knoxville, and in September, 1866, entered Hamilton College, Clinton, New York, where he spent three years, graduating with the class of 1869, being a C. B. K. in that class. Upon graduation he returned to Knoxville, read law with the Hon. Thomas A. R. Nelson, one of the most distinguished lawyers in the state, one of the counsel defending President Andrew Johnson in his impeachment trial and one of the supreme judges of the state.

Mr. Lucky began the practice of the law in the city of Knoxville in the year 1870, just after his admission to the bar, has continuously pursued his profession, never seeking nor holding any public office, but always taking an active interest and part in all civic affairs, city, county, state and national, and in the moral, educational and religious movements of his adopted home.

He and his law firms of Lucky & Yoe, Lucky & Sanford, Lucky, Sanford & Fowler and his present firm of Lucky, Andrews & Fowler have always commanded a lucrative practice, and have been connected with many of the leading cases arising in this section of the state.

Mr. Lucky has always been deeply interested in all of the educational movements in this section—was one of the founders of the first public library in Knoxville, is now a trustee of the Lawson McGhee Library, a trustee of Tusculum College (successor to Greeneville College—where his father graduated), is a member and officer of the Fourth Presbyterian church and a member of the Fred Ault Bivouac.

GEORGE H. BURR. In the development of the business enterprises which accompanied the rehabilitation of the South after the disastrous effect of the Civil war one of the most prominent factors in the city of Knoxville was the late George H. Burr. Mr. Burr was for thirty-five years closely identified with the commercial life and the civic and philanthropic activities of Knoxville, and in his death, which occurred April 29, 1902, that community lost one of its finest citizens. He was a business builder and possessed the rugged strength and enterprising qualities which bring success in that line, but with this half of his character he also combined his finer virtues of citizenship and manhood which are not less essential to the well-being of a city.

The late George H. Burr was a native of Connecticut, born in that state October 15, 1829, and was directly connected with the family which produced Aaron Burr, the former vice-president of the United States, associated with Thomas Jefferson in the office of president and vice-president in 1800, and an eminent American whose position has been subject to many counter opinions, but to whom the maturer judgment of history accords a sanity and worthiness in the enterprise which in early years marked him as almost an enemy of his country, though he was really only in advance of his times. The parents of the late Mr. Burr were Moses and Harriet B. (Banks) Burr, both of whom were natives of Connecticut. Moses Burr was born in Greenfield, Fairfield county, Connecticut, in 1806, and the mother was born in 1809, being a daughter of Thomas and Abigal (Murwin) Banks.

George H. Burr was reared at Weston, Connecticut, and as a boy attained a substantial education in the public and private schools of that place. When a youth he learned the trade of a coach-maker, but after some years in that pursuit it proved too small for his large energies and ambitions, and he sought a better field for his enterprise. With the close of the Civil war he was among the northern men who recognized the great opportunities existing in the new South, and accordingly came to Tennessee in 1867, locating at Knoxville. Here he became identified with the saw milling and general lumber business, and during the succeeding years in the century his name was one of the most prominent in association with this important industry at Knoxville. He occupied a leading place as a manufacturer and dealer in lumber, and was also connected with other local commercial affairs. As a business man he stood in the small group whose resources and influence were the most vital factors in the business community. At his death he left a

Geo. B. Orr

large estate, as in part the measure of his large activities as a business man.

Along with success in business he gave his energies without stint to every movement for the betterment of the city. He was always recognized as a friend of the poor, and gave of his means liberally, not only to individual places of charity but to the organized activities which extend their practical aid to the unfortunate. Among his characteristics was his love for good horses, and during the last fifteen years of his life, which he spent largely in retirement from active business, he was seen almost daily behind a pair of fine drivers. He owned several blooded horses, and was willing to pay a large sum for one that suited his pace.

On October 15, 1853, Mr. Burr married Miss Amelia Andrews, who was born in Connecticut in 1830, a daughter of Jonathan and Abigal (Murwin) Andrews, both of whom were natives of Connecticut. Her father was born in April, 1802, was a farmer by occupation, and died in August, 1848. Her mother was born in 1804 and died in 1854. Mr. and Mrs. Burr had no children. A relative of whom he was very fond, was his half-brother, Lewis S. Burr, of Weston, Connecticut, a farmer of that state, where he was born in 1859. Mrs. Burr, since the death of her husband, has continued to reside at their comfortable home at 208 Prince street in Knoxville, and is now a finely preserved old lady at the age of eighty-two years.

HON. JOHN BAXTER. Up to the time of his death, which occurred at Hot Springs, Arkansas, April 2, 1886, the late John Baxter was the accepted leader of the east Tennessee bar. Both as a lawyer, a judge and a citizen he was a man of many eminent qualities, and in his day was the peer and associate of the strongest individuals in the public and professional life of Tennessee.

The late John Baxter was born in Rutherford county, North Carolina, March 5, 1819. His early life was cast in a period which was notable for its absence of schools and other advantages and facilities which are now deemed essential, but which nevertheless produced through the channels of practical experience and close association with the strong men of the previous generation, many of the ablest leaders known to the last century.

John Baxter had no opportunity for education except as were given in the "old field schools" of the neighborhood of which he lived. For a short time he was a clerk in a country store, but abandoned this for the study of law in the office of Hon. Simpson Bobo of South Carolina, and he quickly showed remarkable ability and talent for the law. In the spring of 1857 he moved to Knoxville, and it was in that city that his most important professional work was done. During the Civil war he was loyal to the government of the United States, and was always a fearless advocate of its cause. In the constitutional convention of Tennessee in 1870 he was a delegate from Knox county, and served as one of the leading members of the judiciary committee. While he himself had been a Union man, it is worthy of note that the majority of the members of the convention had been supporters, if not soldiers of the Confederacy. During the succeeding seven years John Baxter conducted what was probably the most lucrative law practice that any one lawyer has ever enjoyed in east Tennessee. His ability was acknowledged in all the courts of the state.

In 1877 President Hayes appointed Mr. Baxter judge of the circuit court of the United States for the sixth circuit, a position which he filled with great credit and distinction. Death finally relieved him of the duties and responsibilities of the judicial office. As summed up in the various opinions of those who practiced with him and knew his character and ability, the distinguishing characteristic of the late Judge Baxter was force, and in everything he did he was independent, self-reliant and firm. Though sometimes apparently arbitrary and harsh in his manner, he was essentially just, progressive and liberal, and as already stated was the accepted leader of the east Tennessee bar. Without any invidious distinction, it can be asserted that John Baxter was one of the remarkable men of his time in Tennessee.

COL. GEORGE W. BAXTER. A son of the late Judge John Baxter, Col. George W. Baxter is now one of Knoxville's most prominent and well-to-do citizens. He chose a more active life than his father, and has served four years as a lieutenant of the regular army, was for many years a ranch owner, was prominent in the public life of the West, and for the past ten years has been identified with the banking and manufacturing interests of Knoxville.

George W. Baxter was born in the state of North Carolina, January 7, 1855, and was brought to Knoxville as a child in 1857, when his parents moved to that city. He received his education in the University of the South at Sewanee, where he was a student for two years, and was then appointed to the United States Military Academy at West Point, entering as a cadet in 1873 and graduating in 1877. He was commissioned second lieutenant in the Third Regiment, United States Cavalry, but after serving several years resigned his commission to enter business life. His service had taken him into the West and he remained in the Western states and territories for twenty-five years. As a stockman his business took him from Texas to Montana, and he was one of the prominent figures in the dominant industry of the West at a time when the era of the free range had not yet come to an end. In 1902, Colonel Baxter returned to Knoxville to make it his home again, where he has since been engaged in the banking and cotton manufacturing business. President Cleveland appointed him governor of Wyoming territory in 1886.

In 1889 he served as a member of the constitutional convention which drafted the constitution under which Wyoming was admitted to the Union. In that convention he served on the judiciary committee.

Colonel Baxter married Miss Margaret W. McGhee, daughter of the distinguished citizen, Charles M. McGhee, a brief sketch of whose career is given elsewhere. Colonel Baxter and wife were married on January 7, 1880, and they are the parents of five children. The family are members of the Episcopal church, and he is affiliated with the Masonic order. He is also a member of all the social and civic clubs and belongs to several well known clubs in New York City. He is a Democrat in politics, and has always upheld the principles of his party. Colonel Baxter and family reside in their beautiful home at 505 Locust street in Knoxville.

COL. CHARLES M. MCGHEE. One of Knoxville's most prominent and influential citizens was the late Col. Charles M. McGhee, whose death occurred at his home in that city on the fifth of May, 1907. Colonel McGhee was a railroad man, a banker and financier, and both as a business man and as a citizen, his relations were close and intimate with many undertakings that deeply concerned the substantial welfare and progress of his home city and state.

Charles M. McGhee was born in Monroe county, Tennessee, January 23, 1828, one of a family of three children, born to John and Betsy (McClung) McGhee. His father before him was almost equally prominent as a business man and financier, and held extensive landed possessions in Monroe county. The late Colonel McGhee spent his boyhood days on the home plantation, and attended schools in Monroe county. He later graduated from the State University, and then engaged in the banking business at Knoxville. Colonel McGhee for many years was especially identified with the east Tennessee, Virginia and Georgia Railroads, now a part of the Southern System. He was one of the principal stockholders, was vice-president and general manager and took an active part in the development and promotion of this railroad. His varied interests called him much out of the state and from his home city, but he always considered Knoxville his civic and family residence, although in his latter years much of his time was spent in New York City.

Colonel McGhee was for many years a trustee of the State University of Tennessee, and it was largely due to his work and influence that this institution was reopened so soon after the war. He served with distinction as a member of the legislature during 1870-71.

Colonel McGhee first married Miss Isabella M. White, daughter of Hugh M. White. Her father was a nephew of Hugh Lawson White, one of the distinguished men of Tennessee. The only child of this marriage died in infancy, and Mrs. McGhee passed away in 1848. Colonel McGhee then married a sister of his first wife, Miss Cornelia H. White. The children of this marriage are noted as follows: Margaret W., wife of Col. George W. Baxter, above mentioned; May Lawson McGhee, now deceased, wife of D. S. Williams; Anna, now deceased, wife of C. M. McClung; Bettie H., wife of Col. L. D. Tyson, one of the leading members of the Knoxville bar, and one of the largest coal operators of east Tennessee; Elinor W., wife of James C. Neely, of Memphis.

The city of Knoxville has a permanent memorial of the liberality of Colonel McGhee in the beautiful Lawson McGhee Library which stands as a monument to his daughter, May Lawson, and which was built and furnished at a cost of over forty thousand dollars. Though this was the most conspicuous of his benefactions in his home city, Colonel McGhee during his lifetime was always a friend and generous helper in the movements for a better and finer city, and his career was one that left its impress in many ways in east Tennessee.

JOHN J. CRAIG. During the past seventy years the city of Knoxville has had no name better known or honored in general commercial affairs than that of John J. Craig, a name which has been borne by the head of three successive generations. In early years the name was associated with banking affairs in Knoxville, and subsequently the first bearer of the name became a pioneer in the marble business of the eastern part of the state, and it is with the production and distribution of the finer varieties of Tennessee marble that the Craig family has been best known now for many years.

John J. Craig, the first of the name in these three generations, was born in Lauderdale county, Alabama, in 1820 and came to Knoxville in 1839. He was for several years a clerk with the well-known firm of those days, McClung, Wallace & Company, and in 1844 returned to Alabama. In 1847 he married a Miss Lyon of Knox county, Tennessee. In 1852 he removed from Alabama and became cashier of the Knoxville branch of the Union Bank, a position which he filled until the bank was closed by the war. For two years during the war period he resided with his family in Cincinnati, and subsequently was engaged in the banking business in New York City up to 1869. He then returned to Knox county and resided on the old homestead in this vicinity until that place was sold to the state as the location for the present insane asylum, five miles below Knoxville. This John J. Craig was one of the pioneers in the production of the east Tennessee marbles and brought into the market the fine variegated varieties.

John J. Craig, second of the name, for many years identified with business affairs in Knoxville, died at his home in this city in October, 1903. He was a man of exceptional power and ability as a business man and as a citizen. He founded the John J. Craig Company, producers and wholesale dealers in Tennessee marble, and built up the business until it was among the largest of its kind in the South. John J. Craig was born in Knox county, Tennessee, September 20, 1860, and was forty-five years of age at the time of his death. He was a student in the State University, and subsequently graduated in 1879 at the Queen City Commercial College. His business career began as a clerk with the Canton Banking & Insurance Company at Canton, Mississippi, where he remained until December 9, 1880. He was then connected with the banking house of John S. Horner & Son at Helena, Arkansas, as book-keeper until January, 1886. At that date he came to Knoxville and engaged in the marble trade, and gave his best energies to the building up of the business which now bears his name. In 1883 he married Miss Lucy Cage, who was born in Canton, Mississippi.

The late John J. Craig was known and esteemed by hundreds of the leading business men and citizens of Knoxville, and he left behind him only the memories which are associated with a good man and an indus-trious and public spirited citizen. His widow and family reside at 1415 Highland avenue. At his death his body was interred at the Old Gray cemetery, where it now rests.

The son of this late well known citizen, John J. Craig, is now secre-tary and treasurer of the John J. Craig Company. The offices of the company are in the Holston National Bank building. Mr. Craig is one of the prominent young business leaders of Knoxville.

Joe Leon Hughett. The law firm of Hughett & Hughett, with offices in the Holston National Bank building at Knoxville, is in several ways distinctive among the legal firms of this state. The senior member of this firm is Mrs. J. L. Hughett, who was born in Scott county, Tennessee, a daughter of Hon. Laban Riseden, one of the prominent attorneys of that section of the state. Mrs. Hughett received a liberal education and studied for the law, and a few years ago was admitted to practice in all state courts and the Federal court. It is said that she was the first woman in the South to be admitted to practice in the Federal courts. Another noteworthy feature about this firm is that about two years ago it was on Mrs. Hughett's motion that her husband and law partner was admitted to practice in the supreme court of Tennessee. This was the first time in the history of that court that a lawyer was admitted to prac-tice upon the motion of a woman. As a successful law firm none stands higher in the Knoxville bar than that of Hughett & Hughett and the partners have enjoyed a clientage of the highest class and have attained much success in the profession.

Joe Leon Hughett was born in Huntsville, Scott county, Tennessee, December 1, 1883, and was one of a family of five children whose parents were Calvin Hughett and wife. His father was a farmer in Scott county. As a boy he attended the public schools of his native county, and later completed his education in the University of Tennessee, of which he is a graduate. On August 14, 1910, he married Miss Riseden, who, as already stated, was born in the same county, but entered the practice of law somewhat in advance of her husband. Mr. Hughett is affiliated with the Junior Order of United American Mechanics and the Independent Order of Odd Fellows. In politics he is a Republican.

CHARLES H. SMITH. Now assistant division counsel for the Southern Railway Company and representing other large foreign and domestic corporations, Mr. Smith has in less than ten years attained a place in the ranks of the leading attorneys of Knoxville, and his varied and successful experience in the profession has laid a foundation for many larger honors and achievements in the coming years.

Charles Henry Smith was born in the city of Knoxville, Knox county, Tennessee, on the 3rd day of December, 1881, and was the oldest of a family of four children born to Benjamin Franklin and Mary Bogart Smith. His mother was a native of Loudon county, Tennessee, and his father was a native of Campbell county, Tennessee, but since 1880 had made his home and engaged in business in the city of Knoxville, where he was recognized as one of the leading merchants and most influential citizens up to the time of his death, which occurred on the 20th day of August, 1900.

As a boy Charles H. Smith attended the Knoxville public schools and later completed his studies in the University of Tennessee, where he graduated in 1902 with the degree of Bachelor of Arts and in 1903 with the degree of Bachelor of Laws. During the years 1902-1903 he taught school in the public schools in Knoxville, pursuing his study of law in the night class conducted at the University of Tennessee. In June, 1903, he was admitted to the bar in Knoxville, but before beginning the active practice of his profession he taught school another year, being principal during 1903-1904 of the school conducted at Albemarle, Louisiana.

In July, 1904, Mr. Smith returned to Knoxville and began the active practice of law, in which profession he has since been engaged continuously. He was first associated with the law firm of Sansom & Welcker, but in 1905 he formed the law firm of Young & Smith, his partner being Mr. Robert S. Young. Only a few months later, and in the year 1905, a partnership was formed with Judge H. B. Lindsay, and the firm then became Lindsay, Young & Smith, and remained so until 1909, when Mr. W. J. Donaldson became a member of the firm, which continued until 1911 under the firm name of Lindsay, Young, Smith & Donaldson. In August, 1911, Mr. Smith withdrew from this firm and has since been engaged in the practice of his profession alone, having a suite of offices at present in the Holston National Bank building.

In 1908 Mr. Smith was elected secretary and treasurer of the Bar Association of Tennessee, to which position he has been unanimously re-elected each succeeding year, and is at present still occupying this position. Since 1905 Mr. Smith has been connected with the Southern Railway Company as its local counsel for Knox county, and on March 1,

1913, he was appointed assistant division counsel for the Southern Railway Company with headquarters at Knoxville, and having charge of the company's legal business in Blount, Loudon, McMinn and Monroe counties. He also represents several large and influential foreign and domestic corporations, and in addition has an extensive general practice. He is personally interested in several corporations, among which is the Knoxville Savings Bank, of which institution he is a stockholder and director, and is also attorney for this bank.

On the 6th day of November, 1907, Mr. Smith was married to Miss Maude Keller, a daughter of Thomas W. and Laura Lackey Keller. To them one child has been born, a boy who bears the name of his father, Charles Henry Smith, Jr. Mr. Smith and his family are members of the First Cumberland Presbyterian church of Knoxville. He is a Republican and is a member of the Cumberland Club, Cherokee Country Club, American Bar Association, and the Bar Association of Tennessee.

Mr. Smith and his family occupy their beautiful home at 1704 West Clinch avenue on the summit of Fort Sanders, where the historic battle of Fort Sanders was fought.

JAMES ISAAC VANCE, D. D. LL. D.   Though the pastoral service of Dr. Vance has been confined to three or four of the larger congregations of the Presbyterian denomination in the South and East, his name and influence as a preacher, church builder, writer and lecturer are as well known as those of any minister of the South. His talents and his devotion to his profession have brought him into the largest field of efficient Christianity, and his services and career are notable.

James Isaac Vance was born in Arcadia, Tennessee, September 25, 1862, a son of Charles Robertson and Margaret (Newland) Vance. Dr. Vance is a brother of Joseph Anderson Vance, also prominent in the Presbyterian church, and now pastor of the First Church of Detroit. Dr. Vance represents some of the oldest families of the South. His father was a soldier in the Confederate army at the time of the son's birth, and the mother had left her residence in Bristol and was a refugee at her father's home in Arcadia.

The great-grandfather, William Vance, was a resident first at Lexington, Virginia, and then at Jonesboro, Tennessee, and married Kezia Robertson, a sister of Maj. Charles Robertson, who was one of the men appointed to make a treaty of peace with the five Indian tribes. A younger brother of Major Charles was Gen. James Robertson, founder of Nashville, Tennessee. The first member of the Vance family in America was Dr. Patrick Vance from the north of Ireland and a graduate in medicine from the University of Edinburgh. He was a physician in Pennsylvania prior to the Revolutionary war. Some of his descendants moved south along the valley of Virginia to North Carolina and Tennessee. The paternal grandfather of Dr. Vance married Jane Sevier, a daughter of Valentine Sevier, and a granddaughter of Col. Robert Sevier, the latter having been the only officer on the American side to be killed in the battle of King's Mountain. Colonel Robert was the younger brother of John Sevier, who was Tennessee's first governor. Dr. Vance is thus descended from the early settlers of Watauga, and the founders of the state of Tennessee.

On his mother's side, Dr. Vance is descended from the Andersons and Rheas, strong Scotch-Irish families which have given a large number of ministers to the Presbyterian church in America. The maternal grandfather was Joseph Newland, who married Rebecca Anderson a daughter of Isaac and Margaret (Rhea) Anderson. An earlier member of the Rhea family was Joseph Rhea, who was one of the first Presbyterian ministers to come from Scotland to America. To the careful religious training of his mother, Dr. Vance attributes the influ-ence which impelled him to enter the ministry. He was educated at King College in Tennessee, where he graduated A. B. in 1883, and received his master's degree in 1886. It was his intention to enter the medical profession and his course in college was taken with a view to that end. Soon after his graduation, however, his purpose was changed, and in 1883 he entered the Union Theological Seminary of Virginia, at Hampden-Sidney, where he was graduated in 1886. Dr. Vance was made Doctor of Divinity by King College in 1896, and by Hampden-Sidney in the same year. In 1913, King College conferred on him the degree of Doctor of Laws.

Ordained in the Presbyterian church in 1886, his first pastoral charge was at Wytheville, Virginia, where he remained during 1886-7, and was then at the Second Presbyterian church in Alexandria from 1887 to 1891. During his pastorate of four years at Alexandria, a new church building was erected, and he was instrumental in uniting the northern and south-ern branches of the church in that city, the northern society uniting with the southern, and thus making one prosperous congregation. The church was thoroughly organized and its membership substantially increased.

On October 1, 1891, Dr. Vance took charge of the First Presbyterian church of Norfolk, Virginia, where he remained until 1894, and where his pastorate was marked by great prosperity and power. At the end of three and a half years he resigned to accept a larger field, and on February 1, 1895, became pastor of the First Presbyterian church of Nashville, the largest single congregation of the Presbyterian church in the United States, and the largest and wealthiest church in the city of Nashville. In 1900 Dr. Vance left Nashville to take charge of the North Reformed church at Newark, New Jersey, where he remained ten years. Under his ministry this congregation had a rapid development, and when he left it, it was the largest church in the Dutch Reformed denomination. He then returned to Nashville, where he has been pastor of the First church since December 1, 1910, and where he preaches to congregations which crowd his big church to overflowing.

As a platform lecturer Dr. Vance is known throughout America, and he has been only less popularly known as an author, his contributions being both of a religious and moral character. He is the author of "The Young Man Four-Square," 1894; "Church Portals," 1895; "College of Apostles," 1896; "Predestination," a pamphlet, 1898; "Royal Manhood," 1899; "Rise of a Soul," 1902; "Simplicity in Life," 1903; "A Young Man's Make-Up," 1904; "The Eternal in Man," 1907; "Tendency," 1910. Besides these he has been a frequent contributor to magazines and reviews. Dr. Vance is one of the best orators of the South, his powers consisting in his simple and earnest method of presenting his convictions and his concise and forceful language. On December 22, 1886, Dr. Vance married Mamie Stiles Currell of Yorkville, South Carolina, a daughter of William and Agnes (Wilkie) Currell. The children of Dr. Vance and wife are as follows: Margaret, William Currell, Agnes Wilkie, Ruth Armstrong, James Isaac (deceased), and Charles Robertson.

Dr. Vance is recognized as one of the religious leaders of the country, and his influence is not confined to denominational lines. No man is more in demand as a college preacher, and his work has made a profound impression on students. He has made the leading address on many notable occasions of a religious and educational character. The "Brief Statement of Belief" issued by the Presbyterian church in the United States was the result of his leadership and much of it was composed by him. In his views he is a progressive conservative. He has declined frequent invitations to the presidency of colleges, and to the pastorates of leading churches in the largest cities of America.

H. A. DAVIS. Superintendent of the Nashville Railway & Light Company, Mr. Davis is one of the prominent railway and construction engineers of the South, and has been identified with a number of large consultation corporations in various states. He began his career in New York state as a stationary engineer and his natural ability and devotion to the profession which he had taken as a vocation have brought him into prominence. Mr. Davis was born in Oswego, Oswego county, New York, April 3, 1866, a son of Samuel A. and Esther (Parks) Davis, both of whom were natives of Oswego county, the former born there in 1838 and the mother in 1845. The mother now resides with her son H. A. at Nashville. The Davis family came originally from Wales. and was founded in this country by the great-grandfather, Abijah Davis. The paternal grandparents were H. M. and Mary A. (Wilson) Davis, both natives of Vermont, and the former being a prosperous farmer who moved to New York state after his marriage and spent the balance of his life in Oswego county. The maternal grandfather was Nathaniel

Parks, who married a Miss Holly. Nathaniel Parks was a native of New York state and a carpenter by trade. The Holly family were very prominent in both New York and Michigan. Samuel A. Davis was a farmer but also followed the profession of engineer and millwright, and prospered in all his undertakings. He and his wife represented different religious faiths, he being a member of the Adventist church and his wife a Methodist. In politics he was a Republican. There were three children in the family, two of them are now living, and the son, George H. Davis, is a mechanical engineer in New Orleans.

Hiram A. Davis attained most of his early education in a country and high school at Oswego, New York, and was little more than a boy when he began learning all there was to the trade of stationary engineer. When he was nineteen he married Miss Isa May Outwater, a daughter of William H. Outwater. Her father, who was born and reared in New York, was one of the most prominent men of Niagara county and known not only as a pioneer fruit grower in that section, but also as a leader in the temperance cause. It is said that he did more for the promotion of temperance than any other individual in the county. He did much to promote fruit growing on a commercial basis and was influential in many ways in his community. Mr. and Mrs. Davis have two children. Lucy Eudelpha is the wife of Warren A. Holstead, the latter being superintendent of Glendale Park in Nashville. Lloyd E. is now attending school, living at home with his parents in Nashville. Mr. and Mrs. Davis worship in the Baptist church and he is affiliated with Masonry in the Scottish Rite Consistory and the Mystic Shrine. In politics he is independent.

After his early career as a stationary engineer in New York he was given charge of a power house at Long Island City, that being at the time one of the largest power houses for the generation of electricity in the entire country. After this experience he accepted a place as superintendent of equipment on the New Orleans & Carrolton Railway in New Orleans. He had practical management of the entire mechanical department of the road and continued there for five years, being promoted to the place of manager before the road was sold. Mr. Davis came to Nashville on December 5, 1902, his mission here being to construct the power house for the electric light and power system. During this work he was taken sick and was confined in a hospital for one year. On recovering he was given the position of superintendent of the Nashville Railway & Light Company, and now has charge of that important local corporation.

WILLIAM N. HOLMES, M. D. An ex-president of the Tennessee State Medical Society and a practitioner of thirty-five years' standing, Dr. Holmes would be conceded by both the profession and laity a foremost place in ability and success in the field of general medicine as well as in

surgery, in which his special forte lies. Besides his professional prominence, Dr. Holmes has a place in Tennessee history, due to the more than
a century residence of the Holmes family in the state, and its varied
relations with the substantial welfare of both state and nation.

William N. Holmes was born in west Tennessee at a little town named
Holmes, January 27, 1854. The history of the family in America begins
with John Holmes, who came to America with Oglethorpe about the
middle of the eighteenth century. By profession he was a civil engineer
and helped that philanthropic colonizer to lay out the city of Savannah,
Georgia, and he died while living in Georgia colony. This civil engineer
was in the fifth generation from Dr. Holmes. The next in line was James
Holmes, who reached the rank of colonel in the Revolutionary army and
settled in North Carolina, where he remained until his death.

After James Holmes came John Holmes, grandfather of Dr. Holmes,
who was one of the early settlers in west Tennessee, and it is said that
he did more to civilize that country than any other early pioneer. He
was owner of large landed estates and possessed a large amount of
wealth for his day. He died in February, 1851, having been born January 30, 1777. He came to Tennessee in 1806.

The parents of Dr. Holmes were John R. and Eliza Day (McAlexander) Holmes. The latter was born in Virginia in 1815, and died in 1872,
and was a daughter of James McAlexander, a native of Virginia, who
brought his family to Tennessee in 1838, locating in western Tennessee,
where he was one of the big farmers of his time. His father came from
Ireland in 1770 and became a large and wealthy planter of Virginia,
and gave patriotic service to the colonies during the Revolutionary war.
John R. Holmes was born in Bedford county, Tennessee, in 1815, and
died April 21, 1884. He was reared on a farm and when five years of age
moved out to west Tennessee, where his father had taken up a large tract
of land. He spent the rest of his life in that portion of the state. He
and his wife were the parents of eight children, among whom the doctor
was the seventh, and is now the only one living. The father and mother
were members of the Presbyterian church, in which he was an elder and
a very active worker. In politics he was a Democrat.

William N. Holmes received his education in the common schools in
west Tennessee, and later took his collegiate course at Waynesburg,
Pennsylvania, where he was graduated in 1877. He began to study
medicine in 1878, taking his first course of lectures in Cincinnati in 1879.
He spent eight years in practice as a non-graduate, returning to Cincinnati, and graduating M. D. in 1888. He was in practice at Clarksburg,
Tennessee, for three years, after which he returned to his private farm,
which he bought and improved and during his residence there practiced
for six years. His next location was at Milan, Tennessee, where he was
engaged in practice for thirteen years, and in 1901 moved to Nashville.
Since then he has been in active practice in this city, and enjoys a very

large and high class patronage. Though his practice is general, he is especially well known as a skillful surgeon. He performs his operations in different hospitals of the city, and has never been known to lose a case in surgery.

Dr. Holmes was married in 1880 to Margaret E. Learned, a daughter of E. B. Learned of Dresden, Tennessee, a prosperous tobacco manufacturer of that city. The six children born to the doctor and wife are mentioned as follows: Margaret M., who is a teacher of expression in Martin College at Pulaski; John L., a resident of Phoenix, Arizona; William J., also in Phoenix, where he is in the real estate business; Lysander P., an assistant health physician in the city of New York; Sue Day, a graduate of the Ward Seminary, and now living at home; and William N., Jr., in school in Nashville. The family worship in the Presbyterian church. Dr. Holmes belongs to all the medical societies and associations, and for four terms has been chosen president of the Tennessee State Medical Society. He is affiliated with Masonry and with the Knights of Pythias, and is a Democrat in politics. He is prosperous, and holds a high rank in the citizenship of Nashville, and it is an interesting fact that at the beginning of his career he had to acquire his own education and taught school for a number of terms in order to pay his way.

LELAND HUME. To start as a roustabout employe of a grocery house at two dollars a week and eventually rise to the place of vice-president of one of the largest public utility corporations in the South, is an achievement demanding exceptional qualities of individual character. It is not the melodramatic success of Wall street nor of the western gold field. There is something solid, genuine and unimpeachable about such a performance. It begets confidence and admiration. On the way up from the lowly start to the goal there is no place for blundering inefficiency or vacillating decision; anyone with a casual knowledge of American industrialism is sure that no weakling could get far in such a race. The following modest sketch is perhaps the more effective because the details of this advancement are only suggested.

Born in 1864, Leland Hume spent his childhood in the city, and when a boy attained his first regular employment as roustabout for the Orr Brothers' grocery store at the nominal wage of two dollars a week. There he trained for the larger career which was being nursed in his ambition. Some years later he became identified with the Cumberland Telephone Company, and has been in the telephone business ever since, being now vice-president of the Cumberland Telephone Company. When he first went into the business it was a very small and largely local concern, but since then has grown to a corporation with an investment of thirty-two million dollars. Mr. Hume started in the telephone business with three associates, each of whom is a powerful figure in financial life of

Tennessee. The first was James E. Caldwell, president of the Fourth and the First National Banks. Another was T. D. Webb, vice-president of the Fourth and First National Banks, and the third was John W. Hunter, assistant comptroller of the state of Tennessee.

Mr. Hume acquired his education, and has depended upon his own resources ever since he entered business. He went through the public schools of Nashville, and later attended Vanderbilt University. Mr. Hume married Miss Marie Louise Trenholm, a daughter of Dr. George A. Trenholm of Charleston, South Carolina. He and his wife are the parents of three children, namely: Alfred, William and Georgia.

Mr. Hume is a director in the Tennessee Bank & Trust Company and in the Cumberland Telephone Company; is active in the Sons of Confederate Veterans; and is president of the Tennessee Sons of the American Revolution. He was the first president of the Nashville Board of Trade and one of its present directors, and is a member of the Commercial Club, the Golf Club and the Country Club. He has membership in the board of education and is affiliated with the Knights of Pythias.

AMOS L. EDWARDS. Now engaged in the land business and in colonization work on a large scale, with offices in Nashville, Mr. Edwards first gained a place as one of the successful educators of Tennessee. Thirty-five years old, his career has been one of exceptional activity and successful enterprise.

Amos L. Edwards was born in Weakley county, Tennessee, August 19, 1878, a son of William A. and Elizabeth (Howell) Edwards. Grandfather William A. Edwards was born in North Carolina, came to Tennessee in 1835, locating in Dickson county, where he spent his career as a farmer. The maternal grandfather, Jasper Howell, was a Virginian by birth, coming to Tennessee in an early day, and following the pursuits of agriculture. William A. Edwards, the father, was born in Dickson county in 1838, and died in 1909. His wife, who was born in Weakley county in 1850, now resides on the old homestead. The father had his early education in Dickson county, and moved with his parents to Weakley county when he was fifteen years of age. He was known as a substantial farmer, he and his family were members of the Cumberland Presbyterian church, and he was affiliated with the Independent Order of Odd Fellows. In politics he was a Republican, and served as magistrate and on the school board, and other minor offices. There were six children in the family, four of whom are living: Matilda, who married J. W. Pope, a farmer of Weakley county; John A., who lives on a farm in Weakley county; Amos L.; and B. D., who is a farmer in Weakley county.

Amos L. Edwards, outside of his common school training in Weakley county, is largely self-educated, having paid his own way through college and university. He attended the McFerrin College at Martin, Ten-

nessee, and in 1905 was graduated from Vanderbilt University. For
several years he was actively identified with educational work. He had
charge of the Howard Female College in Gallatin for two years, and for
a time was head of the American University at Harriman, Tennessee, also
for one year being head master of the Cumberland City Academy. He
continued as a teacher until 1910, at which time he engaged in the timber
land business, establishing an office in the Stallman building at Nashville. He sells land all over the South, and has conducted several successful colonization enterprises in different directions. Mr. Edwards is
the owner of a Louisiana plantation, and also a farm in west Tennessee.

In 1905 he married Miss Vetress Ramer, a daughter of Dr. D. W.
Ramer, who has been for many years a leading physician of Robertson
county. Mr. Edwards is a member of the Baptist church, is affiliated
with the Independent Order of Odd Fellows and the Modern Woodmen
of America, and was a charter member of the Vanderbilt chapter of the
Phi Kappa Sigma. He has gone through all the chairs in the Modern
Woodmen and filled all the offices in the lodge of the Odd Fellows except
that of Noble Grand. In politics he is an independent Republican.

LEWIS KEMP GRIGSBY. As secretary-treasurer and general manager
of the Lebanon Cooperative Medicine Company, Lewis Kemp Grigsby
has made rapid strides on the way to financial independence, and occupies a place of no little prominence in Lebanon, not because of his
business success alone, but because of his many excellent qualities of
heart and mind and his sterling citizenship as well. He is the representative of two of the oldest southern families extant, and his family, on
the paternal and maternal sides, have borne distinguished parts in the
making of history from colonial days down to the present time.

Born in Winchester, Clark county, Kentucky, on August 30, 1875,
Lewis Kemp Grigsby is the son of J. V. and Mary C. (Robinson)
Grigsby, both of whom were born and reared in Clark county, that
state, which has represented the home of the family for many generations. The father was born there in 1826 and died in 1908, at the fine
old age of eighty-two. He was long identified with the extensive farming
industries of his state, and in later life came to Wilson county,
Tennessee, when he introduced short-horn cattle into the county for the
first time in the history of the state. The date of his settlement here
was in 1887, and Tennessee represented his home from then until the
time of his death. He was a son of Lewis Kemp Grigsby, born in Clark
county, Kentucky, where he spent his entire life. The mother, Mary C.
Robinson, was a daughter of Thomas H. Robinson, who was born in
Jefferson county, Kentucky, and there spent all his life. He at one
time owned an immense body of land in the state of Louisiana and
when he died had an estate valued at $90,000. J. V. and Mary Grigsby
became the parents of six children, of which number three are living

L. K. Grigsby.

today, and of that number L. K. was the youngest born. They were members of the Christian church, and were known for fine and stanch members of the community that knew them, and when they died were mourned by a large circle of friends.

Until Lewis Kemp Grigsby was twenty-one years old he lived on the home farm, attending school in the nearby schools meantime, 'and later graduating from the commercial department of the Cumberland University. When the Spanish-American war came on he enlisted in the First Tennessee Volunteer Infantry and served for nineteen months with his regiment. After the war and his return to his home community, he engaged in the mercantile business in which he continued until 1904, then came to Lebanon and became identified with the drug business. He continued thus until 1912, at which time he organized the Lebanon Cooperative Medicine Company, and engaged in the manufacture of liver medicines. The product of this concern finds a ready market throughout the southern states, and the plant is steadily increasing its output to meet the ever-increasing demands of the trade. It is predicted that this concern will soon take rank with the largest patent medicine establishments in the south. In the management of the plant, Mr. Grigsby has displayed unusual business acumen, and has incontrovertibly proven himself to be possessed of exceptional merit as a business man.

In addition to his interest in this enterprise, Mr. Grigsby has acquired ownership of some four hundred and fifty acres of cotton land in Mississippi, with business houses in Birmingham, where he is extensively interested as a stockholder in one of the more important banking institutions of that city. He also has banking interests in Watertown, Tennessee, and is a director in the Cedar Croft Sanitarium, Lebanon, Tennessee. He has interested himself in oil stock and other investments of a like nature in Texas, and is financially interested in the Union Bank & Trust Company of Lebanon, Tennessee; he is also secretary and treasurer and a controlling stockholder in the Cherokee Glove Manufacturing Company of Lebanon, Tennessee.

Mr. Grigsby is a member of the Christian church, in which his parents reared him, and he is a member of the Knights of Pythias, in which he is past chancellor and master of the exchequer, and is now a trustee of the order as well. He is president of the Lebanon Business Men's Association and a director of the Lebanon National Bank. As a Democrat, he has always taken an active part in the labors of the party, but has never aspired to public office.

On July 4, 1907, Mr. Grigsby married Miss Lizzie Wheeler, the daughter of Dr. Thomas C. Wheeler, a physician of Wilson county for years. He was long a prominent Mason of the county, and was a veteran of the Civil war, serving in the Sixteenth Tennessee Regiment as surgeon throughout the long period of hostilities. He saw much of the horrors of war, and himself was wounded at Perryville, and was captured and held as a prisoner of war in Rock Island prison for some months. He died in 1909, and was known to be one of the wealthy men of the community at the time of his demise. He was the son of Nathaniel Wheeler, who served in the Indian wars, and the grandson of another Nathaniel Wheeler, who gave valiant service to the cause of the colonies in the Revolutionary war.

To the union of Mr. and Mrs. Grigsby two children have been born— Mamie Gates and Bessie Kelton.

THOMAS NEAL IVEY. In 1910 at the General Conference of the Methodist Church South, Thomas Neal Ivey was chosen to the position of editor of the *Christian Advocate* at Nashville, the official organ of the Church. Mr. Ivey is one of the ablest men of the Church South, has given seventeen years of his life to editorial labors, and has been in the ministry since 1888. Thomas Neal Ivey was born at Marion, South Carolina, May 22, 1860, a son of Rev. G. W. and Selina R. (Neal) Ivey. The family origin is traced back to Ireland, from which country, about the middle of the eighteenth century, two brothers came to American soil, landing at Norfolk, Virginia, whence from those two ancestors the large membership of the present family of Ivey in America is descended. The grandparents of Mr. Ivey were Benjamin and Elizabeth (Shankle) Ivey, both of whom were born in North Carolina, the former being a farmer and spending all his career in his native state. He lived during the Revolutionary period of the colonies and gave service to the American cause as a soldier. The maternal grandparents were James and Elizabeth (Moore) Neal, who were also natives of North Carolina. the former having been a successful merchant. The Neal family also came from Ireland.

Rev. G. W. Ivey, the father, was born in North Carolina in 1828, and died in 1902. His wife was born in 1830 and is now living at Statesville, North Carolina, at the age of eighty-three. The father had a common school education, and when a young man took up the work of the ministry, which he followed for fifty-three years. He preached in North and South Carolina, and held charges at Lenoir, Morganton, Newton, Statesville, Clinton and Leasburg. He possessed along with his strong faculties of heart and mind and a thorough devotion to the church a number of quaint characteristics. He was very witty, and was very popular among his people and his advice was as acceptable in secular affairs as in religion. He would go to church to preach in any kind of weather and attended his duties strictly whether anyone else followed him or not. He and his wife were the parents of nine children, six of whom are still living. The father was a Democrat and belonged to the Masonic order.

Thomas Neal Ivey received his collegiate education at Trinity College in North Carolina, where he was graduated A. B. in 1880, and A.

M. in 1882. In 1896 the degree of D. D. was conferred upon him. His
early career was spent in teaching. He was principal of the Shelby high
school in North Carolina from 1880 to 1883, and principal of the Oak
Institute at Mooresville, North Carolina, from 1883 to 1888. Successful
though he was as a teacher, his ambition was to follow in his father's
profession, and having carried on his theological studies, he entered the
active work of the ministry in 1888. During the succeeding years he was
pastor of several charges, at Lenoir Station, North Carolina, in 1888;
Roxboro, North Carolina, from 1888 to 1892, and Wilson, North Carolina,
from 1892 to 1896. His career as an editor began with the *North Carolina Christian Advocate*, published at Greensboro, with which paper he
remained from 1896 to 1898, and was then editor from 1898 to 1910 of
the *Raleigh Christian Advocate*. As already stated he was chosen editor
of the *Christian Advocate* at Nashville, the general organ of the church,
in May, 1910. His relations with the church have been many. He was
a member of the last four quadrennial General Conferences, a delegate
to the Ecumenical Conference at Toronto in 1911, vice-president of
Southern Methodism of the Federal Council of the Church of Christ in
America. He was a trustee of Trinity College, North Carolina, of the
Methodist Orphanage at Raleigh, and a member of the National Editorial Association. He is a Democrat in politics, and an active Mason,
having been grand chaplain of the Grand Lodge of North Carolina for
two years. He belongs to the Kappa Sigma fraternity, his home Chapter
being the Eta Chapter at Trinity College. Since 1896 Mr. Ivey has been
editor of the *Southern Methodist Handbook*, the annual year book of the
Methodist Church South. He is author of "Bildad Akers: His Book."

Mr. Ivey was married in North Carolina August 8, 1883, to Miss
Lenora Ann Dowd, a daughter of James C. Dowd, a North Carolina
farmer. The four children of their marriage are: Mrs. Sam P. Norris,
of Raleigh, North Carolina; Ruth C., at home; Neal D., of New Orleans,
and Margaret P., in school in Virginia.

JOHN LEWIS KIRBY. of the Book Editors' Department of the Methodist Episcopal church South. was born, reared and educated in the city
of Nashville. He is the only son of John Moody Kirby, a native of
Wilson county, Tennessee, but from his twelfth year a resident of Nashville. The father died when the son was less than eleven years of age.
and before finishing his fourth year at the Academy of Gossett & Webb.
the lad found it to be imperative that he should fit himself to aid in the
maintenance of his mother and five young sisters. He chose the printer's
art, of which he readily acquired an expert knowledge under the able
tutelage of the well remembered Anson Nelson and others. During his
apprenticeship, which endured for five years, the opportunity for pursuing his academic studies was eagerly improved. and his interest in an
active literary life began to develop.

While yet a lad in his teens Mr. Kirby frequently did reporting and other writing for his alma mater, the *Nashville Gazette,* and his first real venture into journalism proper was with Col. Thomas Boyers, as co-editor and publisher of the *Gallatin Examiner,* in 1860 and 1861. Physical disability prevented Mr. Kirby from entering the Confederate army, and for the first three years of the war he was connected as writer and business partner with the *Patriot,* the *Press,* and the *Dispatch,* of which William Hy Smith, Edwin Paschal and John Miller McKee were the respective editors-in-chief. These war-time journals within the camp of the enemy obviously gave the news from the contending armies with very meager comment. A noteworthy feat of the young "local" at this time was his report of Andrew Johnson's public address as military governor of Tennessee, in March, 1862—considered to be among the most important speeches of his life. It was heard by a throng of anxious people that packed the hall of representatives to overflowing, and the verbatim report of Mr. Kirby—the only one made—filled two pages of the *Patriot.* Four or five years later he was with President Johnson and his cabinet in the famous "swing around the circle" and reported the speeches, etc., for the *Louisville Journal.* Still later, when Mr. Johnson retired from the presidency, they happened to meet at Gallatin, Tennessee, where Mr. Johnson made an address, and of this the journalist sent telegraphic accounts to the *Courier Journal.*

When the war ended, Mr. Kirby went to Louisville on a visit and was there unexpectedly called to the chief local editorship of the *Journal.* This position he held on the *Journal* and on the *Courier Journal,* in association with George D. Prentice, Paul R. Shipman, Henry Watterson, John E. Hatcher and others, from 1865 to near 1870. In the latter year, his health being seriously impaired, he returned to Tennessee. After two years devoted chiefly to the recovery of his health, and declining all offers to resume newspaper life, he entered the service of the Methodist Publishing House, first as general proof-editor, then assistant Sunday school editor with Dr. W. G. E. Cunnyngham, until 1895, and from that year to the present time assistant editor of books and the *Quarterly Review,* with the late Bishop John J. Tigert and the present editor, Gross Alexander, D. D. Within this long period of time the books edited were many hundreds in number, and the periodicals many thousands—a vast library, indeed, of church, Sunday school and general literature of the highest value. The work of Mr. Kirby has had an undeniable uplifting effect upon the reading community at large, and the results have been of a wider reaching nature than might have been possible had he continued in newspaper circles and work.

JOHN F. JOYNER. The cashier of the Broadway National Bank at Nashville, Mr. Joyner possesses the business qualities which dominate the policy of the big institution with which he is connected—energy and progressiveness. Of the type of man who is architect of his own fortunes, his promotions and achievements in the world of finance have advanced him well to the front rank before reaching the meridian of his career. John F. Joyner is a native Tennesseean born in Sumner county, November 13, 1875, a son of John W. and Veleria L. (Bowers) Joyner. His grandparents were Robert and Martha (Hargraves) Joyner, both Virginians by birth, where they· were married and came to Sumner county, Tennessee, at an early date. The grandfather was a very wealthy man, owning between two and three hundred negroes, and some five or six thousand acres of land. He reared a family of five children, and his death occurred before the Civil war. The maternal grandfather was William T. Bowers, who was born and reared in Davidson county, belonging to a family of early settlers in this county, and he was a well-to-do man and gained a generous prosperity before his death, which occurred when he was still young. Of the four children in the Bowers family, two of the sons went to California early in life and of these T. J. Bowers was eminent as an attorney and at one time served as chief justice of Idaho.

John W. Joyner, the father, was born in Sumner county, Tennessee, in 1833, and died in 1888. His wife was born in Davidson county, in 1838, and died in 1910. Th father was a Sumner county farmer, raised considerable stock, and was very prosperous. There were eight children born to himself and wife, of whom seven are living. The family worship at the Cumberland Presbyterian church, and John W. Joyner was a very enthusiastic member of the Masonic lodge, of which he was a master a number of times. He was a Democrat in politics, and though he held no office he was always generous in supporting his friends and worked for the general success of the party. During the war he was one of the strong supporters of the Southern cause, and was put in prison because of his refusal to take the oath of allegiance. Two of his brothers, Dr. J. H. Joyner and W. H. Joyner, were both soldiers in the war, W. H. having organized a company and serving as captain and major.

John F. Joyner while a boy attended the public schools of Davidson county, and later was graduated from the Jennings Business College in 1896. He began his career as clerk in a general store at Goodlettsville. While in that store he employed all his leisure time in the study of· law, and was admitted to the bar. He then went West and was connected with a law office in Durango, Colorado. On returning to Tennessee, he became assistant cashier of the bank of Goodlettsville, with which institution he remained seven years. He was the active executive of this bank throughout the time, and managed and directed all its business during the seven years. In 1905 Mr. Joyner organized the bank of Greenbrier, and was its cashier for seven years. Then in 1912 he came to Nashville to take the office of cashier of the Broadway National Bank, one of the strongest financial institutions in the state. The Broadway National has a capital stock of two hundred thousand dollars, resources of a million and three quarters and the average deposits run well upwards of a million and a half. The business of the bank is rapidly increasing and during the past two years its deposits have grown by eight hundred thousand in the aggregate. The principal officers are Julian S. Cooley, chairman of the board; A. E. Potter, president; J. H. Bradford, vice-president; and John F. Joyner, cashier.

Mr. Joyner was married in 1902 to Miss Sadie Cunningham, of Goodlettsville, Tennessee. Her father was a merchant and farmer of Goodlettsville, having been in the mercantile business there for thirty-five. years. During the war he fought for four years as a Confederate soldier. Mr. and Mrs. Joyner have one child, Sarah, now nine years of age. Their church is the Methodist South, and he is affiliated with the Masonic lodge, the Independent Order of Odd Fellows. He is a Democrat in politics, but has never been a candidate for office. He acquired his education through his own efforts, and is regarded as one of the prosperous men of Nashville. He is a stockholder in the Broadway National Bank, and also a stockholder and director in the Bank of Greenbrier.

JAMES H. YEAMAN. One of Tennessee's leading architects, Mr. Yeaman has followed his profession with offices in Nashville for the past quarter century. Examples of his work can be pointed out in many of the larger public and semi-public edifices as well as in residences all over the city and in various parts of the county. He was also building contractor for a number of years.

His family is one of the oldest in Tennessee. His great-grandfather was John Yeaman, who came from Scotland in an early day, locating in Spottsylvania county, Virginia, near Danville. He was the father of four sons, two of whom moved to Tennessee, one being Grandfather Yeaman, and both dying a few years after they located in this state. The two other brothers went to Ohio, and from them members of the name spread to the states of Indiana and Missouri.

A son of the first settler was Grandfather Joseph Yeaman, who married Mary Shelton. Both were born in Virginia, moved to Tennessee in early days, locating in Smith county, where Joseph Yeaman died in a few years after his settlement. He and his wife reared a family of seven children, all of whom are now deceased but one.

The parents of the Nashville architect were William J. and Emma (Cooper) Yeaman. The father was born in Virginia in 1835, and died in 1901. The mother was born in Putnam county, Tennessee, in 1845, and is still living. Her father was John C. Cooper, a minister of the Cumberland Presbyterian church, and served as a chaplain during the Civil war. He contracted pneumonia from exposure and died soon after the close of the war. The Cooper family were from England, and the family of Rhoda Patton, wife of John C. Cooper, were from Ireland, and came over the mountains into Tennessee about the same time with the Yeamans. William J. Yeaman, the father, was a carpenter and cabinet maker, and came to Tennessee when a young man with his father. His education was obtained in Virginia. He reared a large family of ten children and gave them all good educations, and eight of them are now living. The father was a member of the Methodist church South, and his wife was a Cumberland Presbyterian. He was a quiet Christian gentleman, supported the Democratic party, but was not active in politics. Several uncles of James H. Yeaman on both his father's and mother's side were soldiers in the Civil war.

James H. Yeaman was born in Jackson county, Tennessee, at Granville, September 3, 1859, was educated at New Middleton in Smith county in what was known as the New Middleton Male and Female Institute, an academic institution well known in its time and having succeeded the old Clinton College of ante-bellum days. The academy had pupils in attendance from every state in the Union. Mr. Yeaman started out in life as a carpenter, and from that practical trade worked himself into his higher position. He devoted himself steadily to acquiring the art of architect, and has practiced that profession more or less regularly for the past thirty years. He opened an office as architect and builder in 1887, but in 1905 gave up the building and contracting end altogether and has since enjoyed a large patronage as an architect alone.

Mr. Yeaman was married in 1882 to Mollie Dandridge, of Nashville, a daughter of Edward Dandridge, who was a Virginian by birth, and who came to Lebanon, Tennessee, when a young man. The Dandridge family were related to George Washington's wife. Mr. and Mrs. Yeaman have one child, Mary Emma, who is a graduate of the Peabody Normal School. The family are members of the Methodist church South, and he is affiliated with Claiborne Lodge of the Masons, and he has filled all the chairs except master, and is a chapter and Knights Templar Mason as well. He also belongs to the Knights of Pythias. In politics he is Democratic.

TONY SUDEKUM deserves the title of a successful young business man. His enterprise enabled him to start on the proverbial nothing, and in a few years become the head of half a dozen companies with an aggregate capital of several hundred thousand dollars, and supplying service and commodities not to the occasional but to the daily wants of many thousands of people.

Tony Sudekum was born in Nashville, August 21, 1880. His parents were Henry and Sarah (Eggensperger) Sudekum. The father was a native of Pittsburgh, and the mother of Nashville. The grandparents were born in Europe but spent their last years in Nashville. The father came to Nashville when a child, and was a baker by trade. For some time he worked as a journeyman in that occupation, and then engaged in business for himself in east Nashville, where he remained for twenty-five years, his plant being located on Cherry and Mulberry streets. He had nothing to start on, but did well financially, and is now living retired. He had little advantages of education, but mastered the fundamentals necessary for a business career, and did well by his children. He and his wife had seven children, all of whom are living, Tony being the oldest. His parents are members of the German Lutheran church, and the father is affiliated with Masonry, being a Knight Templar and a member of Claiborn Lodge. In politics he is a Democrat.

Tony Sudekum, as a boy, attended the Howard School at Nashville, and began his practical career in his father's bakery. He has always continued in the bakery business, although his varied interests in other fields have in recent years occupied much of his time. His actual start on the road to prosperity and in the larger fields of business occurred in 1905 when he established in Nashville a moving picture show. Since then he has built up and extended his interests in this line, and has incorporated the Crescent Amusement Company, and now controls the Elite, the Alhambra, the Fifth Avenue, and the Princess theaters in Nashville, and in other towns of the state he is owner and has the controlling interest in ten other amusement houses. The capital stock of the Crescent Company is one hundred and fifteen thousand dollars. He is also owner of the Princess Amusement Company, with a capital stock of sixty-five thousand dollars. Mr. Sudekum is president and general manager of these companies and they all are directly the result of his keen foresight and business enterprise since he had no capital to speak of when he started eight years ago. Mr. Sudekum is a very busy man, giving all his time to his bakery, and to his other enterprises. He has large interests in the Union Ice Cream Company of Nashville, and is president of the New Southern Milk Condensing Company of Nashville, Illinois, where the company has a large plant and ships its products throughout the southern states.

Mr. Sudekum was married in 1904 to Miss Nettie E. Fesler, a daughter of John Fesler, and a native of Nashville. Her father is a market gardener in this city. Mr. and Mrs. Sudekum have four children, namely: Viola, in school; Elizabeth, in school; Marie and Sarah. The family are communicants of the Lutheran church, and Mr. Sudekum is affiliated with the Corinthian Lodge of Masons, the Woodmen of the World, the Golden Cross, and the Junior Order of United American Mechanics. Politically he is a Democrat.

D. M. SMITH. Publishing agent for the publishing house of the Methodist Episcopal Church South, at Nashville, Mr. Smith has charge of this important position in one of the largest publishing firms in the United States since 1890. He has been connected with the business since 1888, going in as business manager of the Nashville house, and in 1890 was elected by the general conference at St. Louis as one of the two publishing agents, and has acted in that capacity since that date. The business of the Southern Methodist Publishing House has a scope and volume seldom realized, and its publications go from Canada to Brazil and from Norfolk to China. Mr. Smith is a man of self-attainment, having begun as a poor boy and having entered business life as a bookkeeper and office man.

D. M. Smith was born at Knoxville, Tennessee, October 14, 1854, a son of J. R. and Thurza (Young) Smith. The parents moved to the vicinity of Knoxville early in life, where the father was a farmer and where he remained until 1858, when he joined his brother in Arkansas, and made that state his home during the rest of his life. He was a man of moderate means, had a quiet, unassuming character, though he maintained very decided views on moral and general questions. He was of Scotch-Irish descent. The parents had five children, only two of whom are living. Mr. Smith's elder brother, Robert Park Smith, is now in the grocery business in San Angelo, Texas. The parents were members of the Presbyterian church, and the father was a Democrat in politics. He served as captain of a state militia company for a while in Knoxville.

D. M. Smith had his education in private schools and was graduated in 1874 from the Bryant & Stratton Business College at Nashville. Thus equipped for a business career he began as bookkeeper, and followed general clerical work for twelve years, and all in the employ of one firm. He then went with the Southern Methodist Publishing House, as already stated, and his ability as a business getter and in managing the extensive affairs of the publishing house, has caused him to be retained in one of the most responsible business positions in connection with the entire church.

In 1879 Mr. Smith married Miss Virginia Cunnyngham, a daughter of Dr. W. G. E. Cunnyngham, who was a noted minister of the Methodist church. He was sent as a missionary to China in 1854, remained in the East for ten years, engaged in pastoral work until 1875, and then spent the rest of his life in the publishing house of the Southern Methodist church. For nineteen years he was editor of the Sunday school department of the publishing house. The six children born to Mr. and Mrs. Smith are David M., a graduate of Vanderbilt University, and now a student in the University of Chicago; Robert Young, assistant manager in the advertising department of the publishing house; William C., in school; Jessie and Mildred, both at home; and Virginia, in school. The family are all members of the Methodist church South, and Mr. Smith is a Democrat in politics.

WARD-BELMONT—IRA LANDRITH. On June 1, 1913, occurred the
formal consolidation of the Ward Seminary and Belmont College, the
former being the oldest and the latter the largest of Nashville's famous
boarding schools for young women, this event being regarded as one
of the most important and far-reaching in its results of any step which
has been taken in Tennessee educational history within recent years.
The actual negotiations and business arrangements which brought about
this consolidation were concluded early in the year 1913. The full
designation of the new school is "Ward-Belmont, uniting and continuing
Ward Seminary for Young Ladies, founded by William E. Ward, D. D.,
1865, and Belmont College for Young Women, founded by Miss Ida E.
Hood and Miss Susan L. Heron, 1890." The president of Ward-Belmont is Rev. Dr. Ira Landrith, who for eight years was regent and president of Belmont, and for the year preceding the consolidation president
of Ward.

Ward Seminary, the older of the two institutions, was founded in
1865 by the late William E. Ward, D. D. It has enjoyed a very influential career and has educated a great many of the most prominent
women of the present and previous generations. Thousands of its
former students live in this city, the attendance from Nashville alone
exceeding three hundred annually. This fact in itself is regarded as
the highest possible testimony to the work of the institution, particularly since among these are the daughters of leading educators, clergymen, and numerous other citizens of the highest culture who esteem a
school for the educational methods it employs and the ideals to which
it clings. For twenty years Dr. and Mrs. J. D. Blanton had charge of
Ward, Dr. Blanton as the president and Mrs. Blanton as principal of the
home department, and the strong hold they have on the public confidence
and the devotion to them on the part of the faculty and student body
not only kept the school prosperous in spite of the discouragement of a
down-town location, but so bound to them the families of patrons that
the boarding population at Ward the last year was nearly half composed
of daughters from homes that had formerly patronized Ward Seminary.
Dr. Blanton's wisdom in the administration has been equaled by Mrs.
Blanton's fine, strong and beautiful influence in home-making for the
girls.

Belmont College, though younger than Ward Seminary, in its boarding department was more than twice as large, while the day patronage at
Ward was always several times larger than Belmont's day school. Thus
they practically balanced each other in numbers. Miss Ida E. Hood and
Miss Susan L. Heron, school girl friends, are said to have covenanted
in their own student days to unite one day in founding a school for
girls, and Belmont was the fulfillment of that dream. Beginning with
the beautiful old Acklen mansion, "Belmont" in September, 1890, they
year after year had a boarding attendance to the full capacity, during

1912-13 reaching its highest point, about 375. From time to time, as needed, additions were made to the buildings, equipment and faculty, until Belmont became nationally famous as a home school for girls and young women. Belmont always stood for the highest things in character and womanhood, and for earnestness and integrity in training and study. Daughters from representative homes in more than thirty states have been attending annually for many years, every state but four having been represented in its history.

Ward-Belmont had its location on Belmont Hill, and in addition to using the ten buildings of Belmont College, plans and preparations have already been completed for the erection on the campus of two other very handsome halls, one for administration and academic uses and the other as a residence for one hundred girls and teachers. The consolidation of these schools, it should be noted, is the result of the outright purchase of both schools by a new corporation composed of twelve gentlemen, ten of whom had never had any financial interest in either Ward or Belmont. Both schools, therefore, entered the union upon the same terms and basis. Concerning this consolidation and its advantages, one of the local papers said editorially: "It was a source of gratification that neither had absorbed the other, but that the name of each will be perpetuated in the new title of Ward-Belmont. Nashville is proud of both institutions, and of their fame abroad. They have added most materially to its right to be known as the Athens of the South. By the consolidation the management will be able to accomplish results unattainable singly. Two schools of first rank have combined to make one of double lustre. Instead of a division of energy in advertising the two institutions, which might leave a doubt in the mind of the prospective patron as to which school to send the girl to be educated, with perhaps a chance for another school in another city to score, the consolidated college will draw with irresistible force from a wide territory."

Rev. Dr. Ira Landrith, clergyman, and president of Ward-Belmont, was born near Milford, Ellis county, Texas, March 23, 1865. His parents were Martin Luther and Mary M. (Groves) Landrith, of Scotch-Irish stock. During his youth he attained his education in the public schools, and then was a student in Trinity University of Texas, and later in the Cumberland University at Lebanon, Tennessee, where he was graduated in 1888. During the following year he continued a student at Lebanon and was graduated in the law department. The degrees conferred upon this well known Tennessee educator were B. S. in 1888, LL. B. in 1889, LL. D. in 1903 and D. D. in 1904.

Dr. Landrith has spent nearly all his career in educational work, and has enjoyed numerous honors and distinctions in the educational and religious world apart from his most satisfying achievements as head of the two great woman's colleges which have been recently consolidated largely through his own influence and active efforts. He is an ordained

minister of the Presbyterian church in the U. S. A., and in 1903-04 was
general secretary of the Religious Education Association at Chicago.
He was general secretary of the Presbyterian Brotherhood of America
in 1908-09 and was editorial secretary of the Presbyterian Brotherhood
in 1909-1910.   He was moderator of the last General Assembly
of the Cumberland Presbyterian church before its union with the
Presbyterian church.   From 1890 to 1903 he was editor of the *Cumberland Presbyterian*.   In June, 1912, after eight years as president of Belmont College, he resigned and became president of Ward Seminary.
Dr. Landrith was married in 1890 to Miss Harriet G. Grannis.   He is
affiliated with the Knights Templar in Masonry and with the Knights
of Pythias.

ALFRED A. ADAMS.   This prominent lawyer and business man of
Lebanon and leader in the public life of Wilson county is one of the
foremost and forceful men of Tennessee.   Early he set for himself high
and worthy aims in life and how earnestly and successfully he has
endeavored to live up to them is shown in the progress of his career.

Alfred Armstrong Adams was born in Wilson county, Tennessee,
April 9, 1865.   Alfred A. Adams, his father, born in Davidson county,
this state, in 1840, was educated for the profession of medicine but never
became a practitioner, taking up instead the business of a druggist at
Nashville and following that line of endeavor during his brief business
career.   He was remarkably successful and in a very few years of business activity he accumulated considerable wealth.   At the opening of the
war between the states he took service in Company E (Buchanan's company) of the First Tennessee Cavalry (Wheeler's regiment) by enlist-
ment at Donelson, Tennessee, on February 23, 1861, and remained in the
service until discharged at Guntown, Mississippi, on August 29, 1862, on
account of wounds received in battle.   He never fully recovered from those
wounds and from that time until his death in 1867, at the age of twenty-
seven, was practically an invalid.   He wedded Margaret J. Gleaves, who was
born in Wilson county, Tennessee, in 1843, and is yet living, a resident
of Lebanon.   She is a daughter of Guy Trigg Gleaves, formerly of Mt.
Juliet, who was a native of Tennessee and who resided near the Hermitage in Davidson county, and she is a granddaughter of Absalom Gleaves,
an immigrant to this state from Virginia.   Alfred A. Adams, son of Richard Kane Adams, the paternal grandfather of the subject of this review,
was a native of Pennsylvania, born in the city of Carlisle, Cumberland
county, that state, and came to Tennessee in 1813, locating at Nashville.
He was an architect and civil engineer by profession, and was one of the
argonauts that sought the gold fields of California in 1849, but he
remained there only a short time and then returned to Tennessee, where
he passed away in 1854 from cholera.   He was a prominent member of
the Masonic fraternity in this state, was a member of Cumberland Lodge

of Masons at Nashville and was grand treasurer of the Masonic order in Tennessee from 1828 to 1849. Two sons came to the union of Alfred A. and Margaret (Gleaves) Adams: Alfred A., Jr., and Edward E.

Alfred A. Adams, our immediate subject, acquired his earlier education in the public schools of Wilson and Davidson counties and graduated from the Montgomery Bell Academy in Nashville in 1884, as valedictorian of his class. Following his graduation he entered the government service in the auditing department at Washington, D. C., where he remained eight years and during that time pursued the study of law in Georgetown University and in Columbian, now George Washington, University in that city. He was admitted to the bar in 1891 in the District of Columbia and entered upon the practice of law in 1897 in Lebanon, Tennessee, where his ability soon placed him in the front rank of attorneys, admitted to practice in all the courts, and where as years have passed he has become one of the eminent citizens of the community and widely known in politics as a stanch and influential supporter of Democratic policies. The bar has always seemed a stepping stone to political preferment under our American system. It was not long until Mr. Adams' aptitude for public business was discovered, and in 1901 he was elected to the popular branch of the state legislature as the representative of Wilson county. The state still had further need of his services and in 1903 and again in 1911 he represented his district, Wilson and Smith counties, in the state senate. As a legislator he was liberal, high-minded and discreet and took a broad and intelligent view of all public questions. He was also a constructive legislator and his achievements in that connection have been of an important nature. As chairman of the penitentiary committee during his service as state senator he secured the passage of a number of laws for the benefit of prisoners and he was the author of the "Adams law" that put saloons out of all the counties in Tennessee except four. He is not only an able lawyer and a forceful man in public life, but his keen business instincts have made him a man of large and substantial properties, and as a citizen he is of the progressive stamp, alive to every local interest which looks to renewed industry in his community and state. Mr. Adams was one of the original stockholders and is now vice-president and a director of the American National Bank of Lebanon, organized in 1900, which has a capital of $50,000, surplus and profits of $20,000 and deposits averaging $350,000. He also owns a good farm and is interested in live stock. Mr. Adams is distinctly a self-made man and has builded in life out of the resources of his own genius and abilities. He is prominently affiliated with the Masonic fraternity in this state as a Scottish Rite Mason, a member of the Knights Templar and of the Ancient Arabic Order of the Nobles of the Mystic Shrine. He represented the Middle Tennessee Shriners at the national meeting of Shriners at Los Angeles in 1912, and he is called the father of Al Menah Temple at Nashville by reason of his having led ·

in securing its establishment. He has been treasurer and trustee of his commandery of Knights Templar for twelve years and has been a trustee of his Masonic lodge eight years. He also sustains membership in the Knights of Pythias, the Independent Order of Odd Fellows and is a past chancellor commander of the Knights of Pythias and has been a trustee of his local lodge of that order for eight years.

The marriage of Mr. Adams took place in Washington, D. C., in 1889, and united him to Miss Mary Dove Albright of that city. Mrs. Adams is a daughter of Thomas Jefferson Albright, a native of Lancaster, Pennsylvania, who served as secretary and confidential clerk of President James Buchanan and for a while as commissioner of the general land office in the Department of the Interior. Mrs. Adams is a member of the Reformed church, while Mr. Adams is identified with the Presbyterian denomination.

WILLIAM ROSCOE MOORE, a young physician who has but recently located in Tennessee as a medical practitioner at Allen's Creek, Lewis county, has made a thorough preparation for his life work by a full collegiate education and complete medical training, including a year of hospital work. Tennessee is well favored in the number of men of attainments that are to be found in its professional ranks and ever extends a hearty welcome to the young man of ambition and character, and such a one Dr. Moore has proved to be.

He was born April 18, 1885, in Colbert county, Alabama, a son of Dr. Riley Jackson Moore, who was for many years a practitioner at Riverton, Alabama. After completing his literary studies in the Alabama State Normal School at Florence he entered the Memphis Hospital Medical College for his professional training and was graduated in 1908 with the degree of M. D. Following his graduation he served one year as a hospital interne to add practical experience to his preparation and then he returned to his home town of Riverton, Alabama, where he practiced one year. From there he came to Allen's Creek, Tennessee, as physician for the Bon Air Coal & Iron Company, which relation he yet sustains, being also a general practitioner in the village and immediate vicinity. He is a Democrat in political allegiance and his fraternal associations are as a member of Overton Lodge No. 652, Free and Accepted Masons, and of White Oak Camp of the Woodmen of the World. Dr. Moore was married in 1909 to Miss Cecelia Hastings, of Sheffield, Alabama.

Dr. Moore springs from an old family of Alabama, he being a representative of the third generation native to its soil. Dr. Riley Jackson Moore, his father, was born in Alabama in 1851 and passed away in that state in 1908. He wedded Dina B. Terry, who was born in Alabama in 1863 and is yet living, a resident of her native state. To the union of these parents were born nine children, of whom Dr. William R. Moore is fourth in order of birth. Dr. Riley Jackson Moore was educated at the University of Louisville for the profession of medicine and spent his whole career as a practitioner at Riverton, Alabama. He was a Democrat in political views, a member of the Baptist church, and in line with his profession he was affiliated with the American Medical Association.

CAESAR THOMAS. One of the most prosperous business men of Wilson county is Caesar Thomas, who about twenty years ago located at Watertown and opened an office for insurance. The enterprise and energy which he has directed into this business has had very fortunate results, and although he started out in life with nothing, and has had to acquire everything by dint of his own labors and energies he is now enjoying a place among the most influential and prosperous citizens of this county.

Caesar Thomas was born at Statesville, Tennessee, March 1, 1868, a son of Samuel Newton and Drusilla (Sneed) Thomas. The paternal grandfather was James Thomas, a native of North Carolina, who came to Tennessee during the early days and became a settler in Wilson county, where he combined his profession as a minister of the Presbyterian church with the occupation of farmer. The Thomas family is of Welsh descent and has been long represented in America. The maternal grandfather was John Sneed, who was born in Wilson county of parents who had been among the earliest settlers here, and he spent all his life in the county as a farmer and one of the well known citizens.

Samuel N. Thomas, the father, was born in Wilson county in 1820, and died in 1896. His wife, also a native of this county, was born in 1830 and died in 1895. Farming was the occupation which he followed, with more than usual success, throughout his active career. His civil life was interrupted twice by war, and he served in the Mexican conflict during the forties, and subsequently on the Confederate side during the Civil war. He was affiliated with the Masonic order, was a Democrat in politics, and a member of the Presbyterian church, while his wife was a Missionary Baptist. There were four children in the family, and of these James T. lives at Gulfport, Mississippi, while Woods T. is a resident of Batesville, Arkansas.

Caesar Thomas spent only the first fifteen years of his life on the paternal homestead, and during that time he had only meager advantages in the way of schools. At the age of fifteen he ran away from home, and from that time on had to depend on his own efforts to gain a livelihood, and to advance himself into higher places of business activities. On leaving home, at the early age mentioned, he located on the Mississippi gulf coast, where he began to work for himself. He lived there for some years, and it was there he met his wife. He was married in 1892 to Miss Dasie Cropper of Woodville, Mississippi, whose father was Nathaniel Cropper of Woodville, Mississippi. The three children born to Mr. and Mrs. Thomas are as follows: Reid N., who is a graduate of the

Columbia Military Academy, and is now associated in business with his father; Cornelia, at home, she having been born in 1897; and Inez, born in 1900. All the members of the family are communicants of the Baptist church.

Mr. Thomas located at Watertown in 1895, in which year he opened his office in the insurance business. He is state agent for the National Union Fire Insurance Company, and spends a large part of his time in travel and in looking after the interests of the business of this company, which he has built up until it is one of the leading fire insurance companies in the state. Mr. Thomas is a stockholder and one of the directors in the bank of Watertown. For two terms he served as mayor of Watertown, and has also been clerk in the chancery court of Wilson county. He is an influential Democrat in politics, and is affiliated with the Independent Order of Odd Fellows, the Knights of Pythias, the Elks and the Masonic order. He is past grand patriarch for the state of Tennessee in the Odd Fellows, and is the present grand representative of the state in the same order.

ALFRED HESTER. From the telegraph key to the presidency of a financial institution known as one of the most substantial in Sumner county, and the ownership of large farming and business interests, the career of Alfred Hester, of Portland, has been one of steady and continued advancement. Although handicapped in youth, in that he lacked capital, influential friends or special educational advantages, he possessed the much more valuable and desirable gifts of industry, determination and inherent business ability, and with these as a capital has proceeded to work out his own success through the medium of well-directed effort. Mr. Hester was born in Sumner county, Tennessee, July 28, 1871, and is a son of Robert M. and Mary (Groves) Hester.

Robert M. Hester was a native of Kentucky, where he was born in 1843, a son of Martin Hester, a farmer of the Blue Grass state. Educated in Kentucky, as a young man he came to Tennessee, and is now engaged successfully in the drug business at Mitchellville. A Democrat in politics, Mr. Hester has served for twenty-four years as magistrate, being now in his fifth term, and has the distinction of being a veteran of the war between the states, through which he served as a Confederate soldier. He is fraternally affiliated with the Masons and his religious belief is that of the Christian church, while his wife belongs to the Methodist denomination. Mr. Hester was married to Mary Groves, daughter of Alfred Groves, a farmer, merchant and tobacco dealer in Sumner county, and they have three children: Lena, who married Sam Arnett, and lives at Mitchellville; William, who resides in Portland, and Alfred M.

Alfred Hester's educational advantages were limited to those that could be secured in the country schools, and as a youth he learned the

B. J. Tarver

trade of telegrapher, and for twelve years had charge of a key for the Louisville & Nashville Railroad. Being industrious and ambitious, he carefully saved his earnings, invested them wisely and with rare fore-sight, and eventually felt able to enter the produce business. Since 1902 he has been engaged in shipping produce to New York, and this enter-prise has proved decidedly successful. The poor boy who started out to fight his own battles with the world but comparatively a few short years ago, is now the owner of three large farms and president of the Portland Bank, and has numerous other interests, and for ten years has acted in the capacity of postmaster at Portland, at this time being engaged in serving his third commission. In political matters Mr. Hester is a Republican, and his religious connection is with the Methodist Episcopal church, of which his wife and children are also members. Fraternally he holds membership in the Odd Fellows and the Loyal Order of Moose.

On September 25, 1895, Mr. Hester was married to Edna Chisholm, daughter of John Chisholm, an early settler of Simpson county, Kentucky, and to this union there have been born six children: Harold T., Robert V., Mary E., Douglas N. and Hattie Eudora, all attending school, and Edna Estelle, deceased. Mr. Hester has been the architect of his own fortunes in a marked degree, and has always been able to see an opportunity and be able to grasp it, but he has also respected the rights of others, and his operations have been so conducted as to win him the entire confidence of his fellow citizens. In a wide acquaintance gained through many years of business dealings, he numbers numerous friend-ships, and his reputation in business, society and politics is remarkably high.

BENJAMIN J. TARVER. Judge Tarver passed virtually his entire life in Wilson county, Tennessee, and here gained a distinguished place as a jurist and lawyer of splendid talent, the while he left a definite and beneficent impress upon the history of the county, both along civic and material lines. He was a man of exalted integrity of character, broad and tolerant in his judgment, of kindly and sympathetic personality, and entirely free from intellectual bigotry. He made his life count for good in its every relation, was one of the representative and honored citizens of northern Tennessee and it is thus most consonant that in this historical work be entered a tribute to his memory and a brief review of his career.

In Warren county, North Carolina, Judge Tarver was born on the 1st of July, 1827, a son of Silas and Nancy (Harris) Tarver, and was but three years of age at the time of the family immigration to Wilson county, Tennessee, where he passed the residue of his life, his death having occurred at his attractive old homestead in the city of Lebanon, on the 19th of September, 1905, at which time he was seventy-eight years of age. His father became one of the prosperous pioneer agriculturists of Wilson county, was influential in public affairs of a local order and

was one of the loyal and honored citizens of the county until the close
of his life, his cherished and devoted wife likewise having been a resident
of this county at the time of her demise. Both were natives of North
Carolina and both representatives of fine old colonial stock. Benjamin
Tarver, grandfather of Judge Tarver, served in the battle of Guilford
Court House, North Carolina, in the war of the Revolution, and was
but sixteen years of age at the time. Five of his brothers were patriot
soldiers of the Continental line in the great struggle for national independence. The lineage of the Tarver family is traced back to stanch
Welsh origin, and genealogical records extant in England and America
give family data from the time of Oliver Cromwell, the great dictator.

In the common schools of the pioneer era in northern Tennessee
Judge Tarver succeeded in gaining a symmetrical literary education,
which was effectually amplified by self-discipline and constant devotion
to the best of literature. In 1849-51 he pursued his course in the Lebanon
Law School, a department of Cumberland University, and in this institution he was graduated as a member of the class of 1851, in which
year he received his degree of bachelor of laws and was admitted to
the bar of the state. He forthwith opened an office in Lebanon, and
though he initiated his professional career with capitalistic resources of
only ten dollars, he had the self-confidence, the ability and the ambition
that are invariably the concomitants of success, and he soon built up a
substantial and profitable law business, in connection with which he
became known as a specially resourceful trial lawyer and as a counselor
whose opinions were based on thorough knowledge of law and precedent
and upon wise discrimination in determining the points of equity and
justice. It was these same qualities that later gave him much of distinction in his service on the bench. From 1852 to 1878 he was most pleasingly
associated in practice with the late Edward I. Golladay, and their relations were ever marked by mutual confidence and esteem and by the
closest personal friendship. They controlled a large and representative practice, as leaders at the bar of Wilson county, and their alliance
was severed only when Judge Tarver was called upon to serve on the
chancery bench.

In the year 1878, Governor James D. Porter appointed Judge Tarver
chancellor of the Sixth chancery district of the state, to complete an
unexpired term, and he presided on the bench of this tribunal with
all of ability and fidelity. In his law practice he had confined himself
principally to the civil code, in the presentation of causes in the chancery
court, and thus he brought to his judicial office not only marked technical
ability but also large and varied experience in this department of judicial
procedure. He was a man of great business acumen and gained substantial financial success within the course of his long and useful career,
and he was one of the early stockholders and directors of the Tennessee

Pacific Railroad Company, as well as a member of the directorate of the Second National Bank of Lebanon.

Prior to the Civil war Judge Tarver was an old-line Whig in his political allegiance, advocating the policies and principles that had been those of Henry Clay and John Bell, distinguished leaders in the ranks of that party. In the climateric period leading up to and culminating in the war Judge Tarver was vigorously opposed to secession on the part of the southern states and he earnestly labored to prevent the withdrawal of Tennessee from the Union, having made many speeches in behalf of this cause and having urged the same insistently in the private walks of life. When, however, his state gave its decision in favor of the Confederacy, Judge Tarver was loyal to the decision of the majority of its people and laid aside his personal opinions concerning the policy of secession to tender his aid in defense of the cause of the Confederate States. He enlisted as a private in the Seventh Tennessee Infantry Regiment, commanded by Colonel Hatton, and in 1862 he was promoted to the office of lieutenant, while the regiment was in camp at Trousdale, Sumner county, Tennessee. He participated in the spirited campaigns in Virginia and Tennessee, took part in the battle of Murfreesboro and many other important engagements, and proved a gallant soldier and officer. In 1863 impaired health incapacitated him for further service in the field, and he was granted an honorable discharge. In later years he manifested his continued interest in his old comrades by maintaining affiliation with the United Confederate Veterans Association.

In 1866 Judge Tarver was chosen a delegate from his congressional district, in company with Governor William B. Campbell, to the Philadelphia convention called to organize a national political party with which the southern states might consistently affiliate. He took part in the deliberations of that convention and thereafter continued as a stanch advocate of the principles of the Democratic party until the time of his death.

Judge Tarver was a man of broad views, well fortified opinions and utmost civic loyalty. He did all in his power to foster enterprises and measures projected for the general good of the community, took a lively interest in the social, moral, educational and industrial affairs of his home county, and was a frequent contributor to local newspapers, on topics touching political, religious and industrial affairs. He received the three degrees of ancient craft Masonry in 1865 and was also affiliated with the Independent Order of Odd Fellows. His life was guided and governed by the dictates of a specially acute conscience, the approval of which he demanded for his every motive and action, and no man has ever manifested a higher sense of personal stewardship. He was a zealous and liberal member of the Methodist Episcopal Church, South, and of the same his widow likewise has long been a devoted adherent.

On the 28th of July, 1875, in Wilson county, was solemnized the marriage of Judge Tarver to Miss Sue White, who was born in Wilson county, Tennessee, and who is a daughter of the late Dr. James D. and Lucy (Shelton) White, both natives of Virginia and representative of sterling colonial families of the historic Old Dominion. Dr. White was a prominent physician and agriculturist in his adopted state, and upon his removal to Wilson county, Tennessee, he continued to devote his attention to the same lines of endeavor. Both he, and his wife passed the closing period of their lives in this county, secure in the high regard of all who knew them. Mrs. White was a daughter of James Shelton and was a sister of Rev. William Shelton, who was a distinguished clergyman of the Baptist Church, South, and who removed from Nashville, Tennessee, to Kentucky, in which state he passed the residue of his life. Another brother was David Shelton, who was a prominent member of the bar of the city of Jackson, capital of the state of Mississippi, at the time of his demise. The genealogy of Mrs. Tarver is of distinguished order, with collateral kinship with the historic Marshall, Jefferson and Barron families of Virginia. Mrs. Tarver is a woman of distinctive culture and most gracious personality, and she has long been a loved and valued figure in the social activities of her home city. She was graduated in the excellent academy conducted in the city of Nashville by Rev. Collins D. Elliott, D. D., and she has ever continued to devote herself to the best in standard and periodical literature, with a marked familiarity with that of classical and historical order. Deploring all tendencies to pretensions founded merely on family prominence, Mrs. Tarver very highly appreciates the historic insight and realization that is sure to result generally and universally from a study of ancestral records and historic events. She has been especially interested in historic records and to her was due the organization in Lebanon of a chapter of the Daughters of the American Revolution. Of this local chapter she has been historian since 1904, and she is most active in promoting the society and the objects for which it was organized. She still resides in the beautiful old homestead in Lebanon, and the same is not only a center of gracious hospitality but is also endeared to her by the hallowed memories and associations of past years. Judge and Mrs. Tarver not being blessed with children, have fostered and reared many orphaned members of their families. Both Judge Tarver and his wife have, during their whole lives, honored and valued above all else, simplicity of character and humble Christian usefulness.

JOHN MCREYNOLDS GAUT. A distinguished Nashville attorney and official of the Presbyterian church, Mr. Gaut is one of the seniors of the Tennessee bar, having begun practice forty-five years ago, soon after the war. His father before him ranked a peer among the most eminent Tennessee lawyers of his generation. Few families have contributed so many sterling qualities of mind and character to the life and citizenship

John M. Gaut

of Tennessee during the last century as the Gauts. John McReynolds
Gaut was born at Cleveland, Bradley county, Tennessee, October 1, 1841,
a son of John C. and Sarah (McReynolds) Gaut. The Gaut family is of
Scotch-Irish descent, the first member of which immigrated to the colony
of Pennsylvania, and thence to Virginia, finally coming over the mountains to Tennessee. Grandfather James Gaut came to Tennessee early
in the last century, and lived for some time in Jefferson county, where
his son, John C. Gaut, was born in 1813. The late John C. Gaut, who
died in 1895, was educated at Maryville College and at the University
of Tennessee, took up the law as his profession, and began his practice
at Cleveland. Not only as a practitioner, but also in a financial way· he
was unusually successful. For twelve years he served as judge of the
fourth judicial circuit, resigning in 1865 and moving to Nashville, in
which city he began his practice and continued with few interruptions
until his death. In 1866 and 1867 he served as chairman of the state
executive ·committee of the Conservative party, and was a member of
the constitutional convention of 1865, which reorganized the state government. Several times his ability resulted in his appointment as special
judge of supreme court. He had begun practice in Cleveland only the
year following the removal of the Cherokee Indians from Tennessee. In
politics he adhered to the old-line Whig party and stood strongly for the
Union before and during the war. Late in life he became a member of
the Cumberland Presbyterian church, and was also affiliated with the
Masonic order. His wife, Sarah McReynolds, who was born in Tennessee, was a daughter of an early settler in McMinn county. She died in
1873, her death occurring from cholera in the epidemic in Nashville.
The parents had six children, two of whom are now living, John M. Gaut
and his sister Anna E., widow of P. H. Manlove. She resides in Nashville.

John McReynolds Gaut had home surroundings and an example in
his father which proved great inspiration to his early career. He was
liberally educated at the academy in Cleveland and Rutger's College in
New Brunswick, New Jersey, where he was graduated in 1866, A. B.,
took his degree of Master of Arts in 1869, and was awarded the degree
of Doctor of Laws in 1908. The same degree was conferred upon him
in 1907 by the Missouri Valley College of Missouri. After admission
to the bar he began his practice in December, 1867, and has been continuously identified with the Tennessee bar since that time. He has always
enjoyed an extensive practice and for thirty years has been attorney for
the American National Bank of Nashville, and has represented several
other business corporations. During the last seven years his practice has
enlarged in scope and volume. Beginning in 1906 he attained special
prominence as general counsel for the Presbyterian church in the United
States of America in the prolonged litigation over church property
growing out of the union of that church with the Cumberland Presbyte-

rian denomination. As the representative of that church he has appeared before the supreme courts of twelve states, and was successful in ten states out of twelve. He has also had cases in the federal courts in Tennessee and Missouri in the supreme court of the United States. In civil-ecclesiastical jurisprudence, this is probably the most notable litigation of modern times. The Presbyterian committee on legal matters connected with the reunion, in its report to the General Assembly of 1913, say:

"The committee desires to reiterate and emphasize its former expressions as to Judge Gaut's professional ability, also his industry, energy and faithfulness in acting as committee's counsel."

The committee also quote approvingly from a report of Judge Gaut to the committee as follows:

"As you doubtless realize, the litigation to which we have sustained a mutual relation must be recorded in history as the most remarkable known to the judicial history of any country. The United Brethren cases originated in eight states of the Union, and involved much property and questions of great importance. The litigation with which we have been connected arose in thirteen states, involved directly and indirectly probably not less than six millions of dollars of property, affected a very large number of people and involved questions of great importance. It called for a judicial determination of the relation, in this country, between church and state, between ecclesiastical and civil courts, the fundamental nature of ecclesiastical government, and the powers of all ecclesiastical judicatories. A serious indictment was brought against the doctrines of the Presbyterian church in the U. S. A., materially affecting the church's theological standing. It is evident that by this litigation the law of this country relating to the subjects above indicated will be thoroughly settled, and much light from it will radiate across the seas to foreign countries. Many fundamental principles of law affecting religious societies will be established, which are of vital importance to all churches in the United States, and of great importance to churches throughout the world."

Mr. Gaut, in young manhood, served in the city council of Nashville, and his name has been identified with many movements and enterprises of a public nature. He is actively interested in everything that promotes public welfare. For a great many years he has been an elder in the Cumberland Presbyterian church and since the union in the Presbyterian church, and is probably the best known layman of that denomination in Tennessee. In 1870 he became a member of the board of publication of the church, and was officially connected with the publication department for thirty-one years, serving as president of the board for twelve years, and general manager of publication work for ten years. He has attended more than twenty-five sessions of the general assembly. He was a member of the judicial commission of the Presbyterian church,

U. S. A., this body being practically the supreme court of the church. He was also a member of the supreme ad interim executive head of the church, known as the executive commission, and a member of the committee on administrative agencies which existed for several years. He is widely known and beloved throughout the church and generally believed to be the best informed man in the country on civil law, ecclesiastical law and church history, as they are related to each other.

Mr. Gaut in 1870 married Michal M. Harris, a daughter of William O. Harris, who for years was proprietor and one of the editors of the *Nashville Banner*, and a man of prominence in this city. Mrs. Gaut died in 1871. She was a member of the Cumberland Presbyterian church. In 1876 Mr. Gaut married Sallie Crutchfield, daughter of Thomas Crutchfield, who spent most of the years of his life in Chattanooga, where he was owner of the Crutchfield House, now better known as the Read House. He was perhaps the most eminent farmer in the state and member of the agricultural commission of the state. Mr. Gaut's great-grandfather, Isaac Lane, was a soldier of the Revolution and fought in the battle of Kings Mountain. The three living children of Mr. and Mrs. Gaut are: Mrs. Amanda G. Hardcastle, wife of Kendrick C. Hardcastle, who is district superintendent and traffic manager of the Bell Telephone Company; Sarah M. and Mary A. are both living at home. Mr. Gaut is a Democrat in politics, though he recognizes, in theory and in action, that every man's supreme allegiance is to the welfare of the country rather than to any political party.

MARCUS B. TONEY. An exceptional business record is that of Marcus B. Toney. More than forty years ago he was made representative of the New York Central Lines at Nashville. Nominally his position has remained the same in all the succeeding years. Actually his responsibilities have increased in proportion as the commerce and transportation of the nation have expanded in these four decades. Mr. Toney possesses the faculty of being able to adapt himself to the changing conditions of a growing business, and has rendered a valuable service both to his corporation and the public.

Marcus B. Toney, who belongs to an old southern family, was born on a farm eight miles from Lynchburg in Campbell county, Virginia, August 19, 1840. William Henry Clay Toney, his father, was born in Buckingham county, Virginia, and was reared and educated in his native state, where he learned the trade of millwright. In 1842 he emigrated to Tennessee, bringing his family and slaves and making the removal with teams and wagons, and it was three weeks from the time he left Virginia before he reached his destination in Tennessee. After two years spent in the little city of Nashville, he crossed the river and bought ten acres of timbered land on which he built a saw and grist mill in the woods, operating his machinery with horse power. When a road was built past the mill it was known as White Creek Pike, and is now First street of Nashville. He continued to operate his local industries until his death in 1852. His wife was Elizabeth Ann Minton Goodwin, who was born in Amherst county, Virginia, a daughter of George B. and Elizabeth Ann (Minton) Goodwin. The Goodwin family dates in Virginia back to 1616. When William H. C. Toney and wife left Virginia their goal was St. Louis, but on the way they stopped for a time in Nashville, and on account of low waters in the river, and afterwards because of the failing health of the mother, they concluded not to go any further. Mrs. Toney died in Nashville in 1846. She was the mother of four children, three of whom died very young, so that Marcus B. Toney is the only living representative of the family.

Having lost his parents when very young, Mr. Toney was cared for by a negro mammy from the death of his mother until his father died, and then went back to the old family home in Virginia, at Lynchburg, where he attended school. In 1860 he returned to Nashville, and was clerk on a steamboat until the outbreak of the war. At the beginning of that struggle he enlisted in Company B of the First Regiment of Tennessee Volunteers, went into Virginia, fought in the Army of Northern Virginia, under Lee, and was in Stonewall Jackson's command. He was with the regiment in its various marches and battles until 1864. In February of that year he was transferred to the Forty-fourth Virginia Regiment, and fought with that command in the Battle of the Wilderness. On May 12, 1864, he was captured by the Federals and taken to prison at Point Lookout in Maryland, and in the following July was transferred to Elmira, New York, where he was held a prisoner until June, 1865. Being then released, he returned to Nashville, and entered the employ of the Southern Express Company. On December 4, 1868, Mr. Toney was on board the ill-fated steamer United States when it was wrecked on the Ohio river near Warsaw, Kentucky, when one hundred and thirty people lost their lives. Mr. Toney escaped by swimming through the icy waters to the shore. In 1872 Mr. Toney entered the employ of the New York Central Railroad Company as commercial agent at Nashville, and in that capacity has been retained for a period of forty-one years, during which he has faithfully looked after the interests of the great railroad system in Nashville and throughout this section of southern territory.

In January, 1872, he married Miss Sally Hill Claiborne, who was born in Buckingham county, Virginia, a daughter of John C. and Ann (Bransford) Claiborne. Mr. and Mrs. Toney have two children, named Helen and Marion Toney. Helen married Henry W. Skeggs, and her two children are Helen Claiborne and Marion B. Mr. Toney and wife are members of the Methodist church. Since 1866 he has held active membership in the Masonic fraternity, and was the founder of the Masonic Widows' and Orphans' Home near Nashville, an institution to which Col. Ira Baxter donated ten acres of land as a beautiful site. In 1906 Mr. Toney published his war reminiscences, entitled "The Privations of a Private."

JOSEPH STINEFORD CARELS. A long service of quiet usefulness has been performed by Joseph Stineford Carels in the city of Nashville, where he has lived for half a century. Not all the best work of the world is done in the fields of industry and commerce, nor in the usual professions. Invaluable duties, necessary to the proper functions of the world and society, are often discharged with great fidelity and capability by men and women who occupy none of the conspicuous places in life.

Joseph Stineford Carels has for the past thirty years been treasurer and librarian of the Tennessee Historical Society, and also superintendent of the Watkins Institute of Nashville. He was born in Philadelphia, Pennsylvania, August 30, 1825. William Carels, his father, was also born in Philadelphia in 1793. Grandfather Samuel Carels was born in Philadelphia of German parents. The grandfather was a carpenter and builder, and spent all his career in the city of Philadelphia. The father was likewise a life-long resident of Philadelphia, and died at the age of seventy-nine years. The maiden name of his wife was Mary Stineford, who was born in Philadelphia, a daughter of George Stineford, a native of Germany. Her death occurred when she was eighty years old, and she reared twelve out of a large family of sixteen children.

Joseph Stineford Carels graduated from the Central high school of Philadelphia in 1843. In 1851 that school conferred upon him the degree of Master of Arts. After his graduation he began his career as a clerk in a wholesale dry goods store in his native city. Eighteen months later in 1845 he moved to Tennessee, and became clerk in a dry goods house at Murfreesboro, where he remained until 1857. After that he served as bookkeeper and teller in the Bank of Middle Tennessee at Lebanon until the outbreak of the war. He then came to Nashville, and in 1862 presented to the secretary of the United States navy a petition signed by every member of congress requesting a position in the navy. He was accordingly appointed assistant paymaster, and attached to the steamer Clifton in Admiral Farragut's gulf squadron. He remained in the service for about one year, when ill health compelled him to retire and return to Nashville. In this city he was appointed bookkeeper and stamp clerk in the postoffice, and spent about twenty years in the office, serving as assistant postmaster under Postmasters Hopkins, Embry and Hasslock.

Mr. Carels was made a Mason in Murfreesboro, when he joined the Mount Moriah Lodge, A. F. and A. M., in 1843. In 1852 he served as worshipful master of the Murfreesboro lodge. In 1852 he joined Pythagoras Chapter No. 23, R. A. M., and in 1866 took the last degrees in the York Rite and became a member of Nashville Commandery No. 1, K. T.

In 1865 he joined Alminah Temple of the Mystic Shrine, and was a charter member of Emulation Lodge No. 3, A. and A. S. R. For forty-six years he has been secretary of the Cumberland Lodge No. 8 of Masons in Nashville. He has served as captain general, standard bearer and guard of Nashville Commandery No. 1, K. T., and secretary of the Masonic Library and the several Masonic bodies, all at the same time, and for twelve years was librarian of the Howard Library until it was merged with the Carnegie Library.

JAMES A. WILLIAMS. Among the successful agriculturists of Cheatham county, Tennessee, is James A. Williams, who resides near Cheap Hill. Born May 25, 1855, in the adjoining county of Robertson, he is a scion of two of its oldest connections, the Williams and Shearon families, the former of Virginia stock and originally of Welsh lineage, and the latter descended from North Carolina immigrants. Wiley W. Williams, the father of James A., also was a native of Robertson county and spent his entire life there, passing away on April 10, 1865. He was the first county court clerk of Cheatham county elected by the popular vote. He was a farmer by occupation. First a Whig and then a Democrat in politics, he took an active interest in political affairs and served as the first county clerk of Cheatham county after Cheatham county had been formed from a portion of Robertson county. Fraternally he was affiliated with the time-honored Masonic order. His father, Christopher Williams, was born in Virginia and came into Tennessee early in the last century, settling in Robertson county. He was one of the founders of the First Methodist church established in the present limits of Cheatham county, though it was Robertson county at that time. The family had first been planted on American soil by emigrants from Wales. Wiley W. Williams wedded Mary Shearon, who was born in Robertson county, Tennessee, June 22, 1822, and departed life in December, 1910, at the advanced age of eighty-seven years. She was the daughter of Zachariah Shearon, who came into Tennessee from North Carolina about 1800 and settled on a farm in Robertson county, and whose father, Sterling Shearon, was the originator of the family in this state.

James A., the youngest of five children born to Wiley W. and Mary (Shearon) Williams, was reared to farm pursuits and received his education in the country schools of his native vicinity. He took up life independently as a farmer in Cheatham county and has continued to be identified with that vocation to the present time, beginning his business career with no capital save his own native resources. By intelligent effort and well directed energies he has forged steadily forward toward the goal of success and today is the owner of a good farm of 150 acres, with a comfortable dwelling and such other improvements as make it an attractive rural home. Mr. Williams has also taught school in Cheatham county ten years and has entered actively into the public life of his community, having served eighteen years as a magistrate of the fifteenth civil district and being now chairman of the county court. In addition to these public positions he has also been a member of the board of education and represented Cheatham county in the legislature of 1887. In political allegiance he is a Democrat. Through these different relations to society he has become well known in his county and his life and services have been of that order that has won him a high standing in public esteem.

In November, 1886, Mr. Williams was united in marriage to Miss Mary L. Weakley, whose father, William D. Weakley, was a native of Montgomery county, Tennessee, and spent his entire life there. Mr. and Mrs. Williams have six children, named: Cora, Nannie, Mary, Louis, Martha and Benton, the last three of whom are attending school. Mrs. Williams is a member of the Methodist Episcopal church. Mr. Williams is united fraternally with the Independent Order of Odd Fellows.

J. L. DAVIS, M. D., holds a high rank among the professional men of Watertown, Tennessee, and of the surrounding country. He has been in active practice in Watertown for a number of years and the combination of personal charm and technical skill with which he is endowed has won for him many warm friends and admirers. He has been very successful as a physician, and is a land holder as well as a professional man.

J. L. Davis was born in Wilson county, Tennessee, on the 30th day of November, 1865. His father is James H. Davis, who was born in Virginia in 1840, and whose parents were natives of the state of Virginia also. James H. Davis migrated to Tennessee and there met and married Armenia Jennings, a daughter of Riley C. Jennings, who was one of the earliest settlers in Wilson county, where he lived and died. Mrs. Davis was born in Wilson county in 1845 and both she and her husband are living in that county at present. Mr. Davis started out in life with nothing of material means in his possession, and he has succeeded in rearing and educating his large family of children, and is now worth about twelve thousand dollars. With the outbreak of the Civil war he enlisted in the Confederate army and served throughout the four years of the civil conflict under General Hatton. After the war he returned to a desolated farm and set to work to build it up to some semblance of a productive place, with the result already noted. In politics Mr. Davis is a member of the Democratic party, and for a number of years served as a magistrate of the county. Both he and his wife are members of the Baptist church.

John L. Davis grew up on his father's farm, but he had no inclination to the life of a farmer, and as a mere lad determined to obtain an education. He was the third of his father's children and grew up in the years when the father was trying to retrieve his losses caused by the war, so that the lad had to borrow money for his college education. He first attended the Southwestern Baptist University at Jackson, Tennessee, and later entered the medical department of the Vanderbilt University, from which he was graduated in 1893.

Dr. Davis began the practice of his profession at Henderson Cross Roads, in his native state, and for seven years made this his home. In 1900 he removed to Watertown, and established a practice that has grown with the years, until now the doctor has about all the patients he can take care of, though he is one of those men who always have the time and energy to do one thing more. He has never permitted any other interests to intervene between his professional duties and himself, and so is able to accomplish more than many of his confreres.

Mr. Davis was married in 1893 to Stella Hale, a daughter of Dodd Hale. The latter was a native of Wilson county, where he spent many years of his life as a farmer. He was best known, however, as a preacher of the Methodist church. Dr. Davis and his wife are the parents of three children, all of whom are attending school. They are James W., Margaret and Edith.

The doctor is a member and a deacon of the Baptist church, while his wife belongs to the Methodist Episcopal denomination. He takes quite an interest in fraternal affairs, being a member of the Independent Order of Odd Fellows and of the Knights of Pythias. In the latter order he is past chancellor commander. In politics he is a member of the Democratic party, but has never cared to take any active part in the game of political warfare. He owns some valuable bank stock and a fine farm, and should he desire to give up his practice he would be comfortably situated in a financial way. Since the doctor's chief interest lies in his profession, it is but natural that he should take an active interest in the affairs of the state and county medical societies, in both of which he holds membership.

WILLIAM S. SHIELDS. Prominent among the financiers who have conserved the money interests of Knoxville for the past several decades, William S. Shields, president of the City National Bank, has interested himself in various other enterprises of an extensive nature. He entered the banking business in 1888, when he was one of the organizers of the City National Bank, and his wise and careful management of its affairs has made it one of the leading financial institutions of the city. Mr. Shields is one of a family of ten boys born to James T. and Elizabeth (Simpson) Shields, both of whom are now deceased. The father was a prominent jurist of Tennessee, and practiced law in the state for many years. Further mention concerning him is made in a sketch devoted to Hon. John Knight Shields, United States senator from his state.

William Simpson Shields was born in Grainger county, Tennessee, on the 13th day of October, 1853, and his early education was secured in the common schools. On the completion of his studies, he engaged in

stock raising, and some of the best blooded cattle, sheep and swine in the southern states were bred on his farm. Mr. Shields continued in the stock-breeding business until coming to Knoxville in 1888, when he organized the City National Bank, becoming its first cashier and remaining in that capacity until assuming the position of president, having held these positions for twenty-five years. A man of careful and conservative ideas, he is also possessed of the courage necessary to handle affairs of an extensive character and the policy he has used in banking matters has gained him prestige in financial circles and the full confidence of his community. The City National Bank is one of the largest in Knoxville as well as one of the most substantial and prosperous. Mr. Shields is also a partner in the firm of Gillespie, Shields & Company, manufacturers of the "Shield Brand" clothing, the firm consisting of John K. Gillespie, Mr. Shields and E. H. Scharringhaus.

Mr. Shields has served as president of the Cumberland Club, is vice-president of the Knoxville Railway & Light Company, and a director in numerous other large enterprises, which are realizing something of the benefit of his connection with them. Various movements for the welfare of his city have been promoted and fostered by him, and he is especially interested in anything that tends to elevate the young and worthy men of the day.

Mr. Shields was united in marriage on October 30, 1889, to Miss Alice Watkins, the daughter of Arthur P. and Anna (Nielson) Watkins. Mr. and Mrs. Shields are affiliated with the Second Presbyterian church of Knoxville. Their home, located on Melrose avenue, covering three acres, is one of the finest and most beautiful in Knoxville. Essentially a business man, Mr. Shields has not allowed the glamour of the public arena to entice him, although he takes a good citizen's interest in the political affairs of the day. His long and honorable career in Knoxville has made him well known not only in business and financial circles, but in club, social and fraternal life, where his hosts of friends testify to his popularity.

Concerning the family of sons of which Mr. Shields is one, and the eldest, but three others are living today. One is Hon. John Knight Shields, the widely known jurist and senator; another is Samuel G. Shields, a lawyer, and the third is Joseph S. Shields, a jobbing merchant of New York City.

DAVID CAMPBELL KELLY BINKLEY, M. D. The Binkley family originated in Germany, but of their ancestry insufficient data is at hand to make possible a complete record of the family since its establishment in America. It is known, however, that they first settled in Pennsylvania and from there moved to various states of the Union. Two brothers, John and Adam Binkley, came from Pennsylvania and located in North Carolina, thence moving to Tennessee in later years. From these two it is thought that all the Binkleys in Tennessee descended. Of these brothers, John Binkley is the progenitor of Dr. David C. K. Binkley of this review.

John Binkley became the father of Frederic, who was born in North Carolina, but on reaching manhood moved to Tennessee, locating in Nashville, where he followed his trade of carpenter for a number of years. He later moved on a farm in Davidson county, trading his Nashville property for the farm, and there he lived near nature until his death in 1857, when he was eighty-four years of age. He was the father of Joseph Binkley, who spent his life in Davidson county. He followed farming and was a prominent and prosperous man in his community. He was a Whig until in later years when the party was succeeded by the Republican party, when he affiliated with the Democratic faction and thereafter his support and sympathies were centered there. He was born on November 19, 1810, and died in August, 1887. He married Martha Buchanan Steele, born in Davidson county in 1911. She was a daughter of Samuel and Patience (Shane) Steele, North Carolinans by birth, who were interested in agriculture all their lives. The father served in the Indian wars under General Jackson, and in his younger days gave considerable attention to the business of hunting and trapping. He died in 1864 when he was in his eighty-second year of life. Joseph and Martha B. (Steele) Binkley were married in Davidson county in 1832, and they became the parents of twelve children—six sons and six daughters. David C. K. Binkley was the youngest of that number, and five of the family are living today. The wife and mother died in 1859, and in later years the father married Mrs. Elizabeth (Iva) Holland, a widow who had one child. She is now deceased.

David Campbell K. Binkley was born in Davidson county, Tennessee, on the 30th day of June, 1857. He found his early education in the common schools of Davidson county, and later attended a private school in Decaturville, Tennessee, under the tutelage of R. P. Griffith. When he had been sufficiently prepared for higher studies, he went to Vanderbilt College at Nashville, Tennessee, where he took a medical course, finishing his studies in 1878 and graduating with the degree of M. D. at the head of his class, winning two gold medals—the Founder's medal for general proficiency in all branches and also the medal in anatomy given by Dr. T. O. Simmons. His first active practice of his profession was at Hustberg, Tennessee, and so well did he succeed that he continued in that place, which is still the scene of his professional activities and his home as well. In 1891 he engaged in the drug business in connection with his practice, and in that, as in his profession, he has prospered in a pleasing degree with the passing years. His early acquaintance with farm life bred in him a fondness for things agricultural, and when his prosperity made it possible, Dr. Binkley purchased a fine farm in the vicinity of Hurstberg, and later added to his possession a similar property in Davidson county, in both of which he takes a considerable pleasure. In November, 1911, Dr. Binkley suffered a severe fire loss at his store in Hustberg, which constitutes practically the one piece of financial loss of any moment that he has suffered since he has been established in business.

Dr. Binkley is a Republican, not particularly active in affairs of that nature, but withal a good citizen, and one who takes the maximum inter-est in civic movements designed to advance the material and moral status of the community. He is a member of the county and state medi-cal societies and the American Medical Association. Mrs. Binkley is a member of the Methodist Episcopal church.

In 1883 Dr. Binkley was united in marriage with Miss Florence E. Dickson, the daughter of Abner and Mary Jane (Wilkerson) Dickson. She was born in the third civil district of Humphreys county, Tennessee, in 1860. Eleven children came to Dr. and Mrs. Binkley, of which goodly family nine are living today. They are here named as follows: Waldo Bowling. engaged with his father in the drug store; Martha Buchanan, teaching in Alabama; Adelia May, married R. W. Byrn of Hurstberg; Frederick Dickson, attending school at Branam & Hughes; Samuel Fos-ter; Howard Kelly; Florence Rowena; Robert Theodore and Joseph Benjamin, all at home.

COL. GEORGE CAMP PORTER. One of the honored old members of the Tennessee bar, Colonel Porter has for a number of years been engaged in practice at Nashville, and previous to that time was located in different cities of the state. He belongs to one of the old families, and its mem-bers have been honorably represented in this state for a century.

Col. George Camp Porter was born on a farm eight miles north of Summerville in Fayette county, Tennessee, November 15, 1835. His father was Charles Bingley Porter, born in Orange county, Virginia, in 1806, and the grandfather was Col. Charles Bingley Porter, a planter and life-long resident of Virginia. The grandfather had the distinction of being elected to the Virginia house of burgesses over the opposing candidacy of James Madison, afterwards president of the United States. During the Revolution he commanded a regiment of Virginia troops, and led those troops at Yorktown, where Cornwallis surrendered. Charles B. Porter, father of Col. George C., was reared and educated in Virginia, and in 1826 came to Tennessee, locating at Franklin where he was engaged in the manufacture of brick. In 1829 he moved to Haywood county in order to superintend the improvement of the land of Robert C. Foster, and remained in that work until 1834. He then came to Fay-ette county, buying a farm and operating it with slave labor. Leaving his Fayette county land in 1840 he went with his brother John A. to Mississippi. buying a plantation on the river twenty miles above Vicks-burg. In that region he was soon stricken with cholera, and died there in April, 1841, being buried in the Tappan cemetery. He was twice married. His first marriage occurred in Franklin to Miss Martha Ould, who died in Haywood county. He then married Mary Scott of Haywood county. By the first marriage were two children, named Frances and Henry: The second union resulted in three children, named George Camp, Robert S. and Mary Bingley. The mother of the latter children continued to live on the farm in Fayette county until her death in 1847. After that the children went to live with their uncle and guardian, Richard W. Green of Lauderdale county, until 1852. Then another uncle, Robert C. Scott of Brownsville, became their guardian, and in his home George C. Porter lived and attended school until he was well upward of manhood. In 1854 he became an engineer on the railroad between Memphis and Bowling Green, Kentucky, but after a few months' employment in that way entered the Kentucky Military Institute under Col. E. W. Morgan. In 1857 he graduated second in his class and was valedictorian. His ambition led to the law, and at Memphis he took up its study with Yerger, Farrington and Yerger, and was admitted to the bar and began practice in Memphis.

Colonel Porter was in the city of Philadelphia when Fort Sumter fell, and was there when the first regiment of Federal troops from Massachusetts passed through the city en route to Washington. He went to Baltimore on a train that followed that regiment, and in that city saw the first bloodshed in the war. He took a steamer for Norfolk, and while going down the bay the steamer was halted by a Confederate gunboat and searched before being allowed to proceed to Norfolk. Returning to Brownsville, Tennessee, Mr. Porter raised the first company in that county for service. This company was known as the Haywood Blues. It was attached to the Sixth Regiment of Tennessee Infantry, and the organization and muster-in occurred at Jackson. W. H. Stevens was colonel, T. P. Jones was lieutenant, and Mr. Porter was major. The regiment became a part of Cheatham's Brigade. After the battle of Shiloh the regiment was reorganized and Mr. Porter was elected colonel, after which he continued in command of the regiment during its various marches and campaigns and battles until the close. At Murfreesboro the Sixth and Ninth Regiments were consolidated and thereafter were known as the Sixth and Ninth Regiment. At the close of the war Colonel Porter was paroled in Memphis, and soon afterwards formed a law partnership with Hon. David A. Nunn to engage in practice at Brownsville. Four years later Mr. Nunn was elected to congress, and in 1877 Colonel Porter moved to Ripley, where he was engaged in practice until 1891. In that year he returned to Brownsville, but in 1895 gave up his office in that city and moved to Nashville.

As to politics, Colonel Porter cast his first vote as a Whig. In 1856 he voted for Fillmore and Donelson, the Whig candidates during that year. In 1870 he was elected to the constitutional convention and in

1871 he was elected to the state senate, representing Haywood, Madison and Lauderdale counties. In 1877 he was chosen representative to the legislature from Haywood county from the floaterial district which included Haywood, Madison and Hardeman counties. He was appointed in 1895 a member of the board of railroad commissioners, and performed an important service to the state in a time when the work of the commission was largely of a pioneer character. Colonel Porter in 1903 was made superintendent of the state capitol by Gov. B. D. Frazier, and continued to hold that office throughout the administration of the governor.

In 1871 Colonel Porter married Mary Pugh Bond of Haywood county. They have one daughter, Miss Neppie. The family are members of the Episcopal church and Colonel Porter has for a long time been prominent in old army circles. He is a member of Hiram S. Bradford bivouac of the Confederate Veterans, of the John Ingram bivouac at Jackson, and of the Frank Cheatham bivouac at Nashville. As a Mason he has taken the degree of York Rite, including the commandery, and is also affiliated with the Knights of Pythias. At the present time Colonel Porter is a member and financial agent of the Tennessee Historical Society.

PROF. MONROE W. WILSON was born in Union county, Tennessee, December 9, 1867. His father was James H. Wilson and his mother Wineford Wilson, nee Brantley. Monroe was the fourth child of a family of five children. His parents were of the sturdy pioneer stock, who were the bone and sinew of the early settlers of this country, and young Monroe inherited from them those sterling qualities of tenacity, industry and fortitude which have counted for so much in the advancement of his career as a public educator and a gentleman in private life.

His father died in 1870, when Monroe was three years old, leaving him to make his own way in life and educate himself. This orphan boy conceived the idea that he had a mission in life, and that he must have an educaton to fit him for his life work, and, undaunted by the obstacles of poverty, he steeled his heart to his task. He worked in earnest in the public schools and finally qualified himself for a teacher at the early age of eighteen with a heart which was not satisfied with less than the best; he worked his way through college, and in 1896 was graduated from the American Temperance University. He thereafter taught at Cumberland Gap, Tennessee.

In 1897 he was married to Miss Sarah Kathline Bohannon. To this union one son was born, Monroe, Jr.

A year later he moved with his family to Knoxville, Tennessee, and was for years connected with the schools of Knoxville and Knox county. Later he was elected superintendent of the Lonsdale high school, and his efficient service there led to his election in 1911 to the office of superintendent of public instruction for Knox county.

In this office his work was so satisfactory that he was, in January,

1913, re-elected by acclamation. There are nearly three hundred teachers under his supervision, and during his administration he has been instrumental in having erected in the county of Knox three additional high schools, making five in all. These schools are among the best in the state, and are monuments to the excellent work of the superintendent.

During all of these years of incessant professional occupation, the thing which has shown his manhood and endeared him to the hearts of his friends, is the unabated attachment and devotion to his mother; and she has always shared the pleasure and profit of his success.

HON. DAVID D. ANDERSON. Deep and accurate knowledge of law and practice, native shrewdness and ability, and unswerving integrity, made the late Judge David D. Anderson an excellent and successful lawyer and an admirable judge. High personal character, deep religious convictions, a kind heart and a strong sense of duty made him a valuable citizen. For more than forty years a leading representative of the Knoxville bar, he at all times maintained its best traditions, and in his death, which occurred December 5, 1911, bar, bench and public united in expressing their grief at the loss of one whose place was unquestionably a difficult one to fill.

Judge Anderson was born December 9, 1840, in Washington county, Tennessee, one of five children born to Alexander and Eliza Rosa (Deaderick) Anderson, of German and English descent. His father, a leading attorney for many years, became a supreme court judge of California, and in 1840 was elected to the United States senate. Inheriting his father's inclination for the law, David D. Anderson was given a careful education, graduating from the University of Tennessee in 1861 with the degree of Bachelor of Arts. In April of that same year he enlisted for service in Company M, First Regiment, Tennessee Cavalry, in the Confederate service, became captain and senior captain of the regiment, and later was a member of Company B, Nineteenth Tennessee Infantry. His principal engagements were at Shiloh and in Kentucky and southwestern Virginia, and he was wounded at New Hope Church, fifteen miles from Staunton, Virginia, in 1864. On the close of a brilliant military career he engaged in the practice of law, and in 1870 came to Knoxville, where he spent the remainder of his life. He was attorney general of Knox county from 1878 to 1886, and in 1907 became judge of the criminal court of Knox county, in which high office he continued to serve until 1909. His fraternal affiliation was with the Independent Order of Odd Fellows, and he was also a member of the Delaware Society of the Cincinnati, Sons of the Revolution, made up of heirs of officers who participated in the American War for Independence, there being but three members in the entire state of Tennessee.

Judge Anderson was married to Miss Jessie L. Clark, daughter of James Clark, of Morristown, Tennessee.

SAMUEL B. GIFFIN, county trustee or treasurer of Knox county, is one of the able officials of the county where he has spent his entire career. The substantial vocation of farming has always been his regular business, and as one of the popular and successful representatives of the rural communities he was chosen to his present office.

Mr. Giffin, who was one of a family of sixteen children, was born in Knox county, July 16, 1857. His parents were William and Nancy (King) Giffin. The father, who also was a native of Knox county, was a carpenter by trade, and his death occurred in March, 1889. He was well known for his honesty and integrity.

Samuel B. Giffin during his boyhood attended the common schools of the county, and both during and subsequent to his school days was versed in the activities of the farm. He finally engaged in the occupation on his own account, and has long been a substantial producer of the crops of the soil. His farm, comprising some seventy-five or eighty acres of choice land, is situated six miles east of Knoxville.

His first election to his present position of county trustee occurred in 1910, and he was re-elected in 1912. He has one clerk in the office, his deputy being D. A. Giffin. For twenty-two years he served as member of the county court, and has long been one of the influential men in local public affairs. Fraternally he affiliates with the Independent Order of Odd Fellows and the Junior Order of United American Mechanics. His own church is the Baptist, while his wife is a Methodist. Mrs. Giffin before her marriage was Miss Marguerite Cailen, a daughter of E. C. A. Cailen, of Knox county. Their family consists of four children, as follows: Nannie A., Ira S., Margaret A. and Ollie F.

HON. JEROME TEMPLETON. The senior member of the well-known law firm of Templeton & Templeton, of Knoxville, is recognized as one of the strong and representative members of the bar of his state, and as a citizen of sterling attributes of character and utmost civic loyalty. He has served as a member of the state senate and has otherwise received patent evidence of popular confidence and esteem. Associated with him in the practice of his profession is his younger son, Paul E., an able and ambitious young lawyer, who is ably upholding the professional prestige of the family name.

Jerome Templeton is a scion of one of the honored pioneer families of the state of Tennessee and is the second of five children born to Allison and Mahala (Cunningham) Templeton, one of the sons, John C. by name, having been killed in the fight at Peach Tree creek, near Atlanta, in Civil war times. Of the five, three are yet living. The father was born in Rhea county, Tennessee, and he devoted his entire life to the ministry of the Cumberland Presbyterian church. He and his wife were both members of sterling pioneer families of Tennessee, and both were of stanch English lineage. That part of Rhea county wherein Rev. Allison Templeton was born on May 7, 1820, is now included in Meigs county. A man of splendid mental attainments, Rev. Templeton carried on the work of his church with a high order of ability and consecrated zeal. He was ever influential in the councils of his church, and being a man of exalted ideals and purposes, he gained and retained the high regard of all with whom he came in contact, either in his ministerial capacity, or in any of the relations of life. He passed his closing years in Texas, dying in June, 1882, leaving a record of worthy works, and an honored name. His first wife was claimed by death on February 2, 1861. His second wife survives him, and now lives in Dallas, Texas.

Reared under the conditions and influences incidental to farm life, Jerome Templeton early learned the lessons of practical industry, and in the meanwhile he duly profited by the advantages of the public schools of his locality, as he did later of those of the city of Chattanooga, as well as a private preparatory institution. He finally entered Cumberland University, at Lebanon, in which he completed his academic course and was graduated as a member of the class of 1871, with the degree of Bachelor of Arts. He put his scholastic acquirements to practical test and use by turning his attention to the pedagogic profession, and for three years thereafter he continued his labors as a successful and popular teacher in the high school of Loudon county. In the meanwhile he had taken up the study of law, to which he devoted himself with characteristic energy and appreciation, and under the effective preceptorship he was fortunate in having, he made rapid and substantial progress in the absorption and assimilation of the science of jurisprudence, with the result that in 1874 he proved himself eligible for and was admitted to the bar. In September of that year he engaged in practice at Sevierville, where he continued in the successful practice of his profession until November, 1881, when he took up his residence at Knoxville, in order that he might acquaint himself with a broader field of labor. In this city he has continued his successful practice during the long intervening years. Mr. Templeton is a strong and resourceful trial lawyer and has won many important forensic victories, and as a counselor he is conservative and judicious, with a broad and accurate knowledge of law and precedent. He is a valued member of the Knoxville Bar Association, the Knox County Bar Association and the Tennessee Bar Association, and his character and high professional ideals have brought him the respect and confidence of his confreres at the Tennessee bar, while his success in practice has been on a parity with his recognized ability and indefatigable application.

From the time when he attained his legal majority Mr. Templeton has given unfaltering allegiance to the Democratic party, and he has been an effective advocate of its cause. In September, 1904, he was elected representative from Knox county in the state senate, and he proved a valuable working member of the upper house of the state legislature, in which he served one term and in which he was assigned to various important committees. He is affiliated with the time-honored Masonic fraternity and both he and his wife hold membership in the Presbyterian church. The beautiful family home, known for its gracious hospitality, is located on the Kingston turnpike, at a point two miles distant from Knoxville, and Mr. Templeton makes daily trips to his offices, which are maintained in Holston National Bank building, and from which headquarters he and his son control a large and representative law business in and about the city.

On the 29th of January, 1873, was solemnized the marriage of Mr. Templeton to Miss Belle Mabry, eldest daughter of Col. George W. Mabry, now deceased. She was born in Knox county and there reared, her father being a prominent and influential citizen of the county.

Mr. and Mrs. Templeton have two children: Clarence A., a lawyer of Jellico, Tennessee, and Paul E., associated with his father. Clarence Templeton was born in Knoxville in June, 1875, and educated in the Knoxville public schools, in Baker-Himel and the University of Tennessee. After his work at the "hill" he studied at the University of Virginia, and then returned in 1901 to take up the practice of law in his father's office, where he remained two years. In 1903 he located in Jellico, where he is at the present time. Mr. Clarence Templeton married Miss Reese Rodgers, a popular Knoxville girl, and they have a very pleasant home in Jellico, where Mr. Templeton has built up a law practice that engages all his time. At present he represents the Louisville & Nashville Railway and several of the large mining companies in the courts. Although a Democrat, he was elected justice of the peace in a strong Republican district. He is at present chairman of the board of trustees of the high school there. He is an active member of the Methodist Episcopal church at Jellico.

Paul E. Templeton was born in Tennessee on the 24th day of August, 1879, and in the autumn of the following year the family moved to Knoxville, where he was reared to adult age and afforded the advantages of the public schools. In 1899 he was graduated from the University of Tennessee with the degree of Bachelor of Arts, and after reading law under the guidance of his father, he further fortified himself for the activities of his chosen profession by entering the law department of the great University of Michigan, at Ann Arbor, in which he was graduated as a member of the class of 1902, and from which institution he received his well-earned degree of Bachelor of Laws. He has been junior member of the law firm of Templeton & Templeton since 1909, and has ably participated in the legal activities of the firm since that time. In his political proclivities he is a stanch Democrat, like his father, and has been active in the party ranks. In November, 1911, he wedded Miss Kate Copenhaver, a daughter of a well-known resident of Marion, Virginia, and both are popular factors in the social activities of Knoxville.

RUFUS A. MYNATT.   The six years of his service as attorney general
to the criminal court of Knox county have brought Mr. Mynatt recognition as one of the most efficient prosecutors for the commonwealth in
the annals of this jurisdiction.   Mr. Mynatt took high rank as a lawyer
at the outset of his practice, and for fifteen years has been identified
with his profession in Knox county, enjoying a continued success and
growing prosperity in his work.

A native of Union county, Tennessee, where he was born on January
21, 1871, Rufus A. Mynatt was one of the six children born to Joseph
A. and Melvina (Alley) Mynatt, people of Scotch-Irish descent.   The
father, who was born in Knox county, Tennessee, in October. 1829, is
still a resident of this county, and was for many years one of the substantial farmers of this vicinity.

Beginning his studies at the Knox county common schools and finishing them in the high school, Mr. Mynatt was for a number of years
one of the most successful young school teachers of that county, but in
1895 he located at Knoxville and there began to read law under Capt.
W. L. Ledgerwood and with his brother, E. F. Mynatt.   In 1896, before
he had finished his legal studies, he was elected to the state legislature,
and in the following year he was admitted to the bar.   Since that time
he has been one of the ablest representatives of the profession in this
county.   In 1897 he was appointed as assistant attorney-general by his
brother, E. F. Mynatt, who died in 1906, for Knox and Sevier counties,
and assisted in the prosecution of the famous White Cap cases in Sevier
county.   In 1906 he was elected magistrate from the first nine wards
in Knoxville and served until 1910, when he was elected prosecuting
attorney for Knox county.   In that high office he has proved himself
a vigorous prosecutor, but has also shown himself to be one who understands the quality of mercy, and believes there are occasions when it
should be extended.   Prior to his election to the office he now holds, he
had been serving in the office of justice of the peace, but he resigned the
minor office to take the oath of office as attorney general to the criminal
court.

Mr. Mynatt is a member of the county and state bar associations.
In 1896 he married Miss Nola Brock, a daughter of Lewis Brock, and
they have two children, Edward H. and Eugene R. Mynatt.   The family
home is maintained at 2660 Magnolia avenue, and they are members of
the Baptist church.

JOHN M. CURRIER.   Every one is sensible of the fact that in the
present age a rapid change is taking place in every phase of our national
and institutional life.   Efficiency has long been a word of vital importance in the business and professional worlds, but today it is entering
with compelling force into political life.   Parties and their leaders are
being forced into a realization of this, and that they must take account

of both ability and character in selecting their candidates. In 1906 Knox county, Tennessee, chose as its clerk John M. Currier, who was well known thereabouts as an expert bookkeeper and accountant and who as a citizen stood high in public esteem. His first term confirmed the public faith in his efficiency as clerk, and in 1910 he was re-elected to that office without opposition. The people of this county have found him to be the right man in the right place.

Mr. Currier is a native of Knox county, and has spent his entire life within its borders. One of the ten children of John and Mary W. Currier, he was born August 30, 1854, and comes of sturdy Scotch-Irish blood, one of the most highly valued of all strains that have mingled in the shaping of American character. His earlier education was received in the public schools of Knox county and his higher training at Maryville, Tennessee. His business career was begun as a clerk and bookkeeper, and he has long been regarded as one of the best accountants and office experts in the county. To a greater extent than is generally realized the business permanence and legal stability of any modern community is dependent upon the care and accuracy with which public records of all kinds are kept, and the excellence of Knox county records has been no small factor in rendering this section attractive to outside investors. Mr. Currier regards his office as a public trust. By his training, experience and natural abilities he is unusually well fitted for the duties of clerk, and he has met the responsibilities of the office in a manner which reflects credit upon the community as well as upon himself. The unfailing courtesy shown those who have business in his office and the ease and precision with which he discharges his official duties have served to make him one of the most popular and respected officials of the county. In political sentiment he is a Republican. In the way of private business interests he is the owner of a fine farm of 160 acres of choice land in Knox county and he is president of the Mary Moore Coal Mining Company, operating at Excelsior, Kentucky.

Mrs. Currier was Miss Lucy Hudiburg prior to her marriage, a daughter of Mr. and Mrs. John L. Hudiburg, of Knox county. To this union have been born three children, viz.: Miss Mary Louise Currier, William H. Currier and Charles Martin Currier. The family are communicants of the First Methodist Episcopal church at Knoxville.

Rev. John Joseph Graham, pastor of the Church of the Immaculate Conception, of Knoxville, Tennessee, is a native of Erin, born April 13, 1855. He came to the United States in 1871. He became a student in St. Mary's College, in Kentucky, where he was graduated in 1887, and his theological course was completed in Cincinnati, Ohio. On May 28, 1891, he was ordained to the priesthood by the Rt. Rev. Bishop Rademacher, of Nashville, Tennessee, and later of Fort Wayne, Indiana.

He subsequently labored in nearby parts of the state. On February

6, 1902, he came to Knoxville to accept his present charge. Since coming here Father Graham has been the means of many improvements and additions being made in the church and parish.

JAMES C. WOODWARD. At the death of Col. James C. Woodward, on January 5, 1913, there was closed the career of one of Knoxville's best known business men and sterling citizens. He had lived a full life, full of years and replete with practical and useful service in promoting the welfare and common uplift of humanity. Aside from the many material benefits the city of Knoxville derived from his years of citizenship and well directed business activity, there remains as of still greater value his example of worthy and noble living, the heritage of a life spent in helpful deeds.

He was born December 4, 1841, in Lee county, Virginia, a son of Henry and Elizabeth Woodward, and was reared and educated in his native locality. On November 28, 1861, he was joined in marriage to Miss Nannie J. Starnes, who was reared near Rogersville, Hawkins county, Tennessee, not far distant across the border from her husband's native Virginia county. For a number of years their home was in Lexington, Kentucky. From there Colonel Woodward removed to Knoxville, Tennessee, in 1890, and became president of the Fountain City Land Company, which promoted and developed Fountain City, now one of the most populous and most beautiful suburbs of Knoxville. Later he acquired the majority of the stock of the State National Bank at Knoxville and was president of that institution until 1893. In 1899 Colonel Woodward, with his son Hu, bought the Knoxville Business College, with which he was thereafter connected as its president until he retired from business in 1908, his son succeeding him as executive head of that institution. He also had numerous property interests and was numbered among the most substantial men of the city. He was a Mason and a Democrat.

As a churchman Colonel Woodward was very active throughout his career. He was a zealous member of the Church street Methodist Episcopal church, South, and for a number of years served efficiently as superintendent of the Sunday school of that church and also as a member of its board of stewards. At different times he represented his church as a lay delegate at annual conferences of this denomination. One of the philanthropies in which he was especially interested and which he aided very materially with his means was the Methodist orphanage at Greeneville, Tennessee, where a large number of fatherless and motherless children are domiciled and are being educated. Colonel Woodward contributed liberally to this institution, and his wise counsel and advice was sought and heeded in its management. He was a man of very broad sympathies, and other benevolent institutions and many worthy charities were the recipients of his favor and generosity. He believed in doing good for others and made his deeds consistent with this belief, distributing much of his own material riches to relieve need, suffering and distress.

A few months before his death he fell upon the pavement in front of his home and suffered a severe shock, though for several years previous he had been in declining health. A partial stroke of paralysis, added to his generally enfeebled condition and advanced years, brought a speedy end to a long and good life when he passed away at his home at 305 East Fifth avenue, on January 5, 1913, at the age of seventy-one years. He was interred in the Old Gray cemetery at Knoxville. Besides his widow, one daughter and two sons survive him, namely: Mrs. C. B. Proctor, of Memphis, Tennessee; Walter Woodward, of New York City; and Hu Woodward, of Knoxville.

Hu Woodward. Men of efficiency and character are the types of workers the business, industrial and professional worlds of today are eagerly seeking, and it is in recognition of the need and value of special training along certain practical lines that business schools exist. At the head of the Knoxville Business College at Knoxville, Tennessee, is Hu Woodward, a young man of splendid education and himself an example of efficiency, who cannot but inspire those who come under his charge to put forth their best efforts in their work.

Mr. Woodward was born in Lexington, Kentucky, June 7, 1880, and is a son of the late Col. James C. Woodward, who is mentioned individually in this work. His mother was Miss Nannie J. Starnes prior to her marriage, a native of Hawkins county, Tennessee. Mr. Woodward grew up in Lexington, receiving his earlier education in the public schools of that city and later completed a course of study in the Baker & Himel School here. His parents removed to Knoxville, Tennessee, in 1890, in consequence of which he concluded his education in the University of Tennessee. In 1898 Mr. Woodward and his father purchased the Knoxville Business College, of which Colonel Woodward officiated as president until his retirement from active business life in 1908, when his mantle in the executive management fell upon his son. The latter has proved well worthy of the trust and has carried forward the work with a wisdom, tact and ability that has made it a most successful institution. The college was established in 1882, and its present enrollment numbers 150 students.

Mr. Woodward was married September 3, 1902, to Miss Nina C. Marsh, daughter of Henry Marsh, of Greeneville, Tennessee, and to their union have been born two children, Cecil and Pauline. The family residence is at 305 East Fifth avenue. Mr. Woodward is a Democrat in politics, and fraternally is affiliated with the Knights of Pythias.

JAMES B. WRIGHT.   Since 1896 a member of the Knoxville bar, Mr. Wright is one of the prominent young railroad attorneys of east Tennessee, and at the same time enjoys a large and growing general practice. He began his career as a newspaper man, and his broad acquaintance with men and affairs acquired through the work of reporting the news for a city journal was probably the best introduction which any lawyer could attain for successful work in his profession. He has already won a high position in the law, and still has the best part of his career before him.

James B. Wright was born in New Market, Tennessee, November 13, 1875, and is one of a family of nine children whose parents were Ira C. and Martha (Hickey) Wright. The family has been identified with Tennessee for many years, and the father, a native of this state, was a merchant at New Market.

Mr. Wright attended the public schools of New Market while a boy, and subsequently entered the University of Tennessee at Knoxville, where he was graduated in the academic department in 1895 and in the law class of 1896. In the same year he was admitted to the bar, but instead of taking up active practice at once turned his attention to newspaper work, and as a reporter began gathering news for the old *Tribune* and the *Sentinel* at Knoxville. Later he opened an office and began practice, which has since continued with marked success. For several years he was counsel for the Atlanta, Knoxville & Northern Railway, and in 1903 was made district attorney for the Louisville & Nashville Railroad. Mr. Wright maintains large offices in the East Tennessee National Bank building.

On June 14, 1900, he married Miss Dora V. Whittaker, a daughter of Henry C. Whittaker, of Jefferson county, Tennessee. They are the parents of three children. Mr. Wright and family worship in the Methodist church South, and his political affiliations are with the Republican party. His residence is at 517 West Cumberland street in Knoxville.

NATHANIEL BAXTER. In Tennessee Colonel Baxter's name is closely linked with banking and the larger industrial affairs, and for a number of years he has been and still is one of the strongest individual factors in the business life of the South. His has been a notable career. He made a gallant record as a Confederate soldier, afterwards began his career in the law, was once clerk and master in chancery court at Nashville, and from the routine of profession and office his ability led him into the larger field of finance, where he was extraordinarily successful.

Nathaniel Baxter was born at Columbia, Tennessee, in November, 1845, a son of Nathaniel and Mary L. (Jones) Baxter, both of whom were natives of Tennessee. The Baxter family is of Welsh origin, while the Joneses are Scotch. For more than a century the Baxters have been residents of Tennessee. The paternal grandparents, Jere and Catherine

(Baldrich) Baxter, the former a native of North Carolina, the latter of South Carolina, came to Tennessee in 1810, settling near Nashville. After renting a place for a time the grandfather moved to Dickson county, and from there to Maury county, where he died. One of his sons, James, fought under Jackson at New Orleans in the last battle of the War of 1812, being a lieutenant in his company and one of the youngest officers in the service. Montgomery Baxter, another son, died in the battle of San Jacinto, the memorable fight in which the Texans under Sam Houston won their independence from Mexico in 1836.

Nathaniel Baxter, Sr., the father, was born at Charlotte, in Dickson county, was educated at Jackson College in Columbia, took up the legal profession, and began his profession at Columbia. He was elected attorney-general for his district, composed of Maury, Giles and Marshall counties, served six years, then moved to Nashville in 1849, built up a large practice in the capital city, and soon afterwards was elected circuit judge, serving on the bench until the outbreak of the war. He was a Union man in his sympathy, an old-line Whig in politics, but afterwards a Democrat. After the war he served a term of eight years on the judicial bench, and altogether was one of the prominent and most successful members of the Tennessee bar. He and his wife were both members of the Methodist church South, in which his wife took a particularly active part. Mary L. (Jones) Baxter was born near Columbia and was a daughter of John R. Jones, whose native state was North Carolina, whence, after graduating from Chappell Hill College, he came to Tennessee and was one of the largest planters in Marshall county. Previous to the war he owned between 150 and 200 slaves and had an immense estate. There were six children in the family of Nathaniel Baxter and wife, and two of them are now living. Colonel Baxter's sister is Mary L., the wife of Dr. Crouse, of Memphis.

Nathaniel Baxter, Jr., was educated in the schools near Nashville, in one of the private or neighborhood schools of that time. A man named Campbell was the instructor from whom he received most benefit in his early days. In the fall of 1861, though but fourteen years of age, he enlisted in the Confederate army, and served until General Joe Johnston surrendered his troops in North Carolina. He held the rank of first lieutenant in Freeman's battery of artillery and was twice wounded, the first time near Macon, Georgia, and the second time at Chickamauga. Neither wound kept him long from the service, but near Franklin, Tennessee, he was captured and sent a prisoner to Fort Delaware, and remained in a Federal prison for six months.

Following the war he returned to Nashville, where he began the study of law under his father. In 1867 he was admitted to the bar and was in active practice for two or three years. His associates in legal practice were his father and his brother Edward. A little later he was appointed clerk and master in the chancery court at Nashville, an office which he held for six years. After that experience he engaged in the banking business for a year, and at the end of that time his bank effected a consolidation with the First National Bank of Nashville. He was elected president of the consolidated institution, and continued at the head of that well-known old bank for eight or nine years. While president of the bank he also served as clerk of the supreme court. Colonel Baxter's activities in finance and large business affairs will be best remembered for his connection with the Tennessee Coal, Iron & Railway Company, of which important corporation he was president for fourteen years, resigning in 1902, and it is to his credit that he carried the company through two of the worst panics the United States ever had and was the guiding hand in the upbuilding and strengthening of that great corporation. It was during Colonel Baxter's presidency that the company made the first steel ever made in the South and built the first steel rail mill at Birmingham, Alabama, and made the first steel rails in the South. His success in business has brought him rank as one of the substantial business men of Tennessee, but he has used his influence and wealth to worthy ends, and has been an important factor in public and civic affairs.

In 1910 Col. Baxter was elected to the state senate, and was speaker of the senate during that session. In 1912 he was again re-elected, and is now one of the influential members of the upper house. In 1868 he married Miss Laura Lavender, of Memphis. She has always taken and still takes a keen interest in all of Mr. Baxter's enterprises. They are the parents of four children, two still living: Mannie, the wife of Robert F. Jackson, an attorney of Nashville; and Laura, the wife of Robert F. Maddox, of Atlanta, Georgia. They lost two sons in infancy. Mr. Baxter and family worship in the Methodist church, and he is in politics a Democrat. Six miles out from Nashville he owns a very fine farm of twenty-four hundred acres, eighteen hundred acres of which is in cultivation, and it is to this that he at present and for many years has devoted his main attention.

ROBERT SCALES. A good family is a secure foundation for the career of any man, and even without the means afforded by money it takes one far in life. Possessing both an honored family name and ample financial means from youth, Mr. Scales has long been a popular figure in Nashville as a gallant soldier of the South, and is one of Forrest's surviving troopers, and has co-operated in many movements and activities of the city during the subsequent years.

The maternal grandfather Perkins was one of the very first settlers of Davidson county, and Robert Scales still owns a part of the land upon which the pioneer first located in the vicinity of Nashville. Robert Scales was born at Brentwood in Davidson county. His father, Robert Scales, Sr., was born at the old homestead near Cascade, on the line that separates the states of Virginia and North Carolina. Grandfather Henry Scales owned and operated a plantation on the Dam River, a part of that plantation being in Pittsylvania and Henry counties in Virginia and part in Rockingham county of North Carolina, and at that place he lived and died.

Robert Scales, Sr., was reared there, and as a young man came to Tennessee, where he became one of the early settlers of Davidson county. In this county he married Sally Price Perkins, who was born in Virginia, and her father, William Perkins, came from Virginia and had a more than ordinary share in the pioneer development of Davidson county, Tennessee. He secured titles to the land on which he settled from the state of North Carolina, that having been before Tennessee was separately organized as a state. His home was built eight miles from the capital, on what is now the Franklin site. With the slaves who accompanied him to the West he improved large tracts of land and continued to reside there until his death. His wife also was a Virginian. The senior Robert Scales after his marriage located on a part of the Perkins homestead, which had been his wife's dowry, and as he prospered bought the interests of the other heirs until he owned practically all the old Perkins homestead. He was a man of great enterprise, and in the early days before railroads furnished the chief means of transportation, he engaged extensively in the river trade. He built flatboats and took the products of his farm and of other farms down the river to Natchez. These boats were so constructed that the timbers were valuable at the completion of the trip down the river, and he sold them for lumber. He then made his way back, as best he could, sometimes riding horseback, and sometimes coming on foot. The proceeds of his various ventures he invested in lands in Mississippi and Louisiana, and at one time operated two farms in Mississippi. On the old homestead in Davidson county he built a commodious brick house, set back from the pike about two hundred yards, and with most attractive surroundings. That continued to be his home until his death at the age of seventy-two years. His wife died at sixty-two, and was the mother of thirteen children. Mr. Robert Scales is the youngest and the only one now living of this large family. As a boy he attended Robinson Academy and advanced his education in the Cumberland University. He relinquished his studies in order to join the Confederate army in 1861, and became a member of the First Regiment of Tennessee Infantry. With that regiment he went to the front, but after the battle of Shiloh the regiment was so much depleted in numbers that it was reorganized, and Mr. Scales then joined Forrest's Cavalry. Under that noted leader he served in all the campaigns and battles until the close of the war, and then returned home to look after the farm and other interests which fell to him. Since placing his ample estate in good order, Mr. Scales has spent much of his time in travel, and it is safe to say that few men have ever got more enjoyment out of life than he. Davidson county has always been his home, though he usually spends the winters in Florida. He is a popular member of Cheatham Bivouac of the United Confederate Veterans. Mr. Scales has never married. He maintains a good home in Nashville and is a great reader of current and standard literature and an exceedingly interesting conversationalist.

WILLIAM R. JOHNSON. An essentially representative and public-spirited citizen of Knoxville, Tennessee, is William R. Johnson, a prominent business man of this city, mayor of its suburb of Park City, and identified with the group of progressive men that has in charge the National Conservation Exposition of Knoxville.

Born in Lynchburg, Virginia, January 19, 1857, he is one of two children that came to his parents, William R. Johnson and Elizabeth H. (East) Johnson. The father, also a native of the same state and city as his son, was born January 19, 1828, and became a noted artist. He passed away in the city that had been his home from birth.

William R. Johnson, the son, received his education in the public schools of Lynchburg, Virginia, and was graduated from the high school of that city. After attaining manhood he was engaged in the newspaper business four years, and for two years was proprietor and editor of the *Lynchburg Star*. On disposing of those interests he came to Knoxville, Tennessee, where he embarked in the cigar business, and was thus identified until July, 1912. His attention in a business way is now given wholly to his interests in the American Construction & Development Company, of which he is president and general manager. The company is incorporated and has offices in the Henson building. As a citizen Mr. Johnson has always been active and influential in affairs pertaining to the advancement and general good of the city, and besides the firm place he holds in the confidence and esteem of his fellow men he has recognized abilities of leadership. He has been thrice elected mayor of the suburb of Park City, in 1907, 1909 and 1911, each time on the Progressive ticket. When the project of the National Conservation Exposition was launched, Mr. Johnson was chosen a member of the managing board and is commissioner of finance of the same. He is a member of the Travelers' Protective Association and is very prominently identified with its work. He has served as president of the Knoxville Post, two terms as president of the Tennessee Division, served four years as national director, one term as first national vice-president, and was elected unanimously at Savannah, Ga., in 1905 as national president, a distinction never before accorded any member of the Travelers' Protective Association. He was elected again national president in 1907 at Norfolk, Va., on the first ballot, defeating three others who were prominent candidates. He has had the honor of presiding over three national conventions, viz., New Orleans, Buffalo and Milwaukee. He and his wife, who was Miss Della Haynie prior to her marriage, are both communicants of the Methodist Episcopal church.

CPSIA information can be obtained
at www.ICGtesting.com
Printed in the USA
LVHW021401111121
703051LV00004B/51